Mastering the Commodities Markets

Mastering the Commodities Markets

A step-by-step guide to the markets, products and their trading

FRANCESCA TAYLOR

PEARSON

Harlow, England • London • New York • Boston • San Francisco • Toronto • Sydney • Auckland • Singapore • Hong Kong
Tokyo • Seoul • Taipei • New Delhi • Cape Town • São Paulo • Mexico City • Madrid • Amsterdam • Munich • Paris • Milan

PEARSON EDUCATION LIMITED
Edinburgh Gate
Harlow CM20 2JE
United Kingdom
Tel: +44 (0)1279 623623
Web: www.pearson.com/uk

First published 2013 (print and electronic)

ISBN: 978-0-273-76812-8 (print)
978-0-273-77011-4 (PDF)
978-0-273-77012-1 (ePub)

British Library Cataloguing-in-Publication Data
A catalogue record for the print edition is available from the British Library

Library of Congress Cataloging-in-Publication Data
A catalog record for the print edition is available from the Library of Congress

10 9 8 7 6 5 4 3 2 1
16 15 14 13 12

Print edition typeset in 11.5 Garamond 3 LT Std by 30

NOTE THAT ANY PAGE CROSS REFERENCES REFER TO THE PRINT EDITION

About the author

Francesca Taylor

Francesca is Managing Partner of The Matrix Partnership, a Dubai-based firm, specialising in strategic advisory and management services for commodities and natural resources, finance, media and international financial training (www.matrixpartnership.biz). Francesca has been a major player in the international derivatives markets for over 25 years and is a risk management and derivatives specialist and author.

She has written a number of finance books: *Mastering Derivatives Markets*, 4th edition, was published in December 2010, and *Mastering Foreign Exchange and Currency Options* is now in the 2nd edition, both published by Financial Times Prentice Hall. In 2009 Francesca wrote the first of a completely new series for FT Prentice Hall, entitled 'Market Know How: Finance & Markets'.

She commenced her career in London with BICC, the UK cable manufacturer, as a treasury and risk analyst advising on all aspects of currency and interest rate hedging, where she gained her AMCT, with the UK Association of Corporate Treasurers. She then moved into international banking. She was one of the founders of the market-leading Financial Engineering Group at Midland Bank, advising government agencies, major and minor global banks and corporations, and spent time in London as a futures broker on LIFFE.

She has also worked as an OTC derivatives broker specialising in interest rate swaps and is the founder and ex-CEO of Taylor Associates (International) Ltd, the London-based financial training firm, where she personally provided derivatives, treasury and risk training to literally thousands of individuals, worldwide. Clients included tax authorities, exchanges, regulators, information and infrastructure providers, hedge funds, banks, corporations and private individuals.

She has worked with CME and Bloomberg in NYC and ICE in Chicago to create TV- and web-based tutorials in traded options and futures markets.

Her qualifications include:

BSc (Hons) Geology, London University
MBA, Imperial College, London
AMCT, Association of Corporate Treasurers

Contents

Author's acknowledgements

I'd like to thank my publishers Pearson Education and everyone involved in the production of this book. To be asked to write a new book in the Mastering series is a great honour and we have all worked really hard. Commodities are more important now than ever before, with the global population increasingly placing huge pressure on our scarce resources.

Heartfelt thanks go to my specialist contributors, all of whom have full time careers and yet still managed to find time to put pen to paper. These are:

- **Douglas Hansen-Luke**, Managing Partner, HLD Partners
- **Steven McBain**, Crude Oil Trading Manager, Major Commodities firm, Singapore
- **Andrew Pisano**, Senior Manager of Marketing and Development, GreenX, A CME Group Company, New York
- **Jeffrey Rhodes**, Global Head of Precious Metals and Chief Executive Officer, INTL Commodities DMCC, Dubai
- **Fabrice Tayot**, Commodity and Energy Specialist for Thomson Reuters, Dubai

with featured articles from:

- **Victoria Adams**, European Natural Gas Broker, ICAP Energy Ltd
- **Marc-Henri Veyrassat**, AF Founder and Managing Director, African Resources Capital, and **Bruce Danckwerts**, Managing Director, New Venture Farm Ltd, Zambia

Finally, my thanks go to Sandman and Soulcrow91 and everyone at The Matrix Partnership who kept everything running smoothly whilst I was writing.

FST
2012

Publisher's acknowledgements

We are grateful to the following for permission to reproduce copyright material:

Figures

Figure 1.2 Commodity Universe, The Matrix Partnership; Figure 1.4 Benchmark crudes and where they are used, http://dubaimerc.com; Figures 1.5 and 1.6 Contango and backwardation, The Matrix Partnership; Figure 1.7 Illustrating convergence, The Matrix Partnership; Figure 2.1 Exchange data for 2011, World Federation of Exchanges, http://www.world-exchanges.org/; Figure 2.3 Oil swap cash flows, The Matrix Partnership; Figure 3.3 Crude oil production 1990, US Energy Information Administration (EIA); Figure 3.4 Crude oil production 2010, US Energy Information Administration (EIA); Figure 3.5 Oil consumption1990, US Energy Information Administration (EIA); Figure 3.6 Oil consumption 2010, US Energy Information Administration (EIA); Figure 3.7 from *IEA Oil Market Report*, p. 52, 13 December 2011, © OECD/IEA 2011; Figures 3.8, 4.2 and 4.3 from *BP Statistical Review of World Energy 2011*; Figure 3.9 Share of crude oil production, US Energy Information Administration (EIA); Figure 3.10 Share of oil consumption, US Energy Information Administration (EIA); Figure 3.11 OPEC vs non-OPEC output, US Energy Information Administration (EIA); Figure 4.1 Natural gas formation, The NEED Project, www.need.org; Figure 4.6 Two examples of directional drilling, Geology.com, http://geology.com/articles/horizontal-drilling/; Figure 4.7 Horizontal drilling and fracturing, Geology.com, http://geology.com/articles/marcellus-shale.shtml; Figure 4.8 World shale gas reserves, US Energy Information Administration (EIA); Figure 5.1 The coalification process, Kentucky Geological Survey/Stephen Greb; Figure 5.2 from *RockTalk*, Vol. 8 (2) (2005), image courtesy of the Colorado Geological Survey; Figure 5.3 Where is coal found?, World Coal Association; Figure 5.4 from *BP Energy Outlook 2030*; Figure 5.5 from *World Energy Outlook 2004*, © OECD/IEA (2004), p. 177, Figure 5.4; Figure 6.2 from *International Energy Outlook 2011*, US Energy Information Administration (EIA) (2011) p. 11, Figure 15; Figure 6.5 Hydroelectric dam, Tomia, Finland, http://en.wikipedia.org/wiki/File:Hydroelectric_dam.svg, used under the Creative Commons Attribution-ShareAlike License, http://creativecommons.org/licenses/by-sa/3.0/; Figure 6.11 Schematic of a concentrated solar thermal trough power plant, Volker Quaschning, Germany, www.volker-quaschning.de; Figure 6.12 from *Renewables 2011, Global Status Report*, Renewable Energy Network Policy Group for the 21st Century (REN21) p. 32, Figure 11; Figure 6.13 from *The State of Food and Agriculture: Biofuels, prospects, risks and opportunities*, Food and Agriculture Organization of the United Nations, Rome (2008) p. 14, Figure 6; Figure 6.14 Geothermal power production, Australian Geothermal Energy Association, www.agea.org.au; Figure 6.15 Geothermal resources in the US, US Geological Survey, USGS 790; Figure 7.1 Demand curve with social costs, Andrew Pisano, GreenX, a CME Group Company; Figure 7.2 Example of a cap in a two-firm system, Andrew Pisano, GreenX, a CME Group company; Figure 7.3 Economic benefits of cap and trade over command and control, Andrew Pisano, GreenX, a CME Group company; Figure 7.4 EUA spot price and volumes, Point Carbon, 2012; Figure 7.5 California Carbon Allowance future prices, GreenX, a CME Group company; Figure 7.6 CCFE settlement prices, Point Carbon; Figure 7.7 EUA-CER spread 2005–2012, Andrew Pisano, GreenX, a CME Group company; Figure 8.1 Precious metals deficit/surplus, INTL FCStone Inc.; Figure 8.2 Precious metals prices 2001–2011, INTL FCStone Inc.; Figure 8.3 Average gold price, INTL FCStone Inc.; Figure 8.4 When to invest in silver, long term view?, INTL FCStone Inc.; Figure 8.5 When to invest in silver, short term view?, INTL FCStone Inc.; Figure 9.1 Metals and mining equities, HSBC and Thomson Reuters; Figure 9.2 Aluminium forward curve, LME data on Thomson Reuters; Figure 9.3 Aluminium price from 1990 to 2012, LME data on Thomson Reuters; Figure 9.4 2011 bauxite main producers, US Geological Survey; Figure 9.5 Aluminium life cycle, US Geological Survey; Figure 9.6 2011 primary aluminium producers, US Geological Survey; Figure 9.7 2011 main copper producers, US Geological Survey; Figure 9.8 Copper price chart, LME data on Thomson Reuters; Figure 9.9 Copper forward curve in backwardation, LME data on Thomson Reuters; Figure 9.10 2011 zinc producing companies as percentage of world production, US Geological Survey; Figure 9.12 Zinc prices and stock levels since 2005, International Lead and Zinc Study Group (ILZSG) and LME; Figure 9.13 2011 nickel mining production, US Geological Survey; Figure 9.14 Nickel prices 1992 to 2012, LME; Figure 9.15 2011 main lead mining countries, US Geological Survey; Figure 9.16 Lead prices from 1990 to 2012, LME; Figures 9.17, 9.18 and 9.20 from *World Economic Outlook, April 2011*, International Monetary Fund p. 36; Figure 9.19 Asset performance since 2000, Reuters EcoWin; Figure 10.2 Rare earth elements in the periodic table, US Geological Survey; Figure 10.4 from *Critical Materials Strategy*, US Department of Energy (2010) p. 8, http://energy.gov/sites/prod/files/piprod/documents/cms_dec_17_full_web.pdf; Figure 10.5 Key rare earth deposits by country, Alternative-Energy.com.au; Figure 10.6 Uses of rare earth elements, Avalon Rare Metals Inc., www.avalonraremetals.com; Figure 10.8 Share price performance, Tasman Rare Metals Ltd., CVE:TSM, courtesy of Google Finance; Figure 10.9 Share price performance, Avalon Rare Metals, Inc.; Figure 11.1 1992 and 2011 food images, US Department of Agriculture; Figure 11.2 from *Estimating Demand for Agricultural Commodities to 2050*, Global Harvest Initiative

(Kruse, J. 2010) p. 6, IHS, Inc.; Figure 11.3 from *World Health Statistics 2006*, p. 17, http://www.who.int/whosis/whostat2006.pdf; Figure 11.4 from *Economics, Behavior and Biodiversity Loss: Sustainability as a pre-competitive issue*, Jason Clay, SVP, Markets, WWF-US, March 2 2011, The Garrison Institute, p. 12, http://www.garrisoninstitute.org/climate-mind-behavior-project/cmb-video-presentations/cmb-video-2011/1108-jason-clay; Figure 11.6 Returns to listed agricultural companies versus the market, Bloomberg; Figure 12.3 The water cycle, US Geological Survey; Figure 12.6 Sea water reverse osmosis desalination process, http://www.watersecure.com.au/pub/what-we-do/desalination, diagram courtesy of Seqwater 2012; Figure 12.7 Multi stage flash distribution desalination, Wikipedia, http://en.wikipedia.org/wiki/Multi-stage_flash_distillation, used under the Creative Commons Attribution-ShareAlike License, http://creativecommons.org/licenses/by-sa/3.0/

Tables

Table 1.2 Production weightings and components of the S&P GCSI for 2012, http://www.standardandpoors.com; Table 1.3 from *The RICI® Handbook: The Guide to The Rogers International Commodity Index®* (June 27, 2012), http://beelandinterests.com/RICI%20Handbook.html; Table 2.1 Top ten exchanges by number of commodity derivatives contracts traded in 2010, World Federation of Exchanges, http://www.world-exchanges.org/focus/2011-04/m-3-2.php; Table 2.3 Abbreviated contract specification for the ICE Brent Crude Future, http//:www.theice.com*; Table 4.2 Petroleum and natural gas price risks and risk management strategies, US Energy Information Administration (EIA); Table 4.3 European gas hubs, ICAP Energy Ltd.; Table 4.4 Indicative pricing data, ICAP Energy Ltd.; Table 4.5 Pricing data, ICAP Energy Ltd.; Table 5.3 Contract specification for the ICE Rotterdam Coal Futures*; Table 7.1 Examples of CDM and JI project types, Andrew Pisano, GreenX, a CME Group company; Table 7.2 EUA allocations by sector 2005–2010, Point Carbon; Table 7.4 Calculation for clean dark and spark spreads, Andrew Pisano, GreenX, a CME Group company; Table 7.5 Forward hedging of clean clark spread locks in profit, Andrew Pisano, GreenX, a CME Group company; Table 7.6 Spot clean dark spread is unprofitable, Andrew Pisano,

GreenX, a CME Group company; Table 7.7 Utility will be a buyer of power, Andrew Pisano, GreenX, a CME Group company; Table 8.1 Gold supply vs fabrication demand, INTL FCStone Inc.; Table 8.2 Silver supply vs fabrication demand, INTL FCStone Inc.; Table 8.3 Platinum supply vs fabrication demand, INTL FCStone Inc.; Table 8.4 Palladium supply vs fabrication demand, INTL FCStone Inc.; Table 8.5 Precious metals deficit/surplus, INTL FCStone Inc.; Table 8.6 Gold producers and consumers, INTL FCStone Inc.; Table 8.7 Silver producers and consumers, INTL FCStone Inc.; Table 8.8 Platinum producers and consumers, INTL FCStone Inc.; Table 8.9 Palladium producers and consumers, INTL FCStone Inc.; Table 8.10 Global gold prices 2001–2011, INTL FCStone Inc.; Table 10.1 World mining production and reserves, US Geological Survey; Table 10.3 Rare earth elements and their usage, The Matrix Partnership; Table 10.6 TMR advanced rare-earth projects index, Technical Metals Research; Table 10.7 Prices, Copyright Metal-Pages, www.metal-pages.com, Projected Prices, AVL 2015 forecast, www.avalon raremetals.com; Table 11.2 US obesity rates by annual income among national adults aged 18 and older, *Gallup-Healthways Well-Being Index*, Gallup copyrighted material: Copyright © 2010 Gallup, Inc. All rights reserved. The content is used with permission; however, Gallup retains all rights of republication; Table 11.3 Productivity comparisons between nations for cereal production, The World Bank; Table 11.5 Arable value chain, HLD Partners; Table 12.1 from I.A. Shiklomanov, World fresh water resources, in, *Water in Crisis: A Guide to the World's Fresh Water Resources*, pp. 13–24 (Gleick, P.H. (Ed.) 1993), Copyright Oxford University Press, Table 2.1, p. 13, by permission of Oxford University Press, Inc., www.oup.com; Table 12.2 Performance of four water-focused ETFs, Morningstar, Inc.

Text

Extract on page 15 DME recognized criteria, http://dubaimerc.com; Extract on page 23 S&P GSCI, http://www.standardandpoors.com; Extract on page 25 from *The RICI® Handbook: The Guide to The Rogers International Commodity Index®* (June 27, 2012), http://beelandinterests.com/RICI%20 Handbook.html; Extract on page 90 Six reasons for directional drilling, Geology.com, http://geology.com/articles/horizontal-drilling/; General Displayed Text on page 111 Properties of coal, Geology.com, http://geology.com/rocks/coal.shtml; General Displayed Text on page 116 Technical definitions, World Coal Association; Extract on page 130 from *IEA Renewable Energy Working Party* (2002) p. 9, © OECD/IEA 2002; Extract on page 130 from *Renewables 2011, Global Status Report*, Renewable Energy Network Policy Group for the 21st Century (REN21) p. 7; Extract on page 290 10 facts about water scarcity, http://www.who.int/features/factfiles/water/en/; Extract on page 294 from Tiny Pacific Island of Tuvalu calls state of emergency with just two days of drinking water left, *The Daily Mail* (Pickup, O.), 4 October 2011, used with permission of Oliver Pickup.

In some instances we have been unable to trace the owners of copyright material, and we would appreciate any information that would enable us to do so.

Contributors

DOUGLAS HANSEN-LUKE

Managing Partner, HLD Partners

Now an approved parliamentary candidate in the UK, Douglas has spent nearly 20 years living or working in emerging markets and has been involved in the investment and marketing of over $13bn of investments.

He frequently speaks and writes on agriculture and feels passionately that this is an area where investors can be profitable and do good. His interest in the sector has seen him jointly lead the development of the IDB Food and Agricultural Fund, a global food fund for public and sovereign funds, as well as invitations to advise the world's largest institutional investors on food security and speaker slots on Bloomberg, the BBC and CNBC to discuss food and soft commodities.

Most recently as CEO Middle East for the investment arm of the world's leading agri-bank, Rabo, Douglas was responsible for doubling assets managed for central banks and sovereign wealth funds throughout Africa, the Middle East and Central Asia.

His career began with consultants Bain & Company and then moved to emerging market equities for Salomon Brothers. Subsequently he worked for ABN AMRO in Hong Kong, London and then as their seconded CEO for Saudi Hollandi Asset Management in Riyadh.

Douglas maintains a strong interest in the investment challenges involved with emerging markets and in particular those related to agriculture and sustainable investing. He is the founder of HLD Partners, a specialist consultancy advising on best practice investment guidelines for both asset owners and asset gatherers in the fields of development, sustainability and philanthropy.

STEVEN MCBAIN

Crude Oil Trading Manager, Major commodities firm, Singapore

Born in 1973 in Aberdeen, Scotland. Steven left school aged 17 and joined a major oil company in London as an 'A level trainee'. A year later he joined the trading department and spent two further years as an operations trainee before becoming a trading operator in 1993. He moved from operations to trading in 1997 and worked as a crude oil trader in London from this time until the company transferred him to perform the same duties in Singapore in 2002 for their Singapore affiliate.

Steven resigned from the major oil company in 2004 and joined a large Swiss commodities trading house as the crude oil trading manager in Singapore and still currently performs this role.

Steven married his wife Gayathri in 2009 and remains happily so, being also blessed with the birth of their son Charan in 2011. Steven is a budding sports blogger, avid Chelsea FC season ticket holder and in addition to spending time with his family, enjoys travel, wine and cars although not all at the same time.

ANDREW PISANO

Senior Manager of Marketing and Development, GreenX, A CME Group Company, New York

Andrew Pisano is Senior Manager of Marketing and Development for GreenX. Mr Pisano works as part of the team responsible for overseeing the firm's operations and North American sales and marketing efforts. He is also a lead contributor to the development of the firm's global product suite, most recently helping to draft the GreenX California Allowance and Offset Futures Contracts. Prior to GreenX, Mr Pisano worked as a management consultant to a Singapore-based oil and gas corporation where he led a team responsible for driving profitability and energy efficiency improvements in the company's downstream Asian lubricants business. Mr Pisano holds bachelor of science degrees in economics and information systems from Columbia University's School of Engineering and Applied Science and a master of business administration with a concentration in environmental finance from Columbia's Graduate School of Business.

JEFFREY RHODES

Global Head of Precious Metals and Chief Executive Officer, INTL Commodities DMCC, Dubai

With almost 30 years' involvement in the precious metals market, Jeff is a leading figure in the international bullion market. He helped his employers develop their precious metals portfolios in the Middle East region and Indian sub-continent with considerable success, particularly in Dubai's expanding physical gold market. He helped develop the Dubai Multi Commodity Centre, working closely with the Government of Dubai, and has been a member of Dubai's Gold Advisory Group since its inception in 2003. Jeffrey has a regular weekly slot on Dubai's leading morning business radio show, Dubai 103.80, talking about precious metals; he is a frequent guest on regional financial TV and participates regularly as a speaker at major precious metals conferences around the world.

Jeffrey is a past chairman of the Public Affairs Committee of the London Bullion Market Association and was the founding editor of its popular trade magazine *The Alchemist*. He spent 13 years with Standard Bank plc, 11 of which were spent heading up its Dubai office, having joined in 1995 from Credit Suisse, where he worked for eight years. Previously he worked for 15 years at Samuel Montagu, a leading merchant City bank of the 1970s and 1980s and a member of the gold fix.

FABRICE TAYOT

Commodity and energy specialist for Thomson Reuters, Dubai

Fabrice Tayot, Master of International Financial Law from Sorbonne University, has been involved with the commodity and energy sector for almost a decade. He has a diverse background, with roles including Alternative Investment Analyst, Trading Assistant, Energy Analyst, Head of Commodity Research Team among others. After living and working in major financial centres such as London, Paris and New York, Fabrice is now based in Dubai. He is currently the commodity and energy specialist for Thomson Reuters, dealing with leading financial institutions and national oil companies for the last three years. Fabrice is recognised as an active member of the commodity and energy community and travels extensively in the Middle East and North Africa region. He conducts regular workshops on topics such as commodity risk management, asset forward pricing, and other relevant issues, well attended by Chief Risk Officers, Treasurers, Strategists and Heads of Commodity Desk. He has a unique ability to blend theoretical knowledge with the practical aspects of the market, and is sought after by trading desk, buy side research and alternative investment managers. He can be reached at fabrice.tayot@gmail.com.

VICTORIA ADAMS

Commodities Broker, European Natural Gas, ICAP Energy Ltd

Victoria graduated from Nottingham University with a BA Hons in Russian and Hispanic Studies. She joined the Natural Gas desk at ICAP in 2008, bringing with her experiences from the banking industry at HSBC offices in London and Moscow. When she began at ICAP, Victoria more than doubled the revenues generated from their TTF spot business. Four years on she is managing the Dutch and Austrian spot and French curve gas markets: TTF, CEGH Baumgarten and Peg Nord, Peg Sud, Peg TIGF respectively. ICAP Energy, the commodity arm of ICAP plc, provides coverage of base and precious metals, emission credits, crude oil and oil products, electricity, coal, freight, weather derivatives and, of course, natural gas. ICAP is a leader in its field and has consistently received the award for Energy Risk Broker of the Year. Victoria's business involves extensive travel within Europe and she speaks English, Russian, Spanish, some French, German and Serbo-Croat.

BRUCE DANCKWERTS

Managing Director, New Venture Farm Ltd, Zambia

Bruce (56, Zimbabwean) was born in Zimbabwe but moved to Zambia with his family in 1963. Studying Engineering at Cambridge during the oil crisis of 1973 left him with an awareness of sustainability issues. Bruce has been farming in Zambia for 36 years, during which time he has been trying to make his farm in Choma (Southern Province) less and less dependent on fossil fuels.

MARC-HENRI VEYRASSAT

AF Founder and Managing Director, African Resources Capital

Marc-Henri (46, Swiss) has spent the better part of the last two decades doing business and living in Africa, including South Africa, Nigeria, Ivory Coast, Zimbabwe, Zambia and the DRC. He is the founder and managing director of African Resources Capital, a corporate finance advisory firm, specialised in structuring transactions in the SADC region, with a focus on natural resources and agriculture. Marc-Henri holds an MSc in Economics from the University of Lausanne, Switzerland and is based in South Africa.

1

Commodity Fundamentals

Commodities are an asset class in their own right

Range of commodity investments

Market developments and global drivers

Commodity prices and their effect on financial markets

Market participants

How commodities differ from other assets:
storage, transportation/transmission/shipping, spoilage

Economics of commodities: spot and forward transactions

Forward curves: contango and backwardation

Understanding the 'basis'

Commodity hedging, trading, arbitrage

Commodity indices

COMMODITIES ARE AN ASSET CLASS IN THEIR OWN RIGHT

For many years commodities have been relegated to an esoteric backwater but now they have become fashionable; they are volatile, often found in dangerous countries like Afghanistan, can move prices in every other consumer and financial market, yet until comparatively recently were an asset class understood by only a relatively small group of market practitioners.

Every day on the front pages of your newspaper you read about commodities, their prices, their effect on the country and your wallet, coupled with overpopulation, climate change etc.; even our taxi drivers are experts. We regularly hear that commodity markets are driving the capital markets and everyone nods wisely, but let's cut to the chase – what exactly are commodities and why do we need to understand them?

Most readers will be aware of oil and oil products as commodities but it is more than that; in short, a commodity is anything that we consume on this planet. From food and water, to oil and gas, to electricity, to solar and wind power, to metals and minerals, to timber and forests, plastics, paper, plants, animals and fish – they are all commodities, from the rubber in your tyres to the pepper on your table.

As population growth threatens to overwhelm the Earth's natural resources the availability and prices of these commodities will become squeezed in the most dangerous of ways. As an example, it won't just be a matter of, 'it's getting expensive to fill up the car', but maybe there will be no milk in the shops or no fresh meat.

You might not be able to afford the cost of the air conditioner, or the heating in the winter. I am sure you can imagine many more examples – regular power blackouts – no TV, no Internet, no online computer games, no cooking, no air conditioning, no lights, you cannot charge your cell phones. With prolonged situations like these, civil unrest will almost certainly follow, which will spur governments into taking action.

Naturally, this asset class also provides opportunities for investing, hedging and trading both in the physical, equities and derivatives markets. Corporations and individuals that invest in commodities, as well as in the related primary organisations such as the mining and food companies, the energy and power utilities, may do very well, but we must not overlook the spectre of market volatility – love it or hate it, it is a major price and profit and loss determinant.

RANGE OF COMMODITY INVESTMENTS

Commodities can easily be used to diversify a portfolio of financial assets and manage any correlation issues – meaning that the oil or gold prices will not necessarily move in exactly the same way as the stock or financial markets. A compelling research piece from Dr John Lintner in May 1983 demonstrated that if commodities (futures) are added to a portfolio, they significantly increase the return and reduce the volatility and variance. It follows therefore that every portfolio needs some commodities exposure for optimum returns. (For further information please read 'The Potential Role of Managed Commodity – Financial Futures Accounts (and/or Funds) in Portfolios of Stocks and Bonds', delivered at the annual conference of the Financial Analysts Federation in Toronto in May 1983.)

In recent years there has been a marked increase in commodity investment by institutional investors, hedge funds, retail investors and sovereign wealth funds – all of which are looking at the quite depressed traditional investment markets and thinking, 'where else can we put our money?'

Investors can gain exposure to commodities through direct investments in physical commodities, direct investments in commodity-related companies and investments in commodity futures through exchange traded standardised contracts (derivatives) either as separate contracts or via a managed futures fund with exposure to a range of commodities and contracts. You could also invest in countries that produce commodities – including Australia, Canada, New Zealand, Brazil, Russia and the 'Stans' (Kazakhstan, Kyrgyzstan, Uzbekistan and Tajikistan).

Exchange Traded Products (ETPs) are a particular favourite in the commodity markets. They include:

- Exchange Traded Funds (ETFs);
- Closed End Funds (CEFs);
- Exchange Traded Notes (ETNs).

The very first gold ETF was the Gold Bullion Securities ETF, launched in March 2003 by the Australian Stock Exchange.

Another tool in the investor's toolkit is the commodity index. These offer access to a basket of commodities, reducing the risk of investing in a single commodity. There are a number of commodity indices such as the Goldman Sachs Commodity Index (GSCI), now the S&P GSCI, Standard & Poor's Commodity Index (SPCI), the Rogers International Commodity Index® (RICI) and the Thomson Reuters/Jefferies CRB Index (TR/J CRB).

Alternatively, you could invest in indices that are facing towards a certain commodity or groups of commodities; for example, the S&P GSCI has a number of sub-indices, which are discussed later in this chapter.

Commodity assets under management nearly tripled between 2008 and 2011. Inflows into the sector totalled over US$60 billion in 2010, the second highest year on record, down from the record US$72 billion allocated to commodities funds in the previous year. Figure 1.1 shows the comparative performance of bonds using the Barclays Aggregated Bond Index, stocks (equities) using the S&P 500 and commodities using the S&P Goldman Sachs Commodity Index.

Figure 1.1 **Comparison of performance of bonds, equities and commodities**

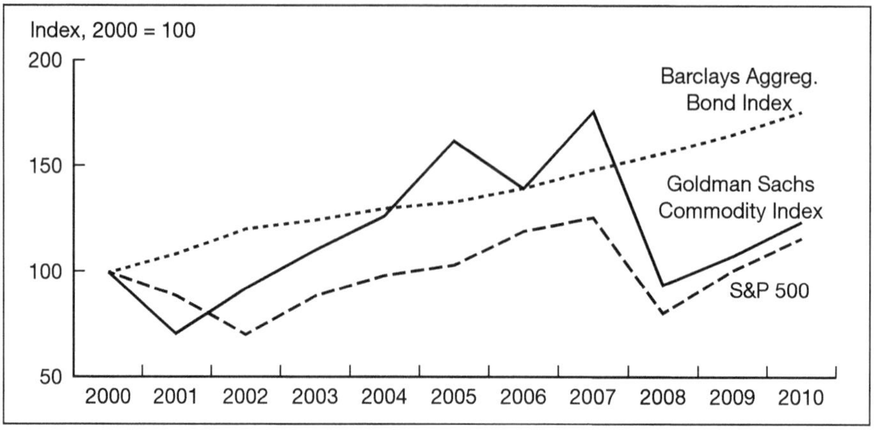

Source: GSCI, Barclays, S&P

The bulk of the funds that went into commodities went into precious metals and energy products. Growth in the prices of many commodities obviously made a contribution to the increased value of commodities funds under management. For example, the price of gold posted a record high during 2011 at over US$1800 per ounce and silver lept to a 30 year high.

A number of factors are behind the recent rise in prices. Emerging economies have driven the demand for various commodities – particularly markets in China, India and the Middle East. Biofuels have boosted the demand for specific food crops, notably sugar cane. A global shortage of rare earth elements (REEs) has driven prices for some REEs skywards. A weakening US dollar and low interest rates have all amplified price pressures, as have increased population pressures.

The sharp rise of commodity prices in recent years is in stark contrast to the 1980s and 1990s when returns on commodities were uncompetitive with either stocks or bonds. Commodity prices, when measured in inflation adjusted terms, reached levels equivalent to their 1930s lows in 1999. Many factors contributed to this downward pressure including:

- falling demand for commodities as a hedge against inflation in market conditions of low inflation;
- consumer spending in the US which dominated global demand and shifted towards services requiring fewer commodities, e.g. banking and finance rather than manufacturing industries.

Currently, exports of commodities continue to play an important role in emerging market economies. The Middle East and North Africa and to a lesser extent sub-Saharan Africa and Latin America have been the main beneficiaries of the recent increase in commodity prices. Fuel exports play the most critical role in the Middle East and North Africa, where they now account for more than one-third of GDP. Latin America depends on exporting both fuel and non-fuel commodities whereas non-fuel commodities, e.g. agricultural products and metals, are particularly important in sub-Saharan Africa.

MARKET DEVELOPMENTS AND GLOBAL DRIVERS

In 2004, commodities market guru Jim Rogers wrote in his book *Hot Commodities* (published by Wiley, 2007, ISBN 978-0-470-51076-6) 'that a new bull market is underway – and it is in commodities'. This market came to be known as the commodities 'super-cycle' and Rogers believes that these cycles typically last around 15 years, and by my reckoning we are just over halfway through.

Listed below are some of the present market drivers.

- Populations are expected to exhibit continued strong growth, especially in emerging markets such as China and India, with the UN forecasting a 47 per cent increase in population over the period 2000 to 2050 to a staggering 8.9 billion.
- Emerging markets and developed economies are projected to spend a significant amount of capital to meet the demands of urbanisation and the replacement of ageing infrastructure.
- Strong emerging market demand will mean that natural resources will essentially remain decoupled from the developed world's economic slowdown.
- Rising demand and constraints in supply will continue to drive commodity prices even higher, particularly for agriculture, in the long term.

Over the last few years, commodities have become a genuine asset class alongside bonds, equities and hedge funds and can provide a positive hedge against inflation. They are typically counter-cyclical and have a negative correlation with other asset classes, whilst also providing broader long-term equity-like returns. Commodities can also exhibit strong price performance during periods of market instability.

Commodity demand in the years ahead is expected to recover fully along with the broader economy, and the rise of ETFs (Exchange Traded Funds) makes investment easier and more openly available. There has been a noted shift by pension funds towards raw materials – e.g. CalSTRS (California State Teachers Retirement System), CalPERS (California Public Employees Retirement System), PGCM and ABP (two of the largest pension funds in the Netherlands) and European Corporate Pension Plans – all of which will add to the price pressures.

Much of the physical trading of commodities is through individually tailored over the counter (OTC) contracts. The most popular physical commodities contracts are:

- Energy – oil, coal, gas products;
- Metals – gold, silver, platinum and palladium (precious) and copper, lead, zinc, aluminium (base/industrial);
- Grains and soy – wheat, barley, corn;
- Livestock, food and fibre – orange juice, cattle, poultry, silk and cotton;
- Exotic commodities – rare earth elements such as neodymium, dysprosium.

A large proportion of OTC commodities' trading is transacted between producers, refiners and wholesalers on the spot market. Trading is delivery based and typically arranged through intermediaries. For most physically traded commodities there is no actual marketplace in, say, a central part of town and if it does exist it typically handles only a small fraction of the total trade.

Commodities are diverse, as shown in Figure 1.2, and appeal to many varieties of investors.

COMMODITY PRICES AND THEIR EFFECT ON FINANCIAL MARKETS

As a discrete asset class, commodities are vital to any diversified portfolio due to their unique characteristics:

- When equity markets fall, commodity markets tend to rise, and vice versa.
- The price of equities can go to zero – not true of commodities.
- There is no credit risk on a commodity.
- Commodity returns are higher than inflation.
- Bonds and equities are negatively correlated to inflation (this increases with the holding period), whilst the opposite is true of commodities – thus commodities provide an inflation hedge.
- Commodities are correlated with inflation, unexpected inflation and changes in expected inflation.
- Commodity prices can rise even if the economy is going nowhere.
- War and terrorism push commodity prices up.
- A precious metal, especially gold, is a safe haven for investors – often replacing cash or treasury bonds as folks become fearful of a weakening US dollar or geopolitical tensions. Gold was priced at US$1000 per ounce in March 2008, yet at the time of writing it is pricing at over US$1800 per ounce!

Figure 1.2

Commodity universe

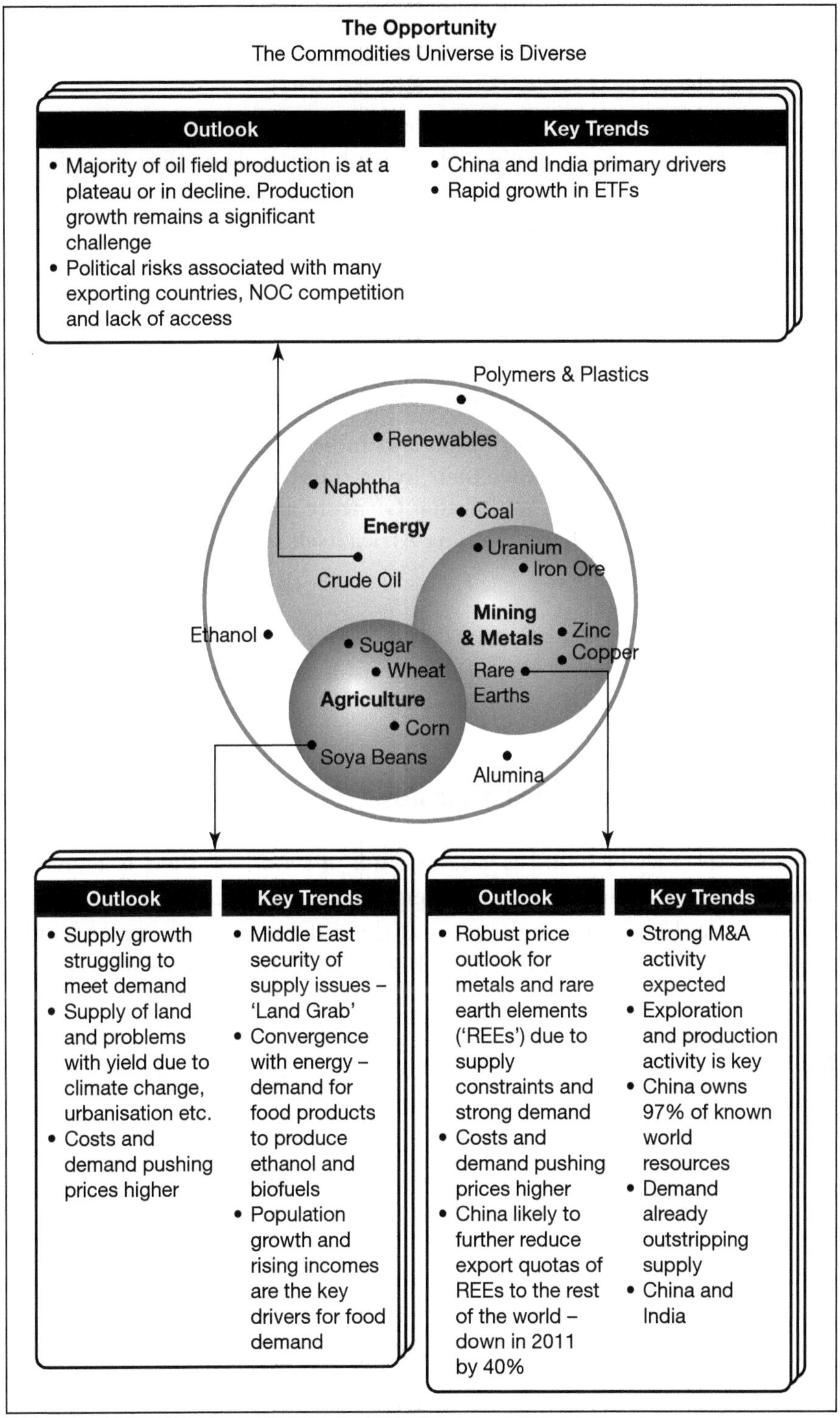

Source: The Matrix Partnership, Dubai, UAE

- Most commodities are priced in US dollars, creating a foreign currency risk to those with non-dollar domestic currencies.
- There is an obvious link between oil prices and foreign exchange generally and the value of the US dollar in particular.
- Currency relationships are very complex. In the short term, a weakening dollar does not affect supply and demand, but it does affect speculation and investment in oil futures markets. As the dollar depreciates, commodities such as oil and gas generally attract investors.
- As population growth soars and pressure intensifies on food and raw materials, the prices of all major consumables will increase, leading to an increase in the cost of living.

As Ivan Glasenberg, CEO of Glencore, said in June 2011:

> **'Over two billion people in China and India need commodities to grow their economies and improve their living standards. Africa is where commodities are found so it is vital that Glencore and other miners are there to develop those resources, helping Africa itself to grow at the same time.'**
>
> (*Wall Street Journal*, 6 July 2011)

Does this mean that investing in commodities is also an investment play on Africa? It might be! It may also be considered to be a proxy China/Asia Pacific play.

Commodities – weights and measures

Commodities may be found as gases, liquids or solids and there is a range of measurements used in the market. Weight often causes confusion in the raw materials market; for example, what is the difference between a ton and a tonne, should we use the terms interchangeably? The answer is no!

Definitions

1 ton	this is a measure used predominantly in the US and is an imperial measure of 2240lb which is equivalent to 1016.0469080kg
1 tonne	this is a metric measure and is predominantly used outside the US and refers to 1000kg

Should copper be priced per kg, per lb or per ton? It depends on the market and the country. Table 1.1 collects together the more popular measures.

Table 1.1

Common weights and measures

Weights and Measures for Commodities			
Name	**Abbreviation**	**Weight**	**Used for**
Fine troy ounce	oz	31.103 grams	Gold
Bar	bar	400 troy ounces ~ 12.5 kg	Gold – Good Delivery Bar
Troy ounce	oz	31.103 grams	Silver
Bar	bar	750 to 1100 ounces	Silver – Good Delivery Bar
Barrel	bbl	42 US gallons, 35 imperial gallons	Oil
Long ton	t	2240 lbs (1016.047 kg)	Coal
Tonne/Metric tonne	tn	2204 lbs (1000.00 kg)	Coal, Rare Earths
Kilograms	kg	2.2 lbs	Rare Earths, Metals
Avoirdupois ounce	oz	28.4 grams (1/16 of lb)	Agriculture
Bushel	1 bushel	Wheat/Soybeans – 60 lbs	Agricultural items
	1 bushel	Corn/Rye – 56 lbs	Agricultural items
	1 bushel	Barley – 48 lbs	Agricultural items
	1 bushel	Oats – 38 lbs	Agricultural items
Carat	Ct	200 mg	Diamonds
Point	Pt	100 points in each carat	Diamonds
Kilowatt	kW	100 watts	Electricity
Megawatt	MW	100 kilowatts	Electricity
Gigawatt	GW	1000 megawatts	Electricity
Terawatt	TW	1000 gigawatts	Electricity
Thousand cubic feet	1 Mcf	1000 cubic feet	Natural Gas
Billion cubic feet	1 Bcf	1,000,000,000 cubic feet	Natural Gas
Trillion cubic feet	1 Tcf	1,000,000,000,000 cubic feet	Natural Gas
Cubic metre	m^3	1 litre = 1 kg	Water

Source: The Matrix Partnership

MARKET PARTICIPANTS

Having started my career as a geologist, I then moved into Treasury and Banking, I have a finance background and it is natural for me to look at commodities and observe where they fit within a financial framework – but that is not the whole story. We also need to consider the participants at the 'sharp end' of the commodities space – literally on the ground. Noted below are the participants that are commonly found in the commodities sector.

Financial participants

Bankers

1. Most large firms have commodities trading desks, where trading either of the underlying physical commodity or of one of the specialised derivatives takes place. Many institutions use the acronym 'FICC' for their trading desks – fixed income, currencies and commodities. However, many banks do not separate out or disclose the results of their commodity trading.
2. Equity trading desks will trade a range of stocks/shares where the core of the stock price is driven by commodities and how they perform, notably multinational organisations, e.g. Royal Dutch Shell, BP, Rio Tinto, Anglo American, Glencore, Schlumberger and Xstrata.
3. Banks with a large investor base will almost inevitably employ economists and investment analysts whose role is to analyse the commodities markets and the companies which are linked to them.
4. Bond trading and origination staff in banks assist a firm to raise funds through the capital markets, possibly through an Initial Public Offering (IPO) or a private placement.
5. Corporate bankers facilitate the day-to-day financial operations of their clients who may require loans for mining or agriculture, or exploration or even logistics.

Commodity traders

These are institutions that trade and speculate on commodities markets – without the need or desire for a banking licence. The well-known firms are Glencore, Trafigura, Vitol and Mercuria.

Brokers

Brokers are the proverbial middlemen, putting together willing buyers and willing sellers, and charging each side (where possible) a fee known as commission or brokerage ('bro'). They are acting as agents, not principals. The early firms had teams of product specialists who literally telephoned their clients or kept them in touch via 'squawk boxes' (intercoms) in their offices – thus earning themselves the description 'voice brokers'. As markets have become more electronic, and with the increasing financial market regulation, it is expected that most of this business will migrate to computerised execution platforms – a process known as 'electronification'.

A full service broker, of whom there are fewer and fewer, will offer a broking service in commodities as well as cash and foreign exchange, e.g. ICAP, GFI Group and Tullett Prebon.

Placement agents

These are individuals or firms that are used to assist in fundraising by commodities firms or funds. An example might be a junior oil company seeking a 'farm in' partner or a private equity fund seeking investors. The agents may be on a monthly retainer or they may operate on a success fee only basis, then they will receive a fee ranging from 1.5 to 5.0 per cent of the funds they raise.

The investor community

The investor community includes a wide range of investors from private equity, to hedge funds, to pension funds, to the private individual. The largest investors by far are the Sovereign Wealth Funds (SWFs). These are organisations that have been formed to manage governmental or state surpluses, an extension of the activity that used to be known as reserves management. Some important examples are:

- Temasek Holdings in Singapore;
- ADIA (Abu Dhabi Investment Authority) in Abu Dhabi;
- SGRF (State General Reserve Fund) in Oman;
- EIA (Emirates Investment Authority) in the UAE.

But there are many others.

All asset managers will look at commodities from time to time, whether they work in a pension fund, a trust or private equity. Also in this category are a group of discreet entities known as 'family offices', formed to look after dynastic monies from some of the world's largest and wealthiest families.

Exchanges

Commodity exchanges have developed from physical markets where deals were originally transacted in warehouses to futures markets (which were vast buildings, but which are now in essence computer-based 'server farms'), allowing for both hedging and trading.

These exchange traded derivatives markets were developed initially to help agricultural producers and consumers manage their price risks. The largest of all the US exchange groups is now called the Chicago Mercantile Exchange Group (CME) but when it was first established in the late 1800s it was known as the Chicago Produce Exchange, latterly as the Chicago Butter and Egg Board, evidencing its agricultural background.

Exchanges are institutions where the trading of 'paper' takes place, usually futures and/or options linked to a specific underlying asset such as Oman crude oil, which trades on the Dubai Mercantile Exchange (DME), West Texas Intermediate (WTI) crude, which trades on the New York Mercantile Exchange (NYMEX), or even carbon, which trades on the GreenXchange. These exchanges operate globally with many diverse members and have strict entry requirements. As Exchange Traded Funds (ETFs) in commodities have grown and become very popular so the exchanges are growing that side of their businesses.

Notable exchanges include ICE (InterContinental Exchange) in Atlanta, NYSE Euronext in Europe, DME in Dubai, CME in Chicago, New York Mercantile Exchange (NYMEX – now part of CME), TSX (Toronto Stock Exchange) in Toronto, SSE (Shanghai Stock Exchange) in Shanghai and GreenX (Environmental Futures & Options) in London.

Non-financial participants

These are individuals, groups or firms involved directly in the physical commodity. In overview they are:

- Geologists – exploring/mapping for the natural resource;
- Surveyors – establishing the extent of the deposit;
- Chemists and metallurgists – investigating the purity of the deposit;
- Miners – to extract the resource;
- Processers – to remove the ore from the deposit;
- Drilling companies – to drill/pump oil/gas from deep wells;
- Refiners – to 'crack' the oil into its component products;
- Logistics, haulage, shipping and transport – to move the resource from where it has been extracted or refined to where the finished goods are required.

Then of course you have the enormous multinational firms that operate along the entire value chain, from exploring for the resource, owning the land, extracting/drilling, transportation/shipping, moving the oil to their refineries, where through various processes they might separate out petrol/gas that is then transported to a garage network for the retail customer, e.g. Shell, Esso, Total.

HOW COMMODITIES DIFFER FROM OTHER ASSETS: STORAGE, TRANSPORTATION/TRANSMISSION/SHIPPING, SPOILAGE

Some of the key differentiators between the commodities markets and other asset classes are the functions of storage, transport and distribution and, in the case of agricultural products, spoilage.

In order to move a currency from one bank to another you simply instigate a SWIFT message and an electronic transfer will transmit the funds. Currency is currency, an equity is an equity, but oil for example comes in many different chemical compositions. If the buyer of a US Treasury bond or US equity lives in Shanghai and the seller lives in the US, we do not need to send the bond/stock on a ship or a plane; we will either use custodians or hold the instruments electronically in a nominee account. There will be a charge in both cases but it will be minor.

Contrast this to physical oil being pumped from reserves off the coast of Oman yet required for use in Singapore; the crude will need to be loaded onto tankers which will then make their way eastwards to Asia. Not only will there be a substantial charge for this shipping, but we also need to consider insurance for the cargo and the time delay in getting the oil from point of origin to ultimate destination.

Many crudes are priced based on their geographical location as well as their sulphur content. Common crude oil benchmarks are:

- Brent – a basket of several crude streams from the North Sea.
- WTI – popular US benchmark but which has become dislocated from the rest of the market, due to overcapacity at Cushing, Oklahoma.
- Dubai – the key Middle East and Asian benchmark.

Another example concerns electricity: how do you store and transport this and what happens if it doesn't arrive on time? Transportation or transmission is along power lines and you can lose up to 15 per cent of the resource during this process. If this 'packet' of power is needed urgently – as in the Texas drought and the fires of 2011, and if it doesn't arrive in time, it is possible to black out entire towns.

With food security being foremost in many governments' thoughts, it is not sufficient to consider whether the food can be grown – this on its own requires water, fertiliser, good weather, harvesting/slaughtering – but it also needs to be stored. Typically, in hot climates a large proportion of food is wasted or spoiled; consequently, in many hot countries spices are used in cooking for their antimicrobial properties. Generally the hotter the climate the more spices are used. Antimicrobial spices which pretty much kill everything include garlic, onion, allspice and oregano.

As a result of the potentially high spoilage issues many Gulf States are considering building new high tech storage facilities with temperature and humidity controls.

ECONOMICS OF COMMODITIES: SPOT AND FORWARD TRANSACTIONS

As seen earlier in the chapter, commodities are different in many ways from traditional financial assets such as bank deposits, foreign exchange or bonds. This affects the way they are priced. However, pricing oil and oil products is markedly different from pricing gold, or indeed soya. Here, I will revert back to first principles of pricing as far as possible.

With most asset classes there are two distinct pricing methodologies: spot and forward markets. A spot rate is a fixed price quoted for delivery in the very near future – today, tomorrow or the next day – and a forward price is a fixed price quoted today for delivery in the future on a forward date. Nevertheless, many commodities are priced using a third method, a fixed term contract, and in the oil market especially this is popular. These longer-term contracts may be linked to a fixed price or a floating price and are often linked to a particular producer. Approximately half of the world's crude changes hands using fixed term contracts with the balance using spot and futures markets pricing.

Spot transactions

A spot transaction is a formal agreement to buy/sell a shipment of oil or a cargo of rare earths, or even bushels of wheat, at a price agreed at the time between the two parties. When the fixed term contracts and futures pricing account for over 90 per cent of the market, spot markets are a way of regulating supply and demand. If a producer has an excess the additional quantity will be offered into the spot market; if a client needs to source additional volumes then oil can be purchased on a shipment by shipment basis. Rising spot levels indicate that more supply is needed and vice versa.

Historically, prices in all commodities have been volatile; oil is a good example as evidenced by Figure 1.3.

Crude oil pricing

The value of any particular crude oil is compared to the appropriate 'benchmark' or 'marker crude' for pricing in the final area of importation. The oil will then be sold at a premium or a discount on the day, with respect to the marker crude being used. Popular crude oil benchmarks are West Texas Intermediate (WTI), Brent, Bonny Light, Dubai and Oman (e.g. Arab light exports to the US at WTI +/– an adjustment factor). The level of the premium or discount will relate to the crude oil itself, while the outright price level is decided by the price of the marker crude. In general, light crudes yield more gasoline and high-value products than heavy crudes.

Figure 1.3

Price of crude oil in 2010 US dollar equivalents, 1869–2011

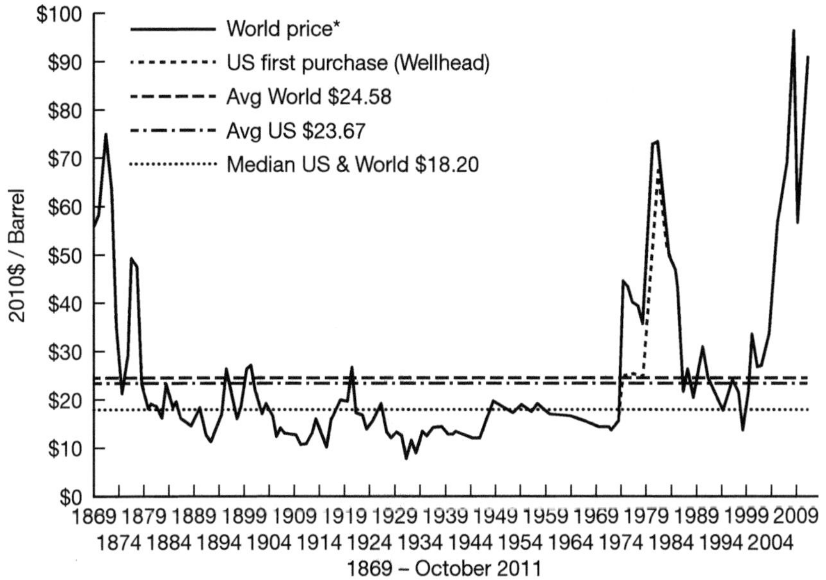

*World price – The only very long-term price series that exists is the US average wellhead or first purchase price of crude. When discussing long-term price behaviour this presents a problem since the US imposed price controls on domestic production from late 1973 to January 1981. In order to present a consistent series and also reflect the difference between international prices and US prices we created a world oil price series that was consistent with the US wellhead price, adjusting the wellhead price by adding the difference between the refiners' acquisition price of imported crude and the refiners' average acquisition price of domestic crude.

Source: WTRG Economics, www.wtrg.com

What determines which crude is used as a marker?

The Dubai Mercantile Exchange (DME) quotes these recognised criteria:

1. Robust long-term production levels (300,000–400,000+ bpd (barrels per day)).
2. Relatively stable daily production levels (e.g. not subject to OPEC cuts, location away from regional hurricane centres).
3. Quality indicative of other regional/substitute crudes.
4. Availability of liquid, freely traded secondary market (e.g. no destination restrictions).
5. Multiple production/access rights, ensuring market access by numerous players.

Figure 1.4 shows where the key marker crudes are typically used.

Figure 1.4 **Benchmark crudes and where they are used**

Historically, Western markets utilised futures traded benchmarks such as Brent and WTI, whereas Eastern markets primarily utilised Dubai crude assessments

- A primary benchmark is used for each of the world's supply/demand regions, reflecting its own unique supply/demand fundamentals.
- Whereas Western benchmarks (e.g., WTI) are principally traded on regulated exchanges (e.g., CME/NYMEX), East of Suez benchmarks (e.g., Dubai) have historically traded in over-the-counter/spot markets, with pricing assessments reported by journalistic agencies.
- The majority of Gulf producers have utilised the average of monthly assessments of Dubai and Oman into their Far East OSP formulas. However, partials market activity has typically been concentrated in Dubai.

Source: Dubai Mercantile Exchange

Forward prices

Calculating forward rates for a commodity

Consider one of the metals, for example copper; assume a client has requested from a bank or a copper trader for a six month forward price. The spot rate at the time of writing is US$8150 per tonne. We need to estimate, not where copper will be trading in six months' time (that would simply be a guess on the spot rate), but what rate the quoting party can live with if it is asked to guarantee the price for physical delivery in six months. The only way to do this safely is for the trader to purchase the copper now at today's known spot rate and factor in all the additional costs (known as cost of carry), including:

- **Financing** – how does the bank/trader pay for the copper now if the client is not going to pay until the maturity date in six months? The money will need to be borrowed for six months at US$ LIBOR, assume 1.0 per cent pa.

- **Storage** – what does the bank/trader do with the copper for 6 months – assume it cannot be loaned to anyone else in the meantime.
- **Transport/insurance** – if appropriate.

Let us assume the additional costs per tonne (at US$8150) are:

- Finance – $40.97 (8150 × 181/360 × 1%)
- Storage – $15
- Transport/insurance – $12

Total = $67.97 = Cost of Carry

The true cost of this transaction to the bank/trader is therefore:

$8150 + $67.97 = $8217.97

This is the fair value of the forward price. It is a theoretical price and a breakeven price – a profit margin will most likely then be added on top. We can summarise this pricing relationship as follows:

Spot + cost of carry = Forward price (theoretical)

There is a very serious drawback with this relationship: it assumes that nothing in that simple formula will change; yet we know it will, so this is not a forecast. Simply, given everything we know today, *where should it be trading?*

Forward pricing for all assets works in much the same way: firstly, ascertain the spot rate; secondly, gather the data for the cost of carry. The forward rate becomes the rate where everything is included – even a risk premium if things go wrong!

One would expect that the forward price of an asset would always be higher than the spot price as there are very real costs incurred for the financing and storage etc. However, in some market conditions the opposite occurs, so it looks as if the forward price is too low; in fact it is more likely that the spot price is too high and it has been bid up due to a market imbalance and folks are scrambling for supplies.

FORWARD CURVES: CONTANGO AND BACKWARDATION

The relationship between the spot and forward rate is known as a forward curve and is a function of multiple inputs – including funding, cost of storage, seasonality, supply and demand and current existing inventories.

The shape of the forward curve may drive physical stocks and inventories. For example, contango markets tend to incentivise stock building whereas backwardated markets encourage stocks to be drawn down (see Figures 1.5 and 1.6).

Figure 1.5 **Contango and backwardation**

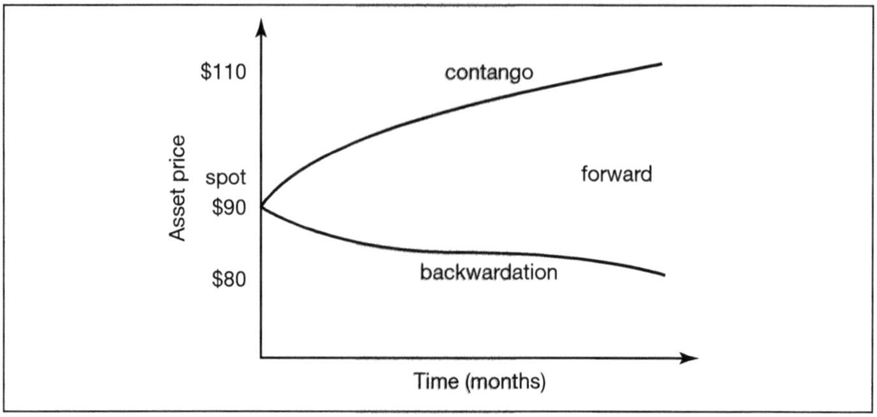

Source: The Matrix Partnership

A commodity forward curve in contango is equivalent to a normal yield curve in the interest rate market. However, in the commodity markets, where you have buyers at the front end of the curve and sellers at the back end of the curve, this tends to move the curve into backwardation.

Spot prices are unpredictable and the buyer may well prefer or indeed require the certainty of holding a guaranteed forward contract now or even holding the physical commodity, and may be willing to pay a premium for the comfort. In the uncertain and volatile commodities markets that we have seen recently, if there is an end user with a continual requirement for a certain input of a stock of goods, a combination of forward (future) and spot buying reduces uncertainty. For example, an oil refiner might purchase 50 per cent spot and 50 per cent forward, averaging his price.

Definitions

Contango

When the forward or futures price is above the expected future spot price. Consequently, the price will decline to the spot price before the delivery date.

Backwardation

When the forward or futures curve is below the expected future spot price. Consequently, the price will increase to meet the spot price before the delivery date.

A backwardated market is equivalent to an inverse or inverted yield curve in the interest rate market. Physical users will pay a premium for prompt delivery; this in turn creates buying pressure at the short end. Producers (sellers) have fewer long-term risks and are more willing to lock in a selling price, creating selling pressure in the longer end of the curve.

If there is a shortage in the market the current spot price will be higher (bid up), also creating a backwardated market. This reflects the 'convenience yield' effect – meaning, I will pay up for the asset now rather than risk it being unavailable in the future. In effect the market has gone into backwardation. A steeply 'backwardated' market implies significant shortages.

Backwardation has no theoretical limit and can coexist with contango in a broken or 'kinked' curve (see Figure 1.6).

Figure 1.6

Contango and backwardation

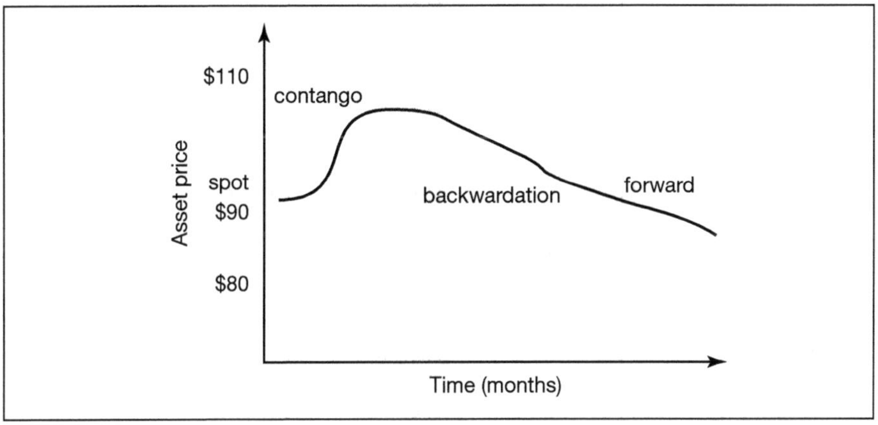

Source: The Matrix Partnership

Backwardation may be used as a leading indicator – for the economists out there! Backwardation usually widens when prices rise and narrows when prices fall.

Convergence

This is the term given when a forward or futures price converges with the then current spot rate.

Futures market convergence is the process where cash market prices and futures market prices come together, or converge, at the futures market expiry date. Theoretically, convergence occurs at each futures contract expiration date for two reasons:

1. All futures and indeed all forward prices are comprised of an underlying spot price for the commodity combined with a 'cost of carry' adjustment that is derived from underlying financing costs, together with transport,

storage and insurance. If you initially purchase a future at US$150 this may have been linked to US$100 spot price + US$50 cost of carry, which is time dependent and includes factors such as financing, storage etc. As time progresses, although the markets will continue to fluctuate, the number of days to maturity will decrease; hence the amount of residual financing will decrease, eventually leading to a spot price which includes zero cost of carry as there are no days left in the transaction. The closer is the expiry date of the futures contract, the closer the futures price should be to the spot rate. The actual futures price may be trading higher or lower than the current spot price.

2. Convergence may also occur due to arbitrage; if spot cash prices remain below futures prices, a market participant could buy in the cash market and sell in the futures market, and make a risk-free profit. Similarly, if the cash price is above the futures price, a market participant could buy in the futures market, take delivery and sell in the cash market, again earning a risk-free profit.

Figure 1.7 shows a diagrammatic representation of convergence.

Figure 1.7 **Illustrating convergence**

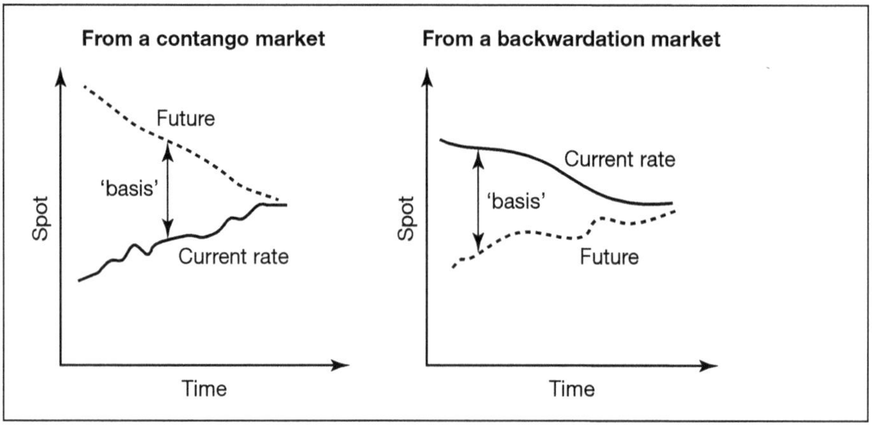

Source: The Matrix Partnership

UNDERSTANDING THE 'BASIS'

This is important when you use futures for hedging.

The 'basis' is the difference between where the future is trading now and where the spot rate is trading now; it is a function of storage, timing and cost of carry. The basis will be different for each futures contract as each one represents a different future date. The basis is continually changing and may be positive or negative depending upon whether the future is trading higher or lower than the current spot rate. It is also incredibly difficult to hedge. The only firm certainty is that by the expiry date of the futures the cash market price and the futures price will converge. Traders may take speculative positions depending on whether they believe that the basis will narrow or widen during the life of the contract.

COMMODITY HEDGING, TRADING, ARBITRAGE

Hedgers

A hedger is someone who wants to manage or mitigate their perceived risk. This may be anyone from a small diesel importer to a large multinational with a stream of crude from an oil well wishing to protect its prices, to a European fund manager who is worried about the domestic stock market falling – much of which contains energy stocks. Hedgers generally will 'buy' the insurance or enter into protection. The tools they use are global market instruments that easily cross borders.

Traders

A trader (or speculator) wants to take risk. The banking and hedge fund community dominates here. Most, but not all traders will make a market, i.e. a bid and an offer. They could be trading supply and demand, or directionally – does the asset go up or down from here? – or even volatility – how the market price is going to fluctuate. Their role is to make markets, in effect to quote prices for anyone who wants them (subject to internal credit criteria), create the asset, run their positions – hopefully at a profit – and hedge themselves. Traders will speculate in the physical commodities and futures markets.

Arbitrageurs

These are individuals or banks that try and identify price discrepancies and profit from them. An example might be someone who can buy Brent crude at US$101.50 and simultaneously sell it at US$104.50. Obviously, this looks too good to be true, but you would take advantage of it nevertheless. In the derivatives market, you would assume that the physical gold price will move at the same speed as derivatives linked to the gold price. This may not always be the case, so there may be profit opportunities from buying one and selling the other.

On the first working day of 2012 the oil price spiked by nearly 5 per cent giving a Brent Crude rate of US$112 and a WTI rate of US$103. This led market commentators and analysts to revisit the 'fat tails' or 'tail-risk' concept (the terminology comes from statistics such as normal distribution/bell curves). These are low probability events that have an outsized impact on prices. At the time of writing the Eurozone is in crisis – which may depress prices – whilst the Iranians are reacting badly to the US and European oil embargos and Israel is watching the developing situation in the Straits of Hormuz where the Iranians are threatening a blockade. The overall political climate in the Middle East and North Africa continues to be challenging following the uprisings during the 'Arab Spring', with conditions worsening again in Syria; and many still have a watchful eye on Egypt, Libya and Iran. Such events can have a profound impact on oil prices, some pushing the prices up, others pushing the prices down, making it increasing difficult for oil traders to try and estimate future price levels. For the statisticians amongst the readers, the 'tail' referred to is the tail of a normal distribution, which is predictable and usually +/– 2.5 per cent if you are working with 95 per cent confidence intervals. It describes price behaviour at the extreme range and 'normally' you would not expect an extreme movement like this in one day. If this occurs it signifies far more volatility than currently built into the market pricing.

COMMODITY INDICES

Many commodities market participants follow closely the movement of commodity indices, of which there are many. Some investment vehicles benchmark themselves against one or more of these indices. Discussed below are just two of the indices:

- The Goldman Sachs Commodity Index (GSCI), now the S&P GSCI
- The Rogers International Commodity Index (RICI®)

S&P GSCI

This is a measure of the performance of the commodities markets over time – it is similar to the FTSE 100 or the S&P 500 equity indices and is a tradable index consisting of 24 well-traded physical commodities active in the futures markets. It is a composite index of sector returns corresponding to a long-only, un-leveraged investment in a range of commodity futures. Originally designed by Goldman Sachs, it became part of the Standard & Poor's suite of products in 2007 (for more information visit www.standardandpoors.com).

> **'The S&P GSCI is a world-production weighted index that is based on the average quantity of production of each commodity in the index, over the last five years of available data. This allows the S&P GSCI to be a measure of investment performance as well as serve as an economic indicator.'**
>
> (Standard & Poor's)

The S&P GSCI index trades OTC and on the Chicago Mercantile Exchange. The 24 commodities come from all commodity sectors – energy products, industrial metals, agricultural products, livestock products and precious metals. This is a passive portfolio of long positions in commodity futures; however, unlike a passive equity portfolio, this contains futures positions that need to be rolled as the contracts expire.

Table 1.2 is an abbreviation of the full table of production weightings and components of the S&P GCSI for 2012 (available at www.standardandpoors.com).

Production weighting is a key attribute for the index to be a measure of investment performance. This is achieved by assigning a weight to each asset based on the amount of capital dedicated to holding that asset just as market capitalisation is used to assign weights to components of the FTSE 100 equity index. Since the appropriate weight assigned to each commodity is in proportion to the amount of that commodity flowing through the economy, the index is also an economic indicator.

The index is based on a basket of futures contracts linked to each of the 24 commodities. The underlying futures contracts are typically front-month contracts and as they approach expiry need to be rolled monthly into the second month. Twenty per cent of the futures contracts are rolled each day during the roll period, that is 5th to 9th of the month.

Range of S&P GSCI returns

The **Excess Return Index** measures the returns accrued from investing in *uncollateralised* front-month commodity futures, whereas the **Total Return Index** measures the returns accrued from *fully collateralised* front-month futures. The total return is completely comparable to returns from a regular investment in the S&P 500 (with dividend reinvestment) or a government bond. The excess return index is comparable to the return on the S&P 500 over cash.

S&P GSCI ER

The S&P GSCI Excess Return Index reflects the S&P GSCI Spot Index returns plus any excess return resulting from the discount or premium generated by 'rolling the futures' as they approach delivery.

Table 1.2

Abbreviated table of components and weightings for S&P GSCI, for 2012

Trading facility	Commodity	Ticker	2011 CPW	2012 CPW	2012 ACRP ($)	Unit	2011 PDW(2)	2012 RPDW
CBT	Chicago Wheat	W	18188.56	18217.58	7.466	bu	3.28%	3.23%
KBT	Kansas City Wheat	KW	4134.2	5004.071	8.333	bu	0.83%	0.99%
CBT	Corn	C	28210.87	29648.15	6.600	bu	4.50%	4.64%
CBT	Soybeans	S	7708.699	8037.317	13.380	bu	2.49%	2.55%
ICE – US	Coffee	KC	16710	17406.22	2.472	lbs	1.00%	1.02%
ICE – US	Sugar #11	SB	340773.4	344724.8	0.278	lbs	2.29%	2.28%
ICE – US	Cocoa	CC	4.015306	4.116321	3085.750	MT	0.30%	0.30%
ICE – US	Cotton #2	CT	51632.55	53411.21	1.410	lbs	1.76%	1.79%
CME	Lean Hogs	LH	70271.76	72823.44	0.865	lbs	1.47%	1.49%
CME	Live Cattle	FC	91458.23	92591.82	1.102	lbs	2.44%	2.42%
CME	Feeder Cattle	FC	13417.1	13596.46	1.279	lbs	0.42%	0.41%
NYM/ICE	Crude Oil	CL	14314	13557.23	94.111	bbl	32.59%	30.49%
NYM	Heating Oil	HO	72571.85	71569.8	2.802	gal	4.92%	4.80%
NYM	RBOB Gasoline	RB	72504.78	73694.1	2.714	gal	4.76%	4.78%
ICE – UK	Brent Crude Oil	LCO	6262.977	6959.701	105.134	bbl	15.93%	17.14%
ICE – UK	Gasoil	LGO	313.6761	359.2745	879.063	MT	6.67%	7.36%
NYM/ICE	Natural Gas	NG	28797.24	28984.31	4.273	MMBtu	2.98%	2.94%
LME	Aluminium	MAL	41.288	42.53	2512.938	MT	2.51%	2.53%
LME	Copper	MCU	16.62	17.14	9194.146	MT	3.70%	3.74%
LME	Lead	MPB	7.574	7.872	2514.708	MT	0.46%	0.47%
LME	Nickel	MNI	1.286	1.352	24796.583	MT	0.77%	0.80%
LME	Zinc	MZN	10.68	11.04	2336.917	MT	0.60%	0.61%

Source: S&P

S&P GSCI TR

The S&P GSCI Total Return Index represents the return on the S&P GSCI ER Index plus any interest earned on the hypothetical fully collateralised contract positions on the commodities included in the index.

Rolling of futures contracts

In essence this process consists of rolling one basket of futures contracts in the nearby month to a basket of futures contracts that is the next in the calendar. With the S&P GSCI this rolling process takes five days and 20 per cent is rolled each day during the period of the fifth to the ninth business day of the month. It is assumed the contracts are rolled at the end of the day at the closing prices.

Process

On the first four business days of the month the basket consists of 100 per cent of the contracts coming up to expiry. At the end of the fifth business day, 20 per cent of futures contracts are rolled: this means we need to sell the existing month's futures contracts and buy them back again in the next closest month. By selling at one price and buying at another there will be a profit or loss on the transaction – this is what generates the additional returns on the index.

At the end of the fifth day we have 80 per cent of the expiring futures and 20 per cent new contracts. By the end of the sixth business day we will have 40 per cent new futures contracts, and so on until all the contracts have been replaced. The process is then repeated on the fifth business day of the next month.

Rogers International Commodity Index®

> 'The Rogers International Commodity Index is a U.S. dollar-based, total return index designed by Jim Rogers. It was designed to meet the need for consistent investing in a broad-based international vehicle; it represents the value of a basket of commodities consumed in the global economy, ranging from agricultural to energy and metal products. The value of this basket is tracked via futures contracts on exchange-traded physical commodities comprised of 37 commodities future contracts, quoted in four different currencies and listed on eleven exchanges in five countries. Indeed, the index's weights attempt to balance consumption patterns worldwide (in developed and developing economies) and specific contract liquidity.'

Source: The RICI® Handbook: The Guide to The Rogers International Commodity Index® (June 27, 2012). Beeland Interests, Inc., the owner and publisher of the RICI®, provides a copy of the RICI® Handbook for download at www.beelandinterests.com

The components of the RICI change rarely and where a future trades on more than one exchange the data generally is taken from the exchange with the most liquidity in that contract. Table 1.3 shows the components of the total RICI® immediately following its June 2012 index roll period.

Table 1.3

Components of the total RICI®

RICI® Contract	Exchange	Currency	Initial Weight (%)
Crude oil	NYMEX	USD	21.00
Brent	ICE EU	USD	14.00
Wheat	CBOT	USD	4.75
Corn	CBOT	USD	4.75
Cotton	ICE US	USD	4.20
Aluminum	LME	USD	4.00
Copper	LME	USD	4.00
Soybeans	CBOT	USD	3.50
Gold	COMEX	USD	3.00
Natural gas	NYMEX	USD	3.00
RBOB gasoline	NYMEX	USD	3.00
Soybean oil	CBOT	USD	2.00
Coffee	ICE US	USD	2.00
Lead	LME	USD	2.00
Live cattle	CME	USD	2.00
Silver	COMEX	USD	2.00
Sugar	ICE US	USD	2.00
Zinc	LME	USD	2.00
Heating oil	NYMEX	USD	1.80
Platinum	NYMEX	USD	1.80
Gas oil	ICE EU	USD	1.20
Cocoa	ICE US	USD	1.00
Lean hogs	CME	USD	1.00
Lumber	CME	USD	1.00
Milling wheat	NYSE Liffe	EUR	1.00
Nickel	LME	USD	1.00
Rubber	TOCOM	JPY	1.00
Tin	LME	USD	1.00
Wheat	KCBT	USD	1.00
Rice	CBOT	USD	0.75
Canola	ICE CA	CAD	0.75
Soybean meal	CBOT	USD	0.75
Orange juice	ICE US	USD	0.60
Oats	CBOT	USD	0.50
Palladium	NYMEX	USD	0.30

Table 1.3 continued

Rapeseed	NYSE Liffe	EUR	0.25
Azuki beans	TGE	JPY	0.15
Milk class III	CME	USD	0.10
			100.00

Source: The RICI® Handbook: The Guide to The Rogers International Commodity Index® (June 27, 2012). Beeland Interests, Inc., the owner and publisher of the RICI®, provides a copy of the RICI® Handbook for download at www.beelandinterests.com

Choosing which commodity index is most appropriate will require the investor to investigate which of the indices has the weighting of index components representing the best fit for the objectives.

Commodities require a different mind set to equities, currency and fixed income products, but are equally rewarding and in many cases portfolios with substantial commodity assets perform better in the long run.

2

Key Commodities Derivatives

Background and context

Market Fundamentals: exchange traded v. OTC derivatives markets

The major commodities exchanges

Exchange traded futures

Market operations

Exchange traded options

OTC commodities derivatives

OTC commodities options (caps)

OTC commodities swaps

Regulatory reform

BACKGROUND AND CONTEXT

Derivatives in the commodities markets are continually receiving bad press. The practitioners who trade futures especially are being blamed for everything from global financial meltdown to increasing the price of food in the shops and fuel at the pumps.

I recall a statistic from the CNN news programme that aired in April 2009, when it was noted that in the previous year 27 barrels of crude oil were being traded on the New York Mercantile Exchange (NYMEX – now part of CME) for every barrel of oil consumed in the United States. The reporter was referring to crude oil futures contracts and if the comment is expanded to total futures traded globally compared with worldwide oil production, the multiplier is now much higher.

As with all other asset classes there is a range of derivative instruments that can be used in the commodity markets – for hedging and trading, for investment and speculation. Each derivative is linked to its underlying asset and as every commodity is different it follows that the choice is almost infinite. There are however a group of derivative instruments which are popular across the whole range of asset classes and they are futures, swaps and options.

Whilst this chapter will give an overview of these products, it is not intended that this is a replacement for a specialised book on derivatives; therefore anyone seeking further information is recommended to read *Mastering Derivatives Markets* – 4th edition, written by Francesca Taylor and published by Financial Times Prentice Hall.

MARKET FUNDAMENTALS: EXCHANGE TRADED V. OTC DERIVATIVES MARKETS

When reviewing derivatives there are two fundamental groups of instruments: exchange traded products with their strict contract specifications, yet superb liquidity; and the over the counter (OTC) instruments that can be specifically tailored to the client's own requirements. OTC instruments are often known as 'off-exchange' instruments. The majority of commodity derivatives trading developed on physical exchanges such as the Chicago Mercantile Exchange (CME) and the London Metal Exchange (LME), rather than OTC. At the time of writing there is increasing regulatory focus on OTC market products in order to try and direct many of the 'standardised' derivatives onto electronic execution platforms and into clearing houses. It remains to be seen how successful this will be, but compared to the interest rate or currency markets the impact in commodities products is likely to be far less.

THE MAJOR COMMODITIES EXCHANGES

Worldwide, there are around 54 major commodity exchanges that trade in more than 90 commodities. 'Soft commodities' – generally regarded as things you can eat – are traded around the world and largely dominate exchange trading in Asia and Latin America, whereas the 'hard commodities' – e.g. metals and energy – are predominantly traded in London, New York, Chicago and Shanghai. Energy contracts are mainly traded in New York, London, Tokyo and the Middle East. More recently a number of energy exchanges have emerged in several European countries. In terms of the number of commodity futures contracts traded, in 2010 China and the UK had three exchanges amongst the largest ten, the US two and Japan and India one each (see Table 2.1).

Exchanges introduce stability, transparency and regulations not found in the physical market and are supposed to create a 'safer marketplace' – or so we are being told. I am sure the traders/investors/hedgers who lost their money in the MF Global collapse in 2011 would argue differently – they were ultimately trading on a regulated exchange (CME) using MF Global as their broker – fully expecting their individual deposit monies to be segregated, not expecting to have these funds seized by the fund administrators.

In 2010 the CME was the largest commodities exchange in the world, followed by the Shanghai Futures Exchange, the Zhengzhou and the Dalian exchanges. The UK's ICE Futures Europe was fifth, and the London Metal Exchange seventh in the top ten commodity exchanges. Trading on exchanges is fairly concentrated. In 2010 the top five exchanges accounted for 85 per cent of the contracts traded (source: World Federation of Exchanges).

China and India have gained in importance in recent years as they have emerged as significant commodities consumers and producers. Over the past decade a number of large exchanges have opened in China and India, such as the Shanghai Futures Exchange, Zhengzhou Commodity Exchange and the Dalian Commodity Exchange in China, and the National Commodity and Derivatives Exchange and MCX in India. Chinese exchanges accounted for more than two-thirds of exchange traded commodities in 2010.

The major exchanges where commodity derivatives trade are:

Energy

- CME Group, which includes New York Mercantile Exchange (NYMEX), which became part of CME in March 2008;
- Shanghai Futures Exchange (SHFE), China;
- InterContinental Exchange (ICE), which acquired the International Petroleum Exchange (IPE) London in 2001;

Table 2.1

Top 10 exchanges by number of commodity derivatives contracts traded in 2010

	Exchange	Millions of contracts traded		% change	Notional Value (bn USD)		% change
		2010	2009		2010	2009	
1	CME Group[1]	843	619	+36%	NA	NA	–
2	Shanghai Futures Exchange	622	435	+43%	9 134	5 399	+69%
3	Zhengzhou Commodity Exchange	496	227	+118%	NA	1 399	–
4	Dalian Commodity Exchange	403	417	–3%	3 085	2 756	+12%
5	ICE Futures Europe	211	161	+31%	NA	NA	–
6	Multi Commodity Exchange of India	197	161	+22%	NA	1 232	–
7	London Metal Exchange	111	112	–1%	NA	6 833	–
8	ICE Futures US	59	50	+19%	NA	NA	–
9	Tokyo Commodity Exchange (TOCOM)	28	29	–5%	807	605	+33%
10	RTS	18	11	+59%	18	8	+124%
	Others	35	40	–15%	NA	NA	–
		3 023	2 262	+34%	57 551	40 456	–

[1] Including OTC business registererd on the exchange
Source: World Federation of Exchanges and International Options Market Association

- Multi Commodity Exchange of India;
- Tokyo Commodity Exchange (TOCOM), Japan;
- RTS Exchange in Russia;
- Dubai Mercantile Exchange (DME), UAE.

Metals

- CME Group, which includes NYMEX and COMEX;
- Shanghai Futures Exchange (SHFE), China;
- Multi Commodity Exchange of India;
- LME – London Metal Exchange, UK;
- RTS Exchange, Russia;
- DGCX – Dubai Gold & Commodities Exchange.

Agriculture

- CME Group – Chicago Board of Trade and Chicago Mercantile Exchange;
- Shanghai Futures Exchange (SHFE), China;
- Zhengzhou Commodity Exchange (ZCE), China;
- Dalian Commodity Exchange (DCE), China;
- InterContinental Exchange – Atlanta and London;
- Tokyo Commodity Exchange (TOCOM), Japan;
- Kansas City (Missouri) Board of Trade, USA;
- RTS Exchange, Russia;
- NYSE Liffe, UK;
- InterContinental Exchange, Canada.

Carbon and emissions

- GreenX – The Green Exchange, London (division of CME);
- ICE – includes European Climate Exchange and Chicago Climate Exchange;
- Bluenext – France.

EXCHANGE TRADED FUTURES

One of the key characteristics relating to exchange traded products is the 'contract specification'; this states clearly the obligations of the buyer and the seller in terms of the quantity, the description of the commodity to which the futures contract is linked, the delivery date and the location, and how settlement (payment) will be effected. This sounds terribly complicated but in fact ensures that everyone knows what they are contracting for; there can be no debate about the quality of the gold or the sulphur content of the crude oil as everything relating to this is pre-specified.

> **'"trading commodities" and "trading futures" are the same thing.'**
>
> (Jim Rogers, *Hot Commodities*, Wiley, 2007)

Futures can be used as pure speculative tools for traders and there is no doubt that large sums of money can be made/lost with a 'naked' futures position. However, if futures are included as part of an overall investment portfolio they can enhance the returns of the underlying basket of stocks and bonds.

A 2004 study, *Facts and Fantasies about Commodity Futures*, published by the Yale School of Management and written by Professor Gary Gorton of the University of Pennsylvania's Wharton School and the National Bureau of Economic Research and Professor K. Geert Rouwenhorst of the Yale School of Management, noted that:

> **'In addition to offering high returns, the historical risk of an investment in commodity futures has been relatively low – especially if evaluated in terms of its contribution to a portfolio of stocks and bonds. A diversified investment in commodity futures has slightly lower risk than stocks – as measured by standard deviation. And because the distribution of commodity returns is positively skewed relative to equity returns, commodities have less downside risk.'**

Another interesting fact is that the returns of commodities futures examined in this study were 'triple' the returns for stocks in companies that produce the same commodities.

Notwithstanding the above comments, as with all investing it is a case of 'caveat emptor' or 'buyer beware'.

Figure 2.1 shows the 2011 turnover data by asset class. Equity derivatives such as contracts linked to FTSE, S&P 500, NASDAQ and Dow Jones account for the majority of trading, with commodities and currencies with an equal but much lower share.

The basics

Positions with futures contracts can be taken to mitigate (hedge) risk or to actively take it; this may be a view on the direction of a particular oil price and a trader's desire to enter into a futures position, allowing a profit to be made from this view (or not). A hedger, however, may seek to take an equal and opposite position in the futures market to offset as much of the price risk as possible on the physical contracts. For example, if we pay US$90 for

Figure 2.1

Exchange data for 2011

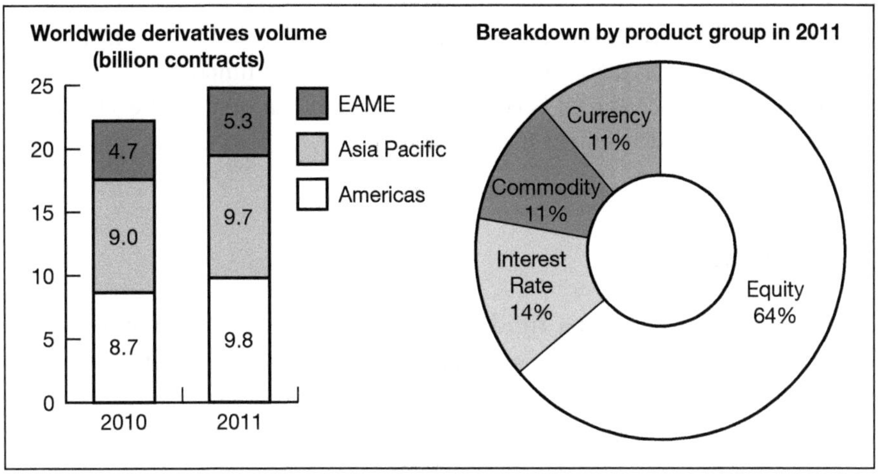

Source: World Federation of Exchanges

a barrel of oil today and then we sell it tomorrow at US$80, we have lost US$10. If we hedge the position we will try to guarantee the price at which it will be sold, in effect to 'lock in' the price.

Terminology

'Long the physical' a firm which has produced/purchased the commodity and is holding it in storage for delivery or use at a later date.

'Short the physical' a firm with an obligation to deliver the commodity on a future date and at a fixed price when it does not already own the commodity.

'Long the futures' a client who has bought futures to open a position.

'Short the futures' a trader who has sold futures without previously owning them.

In order for a company that is 'long the physical' to hedge oil price risk, it will need to 'short the futures', and vice versa (see Table 2.2).

Table 2.2

Basic hedging techniques

Physical position	Price risk	Futures position	Result
LONG	Falling prices	SHORT	Short hedge
SHORT	Rising prices	LONG	Long hedge

Definition

Futures contract

A commodity futures contract is a legally binding agreement to make or take delivery of a standard quantity of a specific commodity at a future date and at a price agreed between the parties on an organised exchange. Cash or physical settlement may be arranged.

Definition discussed

Each futures contract has a rigid contract specification which explains the actions required by the buyer and seller of the future and what obligations they must perform. Each future also specifies a fixed 'contract amount' to facilitate the calculation needed to determine how many futures contracts are required for a particular transaction. The price agreed between two traders today will be for 'delivery' on a particular date in the future as specified in the futures contract. 'Delivery' realistically denotes contract expiry.

Table 2.3 shows an abbreviated contract specification for the ICE Brent Crude future.

Table 2.3 **ICE Brent Crude Oil future – abbreviated contract specification***

Unit of trading	1000 barrels of crude (42,000 US gallons)
Delivery months	Up to 9 years
Expiration date	Trading will cease at the close of business on the business day preceding the 15th day of the month prior to the first day of the delivery month
Quotation	US$ and cents per barrel
Minimum price	One cent per barrel equivalent to a tick value of US$10.00 per contract
Trading hours: UK Hours: Open 01:00 London local time (23.00 on Sundays) Close 23:00 London local time. EST Hours: Open 20:00 (18:00 on Sundays) Close: 18:00 the following day. Chicago Hours: Open 19:00 (17:00 on Sundays) Close: 17:00 the following day. Singapore Hours: Open 08:00 (06:00 on Monday mornings) Close 06:00 the next day.	

*For further contract details, contact ICE, at www.theice.com

Key features

Energy futures contract

Market

Energy futures are traded on regulated exchanges with standard contract sizes and specific delivery dates. A member firm or broker executes the trades.

Contracts

Different contracts are available on each exchange; each is standardised to enhance liquidity.

Pricing

It is a competitive auction-based market, and prices are generally quoted as a bid–offer spread, either in dollars and cents per barrel or per tonne, or in cents per US gallon (pricing for propane and natural gas is a little different).

MARKET OPERATIONS

Buyers and sellers must both put up minimum levels of collateral for each open contract that they hold. This is known as initial margin, and can be viewed as a good faith deposit. The specific level is calculated by the relevant exchange for that particular contract in conjunction with the clearing house. Most exchanges now use an algorithm known as SPAN (Standard Portfolio Analysis of Risk). This is currently in its fourth iteration and was developed by the Chicago Mercantile Exchange in 1988; it is made available under licence, and has become the market standard for portfolio risk assessment, used by over 50 exchanges worldwide and many other market professionals. It is in effect a 'what if' scenario model and marks portfolios to market twice a day.

Once initial margin is placed with the clearing house, interest will accumulate and the deposit plus any accrued interest will be returned to the trader when the position is closed out. The level of margin due on a futures contract can change if market volatility changes.

When the gold price screamed through US$1800 per ounce in August 2011, CME increased initial margins by 22% in one day to US$7425 per contract. This means that overnight your mandatory initial margin amounts were increased by 22 per cent, or an equivalent of an additional

US$1250 for each contract that you held (ignores spread trades and more complex holdings). At the time of writing, each gold futures contract is for an equivalent amount of 100 troy ounces of gold, which at a price of US$1800 makes each futures contract equivalent to a position worth US$180,000. Any participants that could not find the additional finance for the increased margin calls were required to liquidate their positions.

Futures positions are 'marked-to-market' twice daily, managed intraday and profits or losses are crystallised daily. If the position loses money against the daily settlement price, losses must be paid following the close of the trade. If the position is in profit on that day, then payment will be received. These payments are known as variation margin. Many exchanges also have a level known as maintenance margin that is generally 75 per cent of the initial margin amount. As long as the trader has at least the amount of the maintenance margin in his deposit *after* the mark-to-market he will not receive a margin call.

Credit risk

It is the clearing house that will call for margin from market participants and their brokers/Futures Commission Merchants (FCMs), and ultimately each trade will eventually end up as a trade between the buyer/seller and the clearing house.

Availability

There are a number of different oil and gas futures contracts, and it is advisable to check with each exchange exactly which contracts they offer.

Example

A Brent futures hedging transaction

2 November

A trader has bought a cargo of 500,000 barrels of Brent crude, for which he paid US$86.20 per barrel. He has agreed to sell it in mid-January on a Platt's-related basis. Platt's provides reference rates for many different types of oil and oil products, now owned by Standard & Poor's. A Platt's-related trade is based on a continuously variable oil price. It is similar to a LIBOR fix in the interest rate market. The trader is concerned that oil prices may fall and he might make a loss. To manage this position he will need to sell futures to protect against this anticipated fall in prices. He will close out the futures position at the time he sells the cargo.

Assume the trader sells 500 Brent January futures contracts at a price of $85.90. He will put up the initial margin of US$700 per contract – a total of US$350,000 – and the position will be marked-to-market on a daily basis, with profits and losses also crystallised daily.

Example continued

Action – 17 November
The trader sells his cargo at a Platt's reference price of US$85.30 (having previously purchased it at US$86.20), making a loss of US$0.90 cents per barrel or US$450,000.

However, the futures trade has made a profit that will go some way to offset the loss on the physical position. Our trader buys the futures back at the current market level of US$85.40.

Profit from the futures hedge

2 November	Sell 500 contracts at US$85.90
17 November	Close out position by buying the futures back at the current market price US$85.40
Profit	(50 ticks × $10 × 500 contracts) = US $250,000

The hedge is not 100 per cent effective but has narrowed the loss on the transaction to US$200,000 (US$450,000 less US$250,000). This loss of US$200,000 can be accounted for by the narrowing of the basis.

EXCHANGE TRADED OPTIONS

An exchange traded commodity option is an option on the underlying commodity futures contract, and by using a combination of futures and options the majority of risk scenarios can be hedged – but there will always be occasions when the underlying risk is just not manageable with exchange traded products, which is one of the reasons why the OTC markets exist.

An option contract remains the only derivative instrument that allows the buyer (holder) to 'walk away' from the transaction. With energy options, when the option is exercised, it results in the holder being long or short on an energy futures contract, which is then usually cash settled. In effect, the holder of one call option on the energy future will, on exercise, be long on one energy future. An upfront premium is due. The option allows a greater degree of flexibility than a futures contract in that it does not completely take away all the risk, i.e. all the losses and all the profit. Instead it allows a degree of risk management that allows for risk control not risk removal. Options also exhibit 'asymmetry of risk', such that the most that an option holder can lose is the original premium that he paid, whereas the most he can profit is unlimited, the amount of profit governed only by how far the market has moved in his favour.

A seller of options, in contrast, can only hope to keep the premium, but the extent of the losses is potentially unlimited. Put simply, buyers of options have rights, but no obligations, and writers of options have obligations, but no rights.

Definition An exchange traded commodity option gives the holder the right, but not the obligation, to buy or sell an agreed amount of commodity futures at a specified price, on or before a specified date. A premium is due. The option will be cash settled against the corresponding commodity future.

Definition discussed – using traded energy options as an example

An energy option gives the holder, who may be an oil refiner, the chance to secure the oil price in advance. Let me repeat that as these are inextricably linked to an underlying futures contract when you exercise an exchange traded energy option you go long or short by the corresponding number of the underlying energy futures contracts. The holder of the option will choose their own guaranteed rate (the strike) from those specified by the exchange; these are usually in 50 cent increments per barrel. A premium is required, which must be paid upfront to the seller of the option via the clearing house. Although there are both American and European style traded option contracts, the majority of energy options are American style, allowing the holder to exercise on any business day in the contractual period.

NYMEX options and futures on light sweet crude oil are used to hedge positions where the underlying is West Texas Intermediate (see Table 2.4). As with all other options/futures contracts, most open option positions will be closed out or exercised prior to expiry. Any remaining open positions are automatically closed out by the exchange.

Table 2.4 **CME light sweet crude oil option – abbreviated contract specification***

Venue	CME Globex, CME ClearPort, Open Outcry (New York)	
Hours (All Times are New York Time/ET)	CME ClearPort:	Sunday–Friday 6:00 p.m.–5:15 p.m. (5:00 p.m.–4:15 p.m. Chicago Time/CT) with a 45-minute break each day beginning at 5:15 p.m. (4:15 p.m. CT)
	CME Globex:	Sunday–Friday 6:00 p.m.–5.15 p.m. (5:00 p.m.–4.15 p.m. Chicago Time/CT) with a 45-minute break each day beginning at 5:15 p.m. (4:15 p.m. CT)
	Open Outcry:	Monday–Friday 9:00 a.m.–2:30 p.m. (8:00 a.m.–1:30 p.m. CT)
Contract Unit	A Light Sweet Crude Oil Put (Call) Option traded on the Exchange represents an option to assume a short (long) position in the underlying Light Sweet Crude Oil Futures traded on the Exchange.	

Table 2.4 continued

Price Quotation	US dollars and cents per barrel
Option Style	American
Minumum Fluctuation	$0.01 per barrel
Expiration of Trading	Trading ends three business days before the termination of trading in the underlying futures contract.
Listed Contracts	Crude oil options are listed nine years forward using the following listing schedule: consecutive months are listed for the current year and the next five years; in addition, the June and December contract months are listed beyond the sixth year. Additional months will be added on an annual basis after the December contract expires, so that an additional June and December contract would be added nine years forward, and the consecutive months in the sixth calender year will be filled in.
Strike Prices	Twenty strike prices in increments of $0.50 per barrel above and below the at-the-money strike price, and the next 10 strike prices in increments of $2.50 above the highest and below the lowest existing strike prices for a total of at least 61 strike prices. The at-the-money strike price is nearest to the previous day's close of the underlying futures contract. Strike price boundaries are adjusted according.
Settlement Type	Exercise into Futures
Position Limits	NYMEX Position Limits
Rulebook Chapter	310
Exchange Rule	These contracts are listed with, and subject to, the rules and regulations of NYMEX.

*For further contract details, contact CME Group direct.

Key features

Traded energy options

Insurance protection

The client pays a premium to insure against adverse oil price movements. The clearing house agrees to guarantee the agreed rate if/when required by the client.

Profit potential

The risk of adverse oil price market movements is eliminated, while at the same time the buyer retains the potential to benefit from favourable prices. The option can be abandoned or exercised, dependent upon market movements.

Sell-back

Traded energy options cannot be sold back to the exchange, but an opposite position can be transacted at the current market rate with another counterparty.

Key features continued

Exercise

As the counterparty to each deal is the clearing house, if a client wishes to exercise the option he is assigned a counterparty at random.

Cash settlement

The option is cash settled against the corresponding energy future, allowing participants to take profits from favourable movements without having to deal physically in the market.

Terminology

Energy options

Underlying	The price of the asset on which the option is based – contango/backwardation are important factors
Strike price	Specified energy futures price where the client can exercise the right to physical settlement. It will be specified as ATM, ITM or OTM compared to the futures price
Call option	Right to buy the underlying future
Put option	Right to sell the underlying future
Exercise	Take-up of the option at or before expiry
Expiry date	Last date when the option may be exercised
Value date	Date of settlement as determined by the exchange
Premium	Option premium as determined by pricing model
Intrinsic value	Strike rate minus the current market rate
Time value	Option premium minus intrinsic value, reflecting the time until expiry, changes in volatility, and market expectations

Example

Hedging with an option on light sweet crude oil

4 January

An oil producer fears an oil price decline due to warmer winter weather and is worried that he may have to sell his oil too cheaply on the market. He anticipates he will sell approximately 1000 barrels a day in January at a price of about US$65 per barrel. His expected receipts on 25 days of production are US$1,625,000.

The oil producer could use futures that would cost nothing in terms of an upfront premium, but could actually lose him money if his view of the market was wrong. However, there are certain factors in the market that lead him to believe that there may be a short-term market shortage which may well push up prices temporarily. He wishes to profit if the market moves in his favour, but he also wishes to protect his downside.

Example continued

Action 4 January
The current level of the February future is US$64.67 per barrel. The oil producer decides to buy 25 February put options on the CME/NYMEX light sweet crude oil future with a strike at US$65.00 per barrel. This is slightly 'in the money' and the cost will reflect this. His Reuters screen shows that the last trade went through at 59 cents per barrel, the same as yesterday's closing price. Volatility is currently stable, and our oil producer decides to deal through his broker at 59 cents per barrel – a total premium cost of US$0.59 × 25,000 barrels = US$14,750.

February
There are two possible outcomes: oil prices can rise or they can fall. Let us assume that the oil price can move +/– US$5.00.

1. If oil prices rise to US$70.00 the producer will abandon his option and sell his oil at the higher level. This would realise him 25,000 × $70.00, which equals US$1,750,000: an improvement of US$125,000 over his original estimate. But his option premium cost him US$14,750, which must be deducted to give the final figure of US$1,235,250, equivalent to US$69.41 per barrel.
2. If oil prices had fallen to say US$60.00 from their original level, he would exercise the option to sell his oil at US$65.00, netting an income of US$1,610,250 after premium costs. This is absolutely the worst case; if oil prices fall to US$5.00 a barrel, the producer will still be able to guarantee a rate of US$1,610,250 by utilising the option, an effective rate of US$64.41 per barrel.

The oil producer has insured against an adverse oil price movement for a limited and known cost, and preserved his right to benefit if the oil spot market rates move in his favour. This option has guaranteed for the client a worst rate of US$64.41. If rates fall lower than the option strike of US$65.00, the oil producer will always exercise the option. But if the oil producer is lucky, and oil prices rise, then he will abandon the option and sell his oil at the higher price. There is no limit to the amount of profit he can make, it is constrained only by how far the market may move.

Note: It is very rare to achieve a hedge that is 100 per cent effective, owing to the pricing disparity known as 'basis', which in practical terms is almost un-hedgeable.

OTC COMMODITIES DERIVATIVES

Dealing 'off-exchange' or OTC is popular with users and producers who wish to hedge or trade a particular variety of commodity where there is as yet either no exchange traded contract available, it is illiquid, or the contract specification is unsuitable or deemed too rigid. For example, clients may wish to hedge their exposure for a longer period, or to purchase an option with a different strike than that offered by an exchange, or to execute an energy swap where there is no exchange traded equivalent.

The period from 2007 to 2010 saw the notional value outstanding of OTC commodities derivatives fall by approximately two-thirds as investors reduced risk following a five-fold increase in value outstanding in the previous three years. London is one of the main global centres for commodities derivatives trading along with New York and Chicago. While Chicago is predominantly a domestic market, London and New York source a large volume of international business.

The providers of OTC energy derivatives will generally be the large oil companies such as Exxon Mobil, Total, Royal Dutch Shell and Elf, together with the investment banks such as Morgan Stanley and Barclays Capital. Available OTC products are oil swaps, energy options and other option-related products such as oil caps and collars.

An OTC transaction is a bilateral arrangement where each counterparty must bear the other's credit risk. In the wake of the failures of Lehman Brothers, AIG, MF Global and others, this has become an important point. Dealing on an exchange immunises both counterparties from this risk, as once the transaction is executed, both parties are in legal contract with the clearing house, rather than each other. However, unless the user is a large firm with its own clearing capabilities like HSBC, then this function is effectively outsourced to a 'clearing broker' who will hold the client margin monies and who is allowed to invest the monies and keep any interest earned on the funds.

The credit risks attached to OTC transactions are always touted as being greater than the credit risks attached to exchange traded derivatives, but the investors who used exchange traded futures/options via the broker MF Global may disagree, especially after the comment in January 2012 that their missing funds may have 'vaporised'! The story in the *Wall Street Journal* published on 30 January 2012 led with:

> 'Nearly three months after MF Global Holdings Ltd. collapsed, officials hunting for an estimated $1.2 billion in missing customer money increasingly believe that much of it might never be recovered, according to people familiar with the investigation.

> 'As the sprawling probe that includes regulators, criminal and congressional investigators, and court-appointed trustees grinds on, the findings so far suggest that a 'significant amount' of the money could have 'vaporized' as a result of chaotic trading at MF Global during the week before the company's Oct. 31 bankruptcy filing, said a person close to the investigation.'

In comparison, with an OTC contract the users understand that they are susceptible to credit risk and they can agree to take this or not. Unfortunately, with the MF Global scenario, users of the exchange traded products were either unaware that they had a credit risk on the funds held with their broker or chose to ignore the fact.

OTC COMMODITIES OPTIONS (CAPS)

Option products that are most frequently used in the commodity market are caps/floors and swaps. These have exactly the same structure as those in the interest rate markets, but are typically used to cover shorter time horizons.

An OTC cap/floor is similar to a compound option and will have multiple settlements (fixings), with dates that are pre-arranged at the outset, whereas a simple OTC option with only a single settlement, known as puts (the right to sell) and calls (the right to buy), will have a single settlement at maturity if European style and the potential for mid-maturity settlement/exercise if American style. It will perform in exactly the same way as options on stocks or options on currency.

Definition

A commodity cap gives the buyer (or holder) the right, but not the obligation, to fix the price of the commodity on a pre-specified amount of product cargo at a specific rate (the strike) for a specified period. The writer of the cap will guarantee to the holder a maximum price level if/when required, and will reimburse the holder of the cap for any excess cost over the agreed strike rate. A premium is due, typically payable upfront or monthly.

Definition discussed

A cap is simply an option with more than one fixing. Mostly, but not always, in the commodity markets the cap writers or sellers will be the major oil companies, miners, agricultural producers, trading houses and banks. Usually the buyer of the cap is a consumer, for example a user of oil or oil products, such as an airline, or a transport company, or even a supermarket, and in some cases an institution looking to risk manage its positions.

The client will need to choose a strike price for the cap that best reflects actual needs. One noticeable difference between an interest rate cap and a commodity cap relates to the fixings or rollover dates. With an oil cap, the client's floating reference rate is not a particular price on a particular date (as with interest rate caps), such as six-month LIBOR on 21 March, but the average oil price over the period, usually a month. This strike price, index price or fixed rate will be guaranteed for the client if/when required. A reference rate needs to be agreed at the outset for the floating side of the cap: this can be linked to a Platt's rate, or a futures price +/– some premium. The actual monthly averages in the market, as published in Platt's for example, will be compared to the strike rate on the cap, and the appropriate party will make a payment of the difference. Caps with average monthly fixings are sometimes known as 'Asian options'. The benchmark used to compare the strike on the oil cap with the current market rates is the equivalent underlying commodity swap rate.

Key features

Commodity caps

Multiple exercise

A time series of individual commodity options with the same strike rates.

Insurance protection

The client pays a premium to insure against adverse commodity price movements. Premiums can be paid upfront or monthly.

Profit potential

A cap reduces the risk of adverse price movements while retaining profit potential. The instrument can be allowed to lapse (abandoned) if the market has moved in the client's favour.

Cash settlement

Principal funds are not involved. The client is not obliged to make or take delivery from the writing oil company. On exercise, the writer will pay the difference between the strike rate and the average oil/commodity reference rate. Settlement is usually a number of business days in arrears (for oil).

Terminology

Commodity caps

Strike price Specified commodity price where the client can exercise his right to cash settlement. This can be ITM, ATM or OTM.

Terminology continued

Exercise	Takeup of the option on various fixing dates.
Settlement	Usually last business day in the month.
Value date	Usually five business days after settlement date.
Premium	Option premium determined by a pricing model.
Intrinsic value	Strike rate minus the current market rate.
Time value	Option premium minus intrinsic value, reflecting time until expiry, changes in volatility and market expectations.

Example

Hedging with an energy cap

A Singaporean shipping company needs to purchase bunker fuel for one of its small subsidiaries. The company estimates that it will need to buy 1000 metric tonnes per month for September, October and November, and wishes to 'cap' its fuel costs. The index that best suits this customer is based on Singapore IF 180 which is currently trading at US$445/t.

Note: Bunkerfuel is used in car ferries and similar vehicles.

Strategy

The company starts to gather prices from the market makers for a cap with a strike of US$450/t. This is a little OTM, and a major oil company has offered a cap to the shipping company at a premium of US$4.5/t, making a total monthly premium cost of US$4500. This will give full protection starting in September at a price of US$450/t.

Figure 2.2

OTC energy cap

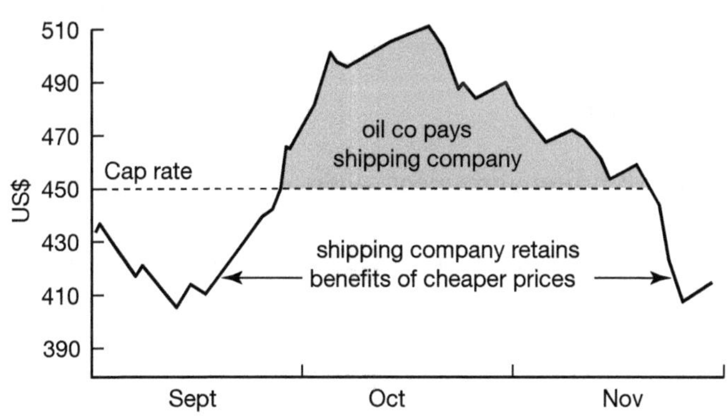

	Sept	Oct	Nov
Average price	$ 420	$ 470	$ 460
Premium	$ –4500	$ –4500	$ –4500
Oil co pays	$ 0	$ 20000	$ 10000
Net	$ –4500	$ +15500	$ +5500

Example continued

Outcome

If the monthly average price is below the strike, the shipping company will buy its fuel at a cheaper price in the market; if the average monthly cost is higher than the strike, the oil company will compensate the company for any excess over and above this rate. An oil cap will therefore fix the shipping company's bunkerfuel costs at a maximum level of US$450/t (see Figure 2.2). The breakeven rate will be achieved at cap price + option premium, a level of US$454.50.

OTC COMMODITIES SWAPS

Introduction

Commodity swaps are one of the fastest growing products on the market and oil swaps in particular are very popular. The mechanics of oil swaps follow those in other swap markets. The big players continue to be the major oil companies and the large international banks, most of which have an interest rate swap capability. Maturities are most likely to be between one and five years, occasionally longer with quarterly or semi-annual resets. In Asia, most oil hedging is carried out using swaps, but in the USA more OTC options are transacted.

Definition

An agreement between two parties to exchange cash flows based on an agreed oil index price for a specified period at agreed reset intervals based on the average price for the period, as noted by a pre-specified independent authority.

Definition discussed

This is a legally binding agreement where an absolute oil price level will be guaranteed. One party will agree to pay the 'fixed index rate'; the other to receive this fixed rate, and pay the 'floating rate' based on the monthly average movement of the same index. The underlying sale or purchase transaction is untouched and may well be with another institution. The only movement of funds is a net transfer of payments between the two parties on the pre-specified dates. However, with oil swaps it is possible to link the swap with a particular physical cargo. The cash flows are calculated based on an agreed notional amount with a cargo which may or may not be delivered.

Key features

Oil swaps

Insurance protection

Through a swap a client can guarantee the rate at which he will purchase (or sell) a pre-specified amount of oil or oil products for a pre-determined period. No premium is required.

Cash or physical settlement

It is normally only the index-linked cash flows that are swapped, with the notional amount of cargo not exchanged. However, physical settlement can be arranged but must be agreed in advance.

Funding optimisation

As the underlying commitment to buy or sell the oil may be with another institution, the client can deal where the best prices are offered. The swap will be negotiated separately.

Credit risk

The credit risk of both counterparties must be carefully evaluated, as each will bear the other's credit risk.

Premium

Swaps are zero-premium instruments and a credit line will be required. On some occasions the client will need to collateralise the swap; that is, to secure the credit risk with cash, either in the form of a deposit, or by way of a variable letter of credit. These arrangements need to be finalised before dealing commences.

Terminology

Oil swaps

Fixed payer Party wishing to pay 'fixed' on the swap, and protect itself from a rise in prices.

Fixed receiver Party wishing to receive 'fixed' on the swap, and protect itself from a fall in prices.

Swap rate Fixed rate agreed between the parties.

Resets Dates when the monthly average floating rate is compared to the fixed rate on the swap. The differences are net cash settled. Settlement is usually five business days in arrears.

Example

Hedging a Brent exposure with an oil swap

15 May

A major European refiner is worried that the price of Brent is rising again and needs to hedge approximately 150,000 barrels per month for one year, commencing in June. The current swap price for the period is US$85.00 per barrel.

Strategy

The company could fix the price of Brent Crude and remove the threat of rising oil prices by using a swap that will need to match the underlying transaction in all respects. In our example, the company wishes to 'pay the fixed and receive the floating' (rate). The company is happy to hedge at the current levels, and a major oil company has offered the swap at the current rate of US$85.00 per barrel against monthly average as quoted by Platt's or Argus.

Outcome

On each of the pre-specified reset dates, the two cash flows will be calculated and offset. If at the beginning of July when we are calculating the settlements for June these were the rates:

Fixed: $85/barrel

Average monthly rate: $87.20

there would be a net payment of $2.20 per barrel from the oil company to the refiner, a total of $330,000 on 150,000 barrels. This offsets the extra $2.20 per barrel that must be paid in the underlying market. Had the monthly average rate been $64.50, there would be a net cash settlement of $0.50 per barrel from the refiner to the oil company, shown in Figure 2.3.

Figure 2.3 **Oil swap cash flows**

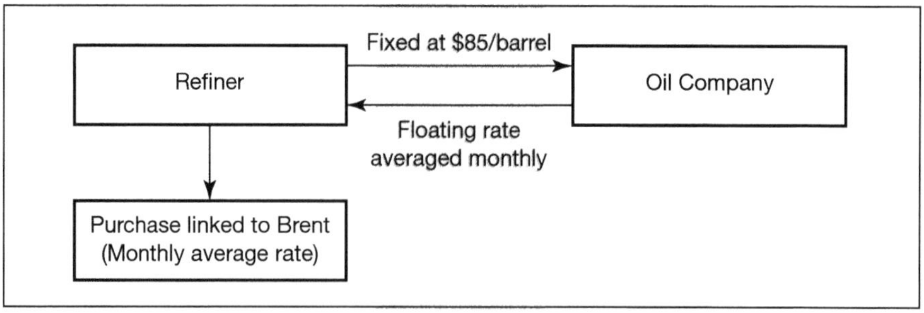

Source: The Matrix Partnership

This illustrates that, as with all swaps, the swap rate becomes an absolute guaranteed rate for the transaction. No improvements on the price level are possible. All risk has been hedged away, even the risk of making a profit.

REGULATORY REFORM

In 2008 the financial markets experienced the near-collapse of Bear Stearns in March 2008, the default of Lehman Brothers on 15 September 2008 and the bailout of AIG. Whilst OTC derivatives were not solely the cause of these problems, they attracted a huge amount of hostile publicity and public ill feeling. In response there has been an international effort to increase stability in the financial market. G-20 leaders agreed in September 2009 that:

> 'All standardised OTC derivative contracts should be traded on exchanges or electronic trading platforms, where appropriate, and cleared through central counterparties by end-2012 at the latest. OTC derivative contracts should be reported to trade repositories. Non-centrally cleared contracts should be subject to higher capital requirements.'

There is no one universal regulation and a whole series of new rules and regulations are now in various stages of being drafted. The following list is not exclusive as many countries are introducing their own, but strategically these new rules and regulations will need to closely resemble each other with similar timings and content or the adverse consequences are likely to include regulatory arbitrage – this is where firms shift certain of their operations to more 'friendly' jurisdictions. These new regulations include:

- The Volcker Rule;
- The Dodd–Frank Act 2010;
- European Market Infrastructure Regulation (EMIR).

The following section is not an exhaustive discussion on the proposed rules and regulations but I hope it goes some way to explaining some of the key issues.

The Volcker Rule

In early 2010, US President Obama stood shoulder to shoulder with Paul Volcker, the ex-chairman of the Federal Reserve, and said that 'Never again would the American taxpayer be held hostage by a "too big to fail bank". This rule became known as the Volcker Rule. In its simple interpretation the Volcker Rule is effectively Section 619 of the Dodd–Frank Act. This is the section that decrees that banks taking deposits, and benefiting from federal deposit insurance, must not indulge in proprietary or speculative trading or invest in private equity or hedge funds. Given the previous few years this was not a surprising statement and Volcker's subsequent ban on 'bright-line' or dedicated proprietary trading led banks such as Goldman

Sachs, JP Morgan Chase, Bank of America and Morgan Stanley to close their proprietary trading desks. However, there has been increasing concern over the literal interpretation of some of the market terminology. For example, the exact interpretation of what are 'market-making' and 'hedging activities' and the assumption that if you do not have an in-house proprietary trading desk, a bank will not need to offer/maintain these activities. But as experienced readers will recognise, every bank needs the ability to hedge itself; after all, where will clients go for the FX, equity, fixed income and commodity prices they require? A bank that is 'market-making' in a particular asset will make two-way prices for the customers to buy/sell their required assets and, following such a trade with a customer, may well require a timely exit/entry into the financial markets to hedge themselves.

A draft of the rule leaked in October 2011 showed no consensus on the detail of its restrictions and a nearly 300-page document was accompanied by some 400 questions that need to be resolved before the rule comes into force. Given how complicated and esoteric the proposed regulations are, the vociferous anti-Volcker Rule campaigners and the increasing competition from outside the banking sector, it is believed that the final version of the Volcker Rule may lack the punch of the original proposals. The initial comment period was extended for three months to four in order to give more time for feedback. Interestingly, one of the longer letters received during the comment period came from the 'Occupy the SEC' group, an offshoot of the 'Occupy Wall Street' movement. The letter was 325 pages long and was written by former financial and banking professionals. Glenn Shorr, Nomura banking analyst, estimates that bank earnings could be reduced by as much as 25 per cent if the rule is passed without amendments (source: *Financial Times*, 19 February 2012).

Dodd–Frank Act, July 2010

In June 2009, the White House sent a series of proposed new financial bills to Congress; over the following six months several revised versions were drafted. Two key individuals, Barney Frank and Chris Dodd, both of whom were involved in the committee stages, were honoured by the conference committee when it voted to name this bill after the two members of Congress.

The Dodd–Frank Act was enacted in July 2010 and this is the Act that is driving most of the global regulatory reform of the OTC derivatives market – although as a piece of regulation it covers more than just derivatives. In brief, Dodd–Frank Title VII is the most important section for the OTC derivatives market; it is also called the Wall Street Transparency and Accountability Act of 2010.

The intention is that the Act will eliminate any remaining loopholes that allow 'risky and abusive practices' to go unnoticed and unregulated in OTC derivatives, asset-backed securities and hedge funds. In the words of Dodd–Frank, these changes need to be implemented:

- **Tighten the regulations**
  The Act will provide the SEC and CFTC with the authority to regulate OTC derivatives so that 'irresponsible practices and excessive' risk-taking can no longer escape regulatory oversight.
- **Implement central clearing and exchange trading**
  The Act will require central clearing and exchange trading for all derivatives that 'can be cleared', and provide a role for both regulators and clearing houses to determine which contracts should be cleared.
- **Increase market transparency**
  The Act will require data from listed and OTC derivatives to be collected and published through clearing houses or swap repositories in order to improve market transparency and provide regulators with tools for monitoring and responding to risks.
- **Add financial safeguards**
  The Act intends to add safeguards to the system by ensuring dealers and major swap participants have adequate financial resources to meet their responsibilities, provide the regulators with the authority to impose capital and impose margin requirements on swap dealers and major swap participants, not end users.
- **Improve business ethics**
  The Act will establish a code of conduct for all registered swap dealers and major swap participants when providing advice to a swap entity. When acting as counterparties to a pension fund, endowment fund, or state or local government, dealers are to have a reasonable basis to believe that the fund or governmental entity has an independent representative advising them.

The Commodity Futures Trading Commission (CFTC) has drawn up a related glossary of terms to assist:

Proposed Dodd–Frank definitions

Swap dealer
Anyone who:

(i) holds itself out as a dealer in swaps;
(ii) makes a market in swaps;
(iii) regularly enters into swaps with counterparties as an ordinary course of business for its own account; or
(iv) engages in activity causing itself to be commonly known in the trade as a dealer or market-maker in swaps.

The Commodity Futures Trading Commission (CFTC) preliminarily (the definition could change as the market evolves) believes the distinguishing characteristics of swap dealers are that they:

- tend to accommodate demand for swaps from other parties;
- are generally available to enter into swaps to facilitate other parties' interest to enter into swaps;
- tend not to request that other parties propose the terms of swaps, rather tend to enter into swaps on their own standard terms or on terms they arrange in response to other parties' interest; and
- tend to be able to arrange customised terms for swaps upon request, or to create new types of swaps at their own initiative.

Major swap participant

Anyone that satisfies any one of the following:

- Someone that maintains a 'substantial position'[1] in any of the major swap categories, excluding positions held for hedging or mitigating commercial risk, and positions maintained by certain employee benefit plans for hedging or mitigating risks in the operation of the plan.
- A person whose outstanding swaps create 'substantial counterparty exposure that could have serious adverse effects on the financial stability of the United States banking system or financial markets'.
- Any 'financial entity' that is 'highly leveraged relative to the amount of capital such entity holds and that is not subject to capital requirements established by an appropriate Federal banking agency' and that maintains a substantial position in any of the major swap categories.

The statutory definition excludes swap dealers and certain financing affiliates.

De minimis exemption from the swap dealer definition

An exemption for those engaged in a de minimis quantity of swap dealing in connection with transactions with, or on behalf of, customers. Must meet all of the following conditions:

- Aggregate effective notional amount, measured on a gross basis, of the swaps that the person enters into over the prior 12 months in connection with dealing activities must not exceed $100 million.
- Aggregate effective notional amount of such swaps with 'special entities' (defined in the Commodity Exchange Act to include certain governmental and other entities) over the prior 12 months must not exceed $25 million.

- Must not enter into swaps as a dealer with more than 15 counterparties, other than security-based swap dealers, over the prior 12 months.
- Must not enter into more than 20 swaps as a dealer over the prior 12 months.

1 A substantial position would satisfy either one of two tests for current uncollateralised exposure and potential future exposure set by the CFTC.
Source: Commodity Futures Trading Commission

At the time of writing, and with the demise of MF Global and the loss of in excess of US$1 billion of customer deposits, it is not entirely clear how the Dodd–Frank regulations will eventually come to be enacted and there are already significant delays in getting the rules onto the statute books.

EMIR, September 2010

The European Market Infrastructure Regulation (EMIR) is the European alternative to the Dodd–Frank Act in the USA. Its aim is to increase stability within OTC derivative markets, by introducing:

- A reporting obligation for OTC derivatives;
- A clearing obligation for eligible OTC derivatives;
- Measures to reduce counterparty credit risk and operational risk for bilaterally cleared OTC derivatives;
- Common rules for central counterparties (CCPs) and for trade repositories;
- Rules on the establishment of inter-operability between CCPs.

(*Source*: Financial Services Authority; for further information please see http://ec.europa.eu/internal_market/ financial-markets/derivatives/index_en.htm)

The key similarities are:

- Mandatory clearing for standardised contracts.
- Scope of derivatives covered.
- Exemptions from clearing for end users.
- Reporting of cleared and OTC transactions by (nearly) all financial counterparties.

The key differences are:

- The 'Volcker Rule' – restrictions on bank proprietary trading not adopted in the EU.

- Swaps 'push-out' rule (swaps business in a separate entity from banking) not adopted in the EU.
- The US has mandatory exchange trading requirements but these are not necessarily going to be replicated in the EU and are being considered separately by the European Commission.
- Clearing organisation ownership rules.

The two proposed regulations (Dodd–Frank and EMIR) are not identical and that in itself will be cause for concern as it may be beneficial for some commodity firms, traders and hedgers to move their operations to a different regulatory environment. If this is complicated by a difference in timing then the financial markets will remain in limbo.

3

Oil

Steven McBain
Crude Oil Trading Manager, Major Commodities Firm, Singapore

BACKGROUND AND CONTEXT

Oil, the oil markets and the geopolitical machinations around it provide a never-ending and much-romanticised James Bond-esque view from the press that often far belies the reality of the situation.

In the simplest of terms, oil is still extracted from the ground in crude oil form and then shipped or piped to refineries where the crude oil is refined into oil products ranging from material for the petrochemical sector at the top to bitumen for roads at the bottom. From the top to bottom of this process are myriad people, all trying to make a profit. Figure 3.1 shows how crude oil prices have moved since April 2004, and highlights the growing price disconnect between two key marker crudes – WTI (West Texas Intermediate), the marker crude for the US markets, and Brent, the marker crude for northern Europe. Excess supplies and surplus storage of WTI at Cushing, Oklahoma have depressed the price of WTI relative to Brent. James L. Williams of WTRG Economics in Arkansas, who compiles this data, is a major source of data relating to all aspects of oil markets (www.wtrg.com).

Figure 3.1 **Crude oil prices 2004–2010**

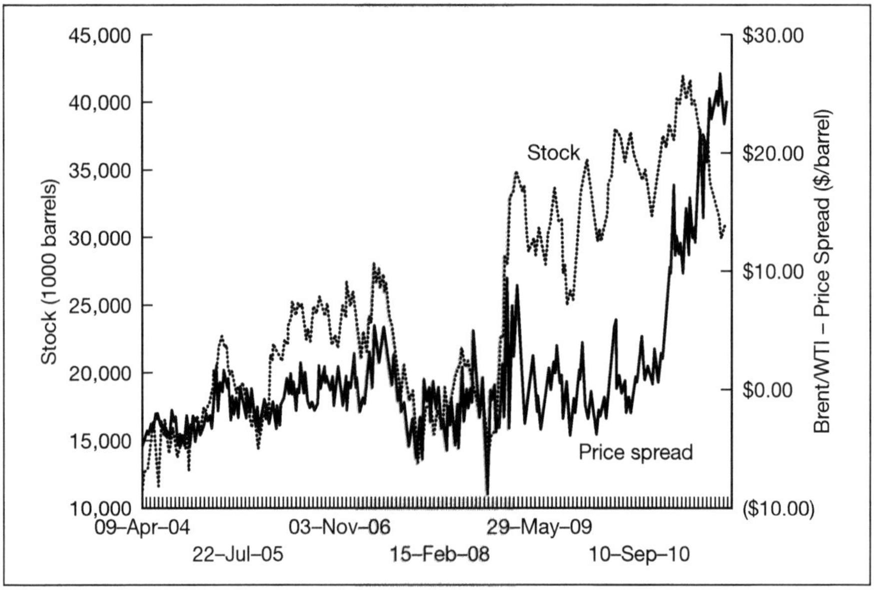

Source: WTRG Economics

In the past, oil markets were dominated by the 'majors' whose rise to power was well documented in the book *The Prize: The Epic Quest for Oil, Money and Power*, by Daniel Yergin (published by Free Press, January 1993). Today, ExxonMobil, BP, Shell, ChevronTexaco and Total remain monoliths in the global sphere.

Oil, alongside other commodities, was seen in the past as a somewhat inferior market to that of, say, equities or fixed income, and oil prices of around \$10/bbl in the mid-1990s did little to add any glamour to proceedings.

Figure 3.2 shows how oil prices have fluctuated since 1947 (priced in 2010 US dollars equivalent) together with major world events.

Figure 3.2

Crude oil prices 1947–2011

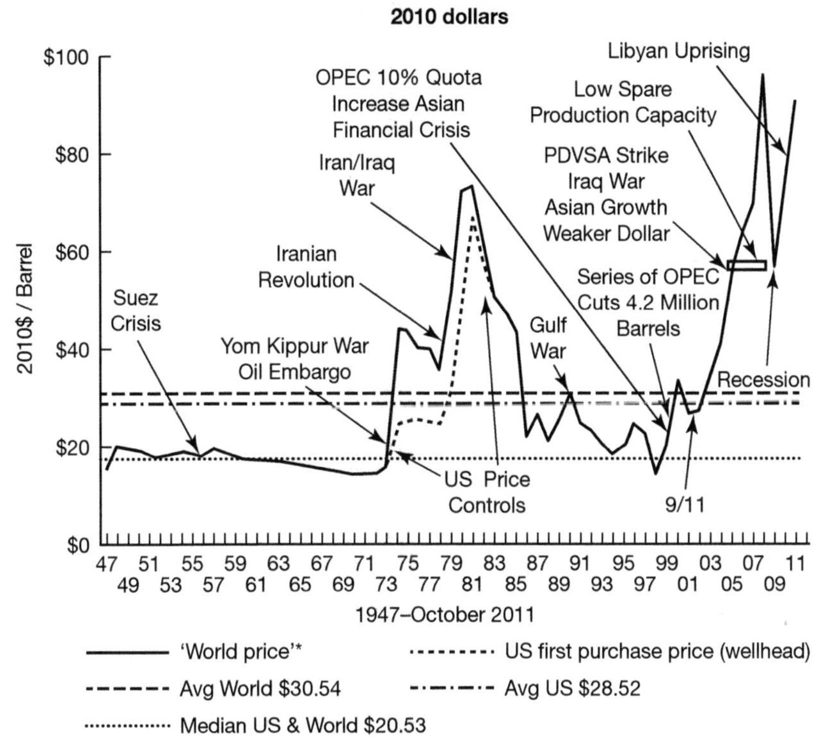

*World price – The only very long-term price series that exists is the US average wellhead or first purchase price of crude. When discussing long-term price behaviour this presents a problem since the US imposed price controls on domestic production from late 1973 to January 1981. In order to present a consistent series and also reflect the difference between international prices and US prices we created a world oil price series that was consistent with the US wellhead price, adjusting the wellhead price by adding the difference between the refiners', acquisition price of imported crude and the refiners', average acquisition price of domestic crude.

Source: WTRG Economics

Whilst oil prices in outright terms were low during this period, markets were evolving and maturing through the late 1980s and early 1990s. A new breed of player in the oil markets emerged – these were the financial players, offering a whole host of risk management and hedging tools as well as themselves speculating on the direction and structure of the markets.

After the Asian crash in the mid-1990s, the commodities market began to enter a bull phase that is still continuing. Oil is no exception and the last decade saw the price of oil rally (and crash) substantially, with many factors playing out. The second Gulf War added clarity to the realisation that oil supplies could, in time, tighten significantly. The West was also waking up to the fact that the strange far-off mystical region called 'Asia' was starting to flex its muscles and show its thirst for all natural resources. Japan had traditionally been the talisman of Asian oil demand but it had always purchased its crude oil in a very passive, safety-first way. The Chinese method of obtaining the hydrocarbons it so craved would soon prove to be anything but.

CRUDE OIL PRODUCTION

As commodities boomed, countries all around the world woke up to the reality that in many cases:

- They were either sitting on a pot of gold – except the gold was black and sulphurous – but they had ceded the rights to their oil reserves to others, or
- At the other end of the spectrum, they were chronically exposed to the price of oil and short of the natural resources that their countries needed to fuel their booming financial and population growth.

Figure 3.3 shows the major oil producers in 1990 and it can be seen that the Middle East (17 per cent), North America and Canada (11 per cent) and the former Soviet Union (FSU) (11 per cent) were the key producers, with Africa at a modest 6 per cent of the total.

Figure 3.3 **Crude oil production – 1990**

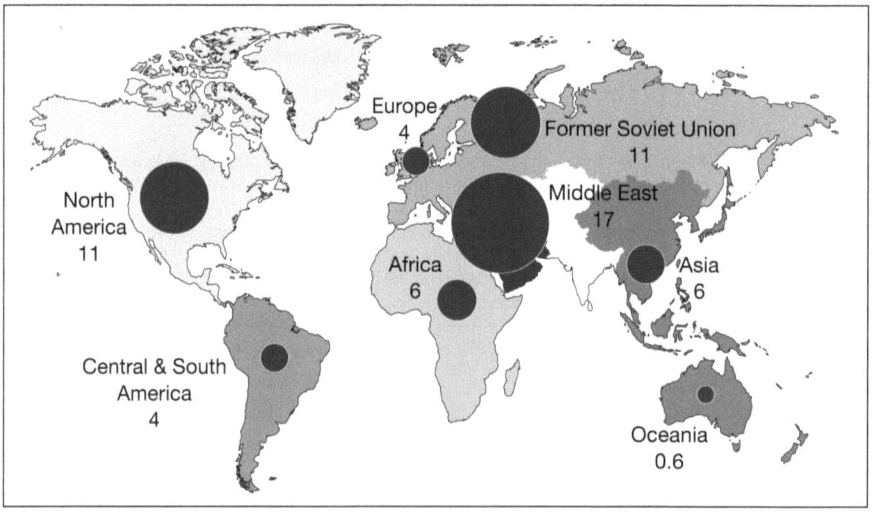

Source: EIA

By 2010, the oil producing landscape had changed with the Middle East then producing 23 per cent of all global oil production. The FSU production had increased slightly to 13 per cent, whilst the US and Canada remained the same at 11 per cent and Africa's production increased slightly to 10 per cent (see Figure 3.4).

Figure 3.4

Crude oil production – 2010

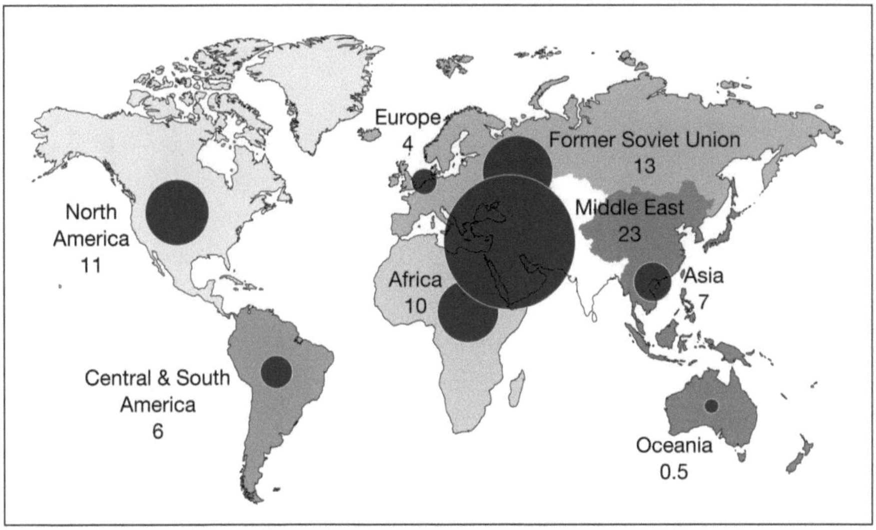

Source: EIA

Previously, the oil markets had typically taken on a fairly predictable pattern. Oil producers either allied with 'the majors' who took the crude oil out of the ground – this oil was then either sold directly to refiners, also known as end users, or to traders who would take a 'position' on the barrels before ultimately selling them to an end user – or the barrels would go to one of the integrated oil companies, typically a major, which could produce, ship and refine the oil itself. Once refined, the finished products would either be destined for domestic use or in some cases they went for export. In addition to the traded crude oil market, there are enormous international traded markets for finished products such as light distillates (LPG, gasoline, naphtha), middle distillates (kerosene, diesel) and heavy distillates (heavy fuel oil, lubricating oils, wax, asphalt). Now, with rising prices, both producers and consumers began to question the deals that were in place as the sums of money involved vastly increased.

On the production side, contracts in countries such as Russia, Venezuela, Ecuador and many in Africa were either renegotiated or simply torn up. The rise in commodities prices was matched by a rising wave of socialism, especially in Latin America.

CRUDE OIL CONSUMPTION

Figure 3.5 shows the global crude oil consumption in 1990, with North America being the largest consumer (20 per cent) followed by Europe (15 per cent) and Asia (13 per cent).

Figure 3.5

Oil consumption – 1990

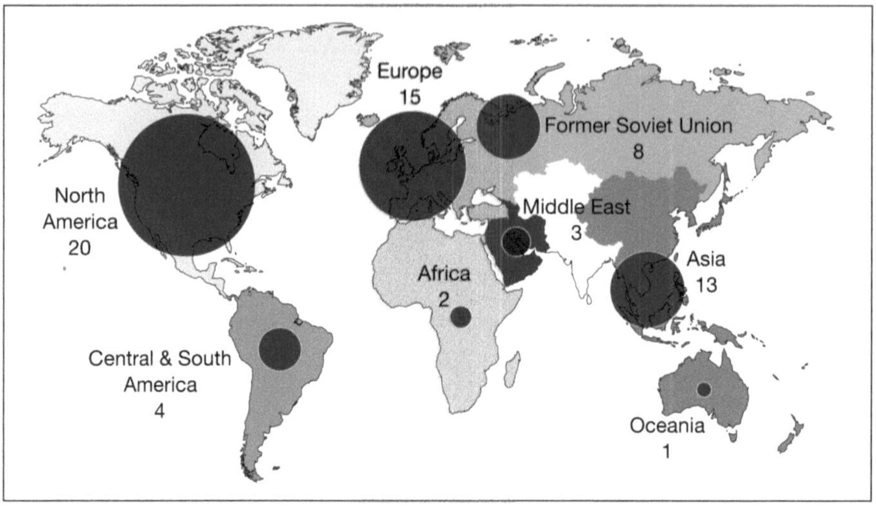

Source: EIA

Twenty years later the map has changed enormously, with Figure 3.6 showing the consumption data for 2010, illustrating the big hike in demand from Asia (mostly China) – up to 25 per cent. North American consumption is up slightly at 23 per cent and Europe's consumption remains static at 15 per cent of the total.

Figure 3.6

Oil consumption – 2010

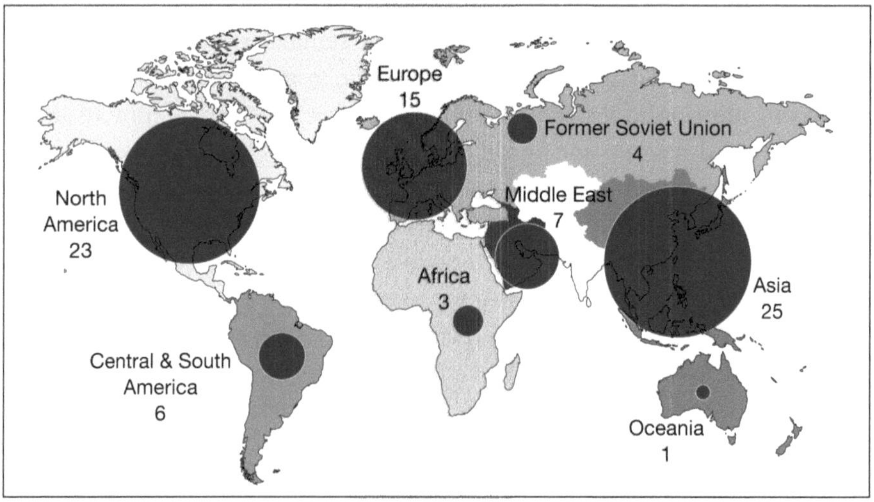

Source: EIA

CRUDE OIL REFINING

Producers also became keen to have more of a say at the consumer end of the market and in the refining sector or 'downstream' part of the business. Saudi

Aramco led the way by adding refining capacity within its own country. This was, firstly, to meet its own growing energy demand and, secondly, to export refined products rather than simply the crude oil, thus capturing the 'refiner's margin' too. This increased refining capacity has been mirrored all around the Middle East.

The previous cycle of low oil prices and poor refining margins – the difference between the cost of purchasing, shipping and refining crude oil and the resultant prices of selling those refined products – had led to a period of chronic underinvestment in oil infrastructure. Refining capacity in particular, after the turn of the century, was found to be lacking both in terms of quality and quantity, making it unable to service the requirements of either the affluent West or the rapidly emerging East. In addition to this, financial stakes have been taken in refineries all over the world in return for supplies of crude oil to supplement the already vast global network of storage facilities owned by countries such as Saudi Arabia and Kuwait, in places ranging from Asia to the Caribbean and Europe. The major oil companies, for so long the backbone of global refining, at the same time as this was happening were happy to pull back from the refining sector, scarred from the years of owning loss-making assets.

Figure 3.7 shows world CDU capacity changes.

World CDU Capacity Changes

Figure 3.7

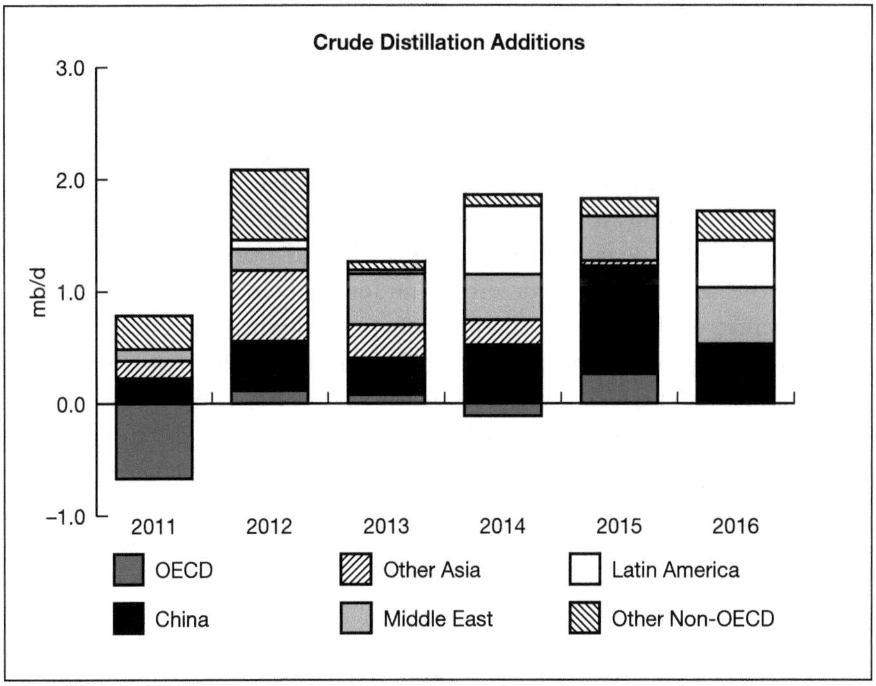

Source: © OECD/IEA 2011

Highly aware of their growing demands, countries such as China, Thailand and India, as well as the Middle East, went on a refinery-building spree that has still not finished. Huge new and vastly superior refineries were and are being built, such as Reliance's enormous gasoline-making machine situated at the port of Jamnagar in northwestern India.

At the same time as the activity in the refining sector, the global demand centres were waking up to their need to secure oil supplies. The result was huge investment from the many consuming countries, with the biggest investor by a long way being China. They targeted the continents of Africa and South America and their associated crude oil production (the upstream part of the market), as the renewed battle for the control of the world's oil reserves began again in earnest.

Figure 3.8 shows how the level of refining capacity has increased since 1990 with the growth of facilities in both China and the rest of Asia.

GEOPOLITICS

For the majors and traders this dual attack on their traditional 'trading sphere' has forced a rethink of strategy on their part. Majors have rationalised and realigned their trading businesses massively – firstly by pulling out of ship owning, and secondly by pulling out from large parts of the refining sector as they were unable to compete with the new refineries in Asia and the many subsidised domestic markets in the developing world. Figure 3.9 shows the global geographical spread of crude oil production, in millions of barrels per day.

Reinvestment in upstream oil and gas has also proved challenging for many companies due to the rising wave of nationalism in many oil-rich countries. The irony of this is that whilst countries such as Venezuela wave the flag for the end of imperialism, the sad reality is that the profits from the sale of their crude oil are no longer being reinvested into the infrastructure of their oil production as happened when there was Western investment. A production graph of Venezuelan oil production is similar to that of an inverted Greek bond yield chart: it is a sorry tale.

For the trading companies, what is clear is that the days of being a middle-man are, in the main, over. Markets are now incredibly efficient with both producers and refiners much more able to service their own needs and incredibly more savvy and aware than before. Trading companies, in many instances, have therefore turned to assets in either the upstream or the downstream sector as they attempt to mirror the behaviour and business models of the majors.

Figure 3.8

World refining capacity

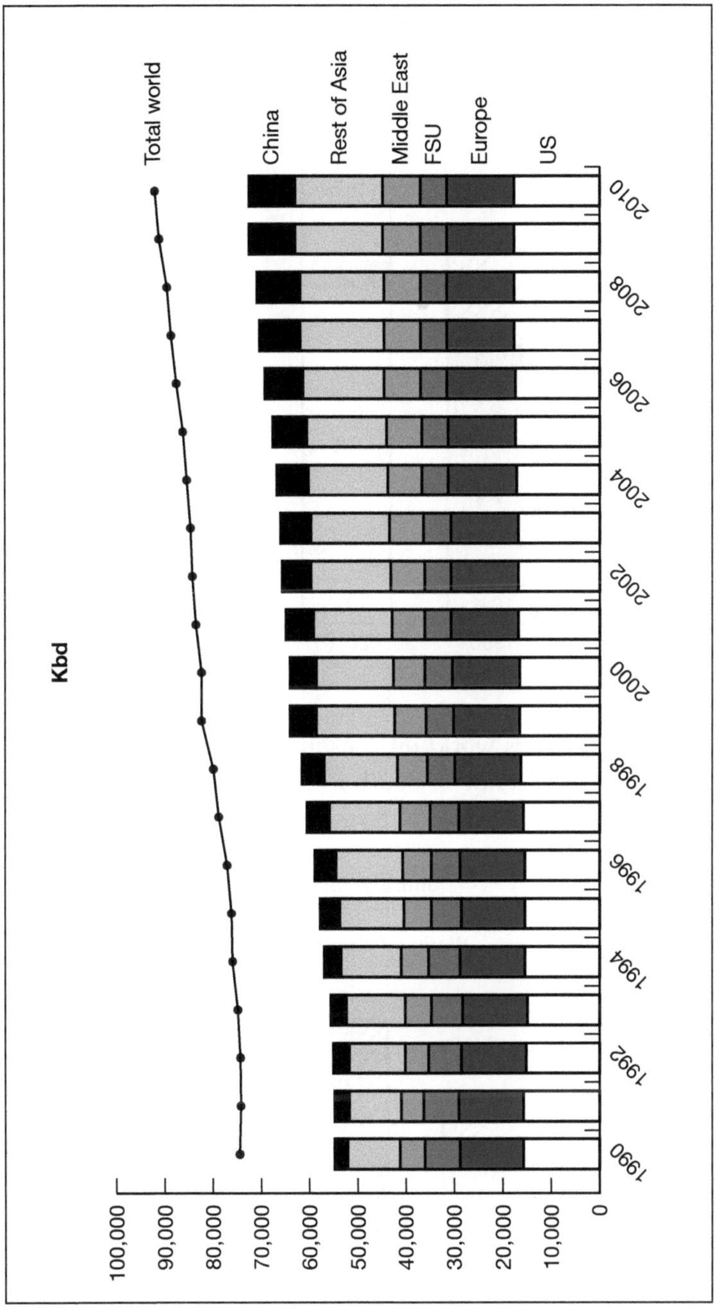

Source: BP Annual Statistics

Figure 3.9

Share of crude oil production

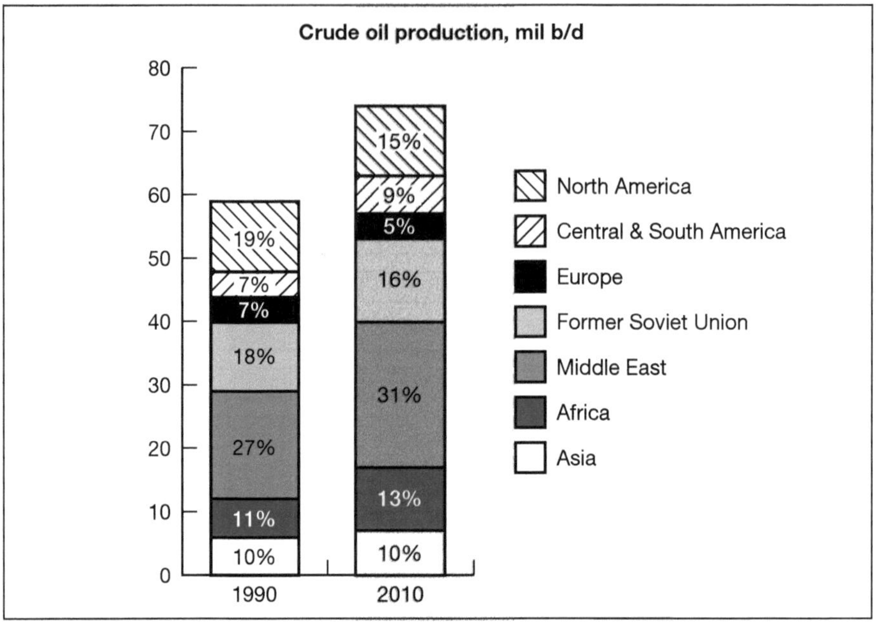

Source: EIA

Figure 3.10 shows world oil consumption in millions of barrels per day, highlighting the decline of South and Central American consumption and the enormous surge in that from Asia.

Figure 3.10

Share of oil consumption

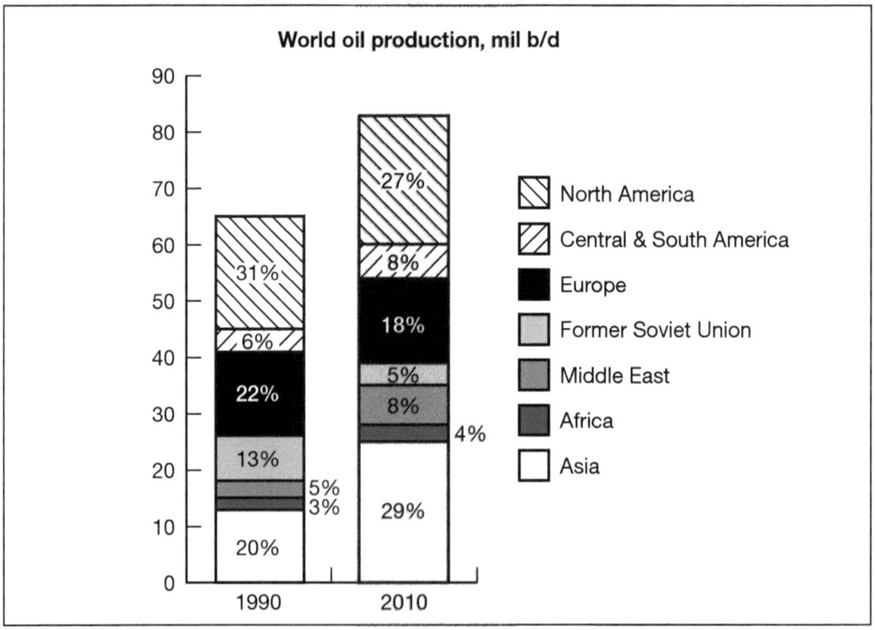

Source: EIA

OPEC

Amongst all of this and forever looming large – or at least attempting to – is the Organization of Petroleum Exporting Companies (OPEC) comprising Algeria, Angola, Ecuador, Iran, Iraq, Kuwait, Libya, Nigeria, Qatar, Venezuela and, most importantly, the UAE and finally Saudi Arabia.

Whilst cartels are effectively outlawed globally, this one operates quite openly and freely with stated aims and price bands that it wishes to achieve. As non-OPEC supply of oil has shot up, so OPEC's effectiveness in controlling the markets has diminished. There are certainly times when it is able to tighten weak markets through the compliance mainly of Saudi Arabia and the UAE, but it proved entirely impotent during the 2008 rally that appeared to be indicative more of a lack of refining capacity than anything else.

Member countries such as Venezuela are in any case entirely incapable of producing their full quota in any respect, and OPEC spare capacity remains an oft-debated subject in terms of establishing how much risk premia should be in a given market. OPEC maintains that it always aims to strike a balance and with the amount of funds its member states have invested in the various Western financial markets and systems, it could be expected that it is cognisant of the need to protect the world from a recession caused by spiralling energy costs.

Figure 3.11 shows the largely static OPEC production and the increases from other sources.

DEFINITIONS AND KEY FEATURES

Within the oil markets there are a number of widely used acronyms and terms that are described below.

The physical markets

Crude oil and sulphur

Crude oils are typically classed as high or low sulphur. Typically the lower the sulphur, the higher the value of the crude.

API (gravity)

Crude oils are also classed as light or heavy. The higher the gravity (or the lighter the crude oil), typically the higher the value of the crude.

Figure 3.11

OPEC vs non-OPEC output

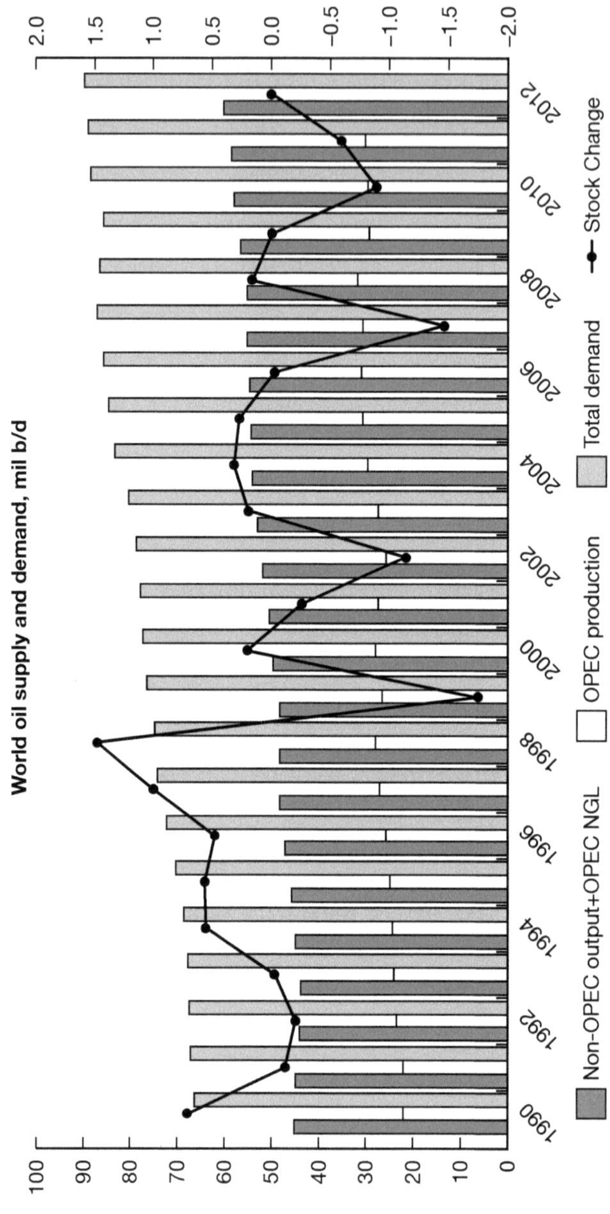

Source: EIA

TAN (acid)

As the world delves deeper for hydrocarbon, more and more acidic crude oils are being found. The higher the TAN (total acid number) is, the more difficult the crude oil is to deal with and process, not least because of the corrosion implications for the kit involved in the production, transportation and refining.

Oil products

Petroleum gas

Used for anything from the production of plastics in the petrochemical sector, to heating and cooking.

Naphtha

Used either as a feedstock or as blending material for the production of gasoline.

Gasoline

Motor fuel for cars.

Kerosene

Fuel for jet engines and tractors, typically.

Gasoil/diesel

Used mainly as diesel fuel or heating oil.

Lubricating oil

Used in motor oil, lubricants and grease.

Fuel oil

Industrial fuel use. Used mainly for direct burning in power generators, and as fuel for the shipping industry.

Residuals

Everything left at the bottom, ranging through coke, asphalt, tar and waxes.

Catalytic cracking

This has largely replaced the old thermal cracking process and is the process whereby crude oil is broken down into its components, from the larger, more complex, long-chain organic hydrocarbons to the simpler, shorter-chain, lighter chemical fractions. This is required as there is far more market demand for the lighter fractions, kerosene and gasoline than for crude itself. Carried out in an oil refinery, it involves many steps and explains why oil refineries cover such a large area. The 'cracking' is done by means of a catalyst that behaves like a fluid when aerated with vapour.

In overview, the crude oil feedstock is heated, mixed with steam and then with the catalyst. The output products are mostly alkylation unit feedstocks, including propylene, isobutene, gasoline and diesel fuel.

Figure 3.12 is a generic schematic showing the cracking process.

Derivatives markets

Exchange traded futures

Predominantly screen-based trading where the market participant either buys or sells a futures contract for a given month of delivery with a fixed expiry period. All futures markets are fully regulated by bodies such as the CFTC (Commodity Futures Trading Commission) and the FSA (Futures and Securities Authority).

OTC swaps

In the oil business this is what is often referred to as the OTC (over the counter) market or swaps market. Participants can buy or sell a plethora of paper swaps that reflect or are linked to either a futures contract or a physical underlying instrument. Most vanilla swaps markets are highly standardised, although more complex tailor-made instruments are also widely traded. Markets are regulated to a large degree.

Options

Options are derivatives which allow the participant to hedge or gain exposure to direction or simply fluctuations in price. Some options are standardised, known as exchange traded or listed options, and can be traded via the exchanges; others are OTC and may be simple (vanilla) or what are known as boutique or exotic – a highly specialised field. Markets are again regulated to a large degree.

Figure 3.12

The cracking process

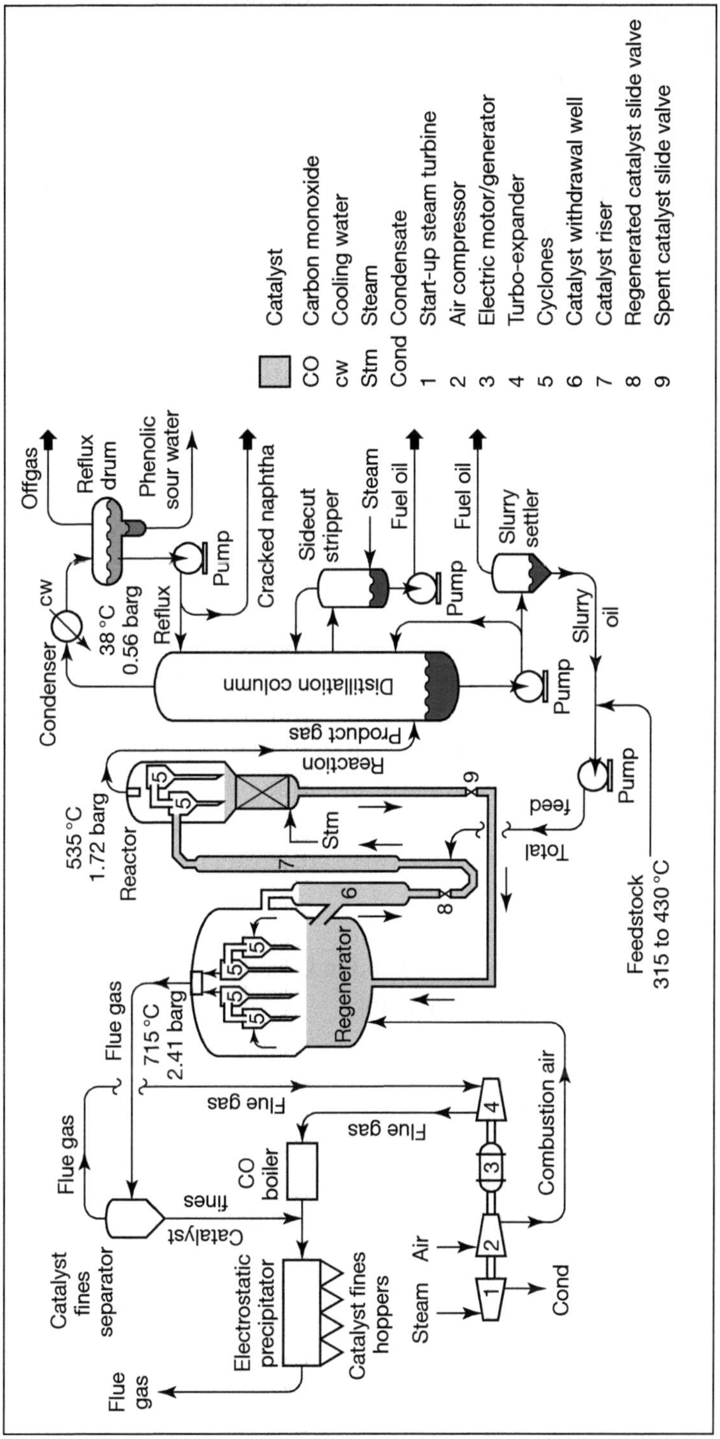

Source: FLEXIM, www.flexim.com

The main oil exchanges

International Continental Exchange (ICE)

Oil futures were until recently traded on open outcry exchanges. When the International Petroleum Exchange (IPE) was acquired by ICE in 2005, the London trading floor was closed down and all the volume was transferred onto screen-based trading via the ICE platform.

New York Mercantile Exchange (NYMEX)

The last bastion of open outcry trading for the oil markets, but the reality is that the success of the screen-based ICE platform forced NYMEX to follow suit.

The main exchange traded oil contracts

Europe

Brent

Brent has myriad jargon and names that follow it. The futures contract is now simply referred to as ICE Brent but the underlying contract is actually called 'BOFE', an acronym for a basket of crude oils that are deliverable into the physical contract. These are Brent, Oseberg, Forties and Ekofisk. This provides the main benchmark for crude oil delivered within Europe, for crude exported from West Africa and for Arabian Gulf deliveries to Europe. It is also used widely now for sweet crude oil produced in Asia.

ICE Gasoil

Like its crude oil cousin, the London Gasoil contract forms the backbone for middle distillate trading in Europe.

USA

NYMEX WTI (West Texas Intermediate)

This is the main benchmark in the Americas. Unlike Brent, WTI has real physical deliverability (not just linked to an underlying physical contract) with the delivery point in Cushing, Oklahoma. ICE runs a successful look-alike contract.

NYMEX RBOB (Reformulated Blendstock for Oxygenate Blending)

This is the gasoline hub for the USA and the only real hedging tool available to gasoline traders, other than crude oil contracts. It can be highly volatile, in respect to seasonality and weather events such as hurricanes.

Middle East and Asia

Dubai/Oman/Upper Zakum

The irony of the huge demand centre of Asia is that the tail often wags the dog and so the oil prices set for that region are expressed in terms of these grades (Dubai, Oman and Upper Zakum) but are effectively set as a differential to Brent.

The Dubai Mercantile Exchange was set up in the past few years in Dubai to offer a futures benchmark for crude oil from Oman. The exchange has proved effective in offering a physical deliverability mechanism for the crude oil but volumes and trading methods have yet to take off in any way remotely close to those found in London or New York.

Oil products in Asia are priced at the same time as the crude oil using a Singapore delivery basis.

OIL RESERVES

The vast majority of the world's untapped crude oil is to be found in the Middle East, with over 50 per cent of the world's proven reserves. Areas such as West Africa and the Former Soviet Union (FSU) also hold vast reserves, as well as the continent of South America. Crude oil is also to be found all over Asia but usually in vastly smaller quantities.

Where these reserves sit is obviously a huge global political issue and we can only speculate on the reasons why dictators in Iraq are removed yet military juntas in Myanmar go untouched. We can again only stop to consider why it was so critical to remove a Libyan regime guilty of humanitarian and war crimes and genocide against its own people whilst nothing was done to intervene in countries such as Rwanda or more recently in Syria. The oil reserves of the countries mentioned are almost certainly coincidental.

The US government, whether Democrat or Republican, has long espoused the need to reduce the dependence on 'foreign oil' or, more pointedly, that from the Middle East. What is interesting is that, in my opinion, they may actually be far closer to this possibility than anyone had previously imagined. Hydrocarbons from (the only slightly foreign) Canadian tar sands abound and with the rapid emergence of the shale gas story there is speculation that the US could become a net exporter of hydrocarbons by 2030, a truly staggering statistic and a shot across the bows for all the long-term dollar bears.

OIL USES AND APPLICATIONS

Hydrocarbons in the form of oil and coal are one of the Earth's most basic yet most important energy resources, mainly in the form of combustible fuels. Hydrocarbons have also, for instance, even replaced chlorofluorocarbons (CFCs) as the propellants in aerosol sprays.

The motor industry has been going through a huge period of upheaval as it strives to meet new emissions targets with hybrid and full electric cars being spawned, as well as many running off LNG or LPG and the vast red herring and driver of food prices that is the misguided biodiesel movement. Whilst it is clear that vast improvements and advancements have been made, gasoline and diesel remain the staple diet of the motor industry and, with car markets rapidly expanding in countries such as China and India, the thirst for hydrocarbons is not going to dissipate any time soon. One trend that has been symptomatic of the recent global financial crisis (felt more keenly in the West) and the increased Asian oil demand is the geographical location of the world's oil refineries. More and more refineries in the West are either closing or being turned into simple storage terminals whilst the Middle East and Asia plough ahead with their vast refinery expansion programme.

This effectively means that, to a large degree, the surplus product that Asia is now producing is being used to supply the hydrocarbon needs of the West. To draw an analogy, it is a little like when you call your credit card company to complain about excess charges only to find out that they have outsourced their call centre to Asia. The big difference here, however, is that the West didn't ask to close their refineries and move them to Asia and nor are they making any money from the whole exercise; quite the reverse.

OIL PRICING AND PRICE DISCOVERY

As mentioned previously, the various prices of crude oil and oil products are set on the international exchanges. This effectively sets what is known as the 'flat price'.

Physical barrels of products or crude can be traded on a fixed price basis, but are typically traded and priced off a series of price quotes established during a date range relevant to the time of loading or delivery. The actual price quotations that are used are defined at the time of the physical or paper (such as swaps) transaction. The most widely used current publication for setting oil prices is Platt's (now owned by Standard & Poor's) which uses a variety of 'mean of close' (MOC) methods in the main oil hubs of Singapore, London and New York to establish the prices that it will publish.

The physical barrels will then price at a premium or discount to the relative quote, be it WTI, Brent or Dubai. Typically cargoes in the West can price around the loading date for a period of five days or for the entire month of loading. In the East, cargoes are typically all priced during the loading month. The methodologies for determining the benchmark pricing are entirely transparent but the differentials for the assorted crude oils are much more opaque given that there are literally hundreds and hundreds of different crude oils. Products markets are typically much more standardised given that there is a fairly usual set of specifications that the products have to adhere to.

FREIGHTING

The other main element of trading physical oil is the freighting (shipping in any other language) of the oil to its final destination. The cost of a shipping transaction is in effect the rate for any given charter (the hire of a vessel). This is determined using a tried and trusted method: Worldscale Freight Rates.

Worldscale (WS) (for more information see www.worldscale.co.uk) is a commercial organisation with its most recent incarnation going back to 1989. The business is linked to the concept of a uniform daily freight rate for a voyage independent of the destination or origin of the cargo and in any vessel. WS publishes a list of 'flat rates' before the beginning of each year that essentially dictates the cost of shipping oil from one port to another. The market rate for tankers then fluctuates by the amount of points of WS that a charter is prepared to pay or that an owner is prepared to lease a vessel at. For example, WS 100 effectively means 100 per cent of the WS rate, which is then multiplied by the tonnage (weight) of the vessel.

On a separate note, the global tanker market is currently enduring a torrid time with a huge amount of new tonnage having being ordered at the peak of the cycle in 2008. These record orders placed with the yards coupled with the global financial crisis that followed have left the market chronically oversupplied and it may take some time yet before the markets recover in any significant way.

HEDGING AND RISK MANAGEMENT

Oil markets have become increasingly volatile, meaning that nearly everyone at some stage needs to employ some risk management and hedging strategies. All trading companies, most refiners and even some producers work in a very sophisticated and largely integrated fashion.

The oil markets are typically traded as a series of curves across the various crudes and products linked by differentials to each other. Taking Brent crude as an example, the flat price would be defined as the outright price of the 'front contract', i.e. the most prompt current futures month. The relationship between the front month and the subsequent months would then be defined by a series of 'spreads'. So, for instance, say the front month is 'April' and the price is US$120.00 (all values are notional). If the price for May delivery is US$119.50 then the spread between April and May (known as apr/may) would be +US$0.50.

When the front of the market is valued more highly than the subsequent months, the market is said to be 'backwardated'. Conversely, if the front of the market is lower than the deferred months, the market is said to be in 'contango'. For more information on contango, backwardation and basis please refer to Chapter 1. It has to be said that much of the trading jargon exists to confuse the layman into believing it is far more complicated than it actually is. You can of course have markets that are in contango at the front of the market yet are backwardated further down the curve: the markets can fluctuate wildly on any given day, meaning that both opportunities and risks abound.

The oil products curves move in much the same way as and at fluctuating levels to the crude oil contracts. The pricing differentials between crude and products are what are known as 'crack spreads' (see Figure 3.12 for a schematic showing the cracking process) and it is these that refiners will attempt to capture when, for instance, prices are very strong in the deferred markets. This in very simple terms allows refiners to lock in the 'refiner's margin' and then run their asset at full capacity, knowing that the supply/demand equation will have no bearing on their margin.

Many producing countries such as those in the Middle East employ little in the way of hedging strategies. Their economies of scale and low sunk costs of production mean that their operations are effectively guaranteed to be profitable, barring the most major of global recessions or catastrophies. Other more 'marginal' producers, such as those in Canada, or independent producers with stakes in blocks in places such as West Africa, have a much higher cost base and therefore a much tighter bottom line. That, and the requirement by the banks providing the financing to lock in that bottom line, dictate that hedging of the forward flat price often takes place. It is sometimes even a banking prerequisite to ensure the viability of the project in the first place.

At the other end of the oil market supply chain lie the consumers, such as airlines with exposure to the jet fuel costs, mining companies with exposure to the diesel costs which form a large part of the cost of any mining operation, and shipping companies which are exposed to the cost of their fuel known as bunker fuel.

ENVIRONMENTAL CONCERNS

Oil at every single point in its journey, from the ground to providing light in your home or the plastic cup that you drink your coffee from, courts huge controversy. Throughout history, there have been numerous large environmental disasters ranging from the Exxon Valdez in Alaska to the Blue Horizon blowout in the Gulf of Mexico that BP recently experienced. There have also been huge losses of life, such as with the Piper Alpha platform explosion in the North Sea many years ago.

Even more recently, the emergence of shale gas in the United States has led to global awareness of the term 'fracking' and all the controversy that is associated with it, ranging from the use of chemicals to allegations that it causes earthquakes.

Safety at all levels is increasingly in focus for the oil industry as a whole but it remains a hazardous business from the wellhead to the refinery and it seems unlikely that we have seen the last piece of news on the subject.

FUTURE MARKET DEVELOPMENTS

Politicians like to describe situations as 'fluid' and in oil the pun is well defined. Oil is driven as much by politics as it is by fundamentals and by regulation as much as it is by speculation. There are many larger scale issues and we have yet to see how they will play out, but we will try to list some longer term issues to ponder, all of which could have a material effect on oil prices.

- The continued US policy, irrespective of the party, on pursuit of non-reliance on foreign oil.
- Continued tension between Israel and Iran and in the wider Middle East.
- Potential for more civil unrest in some of the Arab nations.
- Aggressive Russian policy towards pricing and control of their natural resources.
- Further moves by China to play a bigger role in the production of its hydrocarbon requirements, particularly in Africa, and its wish to determine the price it pays for those requirements.
- Continuation or further tightening of policy by regulators to monitor energy markets in the West.
- The potential rise of a further socialist movement in Latin America.
- Peak oil theory – fact or fiction?

Oil markets are essentially very 'mature' nowadays, with the price highly defined and tracked every second of the day all around the world. The many vagaries and myriad different participants at so many different levels will keep it an entirely fascinating place for some time to come, it would seem.

4

Gas

Including featured section on Trading Natural Gas,
Victoria Adams, European Natural Gas Broker, ICAP Energy Ltd

BACKGROUND AND CONTEXT

Natural gas is found globally, deposits are widespread and most of us have used it at one time or another to heat our apartments, houses or even to cook. It is typically found in association with oil reserves and over the last few decades or so natural gas has been processed to form liquefied natural gas (LNG). Shale gas deposits, which are simply gas deposits that were trapped in rock structures, are now being released through the controversial 'fracking' process. These deposits are now so widespread, especially in the US, that gas prices are falling markedly and the US is well on the way to being self-sufficient in gas.

The main chemical constituent of natural gas is methane, whose more familiar name is marsh gas. It is frequently found in sizeable quantities when associated with large-scale production of oil; in smaller amounts it may rise passively to the surface especially in marshy, damp areas. When this occurs it is known as a gas seep. Historical literature sometimes names these gas seeps as 'will-o'-the-wisps'; in Latin they are known as *ignis fatuus*, or 'foolish fire'. If a naturally occurring gas seep is then ignited, say by a lightning strike, it may be seen for some distance in the dark, prompting warnings to travellers.

Natural gas seeps were first recorded in Iran between 6000 BC and 2000 BC. Around 1000 BC in Greece, a 'burning spring' was discovered. The local population was so in awe of this that they built a temple on the site and a priestess was installed as guardian. She then started to make prophecies – probably encouraged by the gas fumes – and this became the Temple of the Oracle at Delphi. More recently, around 500 BC, the Chinese used natural gas to boil sea water to produce fresh water. The first reported commercial use of gas was in the UK when it was produced from coal to light street lamps in 1785. The first gas well in the US was drilled in the 1820s and connected by pipeline to users in Fredonia, New York.

Some of us cook with gas; we see the blue flames in the gas jets. Most of us are familiar with photographs of excess gas being 'flared' off as a waste product from the drilling for oil. If it is not economically viable for this gas to be transported or used on the rig itself, it is viewed as a dangerous combustible by-product to be disposed of as quickly as possible, usually by flaring the gas. This process of flaring has come under close scrutiny due to the associated waste products that are released back into the atmosphere, and it is now a cause for concern for many environmentalists.

Gas is not easy to transport and it was not until the 1960s when high strength steel pipelines were developed that gas could be transported over long distances. As a result, many countries did not develop the infrastructure to use natural gas. Now it is used mostly for heating and cooking although some gas is used to power gas and steam turbines for electricity generation in preference to coal. Even the word 'gas' has many meanings:

- We put 'gas' in the car (in the UK this is petrol).
- We may get 'gas' if we have indigestion.
- We may cook with 'gas'.

WHAT IS NATURAL GAS?

Natural gas is colourless, shapeless and odourless in its pure form. It is combustible and when burned gives off a great deal of energy. Natural gas burns cleanly and produces 30 per cent less carbon dioxide than oil and 40 per cent less than coal.

Natural gas is a combustible mixture of hydrocarbon gases; it is formed primarily of methane but it can also include ethane, propane, butane and pentane. The composition of natural gas may vary widely, but Table 4.1 shows the typical components of 'raw' natural gas before any refining takes place.

Table 4.1

Typical composition of natural gas

Methane	CH_4	65–90%
Ethane	C_2H_6	0–25%
Propane	C_3H_8	
Butane	C_4H_{10}	
Carbon dioxide	CO_2	0–8%
Oxygen	O_2	0–0.2%
Nitrogen	N_2	0–5%
Hydrogen sulphide	H_2S	0–5%
Rare gases	A, He, Ne, Xe	trace

When natural gas is refined the impurities such as water, other gases (known as natural gas liquids) and sand are removed, leaving almost pure methane. This is an odourless gas to which the commercial gas suppliers add smelly, sulphur-containing organic chemicals called *mercaptans* before onward distribution to end users. This gives the gas its characteristic (rotten cabbage) smell; this is actually a safety measure and aids in gas leak detection. The impurities found in natural gas may be separated out and sold individually – for example propane is used for gas cigarette lighters and to fire up sluggish barbecues.

Natural gas is considered 'dry' when it is almost pure methane (more than 90 per cent pure), having had most of the other commonly associated hydrocarbons removed. When other hydrocarbons are present at a level of over 10 per cent, the natural gas is 'wet'.

GAS MEASUREMENTS

Natural gas can be measured in a range of different ways. As a gas, it can be measured in cubic feet or cubic metres. This is the volume it takes up at normal temperatures and pressures. Gas production and distribution companies commonly measure natural gas in thousands of cubic feet (Mcf), millions of cubic feet (MMcf) or trillions of cubic feet (Tcf). Natural gas may also be measured as a source of energy. Similar to other forms of energy, natural gas is commonly measured and expressed in British thermal units (Btu). One Btu is the amount of natural gas needed to produce enough energy to heat one pound of water by one degree at normal pressure. When natural gas is delivered to a house, it is measured by the gas utility in 'therms' for billing purposes. A therm is equivalent to 100,000 Btu, or just over 97 cubic feet, of natural gas.

NATURAL GAS FORMATION

Natural gas is a fossil fuel. Its formation is very similar to that of oil and is shown in Figure 4.1. Natural gas, oil and coal resources are known as finite or non-renewable, given the millions of years required for their formation. Gas and oil typically form when aquatic biological and plant material are buried by water and mud, then compacted for millions of years at very high temperatures and pressures. Technically, there are three different varieties of natural gas, based on their formation, and a brief description of each is given below.

- Thermogenic;
- Biogenic;
- Abiogenic.

Thermogenic

Thermogenic natural gas is formed in a similar fashion to crude oil: organic particles from decaying animals and plants fall to the bottom of the ocean or lake and are covered in mud and other sediment. Over many millions of years increasing amounts of sediment, mud and other debris are piled on top of this organic matter. This compression, combined with the high temperatures found deep underground, breaks down the carbon bonds in the organic matter. The temperature gets higher and higher as the depth of burial increases. At low temperatures (shallower deposits), more oil is produced relative to natural gas. At higher temperatures, however, more

Figure 4.1

Natural gas formation

How Petroleum and Natural Gas were formed
Tiny plants and animals died and were buried on the sea floor.
Over millions of years, the remains were buried deeper and deeper.
The plant and animal remains turned into oil and gas deposits.

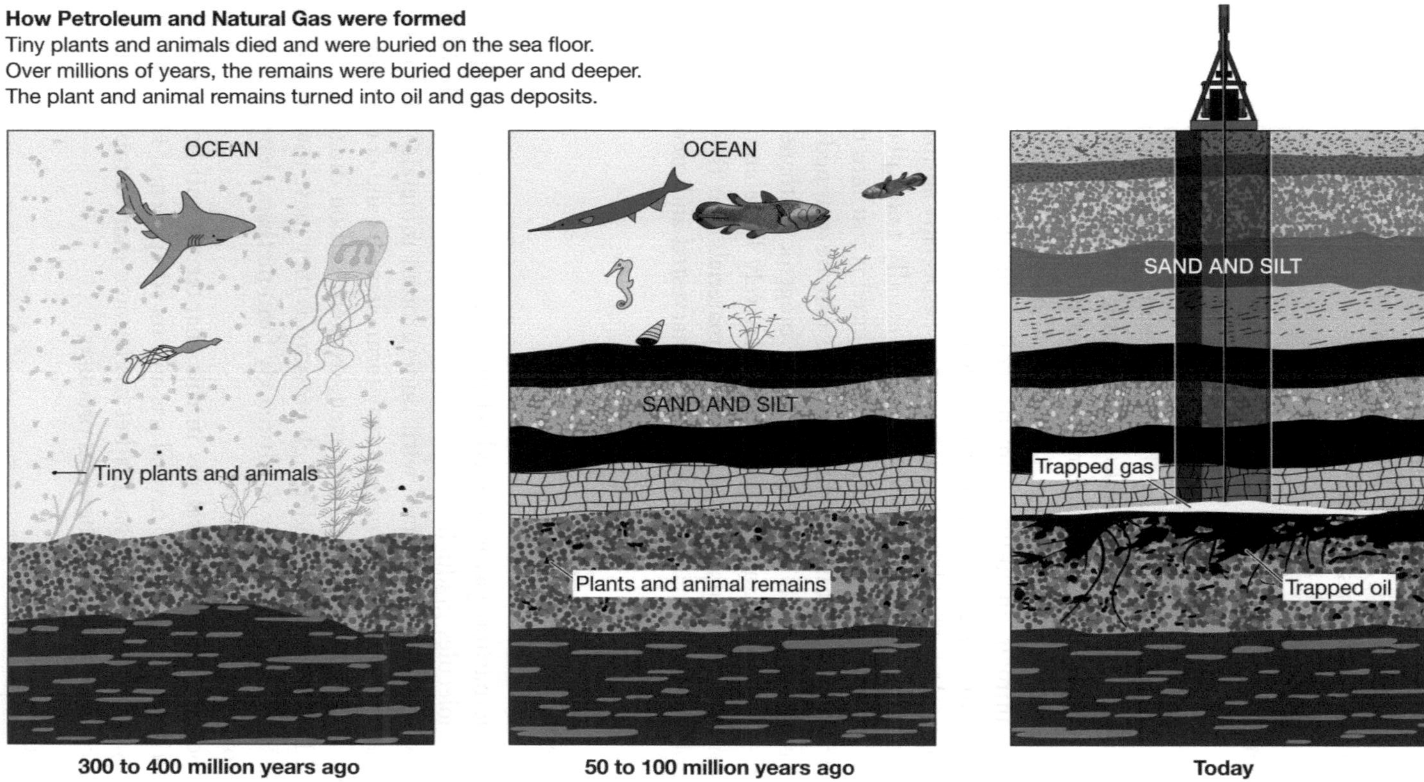

Source: National Energy Education Development, NEED, www.need.org

natural gas is created, as opposed to oil. Consequently, natural gas is usually associated with oil in deposits that are 1–2 miles beneath the Earth's crust. Deeper deposits, very far underground, usually contain primarily natural gas, and in many cases pure methane.

Biogenic

Biogenic natural gas occurs through the transformation of organic matter by tiny microorganisms. Tiny methane-producing microorganisms, known as methanogens, chemically break down organic matter to produce methane. These microorganisms are commonly found in areas near the surface of the Earth that are lacking in oxygen, but they also live in the gut and intestines of most animals, including humans. Following the death of the animal or plant, microorganisms aid in the decomposition process and cause the swelling and bloating often seen in remains, especially animal remains.

Formation of methane in this manner usually takes place close to the surface of the Earth, and the methane produced is lost into the atmosphere. In certain circumstances, this methane can be trapped underground, recoverable as natural gas. An example of biogenic methane is landfill gas. Waste-containing landfills produce a relatively large amount of natural gas from the decomposition of the waste materials that they contain. New technologies are allowing this gas to be harvested and used to add to the supply of natural gas.

Abiogenic

Abiogenic natural gas is formed when existing hydrogen-rich gases and carbon molecules gradually rise towards the surface of the Earth. On their journey they might interact with underground minerals. This chemical reaction in the absence of oxygen may form elements and compounds found in the atmosphere, such as nitrogen, oxygen, carbon dioxide, argon and water. If these gases are under high pressure as they move toward the surface of the Earth, they are likely to ultimately form methane deposits, similar to those of a thermogenic nature.

When we discuss natural gas in this chapter we will be concentrating primarily on thermogenic natural gas and its components. However, in the last few years the natural gas market has become more complex and is often further sub-divided into these gas products:

- Natural gas;
- Liquefied natural gas (LNG);
- Shale gas.

NATURAL GAS RESERVES

There are over 930 major gas fields on Earth. Almost all of them fall within 27 regions, comprising approximately 30 per cent of the land surface, (source: Paul Mann, MK Horn and Ian Cross of the University of Texas, Jackson School of Geosciences). Figure 4.2 shows the world gas reserves by country. However, in the last few months enormous gas reserves have been found in deep water, offshore from Mozambique, Africa, which have been likened in size to those of Qatar. This will surely reshape the supply map.

Figure 4.2

World natural gas reserves by country

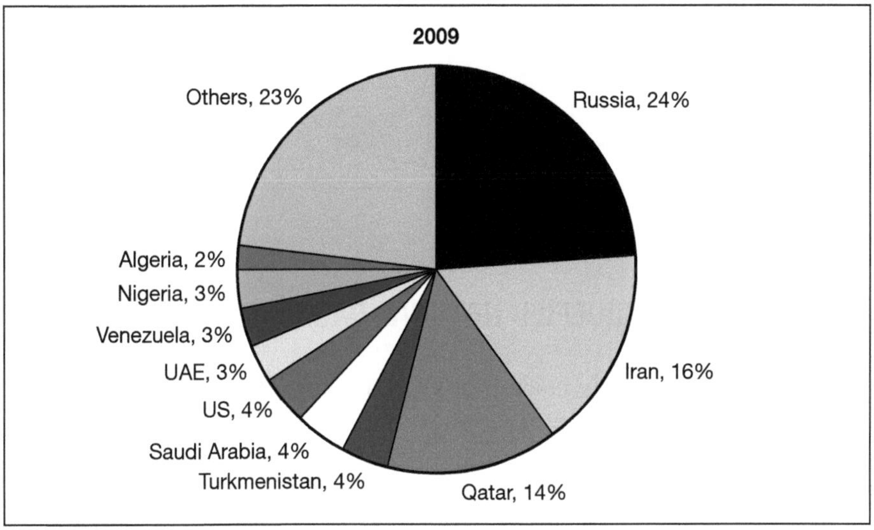

Source: BP Statistical Review

Latest figures show that the Middle East has increased its dominance (see Figure 4.3).

NATURAL GAS PRODUCERS

The US and countries of the former Soviet Union are currently the largest producers of natural gas. The Russian natural gas industry is dominated by Gazprom, which controls 95 per cent of production. In the US, Texas, Louisiana, Oklahoma and Wyoming hold nearly half of the country's reserves. Other major global producers include Canada, Iran, Norway, Qatar, China, Algeria, Saudi Arabia and Indonesia. World natural gas reserves are estimated at 6609 trillion cubic feet (tcf). The Middle East holds 41 per cent of world reserves, while an additional 34 per cent is located in the former Soviet Union, with only 9 per cent held in the OECD countries (source: Deutsche Bank, 'A User Guide to Commodities', May 2011).

Figure 4.3 **Distribution of proved reserves in 1990, 2000 and 2010**

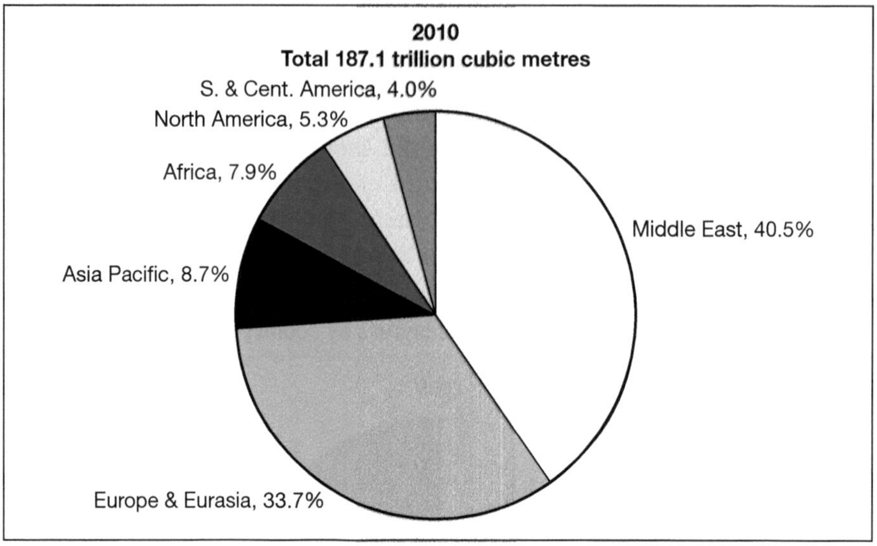

Source: BP Statistical Review 2011

LIQUEFIED NATURAL GAS (LNG)

Natural gas is frequently cooled for ease of transportation and storage. It must be cooled to at least –162°C (–260°F) when it becomes liquefied natural gas, or LNG. It is clear, odourless, non-toxic and non-corrosive. Liquefaction takes place when natural gas is cooled under high pressure, condensed and then reduced in pressure for storage. The resulting liquid is 1/600th of the volume of natural gas, and about half as dense as water.

Mechanics of LNG production

There are a number of processes involved in LNG production:

- Gas is purified by removing condensates such as water, oil and mud, as well as other gases such as CO_2 and H_2S.
- Any trace amounts of mercury are also removed from the gas stream to prevent the mercury combining with aluminium to create amalgam in the cryogenic heat exchangers.
- The resulting gas (mostly methane and ethane) is then cooled down in stages until it is liquefied.
- LNG is finally stored in large storage tanks and can then be loaded and shipped.

Once the gas is in LNG form it can be transported over long distances either by road or sea. A key issue is 'boil-off'; this occurs when the gas starts to warm and is essentially evaporation and may be in the region of 0.10–0.15 per cent per day.

LNG exports

Figure 4.4 shows the major exporters of LNG in 2010. Qatar is by far the biggest exporter of LNG and has developed specific super-sized cargo vessels to carry very large capacities. A standard vessel will carry from 126,000 to 150,000 cubic metres of LNG. However the Qataris have designed the 'Q Flex' vessel that will carry up to 210,000 cubic metres and the 'Q Max' that will carry 266,000 cubic metres. These will be the largest LNG carriers in the world. Qatar gas production is expected to grow in the next few years as the four 'mega-train' (LNG production) facilities have now come on-line, increasing production by a factor of nearly 300 per cent.

Figure 4.4

LNG exports by country – 2010

Exporter	MMtpa	Exporter	MMtpa
Qatar	57.5	Egypt	7.1
Indonesia	23.6	Brunei	6.7
Malaysia	23.1	UAE	5.8
Australia	19.1	Yemen	4.3
Nigeria	18.1	Equatorial Guinea	4.1
Trinidad	15.2	Norway	3.5
Algeria	14.3	Peru	1.3
Russia	10.6	US	0.6
Oman	8.7	Libya	0.2
Total Exports			**223.8**

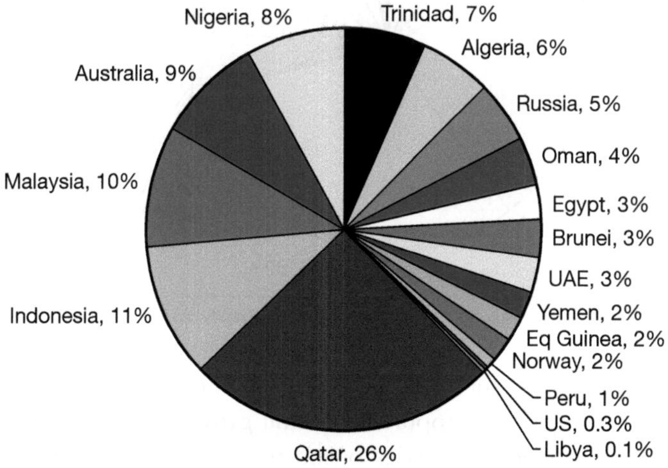

Source: International Gas Union, www.igu.org, based on Waterborne LNG Reports, US DOE, PFC Energy

Australia has recently opened up parts of Queensland for LNG development, extracting methane from coal beds, and is expected to be one of the largest exporters of LNG to the Far East and China within the next few years.

LNG imports

Japan and South Korea together account for nearly half of all LNG imports, as shown in Figure 4.5.

Figure 4.5

LNG imports by country – 2010

Importer	MMtpa	Importer	MMtpa
Japan	70.6	Mexico	4.4
S Korea	34.1	Chile	2.3
Spain	20.5	Portugal	2.2
UK	14.2	Kuwait	2.1
Taiwan	11.6	Brazil	2.0
France	10.5	Canada	1.5
China	9.5	Argentina	1.3
India	9.3	Greece	0.9
US	8.5	Dominican Rep.	0.6
Italy	6.7	Puerto Rico	0.6
Turkey	5.9	UAE	0.1
Belgium	4.5		
Total Imports			**223.9**

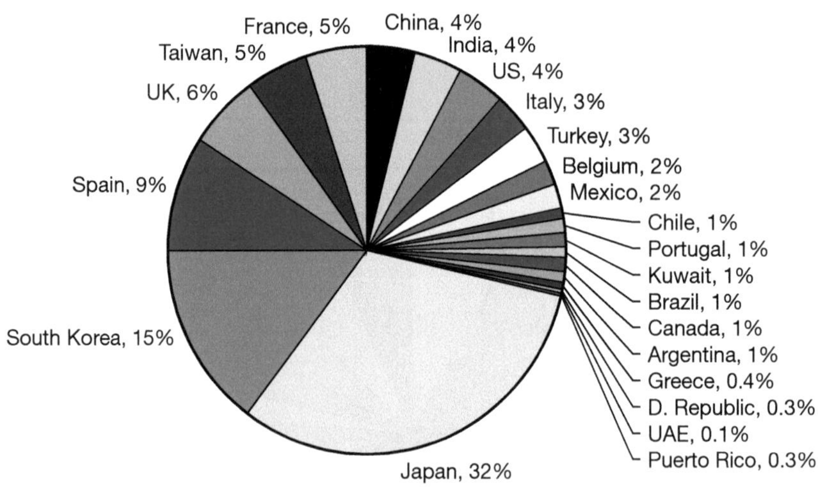

Source: International Gas Union, www.igu.org, based on Waterborne LNG Reports, US DOE, PFC Energy

Gas is increasingly the fuel of choice to supply electricity, provide heating and cooling, and support economic growth. In the last five years (2006–2010), eight new countries began to import LNG to meet domestic needs: Argentina, Brazil, Canada, Chile, China, Kuwait, Mexico and the UAE. Notably, three of these countries are located in South America and two in the Middle East – two regions that previously were not importing LNG. Thailand has also just become an LNG importer, receiving its first cargo from Qatargas in June 2011.

SHALE GAS

Shale is a rock; a very fine grained, organic-rich, sedimentary rock. Geologists have known for years that natural gas may be found in shale rock but until a short time ago it could not be cost-effectively extracted. However, recently we have had:

- Major advances in horizontal drilling;
- Major advances in hydraulic fracturing.

It is possible to combine these processes to form an extraction process known as 'fracking' or 'unconventional' gas production.

Natural gas vs shale gas

Conventional gas reservoirs are created when natural gas moves towards the surface from an organic-rich source formation into highly permeable reservoir rock, where an overlying layer of impermeable rock then traps it. In contrast, shale gas resources form within the organic-rich shale source rock itself. The low permeability of the shale inhibits the gas from migrating to more permeable reservoir rocks and it remains trapped. Without horizontal drilling and hydraulic fracturing, shale gas production would not be economically feasible as the natural gas would not flow from the source at high enough rates to justify the cost of drilling.

Together, both horizontal drilling and hydraulic fracturing have transformed shale formations from marginal to major sources of natural gas. Unfortunately the process itself may be causing environmental damage and there has been a huge public outcry regarding possible contamination and increased seismic activity. There are two main issues; firstly, the water and chemicals that are pumped into the shale to fracture it allow the natural gas to be released but some of the 'lubricants' may escape into the underlying rock and affect the quality of the groundwater. Secondly, increased seismic activity has been linked to the process, as shown in Lancashire in the UK in summer 2011, when minor earthquakes were experienced in an area where fracking was underway and where they were previously unknown.

Mechanics of horizontal/directional drilling

Most wells are drilled straight down. However, there are situations where that option is unavailable, such as in populated areas or to increase the payout of a well. Geology.com lists six reasons why a well might be drilled directionally, which are:

1. **To hit targets that cannot be reached by vertical drilling**
   Sometimes a reservoir is located under a city or a park where drilling is impossible or forbidden. This reservoir might still be tapped if the drilling pad is located on the edge of the city or park and the well is drilled at an angle that will intersect the reservoir.
2. **Drain a broad area from a single drilling pad**
   This method has been used to reduce the surface footprint of a drilling operation. In 2010, the University of Texas at Arlington was featured in the news for drilling 22 wells on a single drill pad that will drain natural gas from 1100 acres beneath the campus. Over a 25-year lifetime the wells are expected to produce a total of 110 billion cubic feet of gas. This method significantly reduced the footprint of natural gas development within the campus area.
3. **Increase the length of the 'pay zone' within the target rock unit**
   If a rock unit is 50 feet thick, a vertical well drilled through it would have a pay zone that is 50 feet in length. However, if the well is turned and drilled horizontally through the rock unit for 5000 feet then that single well will have a pay zone that is 5000 feet long – this will usually result in a significant productivity increase for the well.
4. **Improve the productivity of wells in a fractured reservoir**
   This requires drilling in a direction that intersects the maximum number of fractures. The drilling direction will normally be at right angles to the dominant fracture direction. Drilling at right angles to the dominant fracture direction will drive the well through a maximum number of fractures.
5. **Seal or relieve pressure in an 'out-of-control' well**
   If a well is out of control a 'relief well' can be drilled to intersect it. The intersecting well can be used to seal the original well or to relieve pressure in the out-of-control well.
6. **Install underground utilities where excavation is not possible**
   Horizontal drilling has been used to install gas and electric lines that need to cross a river, a road, or travel under a city.

Figure 4.6 shows two examples of directional drilling.

Figure 4.6

Two examples of directional drilling

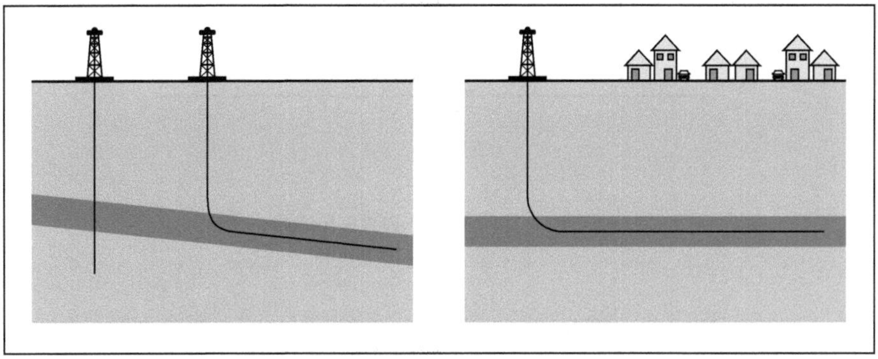

Source: geology.com

Mechanics of hydraulic fracturing

Hydraulic fracturing is used to increase the flow of oil or gas from a well, by pumping liquids into the subsurface rock units under pressures high enough to fracture the rock. The goal is to create a network of interconnected fractures that will serve as pore spaces for the movement of oil and natural gas.

The Barnett Shale formation in Texas is typical of a geological structure where gas was trapped in tiny pore spaces that were not interconnected. The rock had pore space but lacked permeability. Wells drilled through the Barnett Shale would usually have a show of gas but not enough gas for commercial production. This was solved by hydraulic fracturing of the Barnett Shale to create a network of interconnected pore spaces that enabled a flow of natural gas to the well.

Unfortunately many of the fractures produced by the hydraulic fracturing process snapped closed when the pumps were turned off. The Barnett Shale was so deeply buried that confining pressure closed the new fractures. The solution was to add sand to the pumped fluid. When the rock fractured, the rush of water into the newly opened pore space carried sand grains deep into the rock unit. When the water pressure was reduced the sand grains 'propped' the fracture open and allowed a continued flow of natural gas through the fractures.

Mitchell Energy then further improved the yield of its wells by drilling horizontally through the Barnett Shale. Vertical wells were started at the surface, steered horizontally and driven through the shale for thousands of feet. This multiplied the length of the pay zone in the well. If a rock unit was 100 feet thick, it would typically only have a pay zone of 100 feet if the well was vertical. However, if the well was steered horizontally and stayed horizontal for say 5000 feet through the target formation then the length of the pay zone was 50 times longer than the pay zone of a vertical well (see Figure 4.7).

Figure 4.7 **Horizontal drilling and fracturing**

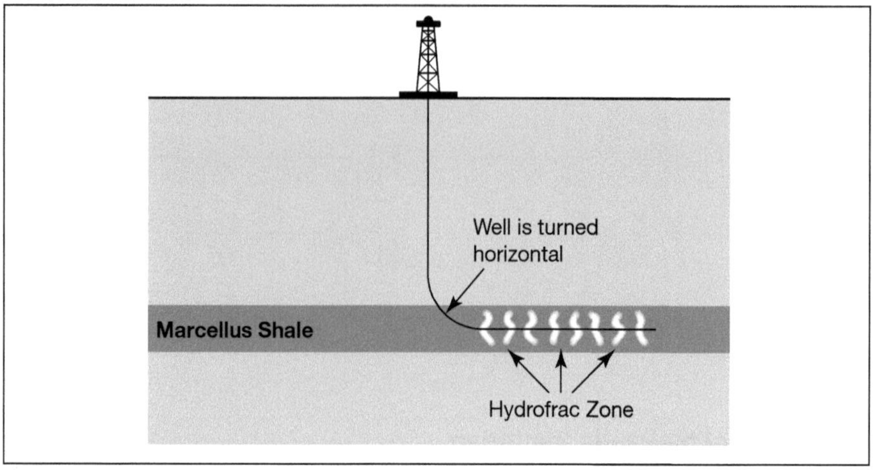

Source: geology.com

A recent report by Advanced Resources International (ARI) noted that high volume shale gas production did not occur until Mitchell Energy and Development Corporation made it a reality with the Barnett Shale in Texas. Following on from that, other shale formations were targeted, notably the Marcellus, Haynesville Eagle Ford and Woodford shales.

Shale gas reserves

The availability of shale gas has increased known gas reserves by 40–50 per cent to 22,600 Tcf. Figure 4.8 shows the currently known and assessed reserves in a subset of 32 countries, which are:

- Canada;
- Mexico;
- Northern South America (Colombia, Venezuela);
- Southern South America (Argentina, Chile, Uruguay, Paraguay, Bolivia, Brazil);
- Central North Africa (Algeria, Tunisia, Libya);
- Western North Africa (Morocco, Mauritania, Western Sahara);
- Southern Africa (South Africa);
- Australia;
- Western Europe (including, France, Germany, the Netherlands, Norway, Denmark, Sweden, United Kingdom);
- Poland, Ukraine, Lithuania and other Eastern Europe countries.

Figure 4.8

World shale gas reserves

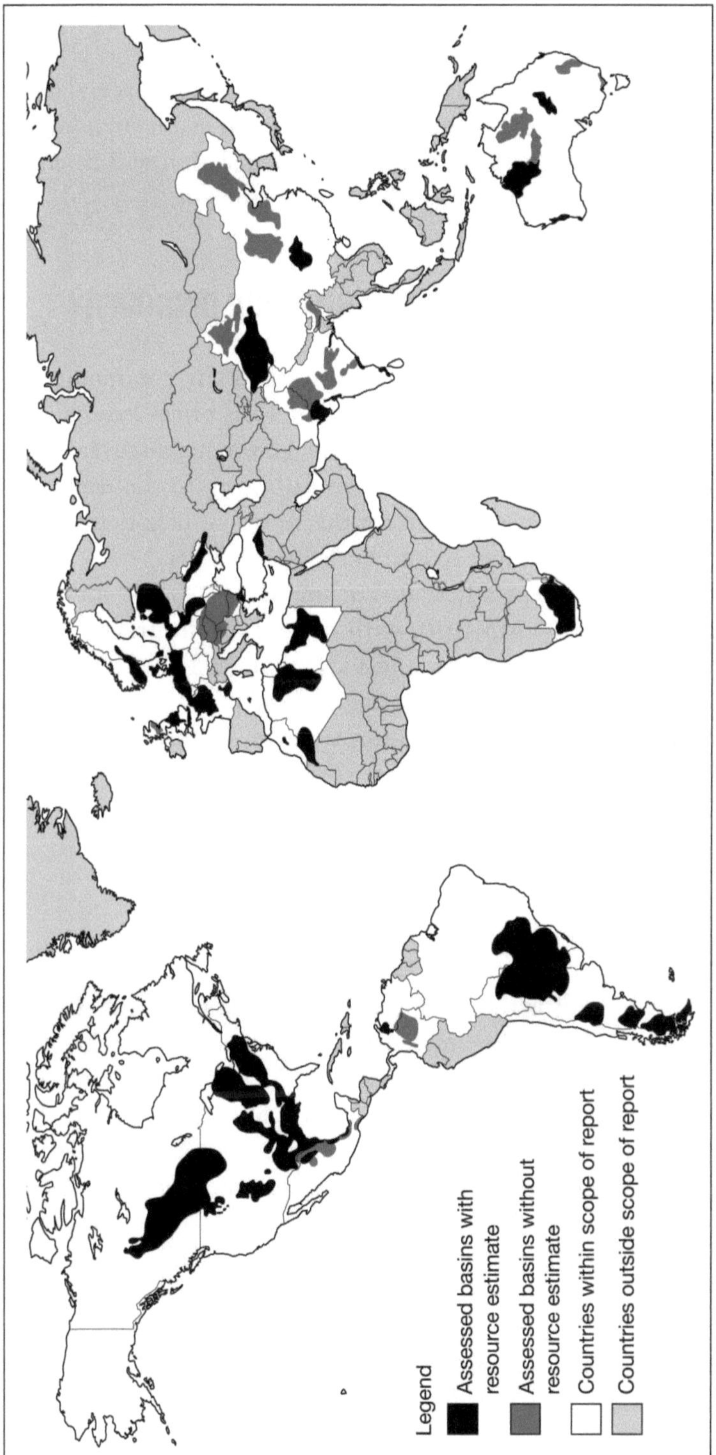

Source: Energy Information Administration

Not included were Russia, the Middle East and large parts of Africa, Scandinavia and Asia, which did not submit data.

At the time of writing there is still much controversy about the actual mechanics of extraction and whether this will cause environmental hazards. It is always possible that environmental legislation will be enacted as a barrier or even an incentive to shale gas development.

GAS PRICING AND PRICE DISCOVERY

Supply and demand are key price drivers in any commodity – financial or otherwise. At the time of writing, natural gas prices have fallen to a 20-year low due to the arrival of LNG and the enormous discoveries of shale gas in North America – all of which is contributing to the debate over whether purchasers should withdraw from the 'norm' of negotiating long-term contracts while it is cheaper to buy in the spot market.

Natural gas is typically traded in amounts of 10,000 million British thermal units (10,000 MMBtu), with natural gas futures traded on NYMEX (now part of CME) and to a lesser extent on ICE. If physical delivery is chosen in the US this is via the Sabine Pipe Line Co. into the Henry Hub in Louisiana (more detail on gas hubs is shown in Table 4.2 below).

Essentially, just like any other commodity, there is spot market trading and forward market trading. The forward markets may be in the terms of long-term contracts or via the financial futures markets.

Spot market trading – gas hubs

The spot market is the daily market, where natural gas is bought and sold 'right now'. Gas hubs are centres of liquidity where gas can be bought and sold using standardised contracts. In Europe the most liquid of these hubs is the National Balancing Point (NBP), located in the UK. Other regional European gas hubs include the Title Transfer Facility (TTF) in the Netherlands, and Zeebrugge in Belgium. In the US there are over 30 market hubs across the country, located at the intersection of major pipeline systems. The main one is known as the Henry Hub, located in Louisiana. In addition to market hubs, other major pricing locations include 'citygates'; these are the locations at which distribution companies receive gas from a pipeline. Citygates at major metropolitan centres can offer another point at which natural gas is priced.

Trading at spot market gas hubs is governed by standard contract terms in order to maximise liquidity.

Terminology

'Gas day' begins at 06:00 in the morning each day.

'Gas year' begins on 1 October of each year.

Commonly traded contracts include:

Within-Day, Day-Ahead, Balance-of-Week, Weekend, Weekdays-Next-Week, Balance-of-Month, calendar months, quarters, seasons (Winter season is defined as 1 October through 31 March, and Summer season is the balance of the year), and calendar years. Seasons are commonly traded in both the UK and the European markets and whilst calendar years are relatively less liquid on the European side, they very rarely trade on the NBP.

The Day-Ahead period is the most popular traded time horizon. When a particular day's gas obligations are finalised, schedulers will work together with counterparties and pipeline representatives to 'schedule' the flows of gas into ('injections') and out of ('withdrawals') individual pipelines and meters. Injections should equal withdrawals (i.e. the net volume injected and withdrawn on the pipeline should equal zero).

Pipeline scheduling and regulations are a major driver of trading activities and the financial penalties inflicted on shippers who violate their terms of service are well in excess of losses a trader may otherwise incur in the market correcting the problem.

Forward contracts

The majority of trading is physical and via long-term forward contracts, up to a maturity of 20–30 years. However, as previously mentioned, with spot prices so low relative to the forward markets, some buyers are switching into the spot markets. Prices in Europe are traditionally indexed to oil products, meaning they are higher than in the rest of the world. We now have a 'disconnect' with prices in the US, where there is no indexation and where gas prices have slumped with the increasing on-line production of the shale gas reserves.

As an example, a Norwegian oil indexation model might price gas at approximately 70 per cent of the price of oil, on a calorific-value basis. If a buyer's annual requirement in any given year falls short of the minimum contractual quantity, the buyer must prepay 75–80 per cent of the cost of the gas at the current oil-indexed price, and then take delivery of the prepaid gas at some point over the following 3–5 years. At the time of delivery, the difference between the prepaid amount and the new oil-indexed price will be collected from or returned to the buyer.

Demand has fallen drastically during the recession and many buyers failed to meet their minimum purchasing obligations in 2011.

Futures markets

The futures markets act as a reference index for gas prices; those futures contracts that trade on NYMEX are linked to the physical delivery of gas at the Henry Hub. Pricing differentials exist between different hubs related to supply and demand at different locations across the country. The difference between the Henry Hub price and another hub is known as the location differential.

The EIA notes a range of gas exposures and the hedging tools that best fit the requirements as shown in Table 4.2.

Table 4.2 **Petroleum and natural gas price risks and risk management strategies**

Participants	Price risks	Risk management strategies and derivative instruments employed
Oil producers	Low crude oil price	Sell crude oil future or buy put option
Petroleum refiners	High crude oil price	Buy crude oil future or call option
	Low product price	Sell product future or swap contract, buy put option
	Thin profit margin	Buy crack spread
Storage operators	High purchase price or low sale price	Buy or sell calendar spread
Large consumers		
Local distribution companies (natural gas)	Unstable prices, wholesale prices higher than retail	Buy future or call option, buy basis contract
Power plants (natural gas)	Thin profit margin	Buy spark spread
Airlines and shippers	High fuel price	Buy swap contract

Source: Energy Information Administration

TRADING NATURAL GAS

Victoria Adams, Natural Gas Broker, ICAP Energy Ltd

Natural gas is more than a traded commodity – it is a physical asset which, when traded and brought to delivery, must be 'nominated', i.e. any gas transactions that have taken place on the spot market must be scheduled and be received in, or delivered to, the relevant pipeline. It is not impossible for a mismatch to occur if any trades are submitted at an incorrect price or volume, or with a false counterpart.

Gas hubs which are critical to gas transport and trading exist in two forms, physical and virtual. The characteristics of these hubs vary in liquidity, depth and transparency, as well as in location and the types of players holding interests (see Table 4.3).

Table 4.3

European gas hubs

Hub	HH	NBP	Zee	TTF	NCG	Gaspool	Peg: Nord, Sud, TIGF	CEGH	PSV
Site	Henry Hub USA	National Balancing Point UK	Zeebrugge Belgium	Title Transfer Facility Netherlands	NetConnect Germany	Gaspool Northern Germany	France	Central European Gas Hub Austria	Punto di Scambio Virtuale Italy
Hub type	Physical	Virtual	Virtual	Virtual	Virtual	Considered as a virtual point, but operated as a physical hub.	Virtual	Physical	Virtual
Operator	Sabine Pipeline LLC	TSO National Grid	Huberator	Dutch TSO Gas Transport Services (subsidiary of Nerelandse Gasunie)	NetConnect Germany	Gasunie Deutschland Transport Services, ONTRAS - VNG Gastransport, DONG Energy Pipelines and WINGAS TRANSPORT	GRTgaz (Gaz de France) and TIGF (Total SA Group)	CEGH	Snam Rete Gas
Units traded	USD/MMBtu	Pence/th	Pence/Th and EUR/MWh	EUR/MWh	EUR/MWh	EUR/MWh	EUR/MWh	EUR/MWh	EUR/MWh
Standard clip size	2,500 MMBtu/ month	25 kt	25 kt	30 MWh	10 MWh (prompt) 30 MWh (curve)	30 MWh	750 MWh/d	10 MWh (prompt) 30 MWh (curve)	30 MWh
Electronic Exchanges	NYMEX	APX, ICE	APX	APX, APX-Endex, ICE	EEX	EEX	Powernext	CEGH Gas Exchange	-

Table 4.3 continued

Hub	HH	NBP	Zee	TTF	NCG	Gaspool	Peg: Nord, Sud, TIGF	CEGH	PSV
Key information	Henry Hub is located in Erath, Louisiana. It interconnects with Gulf South, Sonat, NGPL, Texas Eastern, Sabine, Columbia Gulf, Transco, Trunkline, Jefferson Island and Acadian Gas.	The NBP is the most liquid point in Europe. It is mainly traded outright, but increasingly so in spreads against the TTF (where 25k is equivalent to 30MWh).	Like the NBP, Zee trades in pence per therm. It is connected to the NBP via the Interconnector, and most frequently trades as a spread via the NBP (known as basis).	Linked to the NBP by the BBL pipeline.	The NCG is a virtual trading point, previously known as the E.On Gas Transport (EGT). The NCG came to be in October 2009, which linked the pipelines of 5 network companies. The german market has since grown and liquidity has helped it develop into a fairer and more transparent market. It is traded both outright and spread against, mainly, the TTF.	Formerly known as BEB, trading activity here has increased significantly since it's relaunch in October 2009. It is traded both outright and spread against, mainly, the TTF.	Spot trading here and the number of active counterparties are steadily increasing. Activity along the curve has increased thanks to growing interest in spreads against the TTF (Peg Nord/TTF). Also the OTC Clearing Service provided by Powernext, in which trades brokered by the likes of ICAP are given up to the exchange, has made the market more accessible to counterparties with restricted credit lines, facilitating their scope for trading and improving liquidity for all.	Commonly known as Baumgarten, the hub was originally a subsidiary of OMV Gas International. Despite its ever-growing liquidity, the Baumgarten does remain considerably illiquid in comparison to its North Western European neighbours. Baumgarten was formerly traded at two meeting stations, known as MS2 and MS3 (Trans Austria Gas TAG and West Austria Gas WAG interconnection points respectively). In an attempt to improve and concentrate liquidity a single point was created: the Intergated Trading Area Baumgarten (ITAB).	The PSV is still inadequately liquid (in comparison to even the North Western European hubs). Regional players (i.e. the Italians) are at a considerable advantage, where information (i.e. metering, stock positions, daily gas flows, available capacity) can be limited.

Source: Victoria Adams, ICAP Energy Ltd

Transport

Natural gas is delivered by pipeline. Figure 4.9 shows the main gas pipelines in Europe.

Figure 4.9

Main European gas pipelines

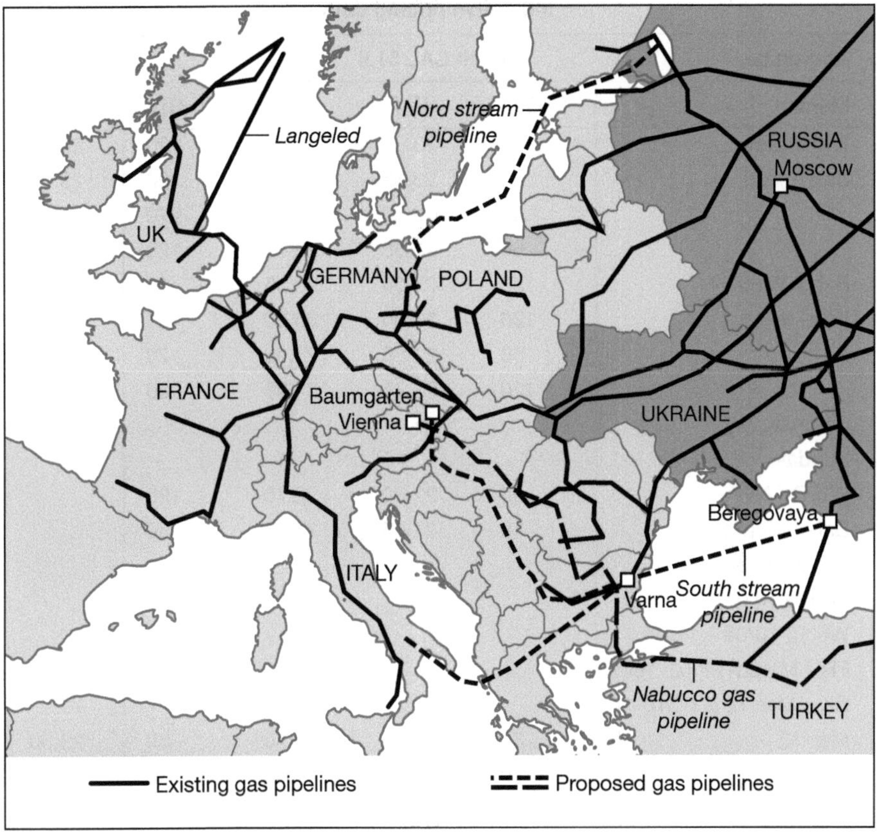

Source: Petroleum Economist

'PROMPT' AND 'CURVE' MARKETS

All gas trades, irrelevant of the location of the gas, are agreed for a specific period. Besides the 10+ year long-term contracts that exist, the brokered gas market is split into two periods: 'prompt' and 'curve'.

The 'prompt' market

The short-term traded market, known as the 'prompt', is made up of contracts such as: Within-Day (WD), Day-Ahead (DA), Balance-of-Week (BOW), Weekend (WE), Working-Days-Next-Week (WDNW) and Balance-of-Month (BOM). These contracts can be traded speculatively, but predominantly as a way of balancing portfolios.

The 'curve' market

The 'curve' is considered to be monthly contracts, quarterly contracts (Q1, Q2, Q3, Q4), seasons (Sum, Win), gas years (GY 1 Oct–31 Sep) and calendar years (Cal 1 Jan–31 Dec). Table 4.4 shows indication prices for these periods.

Table 4.4 **Indicative pricing data**

Aggregate	TTF HI CAL 51.6				
Menu	Qty	Bid	Ask	Qty	Last
Within Day	120	23.00	24.50	120	24.00
Day Ahead	30	23.35	23.40	120	23.35
	60	23.30	23.45	270	
	50	23.30	23.45	120	
Bal of Week	120	23.00	23.35	30	23.30
Weekend	120	23.00	23.30	30	23.10
	60	22.80	23.40	120	
	120	22.75	21.35	60	
Saturday					
Sunday					
WK/DY NW	90	22.00	22.70	120	
Bal of Month	30	21.75	23.60	30	
WE 9 03/03 – 04/03					
WKDS 10 05/03 – 09/0					
WE 10 10/03 – 11/03					
FR – March-12 (01-16)					
BK – Mar-12 (17-31)					
Mar-12	30	23.155	23.40	30	23.30
	30	22.855	23.40	30	
	30	22.85	23.50	30	
Apr-12	30	23.38	23.625	30	23.45
May-12	30	23.23	23.575	30	
Jun-12	30	23.33	23.875	30	
Jul	30	22.98	23.725	30	
Q212	30	23.312	23.691	30	
Q312	30	23.078	24.022	30	
Q412	30	27.025	27.25	30	27.225
Q113					
Sum 12	30	23.50	23.60	30	23.65
Win 12	30	23.40	23.60	30	23.65
Sum 13	30	27.80	28.95	30	
Win 13	30	27.80	28.45	30	
Sum 14			26.35	30	
Win 14			28.75	30	
Cal Yr 13	10	28.275	26.90	10	

Source: ICAP Energy Ltd

Gas can be traded in several ways:

- OTC trades – brokered by phone or, increasingly, electronically (particularly as far as the prompt is concerned).
- Exchange futures and cleared trades – where trading is anonymous.
- Bilateral trades – counterparties with existing relationships trade without the need of a broker or trading platform.

OTC is still the favoured trading method in the gas market, mainly because exchange margins and fees can be costly and counterparties like to know with whom they are trading (for credit and other reasons). Also, OTC is more flexible: if a mis-trade occurs, a broker can remedy it in two minutes.

SPOT TRADING AND BALANCING

The UK and European gas markets have grown considerably since the arrival of electronic broking (see Table 4.3), particularly because 'the screen' has brought greater efficiency to trading on a day-to-day basis. Much like an exchange, traders can leave resting numbers on an electronic screen manned by brokers. These live prices in the format of a bid–ask spread, also known as 'initiated' numbers, can then be 'aggressed' by another trader. Aggressors have the option to trade by clicking on the screen or to pick up the phone and opt to trade a voice-quoted market by one of their brokers. A trader would, naturally, trade where the best market can be found.

Spot trading

There are a range of hubs (see Table 4.2), and the most developed hub is undeniably the USA's Henry Hub (HH) in Louisiana, which is the pricing point for futures contracts traded on NYMEX and for physical delivery at this hub. The UK's National Balancing Point (NBP) differs from HH in that it is not an actual physical location, but a virtual trading point for the pricing and delivery of physical gas and futures contracts. Although the UK is technically part of Europe, the NBP is not classed as European in the gas market; UK gas and European gas are treated as entirely separate arenas, particularly because the NBP is so much more mature. The Dutch Title Transfer Facility (TTF) is unarguably the most developed hub in the continental European gas market. With the exception of the TTF (where calendar year trades up to three years in advance are possible), the remaining continental European hubs are relatively liquid only within the prompt periods. Few or no curve trades are posted frequently enough to provide a basis for speculation or even hedging, and there is a relative lack of available information out there for European players in comparison to that which is offered by the National Grid for NBP.

The liberalisation of the British gas market in the early 1990s revolutionised the trading of natural gas, and mainland Europe is now starting to show similar growth. With reference to the TTF in particular, the ever-growing number of players has contributed to its development, and as liquidity improves the potential for any dominant players to manipulate markets reduces.

National Grid, the network operator in Britain, is responsible for ensuring the integrity of the system and security of supply. In order to do so, the TSO trades to balance the network on a daily basis. With respect to the 'WD NBP' contract (Within Day gas at the UK's National Balancing Point), National Grid has some power to intervene in the market, so that if there is too little gas in the pipelines to meet current demand, it will take action to bring gas onto the system (security of supply). Similarly, if there is too much gas, it will need to take action to reduce the amount of gas in the pipelines (integrity of the system).

Balancing

The WD differentiates itself from other tradable contracts because all nominations for entries/exits into the gas system for DA (Day Ahead) and periods further out are purely projections. National Grid only intervenes with physical flows, i.e. the Within Day. For example, if a shipper is unbalanced at a European hub such as Zeebrugge, fines will be incurred (at roughly 50 per cent of the total gas price). At the NBP, however, there is no fixed penalty as shippers out of balance at the end of the gas day are automatically balanced by 'cashing out'. Before the close at around 4a.m., if a shipper (i.e. trader) is left long or short, they must cash out at the marginal system buy or sell price. The procedure is illustrated below.

A live average price is published throughout the day based upon all trades carried out on APX (the UK's gas exchange which offers an anonymous marketplace within which to trade at the NBP) each gas day. This volume weighted average of all Within Day trades is known as the system average price (SAP), upon which two other numbers are calculated:

System Marginal Buy Price (SMPb) = SAP + 0.84 p/th

System Marginal Sell Price (SMPs) = SAP – 0.95 p/th

Note: These margins are not constant, and can vary as and when the National Grid intervenes. The figures +0.84 and -0.95 are given here for the benefit of illustration.

Example

Balancing

When trading throughout the day, traders must keep in mind that any volumes they have remaining at the close of the day will cash out at the respective price. For example, a shipper short at the end of the gas day must buy gas at the SMPb price:

SAP = 58.15 p/th

SMPb = 58.15 + 0.84 = 58.99 p/th

If a shipper is long at the close of trading, then they will sell the gas at the SMPs:

SAP = 58.15 p/th

SMPs = 58.15 – 0.95 = 57.20 p/th

Intervention

There can however be system action which occurs whenever the system is too long or too short. National Grid comes into the market and physically changes the SMPb or SMPs. When the market is short, the operator will come in and lift the WD to set the SMPs to provide a financial incentive for shippers to cash out, and balance the national transmissions system themselves. The idea is that a higher marginal sell price will encourage more gas onto the system, thus balancing it. The opposite takes place when the National Grid comes into the market and sells down, changing the system marginal price to an attractive SMPb at which shippers will buy and remove gas from an oversupplied sytem. In this case:

Short system (demand outweighs supply)

SAP = 58.50 p/th

SMPs = 58.50 – 0.95 = 57.55 p/th

Oversupplied system (supply exceeds demand)

SAP = 57.50 p/th

SMPb = 57.50 + 0.84 = 58.34 p/th

Occasionally the system is so imbalanced that the differential between the SAP and SMPb or SMPs widens significantly. Thus the above formulas would not be applicable.

Market participants

The types of players active in the gas market include financials, producers, end users (the 'utilities'), other proprietary traders and brokers. The number of active counterparties in the UK and European markets continues to grow, including interest from banks and hedge funds, as well as regional end users that are progressively gaining more direct access to the market. The 'financials' are ever more active members of the gas market, with physical assets of their own to play with: a handful of banks, for example, have access to their own storage and other physical assets, and trading is not purely speculative, as might be assumed. The less liquid hubs tend to be dominated by the players holding physical assets in the region, for example more French players are seen trading the Peg Nord, and Austrian counterparts in Baumgarten. Counterparties may trade for any of the following reasons: physical needs, financial hedging, portfolio optimisation or just plain speculation.

Arbitrage and longer periods

Sometimes the market can be inefficient, to a shipper's advantage – to be more specific, to the shipper who is the quickest to notice! Especially in volatile or illiquid markets, arbitrage is possible. For example, a shipper might trade two periods at a certain price in order to achieve a more efficient market price for the product they are trading. Table 4.5 shows pricing data from ICAP.

Table 4.5 **Pricing data from ICAP Energy Ltd**

TTF HI CAL 51.6					
	Qty	Bid	Ask	Qty	Last
Q412	30	27.00	27.10	30	27.10
Q113	30	27.80	28.80	30	
Sum 12				30	
Win 12	30	27.00	27.40	90	27.35

Markets may be quoted for the following composite periods:

Win 12 = Q412 + Q113

When Q412 = 27.00 and Q113 = 27.80

Win 12 = (Q412 + Q113) ÷ 2 = (27.00 + 27.80) ÷ 2 = 27.40

You can see here that a trader could sell Q412 and Q113 to generate or 'leg in' a Win 12 (gas for winter 2012) sell price at the existing market offer.

EXCHANGE TRADING

As well as trading physical gas, there is a paper market for financial trading, in which the buyer and seller never take physical delivery of the gas. There are two possible motives behind trading in financial natural gas markets: hedging and speculation. The volatility of the price of gas requires the use of financial derivatives to hedge against the risk of price movement. If a trader plans to sell gas on the prompt for the next month, and is worried about falling prices, a variety of financial instruments can be used to hedge against this. Paper trades are also popular for those who wish to speculate about price movements. Great profits might be made if the expectations of a speculator prove correct, but losses can be incurred if these expectations are wrong. A shipper's ability to hedge an asset depends largely upon a market's liquidity. As the NBP is easier to trade than European markets, so too it is easier to hedge than the likes of TTF, NCG, Gaspool and Peg Nord. Let's work with the popular gas index in the UK and European markets, the Heren Index.

Example

A trader can enter into an index trade where he buys or sells at a set price (which is typically at a premium of 0.025) above an index price which is set on a daily basis at the close of trading for products such as DA and Front Month. ICIS Heren publishes an index derived from the trade prices that take place at 16:30 GMT (which is known as the 'market close'). The volumes of indices traded at the NBP dwarf the number of index trades seen at the European hubs, with a spectrum of players involved (including and particularly the banks).

Heren TTF DA Index trades at 0.025
Heren TTF DA Index price is 23.15 at 16:30 GMT
Settlement of the trade between buyer and seller is at 23.175

There is also the London Energy Brokers' Association (LEBA) Index, which is based upon an index derived from all trades throughout the day, and also a window index for which trades struck between 16:20 and 16:30 GMT are included. The 'window' is a set timeframe within which a large proportion of volume trades; in the case of the gas market, this window lasts for 10 minutes. Although not as commonly traded, this is favoured by several market participants because the index price is derived from a volume-weighted average spread across a 10-minute window.

DA TTF LEBA Index trades at 0.025
DA TTF LEBA Index price is 23.163

Settlement of the trade between buyer and seller is at 23.188

It is possible to trade indices as seasonal and calendar trades, however this is very uncommon in the open market, and would tend to be negotiated bilaterally.

5

Coal

Background and context

Range of coals

Mining and production

World production and reserves

Coal pricing and price discovery

Exchange traded markets

Trading with coal futures

Environmental concerns

Coal and carbon issues

BACKGROUND AND CONTEXT

In mid-March 2012, when commenting about rising fuel prices, US President Obama was quoted as saying:

> 'We can't have an energy strategy for the last century that traps us in the past. We need an energy strategy for the future – an all-of-the-above strategy for the 21st century that develops every source of American-made energy. Yes, develop as much oil and gas as we can, but also develop wind power and solar power and biofuels.'

What is noticeable is that coal was not mentioned in any shape or form. Coal is no longer fashionable – if it ever was. *Rolling Stone* journalist Jeff Goodell wrote on 16 March 2012: 'In the world of energy politics, the sudden vanishing of the word "coal" is a remarkable and unprecedented event.'

Coal is big business and big politics, with the major coal-mining states of Illinois, Pennsylvania, Kentucky and Ohio often holding the keys to the White House. The major coal-mining firms, the firms that transport it and the firms that burn it in the US power stations have for many years implied that not burning coal and increasing environmental regulations are bad for business and will eventually lead to power blackouts. The 'Clean Coal' movement was established by the coal majors to try and change the popular image of coal, but has been largely unsuccessful.

Interestingly, in the 2012 presidential campaign, coal is not mentioned at all and this is most likely due to the various environmental lobbies together with the surplus of natural gas largely extracted via horizontal drilling and hydraulic fracturing (see Chapter 4 on shale gas). This surplus and the resulting low gas prices have led many to look to gas to fire up the power stations that traditionally burned coal – and it is cleaner and more efficient. By March 2012, the power generated from US coal-fired power stations was down over 5 per cent. But is the US unique in the switch away from coal or will this be a global shift?

In Australia, coal magnates have been accused of trying to direct government policy. At the same time as the Australian government introduces a carbon tax to reduce greenhouse gases and create a low-carbon economy, it is vastly increasing greenhouse gases by expanding Australian coal mines and supporting the coal seam gas industry – but can coal ever be 'clean'?

Coal is one of the cheapest forms of energy and is still the fuel of choice for most power stations. However, coal waste products are a huge source of pollution, often felt miles away from the power station itself. China's own air pollution is largely caused by its coal-fired power stations and is felt as far afield as central North America. Storms originating in the Chinese Gobi Desert carry pollutants and particulates into Korea and even into Japan via the jet stream and from there into the USA. Some of the lighter particles, such as arsenic, copper, lead, zinc, sulphuric acid and mercury may stay in the jet stream in excess of a week, causing, amongst other things, acid rain and mercury poisoning. I can vouch for this personally, as on a recent vacation to Texas, whilst touring near Seminole Canyon, our guide informed us that the ancient Native Indian cave paintings are being damaged and weathered away and the largest sources of pollution are from US coal-fired power stations and the increased moisture levels from Lake Amistad.

Another interesting fact is that coal-burning power stations contribute as much to global warming as cars, trucks, buses and planes combined. To generate energy from coal requires mining the coal, then transporting it, cleaning and burning it. Water is heated by burning the coal; this converts the water into steam and generates electricity. Each stage of this process generates some pollution. Even so, coal accounts for approximately 28–30 per cent of the world's energy needs – just behind oil at 37 per cent. In most countries the biggest consumers of coal are the electricity industry and coal is the largest single source of electricity worldwide. Coal is used in the production of 70 per cent of the world's steel, and is used by other industrial processes like cement manufacturing.

Coal is one of three key non-renewable fossil fuels, the others being natural gas and oil. They are non-renewable simply due to the passage of time needed to form them. Fossil fuels were formed literally geological ages ago during the Earth's Carboniferous period, approximately 300–350 million years ago. Oil and gas are typically formed from off-shore animal and plant matter, whereas coal tends to be formed from on-shore decaying materials.

Coal formation

When a tree dies, it will eventually rot and the biological components of the tree will break down. In the tree's lifetime it takes in carbon dioxide from the atmosphere and combines it with water to form sugar – a process known as photosynthesis. This sugar is stored energy. The sugar molecules bond together to make more complex strands and it is these strands that start to break down when the tree dies. If the tree just lies fallen on the ground and is exposed to the air the oxygen attacks the links in the sugar chains and stored energy is released into the atmosphere. This is known as an aerobic environment. However, if the tree dies and falls into water or is buried in mud the oxygen cannot attack the tree and any stored energy is retained within the plant remains. This is an anaerobic environment, i.e. no oxygen.

Coal deposits are formed from the decaying remains of early trees and plants which die and are buried by mud and water in areas where there used to be inland seas, lakes, river deltas or even swamps. Submergence in water prevents oxidation of the plant remains. As time progresses, successive layers of mud and organic material are laid down, compressed and, through the continuing course of time, subjected to increasing temperature and pressure. In geological terms coal is a carbon-rich readily combustible sedimentary rock.

In order to form the thick layer of plant material required to produce a coal seam, the rate of accumulation must be greater than the rate of decay. About 10 feet of plant debris will compact into just one foot of coal.

The 40 feet of plant debris needed to make a four-foot thick coal seam requires hundreds of thousands of years to accumulate. During that time the water level of the swamp must remain stable. If the water becomes too deep the plants of the swamp will drown and if the water cover is not maintained the plant debris will decay. The dead plant material is firstly formed into peat, then lignite and then into various types of coal (see Figure 5.1).

Figure 5.1 **Formation of coal**

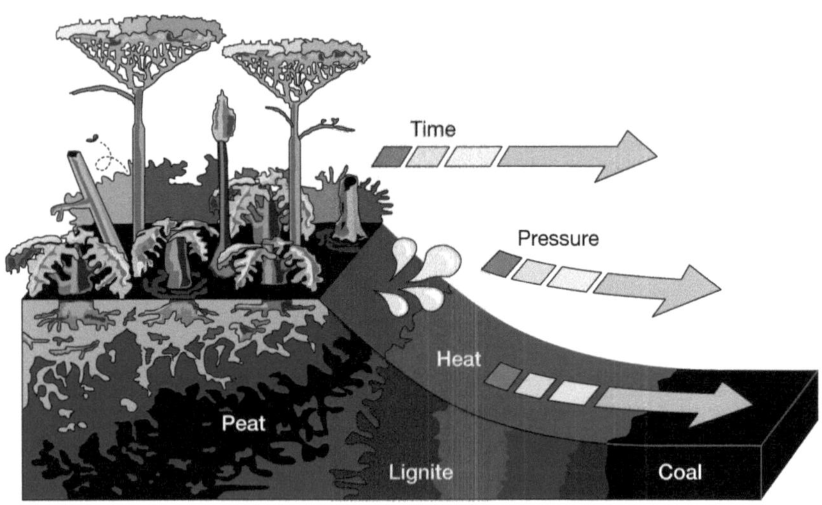

The coalification process from swamp to coal. Note how a thick section of peat is compressed by heat and pressure into a thin section of coal.

Source: Modified from the Kentucky Geological Survey

History

It is generally believed that the Chinese first used coal commercially around 1000 BC as they smelted copper in order to cast their domestic coinage, and Native American Indians used coal to bake their pottery before any European settlers arrived. By the late 1800s many countries had experienced an industrial revolution and coal was the fuel of choice – it was cheap, comparatively easy to obtain and fired the factories in our industrial towns.

For many years coal was tied to power stations and inevitably they were located in close vicinity to each other; in 1882 in New York the first coal-fired electrical power plant commenced operation.

More recently coal has come under the spotlight as the mining and burning of coal is known to pollute the atmosphere and the environment. Many countries and governments are seeking innovative ways to control pollution, mostly via the allocation of carbon and environmental credits (see Chapter 7 on Carbon and Environmental Commodities).

RANGE OF COALS

No two types of coal are exactly alike; heating value, ash melting temperature, sulphur and other impurities, mechanical strength and many other chemical and physical properties all need to be considered. Coal is classified based on its properties and characteristics:

- Peat;
- Lignite;
- Sub-bituminous coal;
- Bituminous coal;
- Anthracite.

Each grade reflects the response of coal deposits to increasing temperature and pressure. The carbon content of coal supplies most of its heating value, but other factors also influence the amount of energy it contains per 'unit of weight'. The amount of energy in coal is usually expressed in British thermal units per pound. A Btu is the amount of heat required to raise the temperature of one pound of water one degree Fahrenheit.

Terminology

Properties of coal

Rank	Properties
Peat	A mass of recently accumulated to partially carbonised plant debris. Peat is an organic sediment. Burial, compaction and coalification will transform it into coal, a rock. It has a carbon content of less than 60% on a dry ash-free basis.
Lignite	Lignite is the lowest rank of coal. It is a peat that has been transformed into a rock and that rock is a brown-black coal. Lignite sometimes contains recognisable plant structures. By definition it has a heating value of less than 8300 British thermal units per pound on a mineral matter free basis. It has a carbon content of between 60 and 70% on a dry ash-free basis. In Europe, Australia and the UK some low-level lignites are called 'brown coal'.

Terminology continued

Sub-bituminous	Sub-bituminous coal is a lignite that has been subjected to an increased level of organic metamorphism. This metamorphism has driven off some of the oxygen and hydrogen in the coal. That loss produces coal with a higher carbon content (71 to 77% on a dry ash-free basis). Sub-bituminous coal has a heating value between 8300 and 13,000 British thermal units per pound on a mineral matter free basis. On the basis of heating value it is sub-divided into sub-bituminous A, sub-bituminous B and sub-bituminous C ranks.
Bituminous	Bituminous is the most abundant rank of coal. It accounts for about 50% of the coal produced in the United States. Bituminous coal is formed when a sub-bituminous coal is subjected to increased levels of organic metamorphism. It has a carbon content of between 77 and 87% on a dry ash-free basis and a heating value that is much higher than lignite or sub-bituminous coal. On the basis of volatile content, bituminous coals are sub-divided into low volatile bituminous, medium volatile bituminous and high volatile bituminous. Bituminous coal is often referred to as 'soft coal', however this designation is a layman's term and has little to do with the hardness of the rock.
Anthracite	Anthracite is the highest rank of coal. It has a carbon content of over 87% on a dry ash-free basis. Anthracite coal generally has the highest heating value per ton on a mineral matter free basis. It is often sub-divided into semi-anthracite, anthracite and meta-anthracite on the basis of carbon content. Anthracite is often referred to as 'hard coal', however this is a layman's term and has little to do with the hardness of the rock.

Source: Geology.com, http://geology.com/rocks/coal.shtml

The harder the coal, the less moisture it contains and the easier it is to burn. Lignite and the softer coals are primarily used for electricity generation – often known as steam or thermal coals, whereas coals such as anthracite are used for high-grade steel production – known in some areas as coking or metallurgical coals.

MINING AND PRODUCTION

The mining or extraction of coal is carried out using one or both of two key methods; the method chosen depends on a number of factors including geology, thickness of coal seam, overburden and environment (see Figure 5.2). In essence if the coal seams are shallow and found close together, surface mining is generally chosen; whereas if the coal seams are thick (greater than 5 feet) and more than 200 feet deep, then nine times out of ten the underground mining method is more economically viable and preferable.

The two key methods – with descriptions from the World Coal Association (www.worldcoal.org) – are shown below:

- Surface or opencast mining, which accounts for approximately 40 per cent globally – but in the US it is closer to 70 per cent.
- Underground mining (60 per cent).

Coal is mined, often by stripping the tops off mountains; unfortunately this may cause water contamination. The coal industry says that it has improved its practices to protect the environment, and that restoring land disturbed by strip mining is a vital part of the mining process. However, coal that is mined via surface mining in the US, especially in the states of Virginia, Kentucky, Montana and Wyoming, is currently one of the prime concerns of the environmental movement.

Surface mining

Surface mining – also known as opencast or open cut mining – is only economic when the coal seam is near the surface. This method recovers a higher proportion of the coal deposit than underground mining as all coal seams are exploited – 90% or more of the coal can be recovered. Large opencast mines tend to be ugly, can cover an area of many square kilometres and use very large pieces of machinery, including:

- draglines, which remove the overburden;
- power shovels;
- large trucks, which transport overburden and coal;
- bucket wheel excavators;
- conveyors.

The overburden of soil and rock is firstly broken up by explosives and then removed by draglines or trucks. Once the coal seam is exposed, it is

Figure 5.2

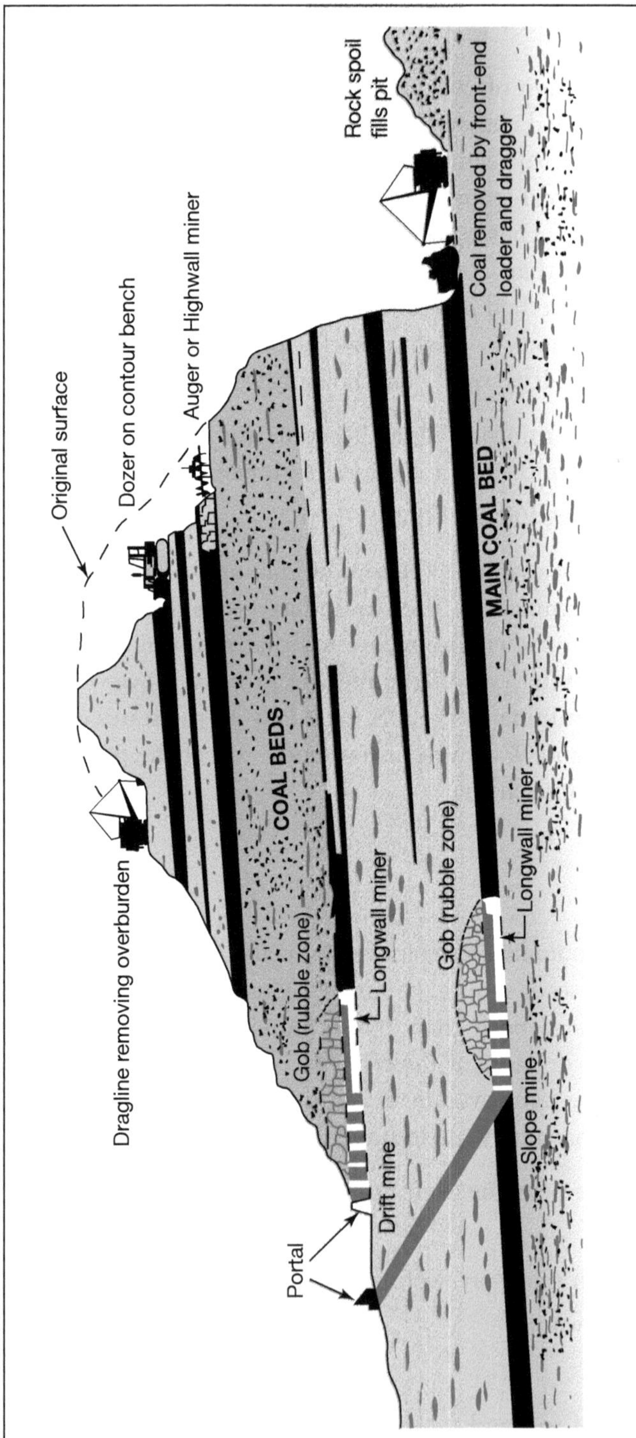

Surface mining v underground mining methods

drilled, fractured and systematically mined in strips. The coal is then loaded onto large trucks or conveyors for transport to either the coal preparation plant or direct to where it will be used. This whole process contributes to an unsightly environment in areas that are/were often designated as 'areas of outstanding beauty'.

Underground mining

There are two key methods of underground mining: room-and-pillar and long-wall mining.

Room-and-pillar mining

In room-and-pillar mining, coal deposits are mined by cutting a network of 'rooms' into the coal seam and leaving behind 'pillars' of coal to support the roof of the mine. These pillars can be up to 40 per cent of the total coal in the seam – although this coal can sometimes be recovered at a later stage.

Long-wall mining

Long-wall mining involves the full extraction of coal from a section of the seam, or 'face', using mechanical shearers. A long-wall face requires careful planning to ensure favourable geology exists throughout the section before development work begins. The coal 'face' itself can vary in length from 100 to 350m. Self-advancing, hydraulically powered supports temporarily hold up the roof while coal is extracted. When coal has been completely extracted from the area the roof is allowed to collapse. It is possible to extract over 75 per cent of the coal in the deposit that may extend a distance of 3km through the coal seam.

WORLD PRODUCTION AND RESERVES

It was estimated in 2011 by the World Coal Association (WCA) that there are over 847bn tonnes of proven coal reserves worldwide, sufficient for around 118 years at current rates of production. In contrast, proven oil and gas reserves are equivalent to around 46 and 59 years respectively at current production levels. According to the WCA, consumption of coal is projected to grow by approximately 1.5 per cent per annum until 2030, with Asia being the biggest market (around 60 per cent of global production – the bulk of which is for China) (see Figure 5.3). Most countries in the region supplement their existing reserves with additional seaborne coal supplies from Japan, Taiwan and South Korea.

Figure 5.3

Where is coal found?

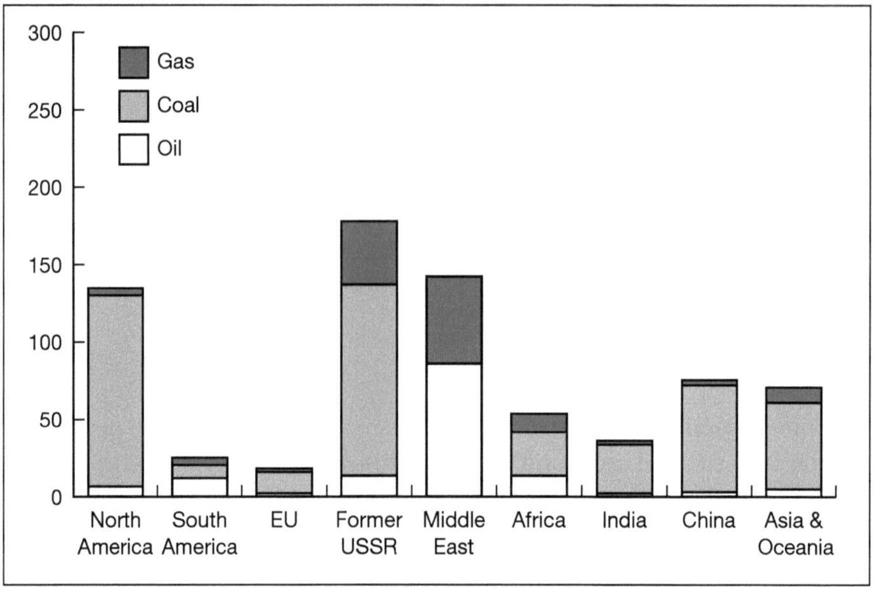

Source: World Coal Association

Coal reserves are available in almost every country worldwide, with recoverable reserves in around 70 countries. The biggest reserves are in the USA, Australia, Russia, China and India. The location, size and characteristics of most countries' coal resources are quite well known, but where there is some confusion relates to differences between the assessed levels of the resource – i.e. the potentially accessible coal in the ground – and the proven recoverable reserves. Proved recoverable reserves is the tonnage of coal that has been proved by drilling etc. and is economically and technically extractable; see box for the technical definitions.

Definitions

Resource

The amount of coal that may be present in a deposit or coalfield. This does not take into account the feasibility of mining the coal economically. Not all resources are recoverable using current technology.

Reserves

Reserves can be defined in terms of proved (or measured) reserves and probable (or indicated) reserves. Probable results have been estimated with a lower degree of confidence than proved reserves.

Definitions continued

Proved reserves

Reserves that are not only considered to be recoverable but can also be recovered economically. This means they take into account what current mining technology can achieve and the economics of recovery. Proved reserves will therefore change according to the price of coal; if the price of coal is low, proved reserves will decrease.

Source: WCA

The AME Group in Australia has compiled export/import data for 2010, shown in Table 5.1.

Table 5.1

Exporters and importers of coal in 2010

Top Coal Exporters (2010e)			
	Total of *which*	Steam	Coking
Australia	298Mt	143Mt	155Mt
Indonesia	162Mt	160Mt	2Mt
Russia	109Mt	95Mt	14Mt
USA	74Mt	23Mt	51Mt
Colombia	69Mt	68Mt	1Mt
South Africa	70Mt	69Mt	1Mt
Canada	31Mt	4Mt	27Mt
Top Coal Importers (2010e)			
	Total of *which*	Steam	Coking
Japan	187Mt	129Mt	58Mt
PR China	177Mt	129Mt	48Mt
South Korea	119Mt	91Mt	28Mt
India	90Mt	60Mt	30Mt
Chinese Tapel	63Mt	58Mt	5Mt
Germany	48Mt	38Mt	8Mt
Turkey	27Mt	20MT	7MT

Source: Based on data from IEA Coal Information 2011

Changing coal consumption

Within the countries of the OECD, coal consumption is gradually declining (–1.1 per cent p.a. 2010–30); however this is offset with a small amount of growth in the non-OECD countries (2.1 per cent p.a.). Overall there is projected to be growth of just 0.5 per cent p.a in the period from 2020 to 2030 (see Figure 5.4). It seems both China and India will struggle to mine sufficient resources domestically for their own requirements and will increasingly need to tap the export markets.

Figure 5.4 **Changing coal consumption**

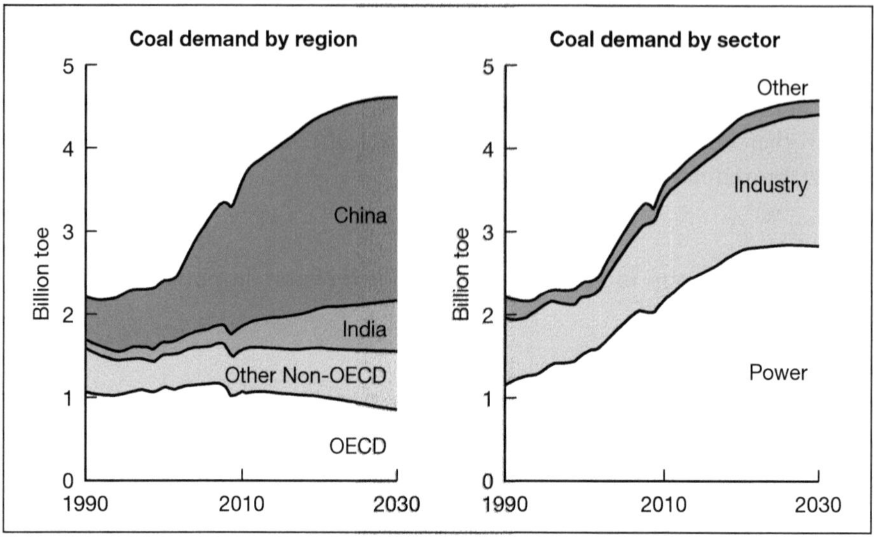

Source: BP Energy outlook 2030

COAL PRICING AND PRICE DISCOVERY

The majority of coal is mined and used domestically but in almost every country additional coal supplies are required. Coal might be transported over vast distances as users seek specific grades of coal for their differing requirements. Transport is most often in bulk carriers by sea, hence the given name of seaborne coal.

Transportation costs account for a large share of the total delivered price of coal; therefore international trade in coal is effectively sub-divided into two regional markets – the Atlantic and the Pacific. The Atlantic market is made up of importing countries in Western Europe, notably the UK, Germany and Spain. The Pacific market consists of developing and OECD Asian importers, notably Japan, Korea and Chinese Taipei. The Pacific market currently accounts for about 60–70 per cent of the world coal trade. Markets tend to overlap when coal prices are high and supplies are plentiful. South Africa is a natural point of convergence between the two markets. Shown in Figure 5.5 is the summary of an analysis carried out by IEA regarding how the trade flows in coal will most likely change by 2030.

Coal pricing

Coal is priced according to its calorific content measured as kilocalories/kilograms with the standard level set at 6500kcal/kg. Most coal is procured through negotiated annual contracts between producers and consumers. In the Asia-Pacific market, annual contracts have historically been set up

Figure 5.5

Major trade flows: 2002 and projected 2030

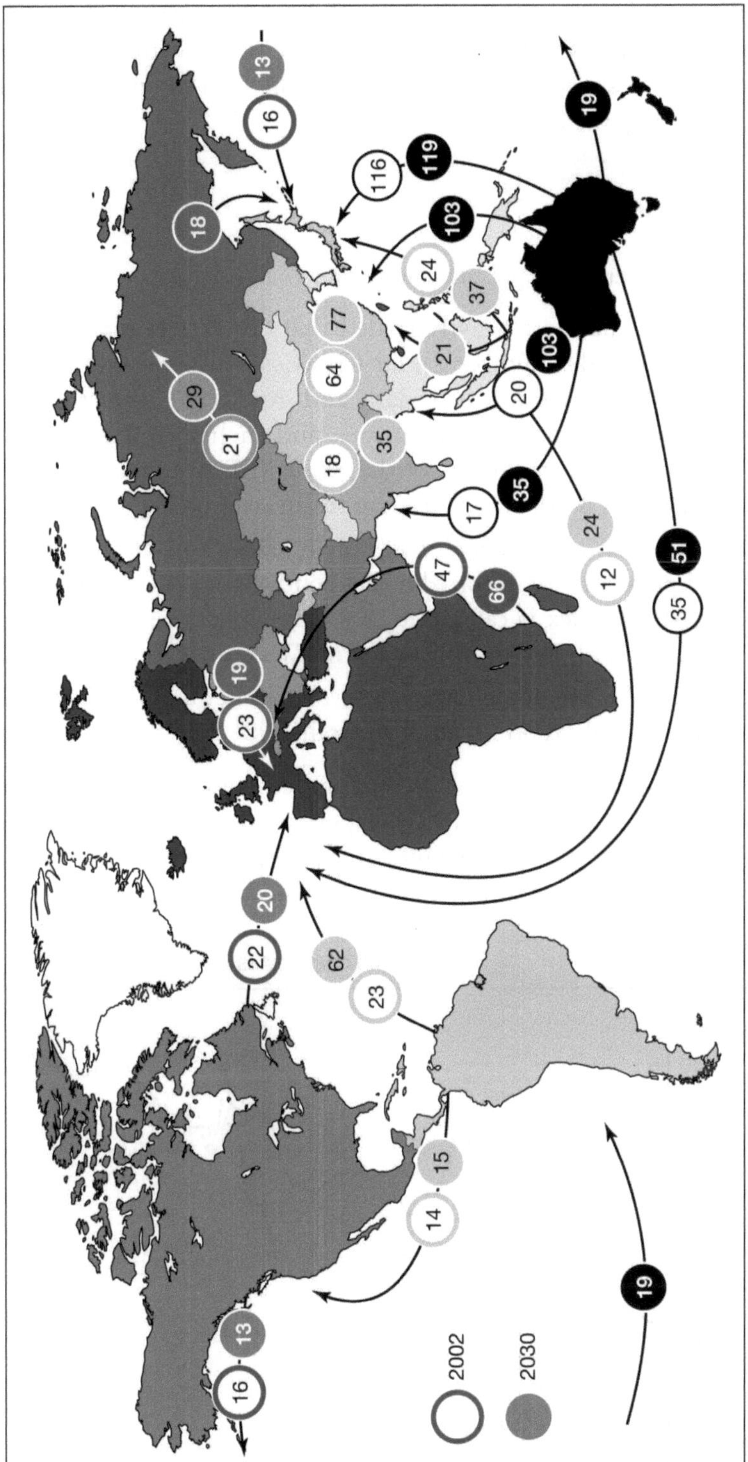

Figures in circles denote trade in Mt (metric tonnes)
Source: IEA, 2004

between Japanese power utilities and Australian producers on a Japanese financial year basis. The European market is dominated by South African supply, with supply prices that are generally priced on a spot basis highly influenced by the Asian price.

Coal indices

There are a variety of popular indices for coal, notably:

- API 2 – The most heavily traded coal derivatives market, API 2 (All Published Index number 2), for CIF (Cost, Insurance, Freight included) ARA (Amsterdam, Rotterdam and Antwerp), this represents coal imported into north-west Europe and inclusive of freight costs and insurance. It is an average of the Argus CIF Rotterdam assessment and McCloskey's north-west European steam coal marker.
- API 4 – This is the second most heavily traded coal market and the benchmark price for coal exported out of South Africa's Richards Bay terminal. The API 4 index is calculated as an average of the Argus FOB (Free on Board) Richards Bay assessment and McCloskey's FOB Richards Bay marker.
- API 6 – An average of Argus and McCloskey's FOB Newcastle assessments for coal exported out of Australia.

Different markets require different indices and shown in Figure 5.6 are some of the thermal coal prices experienced from mid-2011 until early 2012. QHD refers to the Chinese port of Qinhuangdao and Newcastle is the key centre for coal exported out of Australia.

Figure 5.6

Thermal coal prices

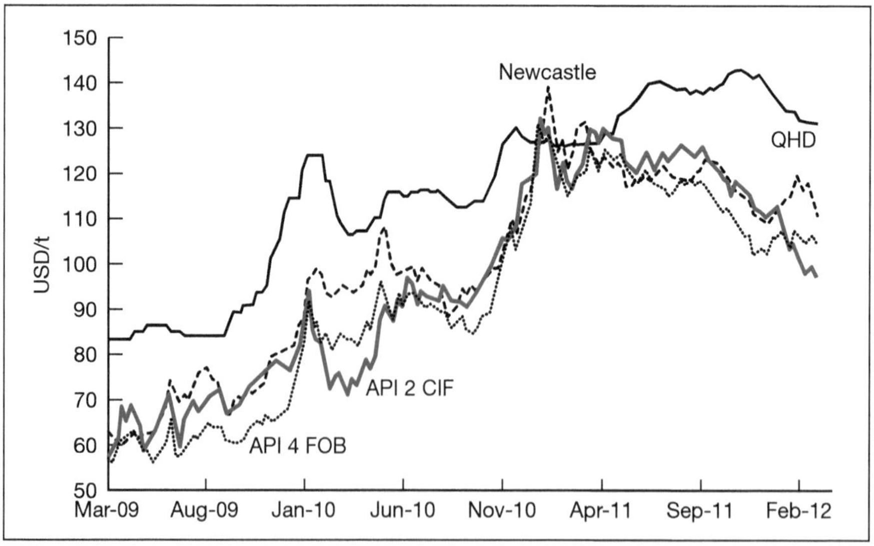

Source: McCloskey, Sxcoal, Standard Chartered Research

EXCHANGE TRADED MARKETS

Most coal futures are traded on two major exchanges: CME and ICE. One of the most popular coal contracts trades on NYMEX – now known as a designated contract market (DCM) of CME.

The key US coal futures contract is based on Central Appalachian Coal and trades in contract sizes of 1550 tons per contract and is priced in US dollars per ton. This is a physically settled contract with coal actually being delivered.

In contrast, the ICE contracts are cash settled to an index price, lending themselves more to speculative rather than hedging counterparties.

Note: Central Appalachian Coal is coal produced in the Central Appalachian region of the USA which comprises the counties located in southern West Virginia, eastern Kentucky, south-west Virginia and eastern Tennessee. West Virginia and Kentucky are considered to be the two largest US coal producers. Production by both states represented 89 per cent of the region's coal production in 2008.

Table 5.2 is a contract specification from NYMEX for the Central Appalachian Coal Future and shows just how specific the contract is on the delivery grade of coal.

Example

Table 5.2

Contract specification
NYMEX Central Appalachian Coal Future – physically settled

Product symbol	QLD, Clearing: QL	
Venue	CME Globex, CME ClearPort	
Hours (all times are New York time/ET)	CME Globex	Sunday–Friday 6:00 pm–5:15 pm (5:00 pm–4:15 pm Chicago Time/CT) with a 45-minute break each day beginning at 5:15 pm (4:15 pm CT)
	CME ClearPort	Sunday–Friday 6:00 pm– 5:15 pm (5:00 pm–4:15 pm Chicago Time/CT) with a 45-minute break each day beginning at 5:15 pm (4:15 pm CT)
Contract size	1550 tons	
Price quotation	US dollars and cents per ton	
Minimum fluctuation	$0.01 per ton	
Termination of trading	Trading terminates on the fourth last business day of the month prior to the delivery month	
Listed contracts	Trading is conducted in the current year and the next four years. Contracts for each new year will be added following the termination of trading in the December contract of the current year	

▶

Table 5.2 continued

Settlement type	Physical
Delivery period	The seller may not schedule delivery of coal earlier than the first calendar day and not later than a date such that there are a minimum of seven calendar days remaining in the delivery month. The seller may not complete delivery of coal later than the last calendar day of the delivery month.
Grade and quality specifications	*Coal delivered under this contract shall meet the following quality specifications:* ■ Btu: Minimum 12,000 Btu/lb, gross calorific value, with an analysis tolerance of 250 Btu/lb below (ASTM D1989); ■ Ash: Maximum 13.50%, with no analysis tolerance (ASTM D3174 or D5142); ■ Sulphur: Maximum 1.00%, with an analysis tolerance of 0.050% above (ASTM D4239); ■ Moisture: Maximum 10.00%, with no analysis tolerance (ASTM D3302 or D5142); ■ Volatile Matter: Minimum 30.00%, with no analysis tolerance (ASTM D5142 or D3175); ■ Grindability: Minimum 41 Hardgrove Index (HGI) with three-point analysis tolerance below (ASTM D409); ■ Sizing: Three inches topsize, nominal, with maximum 55% passing one quarter inch square wire cloth sieve to be determined basis the primary cutter of the mechanical sampling system (ASTM D4749). *The tests for grindability and sizing are at the buyer's option, with the buyer required to*: Direct its inspection company to collect whatever additional samples are necessary for these tests to be performed according to the specified ASTM guidelines. The buyer will bear any costs for additional sample collection. Notify the seller whether the test is to be conducted pursuant to Rule 260.13(D)(1)(b).
Position limits	NYMEX Position Limits
Rulebook chapter	260
Exchange rule	These contracts are listed with, and subject to, the rules and regulations of NYMEX.

Source: Courtesy NYMEX

Hedging using the NYMEX Coal futures contract

Example

A major US utility company has estimated that it will need to source 310,000 tons of coal in two months' time. The prevailing spot price for coal is US$80.55/ton while the price of coal futures for delivery in two months' time is US$71.27/ton. The market is in backwardation. The utility does not wish to purchase the coal now due to storage considerations and wishes simply to have it available when it is required in two months' time. To hedge against a possible rise in the coal price, the utility company decides to lock in a price for the coal of US$71.27/ton, which is where the futures are currently trading. The strategy is executed by taking a long position in the required number of NYMEX coal futures contracts. As each NYMEX coal futures contract covers 1550 tons of coal and the utility will need to buy 310,000 tons of coal, it will need to purchase (go long) 200 futures contracts.

This strategy will guarantee that the power company would be able to purchase the 310,000 tons of coal at US$71.27/ton, making a total amount of US$22,093,700.

As every reader knows, market prices can go up and/or down in the intervening period and I am making the assumption that markets could be higher/lower by 10 per cent at the maturity date in two months' time.

Spot coal price rises by 10 per cent from US$80.55 to US$88.60

If spot prices increase, the utility must pay more for its coal on the physical market. Using the assumption above, the new price for the coal purchase will be US$27,466,000 – an increase of US$5,372,300. However, the increased purchase price will be offset by the gains on the futures contracts.

By the delivery date, the coal futures price will have converged with the coal spot price and both will be trading equal to US$88.60. The original futures position was entered into at the lower price of US$71.27/ton: it will have gained US$88.60 – US$71.27 = US$17.33/ton. With 200 contracts covering a total of 310,000 tons of coal, the total gain from the long futures position is US$5,372,300 ($15.50 per contract × 200 contracts × 1733 ticks).

In the end, the higher purchase cost is offset by the gain in the coal futures market, resulting in a net payment amount of US$27,466,000 – US$5,372,300 = US$22,093,700. This is equivalent to the amount payable when buying the 310,000 tons of coal at US$71.27/ton.

Example continued

Spot coal price falls by 10 per cent from US$80.55 to US$72.50
With the spot price having fallen to US$72.50/ton, the utility company will need to pay only US$22,475,000 for the coal. However, any loss/gain in the futures market will normally offset any savings/costs made in the physical markets.

The assumption is that coal futures prices will have converged with the current coal spot price and are now trading at US$72.50/ton. The long futures position was entered into at US$71.27/ton: it will have made a small amount of profit, notably US$72.50 – US$71.27 = US$1.23/ton. With 200 contracts covering a total of 310,000 tons the total income from the long futures position is still positive at US$381,000 ($15.50 × 200 × 123 ticks). The net amount payable will be US$22,475,000 – US$381,000 = US$22,094,000. Once again, this amount is equivalent to buying 310,000 tons of coal at US$71.27/ton.

Outcome
The downside of the long futures hedge is that the coal buyer would have been better off without the hedge if the price of the commodity had fallen, but as no one has a crystal ball this outcome is not 100 per cent certain. By hedging with futures contracts at least the utility has locked in a fixed price. Options would have proved to be a better hedging tool as the hedge could be abandoned when the price fell; however, that strategy requires the payment of an up-front premium.

TRADING WITH COAL FUTURES

The ICE contract, which is a cash settled contract, is linked to a final closing price which is an index. As the coal does not need to be physically transported these types of cash settled contracts lend themselves to trading rather than hedging. Coal futures are cash settled via one of the key Argus indices (Argus is one of the key information providers in the commodities markets).

- API 2 – The standard reference price benchmark for coal imported into north-west Europe.
- API 4 – The benchmark price for coal exported out of South Africa's Richards Bay terminal.
- API 6 – An average of Argus and McCloskey's FOB Newcastle assessments for coal exported out of Australia.

Table 5.3 shows the Rotterdam Coal ICE futures contract.

ICE Rotterdam Coal Futures: contract specifications

Table 5.3

Description: The Rotterdam Coal Futures contracts are financially settled based on delivery to Rotterdam in the Netherlands. They are cash settled against API 2 as published in the Argus/McCloskey Coal Price Index Report.

Trading period/strip: Up to 72 consecutive contract months. Up to 18 consecutive quarters – quarters are strips of three individual and consecutive contract months. Quarters always comprise a strip of January–March, April–June, July–September or October–December contract months. Up to six consecutive calendar years – calendar years are strips of 12 individual and consecutive contract months comprising January–December. On expiry of a December monthly contract an additional 12 months, four quarters and one calendar year are added.

Expiration date: The month contracts cease trading at the close of business on the last Friday of the contract delivery period. The quarters, seasons and calendar years cease trading as a quarter/season/calendar year at the close of business on the last Friday of the first month contract in that quarter/season/calendar year.

Contract security: ICEU guarantees financial performance of all ICE Futures contracts registered with it by its clearing members. ICE Futures members are either members of ICEU, or have a clearing agreement with a member who is a member of ICEU.

Trading hours: Open 07:00, Close 17:00 (London local time).

Contract size: 1 lot equals 1000 tonnes of coal.

Quotation: The contract price is in US dollars and cents per tonne.

Minimum price flux: 5 cents per tonne.

Maximum price flux: There are no limits.

Settlement price: The weighted average price of trades during a 15 minute settlement period from 16:00:00, London time.

Daily margin: All open contracts are marked-to-market daily, with variation margin being called for as appropriate. This process compares the settlement price, established by ICE Futures with the previous day's settlement price (or traded price for new contracts).

Position limits: There are no position limits.

Trading methods: ICE Rotterdam Coal Futures are supported for trading on the ICE platform or by submission of exchange of futures for physicals (EFPs), exchange of futures for swaps (EFSs) or blocks.

Delivery/settlement basis: The ICE Futures Rotterdam Coal Futures contract is cash settled at an amount equal to the monthly average API 2 index as published in Argus/McCloskey's Coal Price Index Report.

Source: Courtesy of ICE

Example

Long Coal Futures trade

A trader decides to go long 10 March ICE Coal Futures contract at the price of US$78.40/tonne. Since each ICE Coal Futures contract represents 1000 tonnes of coal, the value of the 10 futures contracts is US$784,000. Instead of paying the full value of the contract, the trader is required to deposit an initial margin of ten times the pre-set initial margin amount – assume this is US$4950, therefore we need US$49,500 to open the long futures position.

Assume that a month later, the price of coal has risen and the price of coal futures has also increased to US$82.90/ton. Each single contract is now worth US$82,900. If the trader sells the 10 futures contracts now, he can exit his long position in coal futures with a profit of US$45,000.

Long Coal Futures Strategy: Buy LOW, Sell HIGH	
BUY $10,000 tonnes of coal at $78.40/tonne	$784,000
SELL 10,000 tonnes of coal at $82.90/tonne	$829,000
Profit	$45,000
Investment (initial margin)	$49,500
Return on investment	91%

Margin requirements and leverage

In the examples shown above, although coal prices have moved by only 5.73 per cent, the ROI generated is 91 per cent. This leverage is made possible by the relatively low margin amount required to control the large amount of coal represented by each contract.

Leverage is a double-edged weapon. The above example only depicts positive scenarios whereby the market is favourable towards you. If the market turns against you, you will lose and be required to top up your account to meet margin requirements in order for your futures position to remain open.

ENVIRONMENTAL CONCERNS

Water pollution

The production and mining of coal requires large quantities of water, affecting the habitats of water- and land-based wildlife as well as the folks who use these water resources. Water that comes into contact with coal during the processes of extraction, cleaning, storage or energy production collects heavy metals like lead and arsenic. This polluted water might contaminate groundwater and nearby streams and lakes.

Air pollution

The process of burning coal for energy produces greenhouse gases as well as other pollutants, including carbon dioxide, mercury compounds, sulphur dioxide and nitrogen oxides. Coal produces more pollution per unit of electricity than any other fuel source, according to the US Environmental Protection Agency. In addition, every step of coal energy production – from the mining to the transportation and cleaning – produces greenhouse gas emissions. Coal contains methane, a combustible and potent greenhouse gas, which has caused many mine accidents over the last few years.

Note: Methane's global warming potential is 23 times greater than carbon dioxide.

Additional environmental impacts

Coal mining operations radically alter local ecosystems and wildlife habitats by introducing roads, clearing trees and removing large sections of land. The burning of coal generates ash, a solid waste containing alkali and metal oxides. New recycling processes are being investigated in order to use coal ash for building material, such as cement, but the majority of ash still contributes to landfills or remains in abandoned mines.

COAL AND CARBON ISSUES

Coal is the single most important fuel for producing electricity globally – but it is also the most controversial. As the greatest source of carbon dioxide of all fuels, environmentalists say it is critical to reduce the world's dependence on it in order to stem global warming.

As the economies of Asia, particularly China, rebounded from the 2008 global slowdown, their imports of coal soared, pushing prices up. By 2010, China was using half of the 6 billion tons of coal burned each year, and the price had doubled over five years.

In a few places, particularly South Africa, gasification of coal produces synthetic fuels. The Fischer–Tropsch synthetic fuel process was first used on a large scale by Germany to produce fuels for World War II. No one doubts that coal is a versatile and cost-effective fuel, but is the current rate of consumption harming the planet? This book is not about to debate that issue.

There are currently about 600 coal-fired power plants across the United States. Coal has long been considered a reliable and inexpensive source of energy in the United States, but it is facing an uncertain future due to growing political pressure on American politicians to impose new regulations controlling its growth. While state and local governments have been blocking the development of new coal plants across the country in the last few years, coal executives are now preparing for eventual carbon taxes or a cap-and-trade system like that already in place in Europe (see Chapter 7 on Carbon and Environmental Commodities).

6

Alternative Energy

BACKGROUND AND CONTEXT

What exactly are alternative energy resources? Are these the same as renewable energy resources or Green Energy? The International Energy Agency (www.iea.org) defines renewables as:

> 'Renewable energy is derived from natural processes that are replenished constantly. In its various forms, it derives directly from the sun, or from heat generated deep within the earth. Included in the definition is electricity and heat generated from solar, wind, ocean, hydropower, biomass, geothermal resources, and bio-fuels and hydrogen derived from renewable resource.'

According to the Bureau of Ocean Energy Management, Regulation and Enforcement (www.boem.gov), however, 'alternatives' are defined as:

> 'Fuel sources that are other than those derived from fossil fuels. Typically used interchangeably for renewable energy. Examples include: wind, solar, biomass, wave and tidal energy.'

I will use both terms interchangeably in this chapter; both are also colloquially known as 'green energy'.

One interesting fact is that sunlight falling on the United States in one day contains more than twice the energy the US consumes in an entire year.

A leading industry group is REN21 (Renewable Energy Network Policy Group for the 21st Century), established in 2005 to bring together international leadership and a variety of stakeholders to enable a rapid global transition to renewable energy. REN21's Renewables Global Status Report (GSR) was first released later that year; it grew out of an effort to comprehensively capture for the first time the full status of renewable energy worldwide. In REN21's own words, the report also aimed to align perceptions with the reality that renewables were playing a growing role in mainstream energy markets and in economic development.

> 'Renewable sources have grown to supply an estimated 16% of global final energy consumption in 2010. By year's end, renewables comprised one-quarter of global power capacity from all sources and delivered close to one-fifth of the world's power supply. Most technologies held their own, despite the challenges faced, while solar PV surged with more than twice the capacity installed as the year before. No technology has benefited more than solar from the dramatic drop in costs.'

(Mohamed El-Ashry, Chairman, REN21
REN21, Renewables 2011, Global Status Report)

Figure 6.1

Global energy consumption 2009

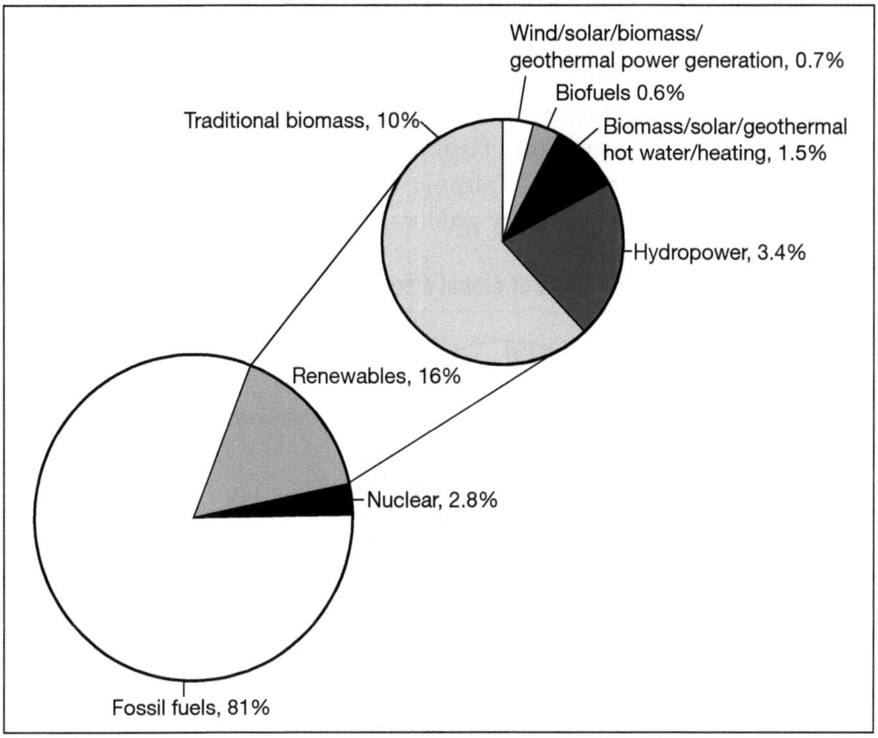

Source: REN21, Renewables 2011 Global Status Report

Figure 6.1 shows how the 16 per cent of global consumption that is 'renewables' is broken down into its component parts. (Note: Traditional biomass is how we define cooking and heating in rural areas.) Renewables offer huge potential for development and shown in Figure 6.2 are the projected (estimated) figures for global energy usage from a variety of fuels

Figure 6.2

Global energy use by fuel 1990–2035

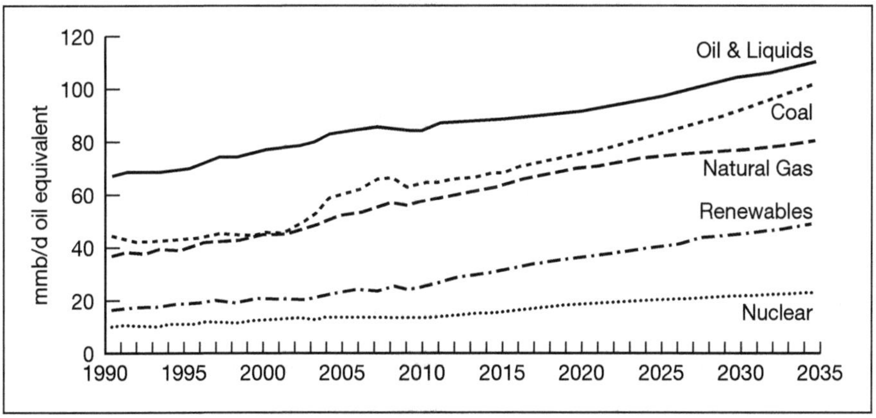

Source: US DOE/EIA

covering the period 1990–2035. The data show that by 2035 the usage of renewables has exhibited a marked increase.

Electricity generation is typically driven by fossil fuels like coal, oil and natural gas; however, these resources are being rapidly depleted. In essence there are two key reasons why the hunt is on for 'alternative' forms of energy: firstly the financial cost of using traditional fossil fuels and secondly the cost to the environment of burning these fuels. Figure 6.3 shows how the renewables share of electricity production is broken down.

Figure 6.3 **Renewables share of global electricity production, 2010**

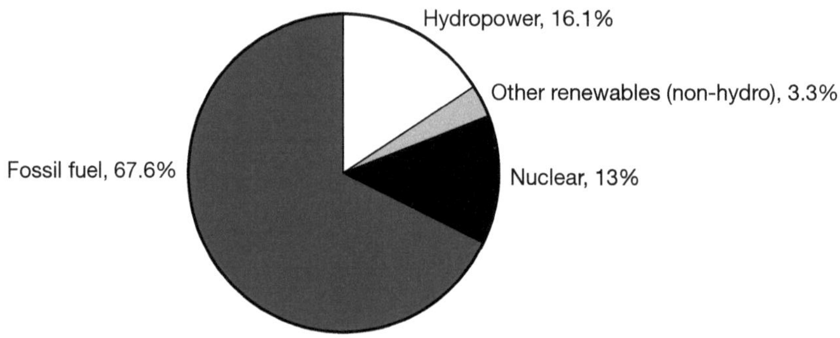

Source: REN21, Renewables 2011 Global Status Report

MEASUREMENTS OF ELECTRICITY

Electricity is measured in watts (named after the Scottish mechanical engineer James Watt). Shown in Table 6.1 are the units in common usage.

Table 6.1 **Measurements of electricity**

Value	Symbol	Name
10^1 W	daW	decawatt
10^2 W	hW	hectowatt
10^3 W	kW	kilowatt
10^6 W	MW	megawatt
10^9 W	GW	gigawatt
10^{12} W	TW	terawatt
10^{15} W	PW	petawatt
10^{18} W	EW	exawatt
10^{21} W	ZW	zettawatt
10^{24} W	YW	yottawatt

Table 6.2 shows the approximate cost to generate power across a range of renewable energy sources.

Table 6.2

Table 6.2 Cost of generating power

Technology	Typical characteristics		Typical energy costs (US cents/ kilowatt-hour)
Large hydro	Plant size:	10 MW–18,000 MW	3–5
Small hydro	Plant size:	1–10 MW	5–12
On-shore wind	Turbine size:	1.5–3.5 MW; Rotor diameter: 60–100 metres	5–9
Off-shore wind	Turbine size:	1.5–5 MW; Rotor diameter: 70–125 metres	10–20
Biomass power	Plant size:	1–20 MW	5–12
Geothermal power	Plant size: Types:	1–100 MW; binary, single- and double-flash, natural steam	4–7
Solar PV (module)	Efficiency:	crystalline 12–19%; thin film 4–13%	–
Solar PV (concentrating)	Efficiency:	25%	–
Rooftop solar PV	Peak capacity:	2–5 kW peak	17–34
Utility-scale solar PV	Peak capacity:	200 kW to 100 MW	15–30
Concentrating solar thermal power (CSP)	Plant size: Types:	50–500 MW (trough), 10–20 MW (tower) trough, tower, dish	14–18 (trough)

Source: REN 21, Renewables 2011 Global Status Report

ENERGY DEFINITIONS

In addition to understanding how power and electricity is measured, e.g. watts, it is also advantageous to understand different types of energy.

Terminology

Potential energy Equal to stored energy and in hydropower this is proportional to the height above ground.

Kinetic energy Equal to the energy of motion and is proportional to the velocity.

Creating kinetic energy

- A ball resting at the top of an incline has no motion and thus no kinetic energy.
- With a little push, the ball rolls down the incline, picking up speed as it rolls.
- At the bottom, the ball has its highest speed but can fall no further.
- This is an example of converting potential energy to kinetic energy. (See Figure 6.4).

Figure 6.4 **Converting potential energy into kinetic energy**

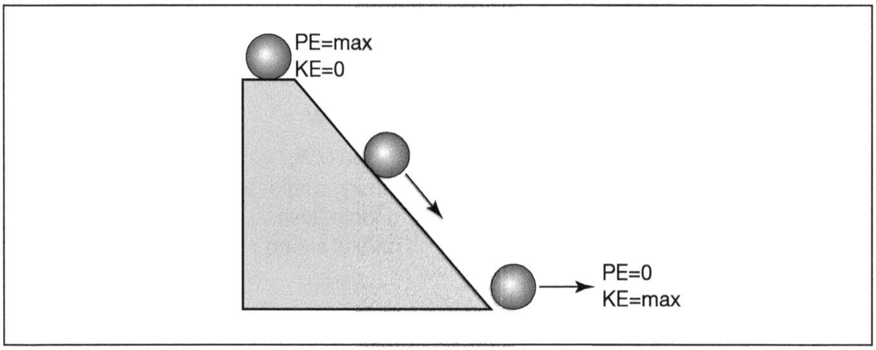

Nearly all forms of alternative energy sources involve turbines that convert the kinetic energy through various processes into electricity.

HYDROPOWER

This is the most popular and mature of all renewable energy sources and accounts for about 16 per cent of world electricity production. It has been around for thousands of years, historically used in agriculture for irrigation and grinding of corn. In today's hydro industry water typically falls with gravity and pushes the blades in a turbine to produce electricity. As a country China currently holds the largest hydropower capacity with 263 GW or 20 per cent of the world's total and has the largest active hydropower industry. Globally, there are hundreds of small entrepreneurs and municipal governments, as well as a number of large players. India also has a wide manufacturing base for small-scale hydropower equipment, with 20 active domestic manufacturers. The European Union (EU-27) holds the bulk of the world capacity with 580 GW or 59 per cent of the world's total.

Tidal power can also be a source of hydropower, where a machine that looks like an upside-down wind turbine spins from the motion of currents, generating electricity. Other forms of marine energy are being tested, including those that capture kinetic energy from underwater currents and the movement of surface waves.

Definition

- Power = Flow × Head × Constant
- Power is measured in megawatts (million watts)
- Flow is measured in cubic feet per second
- Head (height) is measured in feet
- Constant is a function of the turbine's efficiency

Example

Grand Coulee Dam, Colombia River, Washington State

- Flow is 100,000 cubic feet per second
- Head is 328 feet
- Constant is 0.075
- Power = 100,000 × 328 × 0.075 = 2460 megawatts

Mechanics of hydroelectric power generation

Conventional hydroelectric power generation comes from constructing a major dam across rivers which then back up and form lakes. The water is then forced through a narrow intake valve(s). The actual mechanics of hydropower generation are shown in Figure 6.5.

The Hoover Dam, one of the best-known examples of a dam, can produce a maximum of 2080 megawatts of power, making an average annual generation of 4.2 TWh per year.

The movement of water as it flows downstream creates kinetic energy that can be converted into electricity. A hydroelectric power plant converts this energy into electricity by forcing water, often held at a dam, through a hydraulic turbine that is connected to a generator. The water exits the turbine and is returned to a stream or riverbed below the dam. Hydropower is mostly dependent upon rainfall and elevation changes; high precipitation levels and large elevation changes are necessary to generate significant quantities of electricity.

Figure 6.5 **Hydroelectric dam**

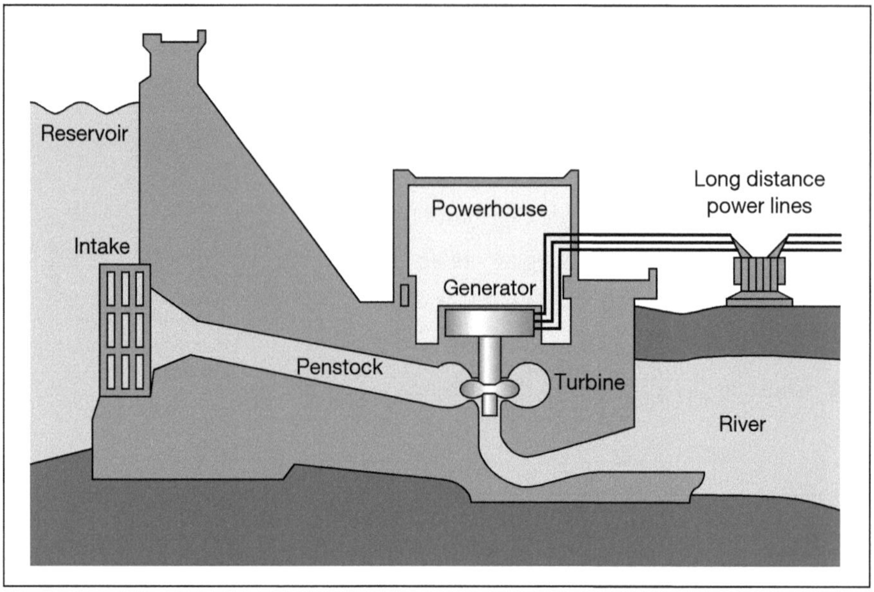

Source: Tomia, Finland, Wikimedia Commons

Environmental impact

There are environmental impacts even with this type of 'clean energy'. Hydropower usually requires the construction of dams, which can greatly affect the flow of rivers, altering ecosystems and impacting on the wildlife and people who depend on those waters.

Often, water at the bottom of the lake created by a dam is inhospitable to fish because it is much colder and has less oxygen compared with water at the top. When this colder, oxygen-poor water is released into the river, it can kill fish living downstream that are accustomed to warmer, oxygen-rich water. In addition, some dams withhold water and then release it all at once, causing the river downstream to suddenly flood. This action can disrupt plant and wildlife habitats and affect drinking water supplies.

One of the most extreme cases of negative consequences is seen at the Three Gorges Dam in China, where the weight of the water behind the dam caused immense pressure on tectonic plates, leading to earthquake tremors and landslides in the area.

WIND POWER

In 2010 for the first time the majority of new wind power capacity was added by developing countries and emerging markets, driven primarily by China, which accounted for half the global market. In the United States by the end of 2010, wind accounted for 2.3 per cent of electricity generation (up from 1.8 per cent in 2009), enough to supply electricity for more than 10 million US homes. In fact the state of Texas, with 10.1 GW, has more than 25 per cent of all existing US capacity. Germany maintained the lead in Europe with a total of 27.2 GW operating at the end of 2010, generating 36.5 TWh of electricity during the year. Figure 6.6 shows wind power capacity in the top 10 generating countries.

Figure 6.6

Wind power capacity, top 10 countries

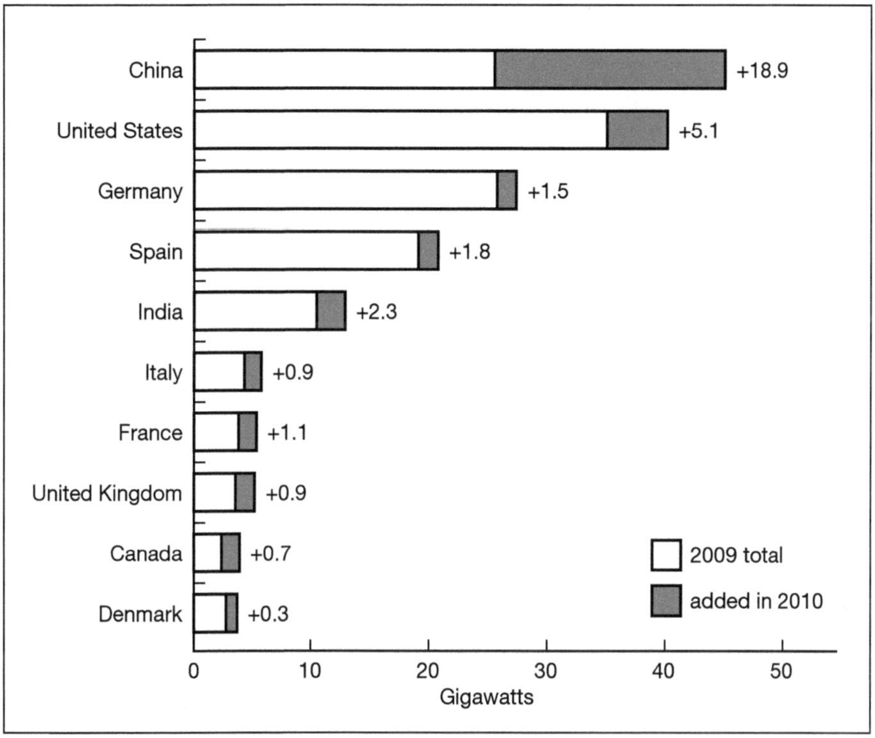

Source: REN21, Renewables 2011 Global Status Report, GWEC, WWEA, EWEA, AWEA, MNRE, BMU, BTM Consult, IDAE, CREIA, CWEA

Figure 6.7 shows the increasing growth in wind power capacity.

Mechanics of wind power generation – how does a wind turbine work?

A wind turbine generates electricity by harnessing the kinetic energy in the wind and as the wind speed increases so does the power output of the turbine. This can lead to complications and some UK readers may recall a photograph of a wind turbine in flames, the result of overheating during the storms in Scotland in December 2011. Just a few weeks later in 2012

Figure 6.7 **Growth in wind power capacity**

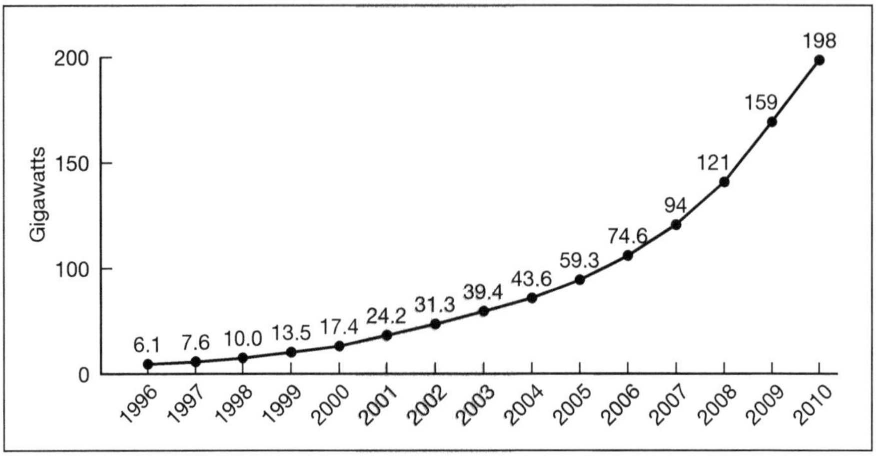

Source: REN21, Renewables 2011 Global Status Report, GWEC, WWEA, EWEA, AWEA, MNRE, BMU, BTM Consult, IDAE, CREIA, CWEA

a number of land-based wind turbines were again badly damaged by high winds in England, leading to local residents calling for them to be removed as the pieces flying off were a safety risk and someone could have been killed.

Reputedly the earliest windmills were built in Persia in the seventh century, and in the Middle Ages windmills in the Netherlands and Belgium were built to pump water from low lying areas.

Today's wind turbines may reach up to 300 feet above the ground, with the diameter of the rotor and blades reaching more than 250 feet. Lying flat on the ground, a three-bladed rotor can almost cover a football field! Wind turbines consist of three main parts: the tower, the blades and the nacelle. A nacelle is the size of a small truck. The nacelle houses the generator, which transforms wind into electricity. Turbines are built on a tower as wind travels faster above the ground and is less turbulent. Turbines catch the wind's energy with their propeller-like blades. Usually, two or three blades are mounted on a shaft to form a rotor.

The blade acts much like an aeroplane wing. When the wind blows, a pocket of low-pressure air forms on the downwind side of the blade. The low-pressure air pocket then pulls the blade towards it, causing the rotor to turn. This is known as lift. The force of the lift is actually much stronger than the wind's force against the front side of the blade, which is called drag. The combination of lift and drag causes the rotor to spin like a propeller, and the turning shaft spins a generator to make electricity. Figure 6.8 shows the basic features of a wind turbine.

Wind turbine

Figure 6.8

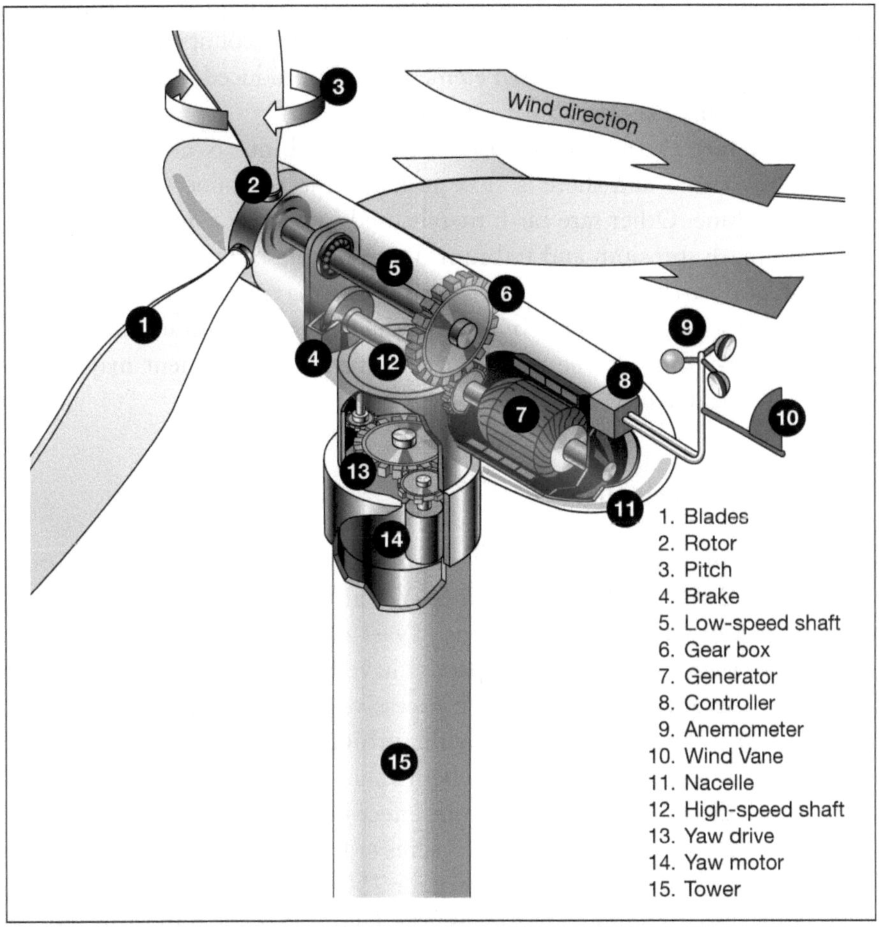

Source: Alternative Energy News, Australia, www.alternative-energy-news.info

In order for wind turbines to capture the wind from any direction, all wind turbines have computer-controlled *yaw systems* that automatically turn the wind turbine and align the blades into the wind. There are two main versions of wind generators: those with a vertical axis and those with a horizontal axis. Wind turbines can be used to generate large amounts of electricity in wind farms both onshore and offshore.

Wind power and rare earth magnets

The Global Wind Energy Council (GWEC) recently predicted that global wind power capacity will increase by 100 per cent in the next few years, with global installed wind capacity estimated to reach 409 GW by 2014. The new generation of wind turbines include rare earth magnets to increase their efficiency, and if the GWEC figures are proved to be correct, approximately 160,000 tons of rare earth magnets will be required to meet this expansion in capacity – unfortunately China, which accounts for 95 per cent of world production of rare earth elements, only produced 150,000 in total in 2009 and only exported 5 per cent of that.

The key rare earth element used in wind turbines is neodymium – a heavy rare earth – and there is close to half a metric tonne of the element for each turbine. Other rare earth metals used in wind turbines include praseodymium, dysprosium and terbium. It is possible to build wind turbines without rare earths, but the older permanent magnet technology is very much less efficient than those built with the newer neodymium-based magnets, and depending on the project, their return on investment may be too low to be considered.

Environmental concerns

A key trend is the increasing size of turbines, with some manufacturers launching 5 MW and larger machines. Yet although this clean fuel is seen as ecologically friendly, wind farms – vast collections of wind turbines, often more than 100 in a small space – have been increasingly accused of damaging the environment through excessive noise and being a blight on the landscape. There are reports about turbines falling over, catching fire after being struck by lightning, ice being shot from the blades, the noise – likened to a disco bass – and the strobe effect in sunlight.

The average wind farm requires 17 acres of land to produce one megawatt of electricity, about enough electricity for 750 to 1000 homes. On the plus side, farms and cattle grazing can use the land under the wind turbines, if they can stand the noise.

Wind farms may also cause erosion in desert areas. Often wind farms affect the view because they tend to be located on or just below ridgelines. There is increasing concern that these wind turbines which have been erected to reduce our dependence on fossil fuels and thus save the planet are instead damaging it. In Hawaii many wind turbines are now rusting and silent on the South Island – which weather-wise would seem to be perfect with almost year-round high winds – a legacy of a 27-year-old wind farm which has now been shut down.

In the US, turbines were built across several states, with the majority in California. Most of these were concentrated in three enormous wind farms: Altamont, east of San Francisco; Tehachapi, on the edge of the Mojave desert; and San Gorgonio near Palm Springs. They had the advantage of the 'right sort of wind' – strong and almost continual. But birds were known to be casualties, especially in Altamont, and the National Audubon Society,

America's RSPB, called this 'probably the worst site ever chosen for a wind energy project'.

Its figures show that an estimated 10,000 birds, including up to 80 protected golden eagles, 380 burrowing owls, 300 red-tailed hawks and 330 falcons, and thousands of bats were being shredded each year in Altamont's turbine blades. Four years ago, angry conservationists launched an action against America's 'deadliest' wind farm. Now the blades stop turning for four months every year to avoid causing more deaths during the annual migration season. The issue for the larger birds such as the golden eagles is that their size makes it difficult for them to maneuvre through the turbine blades that are rotating at speeds of up to 200mph, especially when the birds are looking down and hunting for prey. The American Bird Conservancy estimates wind turbines kill between 75,000 and 275,000 birds each year.

Notwithstanding the environmental concerns, wind energy is gaining worldwide popularity as a large-scale energy source, although it still only provides a very small amount of global energy consumption – less than 1 per cent.

SOLAR POWER

Solar power is the term used for converting power from the sun into other forms of energy, such as heat and electricity. The sun and other stars are responsible for all our energy, including nuclear energy. When an exploding star goes nova it creates the uranium atoms needed in nuclear fusion to power nuclear power stations.

You would expect that countries without much in the way of sun but with a surplus of dense cloud cover – such as the UK, parts of Northern Europe and Scandinavia – would find solar energy a challenge. In parts of the UK, domestic homeowners were encouraged to install solar panels and sell any excess electricity they generated to the local provider – with an incentive of 43 pence per kilowatt hour, which was reduced to 23 pence in March 2012. This so-called 'Feed in Tariff' (FIT) generated up to £1100 per household and reduced electricity bills by as much as £90 per annum. This has led to a far greater takeup than the UK government expected and a shortage of photovoltaic panels.

Countries nearer the sun belts around the equator where there is a high level of insolation (solar radiation) are embracing solar technology and new solar panel farms in the Gulf and surrounding regions are under construction.

There are a range of different solar power technologies.

Solar photovoltaic

Solar energy is converted into electricity using photovoltaic (PV) devices or solar power plants. Photovoltaic or solar panels generate electricity directly from sunlight and can vary in size from a panel the size of the one in your calculator or watch to the one on the roof of your house to a field full of them. Full-scale solar power generation requires a number of solar cells all containing photovoltaic material to be linked together (see Figure 6.9).

Figure 6.9 **Grid tied PV element**

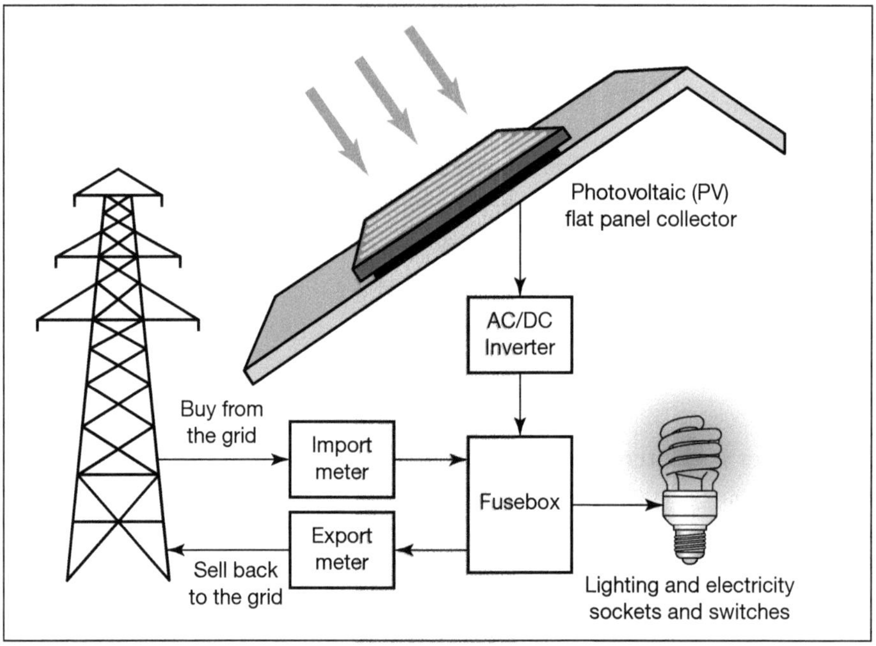

Source: In Balance Energy. www.inbalance-energy.co.uk

Mechanics of solar PV power generation

When sunlight strikes a solar cell, electrons are knocked loose and move towards the treated front surface. This creates an electron imbalance between the front and back of the cell. When a wire connector joins the two surfaces together a current of electricity flows between the negative and positive sides. Individual solar cells are arranged together in a PV module and the modules are then grouped together to form an array. Some arrays are set on tracking devices to follow the sun all day long or attached to orbiting satellites for maximum solar exposure.

The EU dominates the global PV market with 80 per cent of the world total, led by Italy and particularly Germany, which installed more PV in 2010 than the entire world did the previous year (see Figure 6.10).

Figure 6.10

Solar PV capacity – top 10 countries

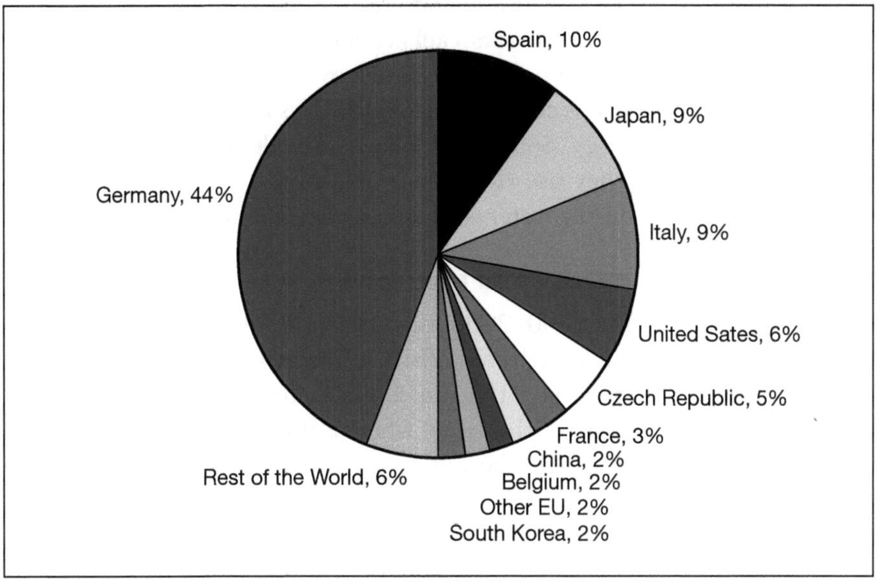

Source: REN21, Renewables 2011 Global Status Report, EPIA, BMU, IDAE, GSE, KOPIA, CREIA

Concentrated solar power

These systems use mirrors and lenses to concentrate a large area of sunlight into a small area. Electrical power is then produced when the concentrated light is converted to heat, which in turn drives an engine, usually a steam turbine connected to a power generator. Different versions exist including:

- Parabolic trough power plants (most common, over 90 per cent);
- Solar thermal tower power plant.

CSP growth is expected to continue at a fast pace, with Spain leading the way with new capacity. Interest has also been shown in North Africa and the Middle East, as well as India and China. In an industry that is fashionable, it was unexpected when in December 2011 BP Solar announced it was closing down its operation and withdrawing from an industry that's facing oversupply and price pressures after Chinese competitors increased production. BP was unable to remain profitable; in addition, the prices of solar panels fell nearly 50 per cent in the US alone, leading to some high-profile bankruptcies.

Mechanics of CSP generation – parabolic trough power plant

A highly curved mirror known as a parabolic trough focuses the sunlight on a pipe running down a central point above the curve of the mirror. The mirror focuses the sunlight to strike the pipe, and it gets so hot that it can boil water into steam. That steam can then be used to power a turbine and make electricity. If you link a group of these together, such as has been done in the Mojave Desert in California, you create 'solar thermal power plants' where huge rows of solar mirrors can generate electricity for more than 350,000 people (see Figure 6.11). The problem with solar energy is that it works only when the sun is shining. On cloudy days and at night, the power plants can't create energy. Some solar plants include 'hybrid' technology. During the daytime they use the sun. At night and on cloudy days they burn natural gas to boil the water so they can continue to make electricity.

Mechanics of CSP generation – solar tower plant

A tall tower is built and 1800–2000 mirrors are arranged in concentric circles around it. Sunlight is reflected off these mirrors, known as heliostats, as they move and turn to face the sun. Light is reflected back to the top of the tower in the centre of the circle where a fluid is boiled by the sun's rays. That fluid can be used to boil water to make steam to turn a turbine and a generator.

Environmental impact

As in hydro and wind power, the search for more environmentally friendly energy sources is not without pain. Solar thermal energy plants requiring the collection of solar rays through huge mirrors need large tracts of land to act as a collection site. This affects the natural habitat. The environment is also affected when the buildings, roads, transmission lines and transformers are built. Some of the fluids used with solar thermal electric generation are themselves very toxic and spills may happen.

Solar or PV cells use the same technologies as the production of silicon chips for computers. The manufacturing process itself uses toxic chemicals. Toxic chemicals are also used in the making of batteries to store solar electricity through the night and on cloudy days; manufacturing this equipment has environmental impacts too. The renewable power plant doesn't release air pollution or use precious fossil fuels, but it still has an impact on the environment.

BIOFUELS

Biofuels are fuels that derive from any plant or animal material – known as biomass – and include wood, charcoal and animal waste, all of which when processed are traditionally used for energy production by those in rural areas or in extreme poverty. Biofuel may also come from agricultural crops, or it may be derived from forestry, agricultural or fishery products or municipal waste, as well as from agro-industry, food industry and food service by-products.

Figure 6.11

Schematic of a concentrated solar thermal trough power plant

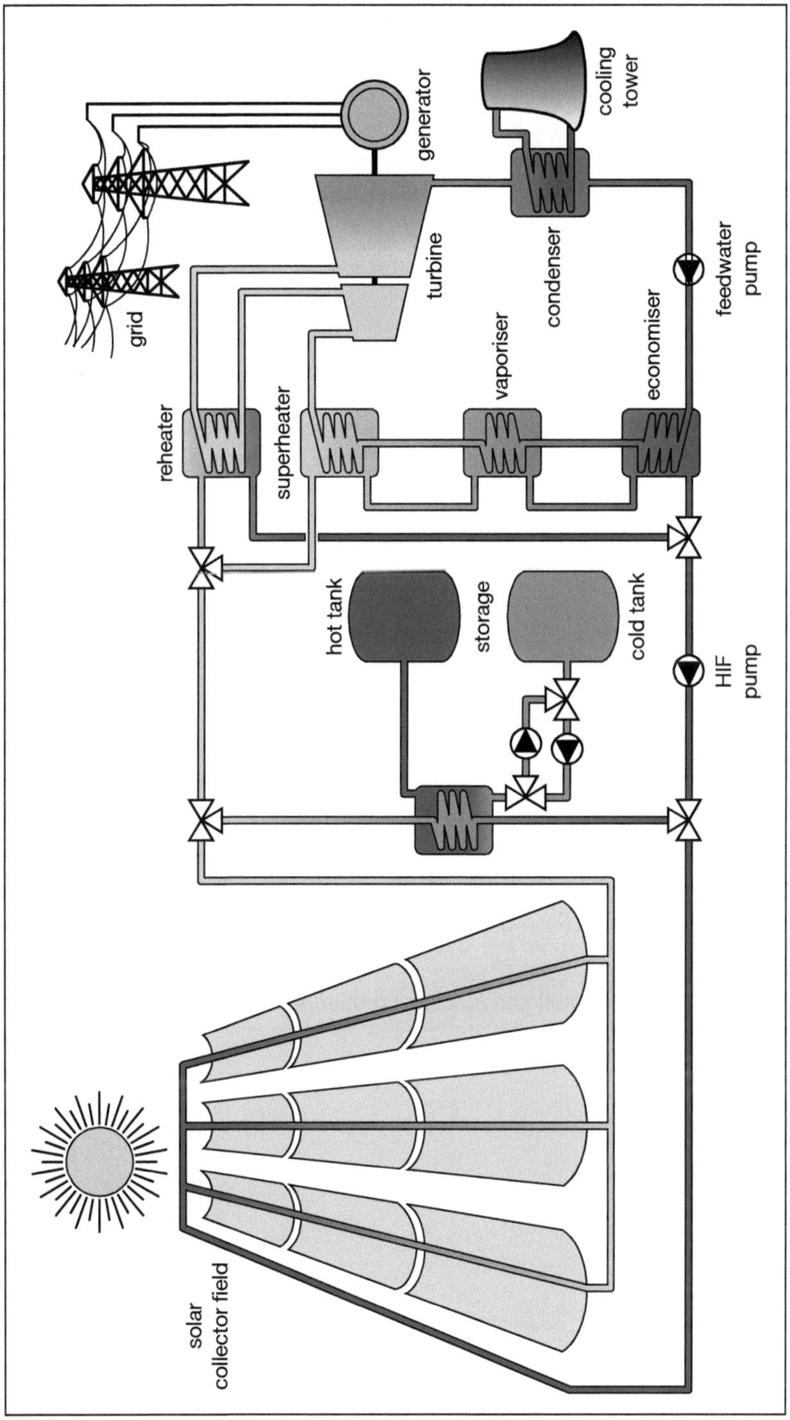

Source: Volker Quaschning, Germany, www.volker-quaschning .de

It is possible to sub-divide biofuels into those which are unprocessed (primary) biofuels, e.g. wood, and those which are processed (secondary) biofuels, e.g. ethanol and biodiesel. The dominant use of secondary biofuels is for transportation, where it used instead of petrol (gas).

Primary biofuels

Wood, including

- **Fuelwood:** wood in the rough, e.g. branches, twigs, logs, sawdust and pellets.
- **Wood residues**: wood left behind in the forest and wood by-products from wood processing, such as wood chips, slabs, edgings, sawdust and shavings.
- **Wood pellets:** small particles used for energy generation made from dried, ground/pressed wood. Wood pellets are originally produced from wood waste (sawdust and shavings), rather than whole logs. The material is dried, shaped and extruded under intense pressure into pellets.

Secondary biofuels – ethanol and biodiesel

Both ethanol and biodiesel are known as first-generation biofuels as only the sugar/starch component of the plant material is used, whilst leaving behind the cellulose. Second-generation products that are still in their relative infancy will aim to utilise the cellulose. Figure 6.12 shows the increasing world production of ethanol and biodiesel.

Figure 6.12

Ethanol and biodiesel production 2000–2010

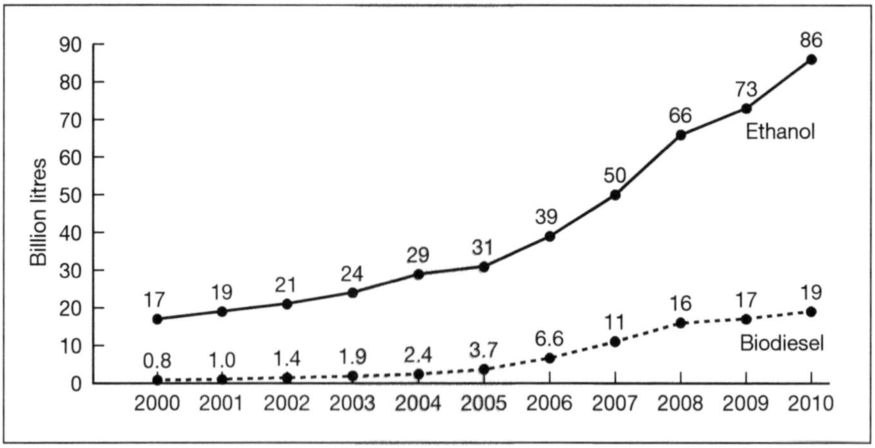

Source: REN21, Renewables 2011 Global Status Report, based on F.O Licht

Ethanol

Ethanol is an alcohol produced using any crop consisting of significant amounts of sugar or starch, e.g. sugar cane, sugar beet, maize and wheat. Sugar is directly fermented to alcohol whereas starch needs to be converted to sugar first. The process is similar to that used to make wine or beer, and pure ethanol is obtained by distillation.

Ethanol can be blended with petrol or burned in nearly pure form in modified spark-ignition engines. One litre of ethanol contains approximately two-thirds of the energy provided by a litre of petrol/gas. However, if it is mixed with petrol, the combustion performance of the engine improves and decreases emissions of carbon monoxide and sulphur oxide. Ethanol is mostly produced in the Americas.

Biodiesel

In contrast, biodiesel is produced, mainly in the European Union, by combining vegetable oil or animal fat with alcohol. It can be blended with traditional diesel fuel or burned in its pure form in special compression ignition engines. The energy content is somewhat less than that of diesel (88 to 95 per cent). Biodiesel can be made from a wide range of oils, including rapeseed, soybean, palm, coconut and jatropha oils (see Figure 6.13).

Diesel engines can also run on vegetable oils and animal fats, for instance used cooking oils from restaurants and fat from meat-processing industries.

In 2010, liquid biofuels provided about 2.7 per cent of global road transport fuel and production increased by 17 per cent in response to rising oil prices. The United States and Brazil accounted for around 88 per cent of global ethanol production, and after several years as a net importer the United States overtook Brazil to become the world's leading ethanol exporter. The EU remained the centre of biodiesel production in 2010, but due to increased competition with relatively cheap imports, growth in the region slowed.

Environmental impacts

One of the major reasons for using biofuels is to reduce greenhouse gas emissions and to manage more efficiently the effects of global warming, produced largely from the burning of fossil fuels. Nevertheless, the Food and Agriculture Organization (FAO) of the UN has projected some unintended impacts of biofuel production on biodiversity, land and water. The production of these biofuels is ultimately from agricultural production and if this is intensified then the side effects are even worse. There is a common misconception that growing crops for biofuels will offset the greenhouse gas emissions because they directly remove carbon dioxide from the air; no,

Figure 6.13 **Converting agricultural feedstock to biofuels**

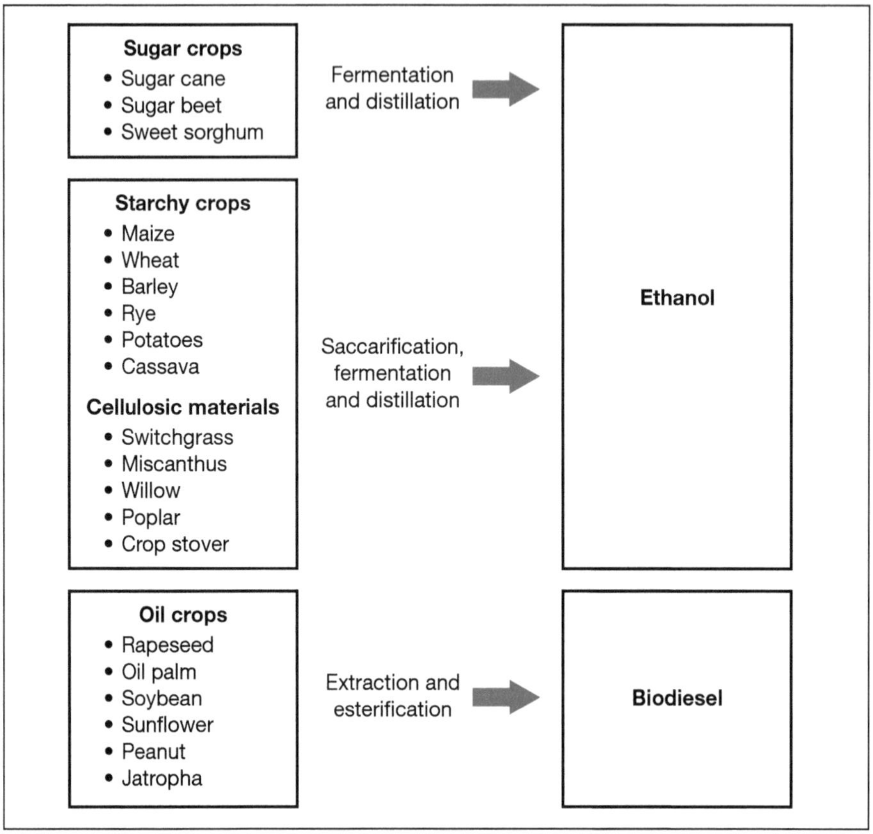

Source: FAO 2008

they won't. The FAO in its *The State of Food and Agriculture 2008* report notes that some crops may even generate more greenhouse gases than do fossil fuels. It cautions that nitrous oxide released from the fertilisers that may be used will have 300 times more global warming effect than carbon dioxide. There is also a difference in the greenhouse gas savings of different crops as maize produced for ethanol has an annual greenhouse gas saving of about 1.8 tonnes per hectare, according to the report, but switchgrass, which is a second-generation crop, has a saving of 8.6 tonnes. A balance has to be drawn between the greenhouse gas emissions produced in the production and burning of biofuels and the production and burning of fossil fuels. These balances can vary between different feedstocks and different locations and production methods.

Interestingly, in the 2008 report the FAO says the impact is at the beginning of the production cycle and any change in land use might take years to balance out the effects and in some cases could show fossil fuels to be more efficient than the biofuels: 'this would be particularly relevant if rainforest, peat-lands, savannahs or grasslands are used to grow feedstocks to produce ethanol or biodiesel'. Alarmingly, studies have shown that in some cases more carbon would be concentrated by converting cropland used for a biofuel feedstock to forest than the production of the fuel itself. 'If the objective of biofuel support policies is to mitigate global warming, then fuel efficiency and forest conservation and restoration would be more effective alternatives', the report says.

GEOTHERMAL POWER

Unlike wind and solar resources, which are more dependent upon weather fluctuations and climate changes, geothermal resources are available 24 hours a day, 7 days a week. The temperature at the centre of the Earth is around 5000 degrees Celsius – hot enough to melt rock. Even just a few kilometres down the temperature can be over 250 degrees Celsius. In general, the temperature rises one degree Celsius for every 30–50 metres you go down, but this varies depending on location.

At the time of writing geothermal power is in its infancy, with the US and Japan leading the way in terms of production. Iceland is totally self-sufficient in geothermal power and electricity and is already heating a large number of homes with this power source. It is using surplus electricity to attract investment and jobs from the energy-intensive aluminium smelting industry. This is now so cheap that it makes economic sense for smelting companies, including Alcoa and Rio Tinto Alcan, to produce aluminium in Iceland, despite its isolated location. Even Google is investing in it. The potential for geothermal power is enormous. It is estimated that using this technology, just 2 per cent of the heat below North America would easily supply all of the United States' current energy needs, and in December 2011 an Australian government scientist stated that 1 per cent of the nation's untapped geothermal potential could create enough energy for 26,000 years! Canada is in a curious position where despite having geothermal resources estimated at more than 1 million times its energy needs, there's not one single geothermal power plant up and running, as at March 2012.

For the technically minded, geothermal energy is heat energy emitted from within the Earth's crust, usually in the form of hot water or steam, which can be used to produce electricity or as a direct heat source for buildings, industry and agriculture. In addition, some ground-source heat pumps use shallow geothermal heat sources to heat and cool water. Shallow heat is found at around 20 metres depth; this may also be referred to as stored solar heat.

Mechanics of geothermal power generation

Holes are drilled in the rock down to the hot region; steam comes up, is purified and used to drive turbines, which drive electric generators. Natural 'groundwater' may be present in the hot rocks anyway, or more holes may need to be drilled and water pumped down.

Figure 6.14 shows how this works.

Figure 6.14 **Geothermal power production**

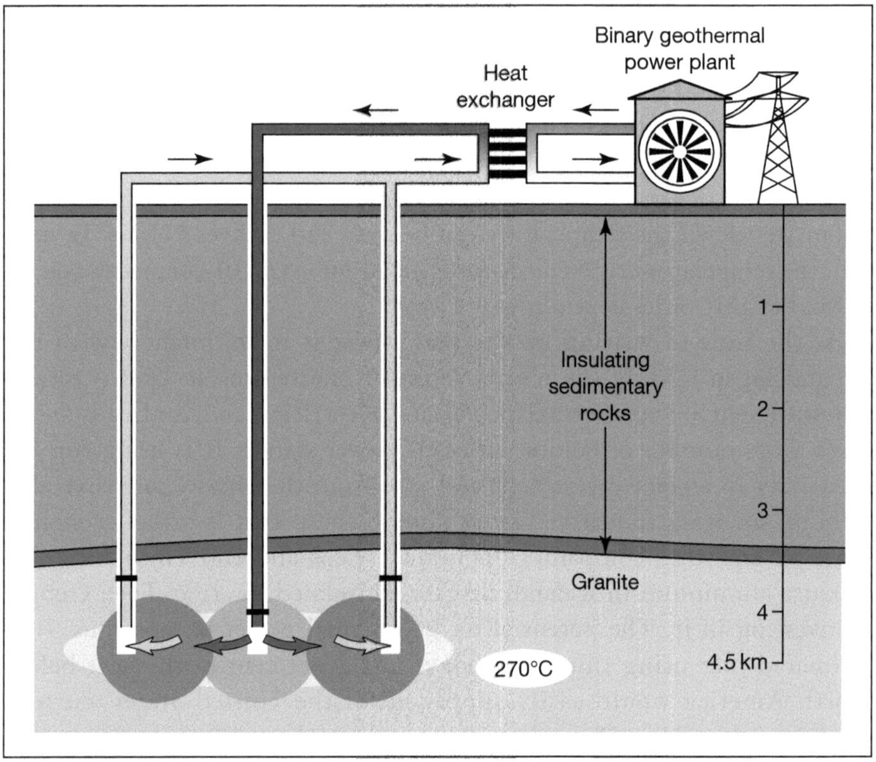

Source: Australian Geothermal Energy Association

Supply and demand

Geothermal power plants can generate electricity economically when the host rock resource temperature rises above approximately 212°F (100°C) or is at depths of roughly 4km or less. However, when you consider that oil rigs regularly drill in excess of 6km depth and in hostile environments, perhaps 6km is a better indicator of resource potential. If just 2 per cent of the estimated thermal energy 3–5km beneath Australia is recovered, there is a generation potential of 417,000 MW – more than 10 times the power currently generated from coal or gas of 40,647 MW current installed generation capacity in Australia (source: Hot Dry Rocks Pty, see www.hotdryrocks.com). Figure 6.15 shows a geothermal map of the USA indicating where power generation is possible. The figure illustrates that most of the US is suitable for power generation.

Geothermal resources in the US

Figure 6.15

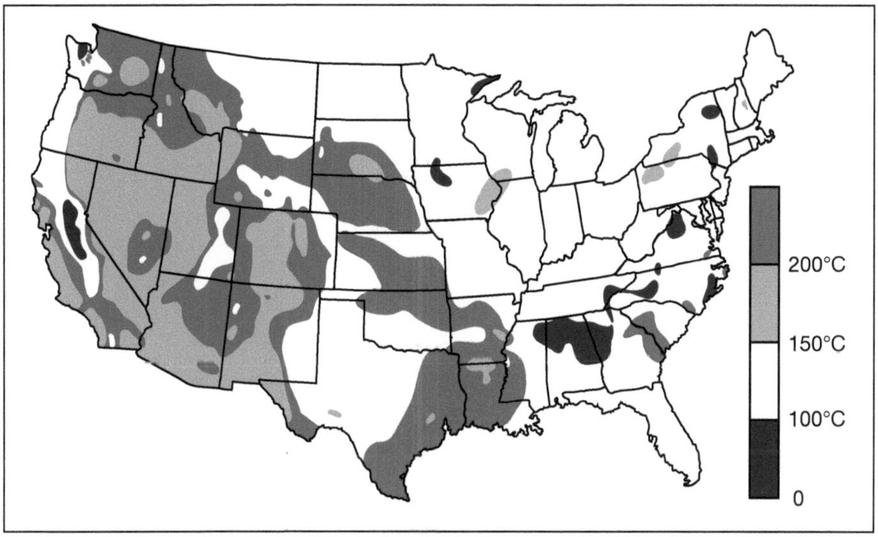

Estimated temperatures at 6km depth
Source: US Geological Survey, USGS 790

Environmental impacts

Geothermal energy does not produce pollution and does not contribute to greenhouse gases. No fuel is needed and only minimal pumping is required; once this power station is built it is almost free to run. However, there are very few places where you can build a geothermal power station. The rocks must be of the correct variety – hot rocks – but at a depth where they can be drilled. The overburden covering these rocks is also important in that it must be of a type that can be easily drilled.

One major downside to geothermal heat is that occasionally hazardous gases and minerals may seep from underground, and can be difficult and expensive to safely dispose of. But an upside is that geothermal plants may produce solid waste materials, or sludges requiring disposal in approved sites. Some of these solids, including zinc, silica and sulphur, are now considered valuable and are being sold separately, making the geothermal resource even more valuable and environmentally friendly.

7

Carbon and Environmental Commodities

Andrew Pisano
Senior Manager of Marketing and Development, GreenX,
A CME Group Company, New York

BACKGROUND AND CONTEXT

In February of 2003, Shell Trading and Nuon Energy Trade (now a subsidiary of European electricity giant Vattenfall) completed the first ever trade of a European carbon allowance, signalling the beginning of a new commodity market. Over the next several years, the market continued to develop: multinational energy companies, investment banks and hedge funds expanded their energy trading desks to include carbon traders, whilst the top commodity exchanges developed standardised derivative contracts, promoting transparency and liquidity in the marketplace. What happened in Europe was imitated in other parts of the world. Niche carbon markets progressed in North America, New Zealand and even in the developing world. Carbon, along with other greenhouse and hazardous gases, collectively made up the fastest growing class of commodities over the past decade: emissions. Today, nearly 10 billion tonnes of gas worth nearly €100bn are traded every year. In this chapter we will investigate how these commodities are created, explore the emissions trading programmes that give them value, and delve into how a firm might manage its exposure to these environmental risks.

ECONOMICS OF CLIMATE CHANGE

In 2006, British economist Lord Nicholas Stern claimed that 'Climate change is the greatest market failure the world has seen' (*The Stern Review*, Cambridge University Press, 2007). In his 700-page review on the economics of climate change, Lord Stern paints an apocalyptic picture of a planet that fails to curb global greenhouse gas (GHG) emissions. The fundamental tenet of Stern's theory is that carbon and other GHGs are negative externalities: costs that are not reflected in the price of a good or service which are borne by society rather than the individual or firm. In the case of climate change, every citizen of the Earth – current and future generations – will share the cost of global warming.

Negative externalities are effectively priced when producers bear these social costs. Figure 7.1, a generic diagram, illustrates how inefficient pricing of negative externalities causes the producer's private marginal cost curve to lie below society's. The effect is that price (P) is too low to cover the true costs of production and an excessively high quantity (Q) is produced. Factoring in social costs causes the optimal price (P*) to be higher, resulting in less output (Q*).

Figure 7.1

Demand curve with social costs

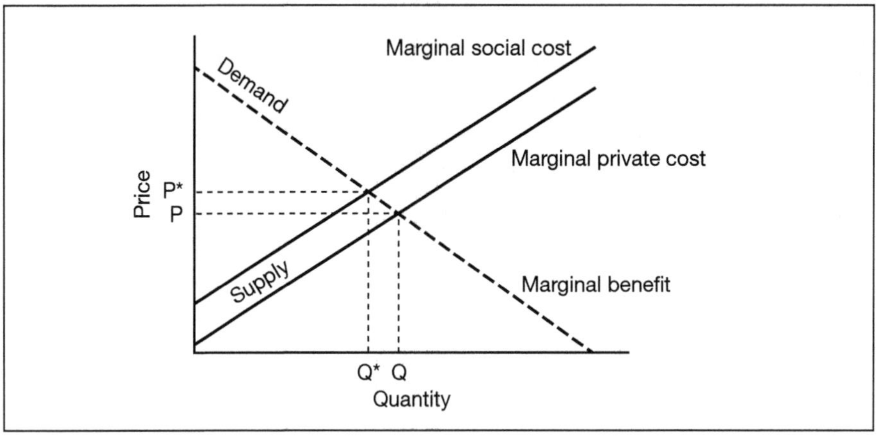

Source: Andrew Pisano, GreenX, a CME Group Company

There are several approaches to establishing a price on carbon. Command and control regulations, taxation and market-based solutions are various ways to skin the cat, but the goal of each is, as much as possible, to factor in the full social cost of polluting, thereby motivating individuals and firms to embrace a change to a low-carbon economy.

Arguments can be made for and against each methodology, but from an environmental and economic perspective, market-based solutions provide the best opportunity for achieving emissions reductions at the lowest cost to society. Well-designed and well-regulated emissions trading programmes harness the power of the market, efficiently driving capital to cleaner technologies. It's important to note that trading programmes can be designed to solve a number of environmental issues, all stemming from the inability to price pollution. The largest and most common market-based solutions address carbon dioxide and the other GHGs (e.g. methane, nitrous oxide, hydrofluorocarbons, perfluorocarbons and sulphur hexafluorides); however, other programmes exist to control acid rain and water pollution. Through the implementation of emissions trading programmes around the world, new asset classes are born: environmental commodities. Before we dive into the tools of the trade, it's important to first understand the fundamentals of emissions trading and how these commodities are created.

AN OVERVIEW OF EMISSIONS TRADING

Emissions trading is comprised of two different types of markets: allowance markets and credit markets.

Allowance market trading

Terminology

Allowance	A legally defined unit, e.g. AAU, RGA, EUA, allowing the holder to emit one tonne of CO_2, or another specific unit of greenhouse gas. These are also known as emission allowances or emission permits.
Greenhouse Gases (GHGs)	Gases found in the Earth's atmosphere that absorb infra-red radiation. Some GHGs are man-made whilst others occur naturally. Under the Kyoto Protocol, six GHGs are covered – carbon dioxide (CO_2) *most important*, hydrofluorocarbons (HFCs), methane (CH_4), nitrous oxide (N_2O), perfluorocarbons (PFCs) and sulphur hexafluoride (SF_6).

In an allowance market, the fundamental and essential trading mechanism is known as cap and trade. Using historical emissions data[1] as a benchmark, a government or regulatory authority will set a total market limit, or as the name implies a 'cap', on the amount of pollution it will allow over a specific amount of time, generally a year. Over time, the cap will decrease, eventually reaching a target emissions level. The cap is then allocated or auctioned to regulated entities in the form of allowances. Think of an allowance as an emissions permit, or the right to pollute by a given quantity of emissions; typically, one allowance gives the holder the right to emit one tonne of that particular pollutant. The total number of allowances in the system will thus equal the cap. Figure 7.2 illustrates the basic relationship of emissions and a cap in a simple system. Where Firms A and B have the same cap level, Firm A may exceed the cap, but the overage will be offset by Firm B reducing its emissions below the cap level.

All firms that have obligations under the cap are then required to monitor and report their emissions to the regulating authority. For many industrial processes, emissions can be physically measured by sensors that are attached to chimneys and smokestacks. Where this is not feasible, regulators rely on theoretical formulas to estimate emissions levels based on the thermal capacity of the unit and the amount and type of fuel used in the combustion process. Importantly, all emission reports are assessed by independent third party verifiers according to regulatory procedures. At the end of the year, each entity reports how much it emitted and is then required to

[1] Using historical emissions as the method of allocation is referred to as grandfathering. Another way of setting the cap includes best available technology benchmarks, to be used in EU ETS phase 3.

Example of a cap in a two-firm system

Figure 7.2

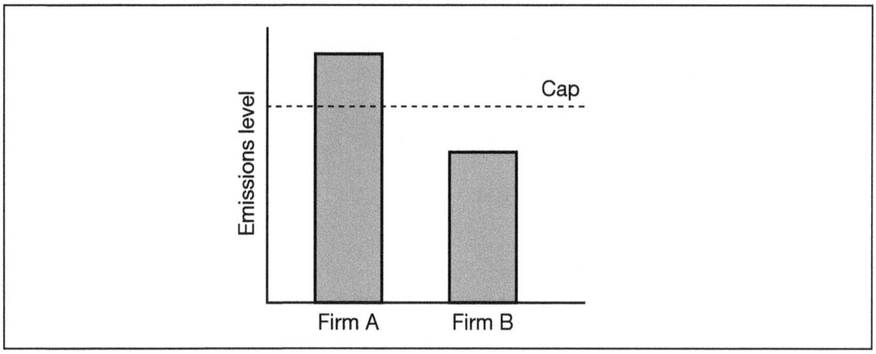

Source: Andrew Pisano, GreenX, a CME Group Company

surrender enough allowances to cover its emissions for the year. Entities have a few choices on how to comply with the cap-and-trade regulation. Firstly, an entity could decide to emit less, thereby lessening its need for allowances – potentially even below the cap, thus generating surplus allowances that could be sold on the market. The firm could do this by decreasing production or by becoming more efficient, say by installing cleaner technologies at its facilities. Secondly, a firm could continue polluting at its current rate and purchase, or trade for, allowances from another entity. This ensures that while emissions for some entities may increase, the total amount of emissions for the entire system does not exceed the cap.

The economic theory is that the reductions will occur at firms where the marginal abatement cost (i.e. the cost of eliminating an additional unit of emission) is cheapest. These firms can then trade their surplus allowances to those entities where those reductions would be more expensive to achieve. It is this trading mechanism that enables the desired amount of reductions to occur at the lowest cost to the system. Also, some programmes allow entities one additional level of flexibility: the ability to save, or 'bank', allowances for use in future compliance periods. Figure 7.3 is a simple diagram that shows the economic benefits of cap and trade versus a command and control approach. In command and control regulation, governments specify how a company will meet its environmental goals. A regulator, for example, could require a firm to install emissions-reducing scrubbers at a facility, which could be costly. In the cap and trade model, the entity can meet its goal through internal abatement measures, trading for allowances, or a combination of both.

Figure 7.3 **Economic benefits of cap and trade over command and control**

No trading (command and control approach)			
	Firm A Reduce emissions 10% to 90 Mt CO2e Expected emissions: 100 Mt CO2e Marginal abatement cost: €20/tonne	**Firm B** Reduce emissions 10% to 90 Mt CO2e Expected emissions: 100 Mt CO2e Marginal abatement cost: €10/tonne	**Total of system**
Cost of compliance	€200,000,000	€100,000,000	€300,000,000
Total emissions	90 Mt	90 Mt	180 Mt
With trading (cap and trade approach)			
	Firm A Cap: 90 Mt CO2e Expected emissions: 100 Mt CO2e Marginal abatement cost: €20/tonne	**Firm B** Cap: 90 Mt CO2e Expected emissions: 100 Mt CO2e Marginal abatement cost: €10/tonne	
	Firm A does not reduce emissions, but buys 10 Mt of allowances from Firm B at €15/tonne	Firm B reduces 20 Mt internally and sells 10 Mt of excess allowances to Firm A at €15/tonne	
Cost of compliance	€150,000,000	(20 Mt x €10/tonne) – (10 Mt x €15/tonne) = €50,000,000	€200,000,000
Total emissions	100 Mt	80 Mt	180 Mt

Note: Global warming potential of greenhouse gases is measured in MT CO2e, or metric tonnes of carbon dioxide equivalent.

Source: Andrew Pisano, GreenX, a CME Group Company

Credit market trading

The second type of emissions trading market is a credit market, often introduced in conjunction with a cap and trade market. In a credit market, regulators allow firms to offset their emissions by funding emissions reduction projects outside of the capped system, in non-trading sectors or even in other countries. To ensure that the environmental goal of reducing emissions is met, the credits must come from projects that are verified and validated through an accredited process and are 'additional', meaning the projects would not have occurred without the credit market mechanism. The types of emissions credits generated from these investments are called offsets and are an important design function of emissions trading for a number of reasons. Firstly, as it allows companies to tap into cheaper emission reductions in non-trading sectors or in the developing world, it provides a cost-effective alternative for compliance entities instead of reducing internal emissions or by trading for an allowance. In the fight against global warming, it doesn't matter where in the world the reductions take place – a tonne reduced in the US or in India will have the same impact on the atmosphere. Secondly, offsets allow for the transfer of clean energy technologies and know-how from the developed to the developing world, while promoting economic development outside the capped sectors. It should be noted that there are often limits on the amounts of offsets that can be used in a cap and trade system, to ensure that a meaningful amount of emission reductions takes place in the trading sector. We'll explore offsets in more detail when we discuss the specific programmes in the next section.

EMISSIONS TRADING SCHEMES

The European Union Emissions Trading Scheme

Bragging rights for the largest carbon market in the world (€76bn in 2011, source: Point Carbon) belong to the Europeans. Launched in 2005, the European Union Emissions Trading Scheme (EU ETS) covers more than 10,000 installations in the electricity generation and industrial sectors. The currency of the EU ETS is the European Union Allowance, commonly referenced as the EUA. The programme is divided into three multi-year trading periods, although the programme has no sunset clause and will in principle continue beyond these three periods.

The first phase (2005–2007), which covered nearly 40 per cent of EU GHG emissions, was essentially a trial period. This period was oversupplied with allowances and EUA prices collapsed as the period expired. In the second phase (2008–2012), the scope of the programme expanded significantly as Iceland, Liechtenstein and Norway joined the scheme, and the use of offsets as a compliance mechanism proliferated. Figure 7.4 shows EU ETS allowance prices and OTC/exchange traded volumes since 2004.

Figure 7.4

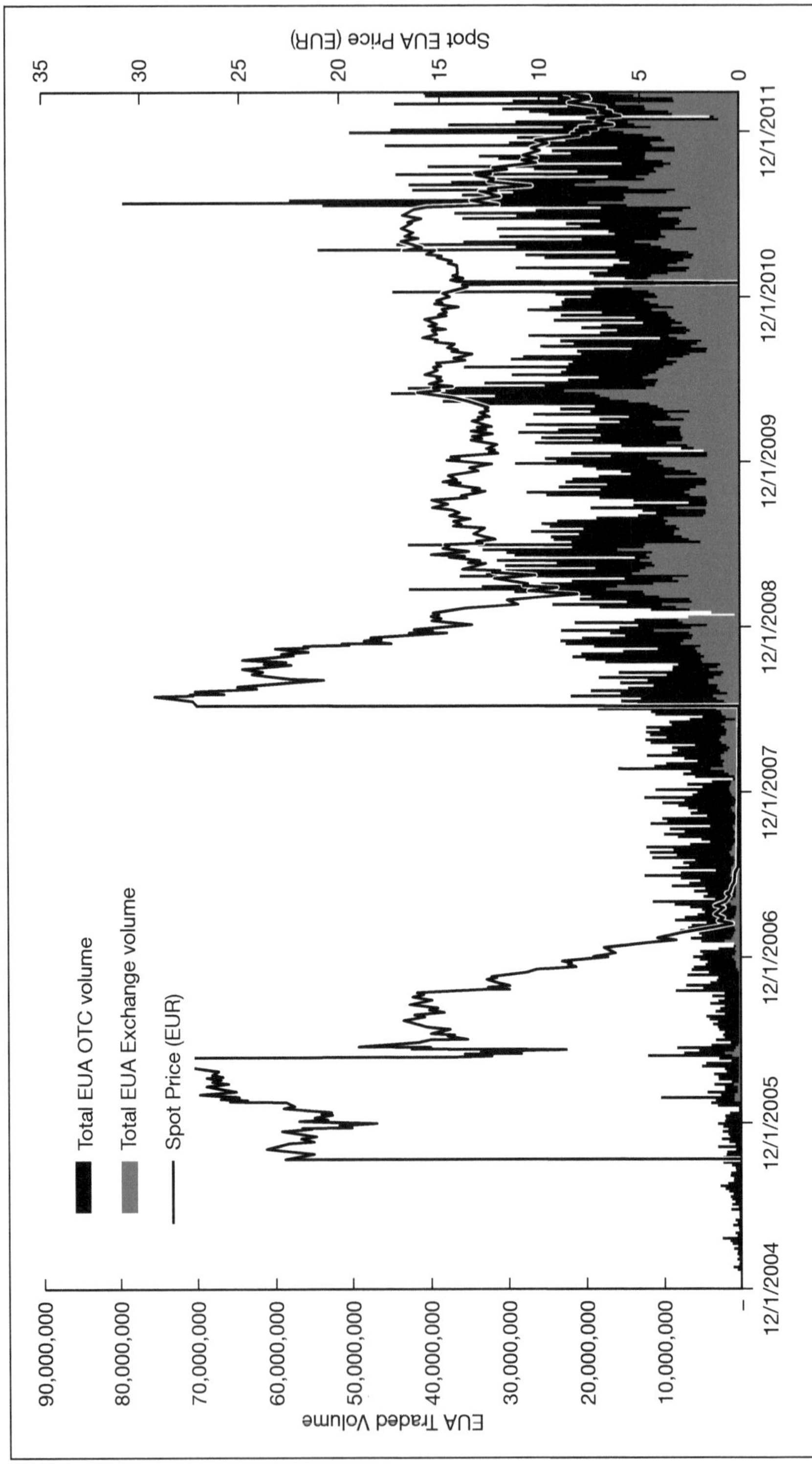

Source: Point Carbon, 2012 (Thomson Reuters)

Terminology

Offset credits or offsets	These include CERs and ERUs. These result from activities which can be used to meet compliance or voluntary objectives. Rather than reduce one's own emissions, these can also act as an alternative or supplement. Instead of allowances, Cap-and-trade schemes allow offsets to be used.
European Union Emissions Trading Scheme (EU ETS)	Launched on 1st January 2005, this trading scheme operates within the European Union and is the largest cap and trade program in the world.
European Union Allowance (EUA)	Under the EU ETS, this is a tradeable unit. Each EUA equals 1 tonne of CO_2.
Joint Implementation (JI)	Under the Kyoto Protocol, JI is one of three flexible mechanisms for transferring emissions permits from one Annex B country to another. ERUs are generated by JI and this is based on emission reduction projects which lead to quantifiable emissions reductions.

Through the EU's 'Linking Directive', compliance entities, i.e. companies covered under the EU ETS, were allowed to use offsets from the Kyoto Protocol's two credit flexibility mechanisms, the Clean Development Mechanism (CDM) and Joint Implementation (JI). The CDM allows for the creation of emission reduction projects in developing or industrialising countries (e.g. China, India and Brazil). JI gives EU ETS entities the opportunity to benefit from emissions reductions achieved from projects registered in transitional economies (e.g. Russia and Ukraine). Offsets generated from CDM and JI projects are called Certified Emission Reductions (CERs) and Emission Reduction Units (ERUs), respectively. Table 7.1 provides examples of CDM and JI project types.

Table 7.1 **Examples of CDM and JI project types**

Examples of Clean Development Mechanism Projects

- Capturing methane emitted at a landfill in Africa and using the gas to generate electricity
- Destroying nitric acid (N_20) waste gas at a chemical plant in India
- Substituting clinker with volcanic ash at a cement facility in Brazil
- Collecting methane from livestock at a farm in Mexico and generating electricity from the gas
- Installing a wind farm in rural China

Examples of Joint Implementation Projects

- Building a run-of-river hydroelectricity plant in Bulgaria
- Replacing heavy oil fired boilers with biomass fired boilers at a Ukrainian industrial site

Source: Andrew Pisano, GreenX, a CME Group Company

Beginning in 2012, the aviation sector will be included in the European cap and trade programme. Airlines will have their own separate tradable asset, European Union Aviation Allowances (EUAAs); however, airlines can meet their compliance obligations with EUAAs as well as EUAs and, to a limited extent, CERs and ERUs.

In Phase III of the EU ETS (2013–2020), entities have to comply with a more stringent cap as well as tighter restrictions on the use of offsets. Additionally, at least half of all allowances will be auctioned, decreasing a firm's reliance on free allocations.

Terminology

Emission Reduction Unit (ERU) An offset realised through a Joint Implementation project.

Clean Development Mechanism (CDM) Another Kyoto mechanism for project-based activities to reduce emissions in developing countries. Certified emission reductions or CERs occur from projects that lead to reductions in emissions that would not otherwise occur.

European Union Aviation Allowance (EUAA) Tradable unit under the EU ETS specifically for the aviation sector, each EUAA equals 1 tonne of CO_2.

Terminology continued

Certified Emission Reductions (CERs)	Carbon offsets generated through the UN's Clean Development Mechanism. CERs are realised from emission reduction projects in developing countries
California Carbon Allowance (CCA)	The tradable unit under the California ETS Each CCAA allowance equals 1 tonne of CO_2.
Carbon Dioxide Equivalent (CO_2e)	To illustrate the global warming potential (GWP) of greenhouse gases, this unit of measurement is used. Carbon dioxide is the reference against which other greenhouse gases are measured.

The California Emissions Trading Scheme

On 20 October 2011, the California Air Resources Board (ARB) finalised the rules for the state's greenhouse gas market-based compliance programme. The California Emissions Trading Scheme (Cal ETS), which will govern sources that attribute approximately 85 per cent of California's emissions, is scheduled to begin on 1 January 2013, after being delayed one calendar year. With 2.5 billion allowances under the cap between 2013 and 2020, California's cap and trade programme will be the largest in North America, and second only to the EU ETS in the world.

This programme is also divided into three multi-year compliance periods. The first compliance period (2013–2014) will cover electricity generating and industrial facilities exceeding 25,000 MT CO2e per year. The second (2015–2017) and third (2018–2020) compliance periods will include transportation fuels.

The newly created greenhouse gas asset is referred to as the CCA, or California Carbon Allowance. Similar to the EU ETS, California's programme will allow for the use of offsets. Covered entities can use up to 8 per cent of their cap with offsets. At the time of publication, four offset project types, or protocols, were approved by ARB:

- Forestry;
- Urban forestry;
- Agricultural methane;
- Ozone depleting substances.

ARB-approved projects must be sourced from reductions that occur in the US, Canada or Mexico.

Even though the programme is expected to begin on 1 January 2013, over the counter trading in allowance forward contracts started in early 2011. Exchange trading kicked off on 29 August 2011 with the first trade CCA futures deal booked on GreenX. Prices for the December 2013 delivery peaked (US$24.75) in the second week of trading but have since settled between US$13.50 and US$20.00 per allowance. Figure 7.5 shows CCA prices at the onset of trading.

Figure 7.5 **California Carbon Allowance futures prices**

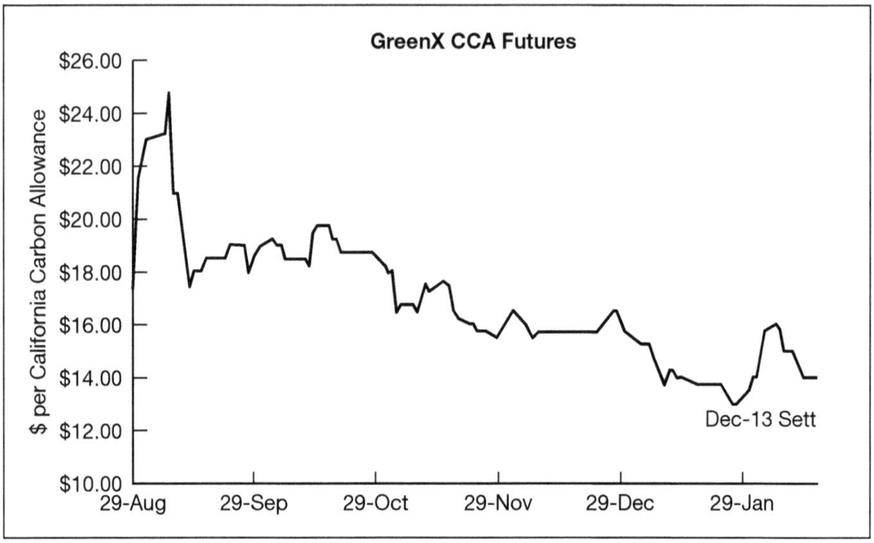

Source: Green Exchange, GreenX, a CME Group Company

Under the framework of the Western Climate Initiative (WCI), the Cal ETS has the ability to link, or join, with other state and provincial cap and trade programmes in the US and Canada. By permitting allowances to be fungible across jurisdictions, the linking mechanism immediately expands the size of the markets, thereby reducing the overall cost of compliance.

Regional Greenhouse Gas Initiative

Established in 2005, the Regional Greenhouse Gas Initiative (RGGI) is the first mandatory, market-based CO_2 emissions reduction programme in the United States. The nine Northeast and Mid-Atlantic signatory states[2] – Connecticut, Delaware, Maine, Maryland, Massachusetts, New Hampshire, New York, Rhode Island and Vermont – have agreed to reduce electricity-generated CO_2 emissions by 10 per cent by the year 2018. The first three-year compliance period began on 1 January 2009.

[2] New Jersey participated in Phase 1 of the programme.

RGGI applies to approximately 200 electricity generators across the nine states. Each state sets carbon emissions limits for its own power sector and enforces compliance through state regulation. However, the states agree that all CO_2 allowances from RGGI states are fungible with one another. In effect, the individual state programmes function as a single, regional cap and trade market for carbon emissions. The combination of a weak cap and economic recession contributed to a surplus of allowances in the first compliance period, resulting in depressed prices and little trading. Figure 7.6 tracks RGGI settlement prices on the Chicago Climate Futures Exchange (CCFE) from 2008 to 2011. Supplemental programme reviews (i.e. lowering the cap) have the opportunity to revive the programme and stimulate trading in future years.

Figure 7.6

Chicago Climate Futures Exchange settlement prices

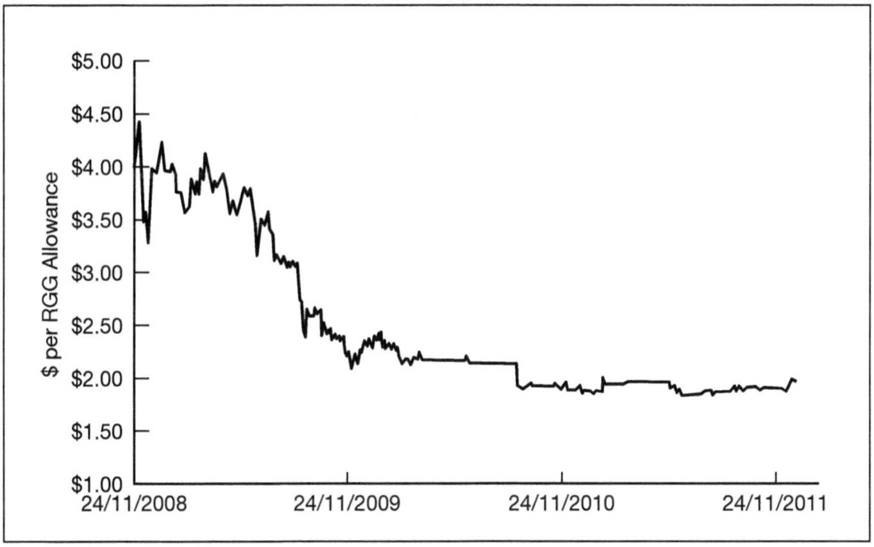

Source: Point Carbon (Thomson Reuters)

NO_x and SO_2

While the largest and best-known emissions trading programmes in the world focus on greenhouse gas emissions, the US Environmental Protection Agency's (EPA) Acid Rain Programme was the first federal cap and trade programme to achieve emissions reductions of nitrogen oxides (NO_x) and sulphur dioxide (SO_2) in the electric power industry. Under the programme, SO_2 emissions are set at a permanent cap requiring a 50 per cent reduction from 1980 emission levels by 2010. The Acid Rain Program was established as part of the 1990 reauthorisation of the Clean Air Act (CAA), which set a goal of reducing annual SO_2 emissions by 10 million tons below 1980 levels. In addition, the EPA NO_x programme requires a reduction of 10 million tons of NO_x per year below 1980 emissions.

In May 2005, the US EPA created the Clean Air Interstate Rule (CAIR). The CAIR programme is directed at further reducing NO_x and SO_2 emissions from the electric power sector across a 28-state region of the Eastern United States and the District of Columbia. The EPA required these states to revise their state implementation plans to include control measures to reduce emissions. The EPA developed a model cap and trade programme for the states to achieve the milestones set by CAIR. The existing Acid Rain Program continued with the overlay of a new CAIR SO_2 obligation, requiring 2010–2014 allowances to be surrendered at a 2:1 ratio and 2015 and later allowances to be surrendered at a 2.85:1 ratio. The CAIR programme was remanded by the US Court of Appeals in 2008, replaced by the Cross-State Air Pollution Rule (CSAPR) trading programme, and then later reinstated in 2012.

Terminology

Regional Greenhouse Gas Initiative (RGGI)	Cap and trade system operating in Connecticut, Delaware, Maine, Maryland, Massachusetts, New Hampshire, New York, Rhode Island and Vermont. Others are observing, notably, District of Columbia, Pennsylvania, the Eastern Canadian Provinces, and New Brunswick. This initiative monitors CO_2 emissions from power plants in the region, and by 2018 is seeking to reduce emissions by 10 per cent.
Emissions-to-cap (E-t-C)	To calculate this, subtract the seasonally adjusted cap from emissions (actual or forecasted). This will give an idea as to whether the market (for a specific period) produces more or less than the seasonally adjusted cap for that same period. If you do not take offsets into account, a positive (negative) E-t-C will mean that the market is short (long), which suggests a buy (sell) signal. E-t-C are also called Gap-to-cap.
Nitrogen oxides (NO_x)	Gases which are released when fossil fuels such as coal, gas and oil are burnt. This causes acid rain and other environmental problems, which include smog and excess plant growth in coastal waters. Various programs are aimed at reducing NO_x emissions, including the Acid Rain Program and NO_x cap and trade programs.

Terminology continued

Sulphur dioxide (SO_2)	Burning fossil fuels, such as oil and coal releases sulphur dioxide into the atmosphere which is the primary cause of acid rain. Selective EPA programs are aimed at reducing SO_2 emissions.

PRICING AND PRICE DISCOVERY – SUPPLY AND DEMAND

For the purpose of supply and demand analysis, we will focus on the EU ETS market. Like most commodities, the price of an emissions allowance or offset depends on a number of macroeconomic and microeconomic drivers.

Supply

The supply side in an allowance market is relatively straightforward. Since the cap is defined and fixed at the onset of a programme, supply is essentially set in stone (that is, of course, unless the government changes its mind and 'tweaks' the programme to achieve a greater or lesser target).

Allowances are created and distributed by the central regulating authority, the European Commission, according to member state national allocation plans (NAPs). In Phase III of the EU ETS, the allocation methodology will be centralised and utilise benchmarks rather than NAPs based on historical emissions. In addition, auctions will be the predominant method for supplying the market with allowances.

For credit markets, offset supply is primarily a function of market price in the EU ETS and the physical availability of suitable projects. As individual projects have unique financing structures, risk profiles and income streams, the profitability of a project is often determined by the price a project developer can receive for a CER or ERU in the secondary market. As allowance and offset prices decline, so too does the profitability of the underlying emissions reduction project. Not surprisingly, project developers are reluctant to launch projects when prices are deflated. Other factors that influence the supply of offsets include limits applied to the total usage of offsets, regulatory decisions on what offset projects are allowed, as well as the approval and issuance procedure for offsets, although this latter point mostly concerns the timing rather than the volume of offsets.

The emissions-to-cap ratio is a useful indicator for determining whether an entity, a particular sector or the entire system is long or short. The ratio is calculated by subtracting the seasonally adjusted cap from actual or forecast emissions. A positive emissions-to-cap ratio indicates that the market is fundamentally short, while a negative ratio means the market is long. When analysing supply, it's important to consider not only current and future supply, but also historical emissions levels and supply. Since entities are permitted to bank, or carry forward, allowances to future years and compliance periods, the impact of supply during periods in which the programme was 'long' needs to be assessed. The system is considered long when emissions for a given period of time fall below the level of the cap.

Demand

The demand side, on the other hand, is a little more complicated. Before we get into the drivers, it's important first to understand who are the buyers of compliance instruments; that is, who are the regulated entities. In the EU ETS, 73 per cent of the covered emissions in 2010 came from combustion installations, i.e. electricity generation. Various industrial processes – oil refining (7 per cent), steel manufacturing (6 per cent), and cement manufacturing (8 per cent) – contribute to the remainder of emissions. Table 7.2 shows EUA allocations by sector from 2005 to 2010.

Table 7.2 **EUA allocations by sector 2005–2010**

Year	2005	2006	2007	2008	2009	2010*
Combustion installations	1459	1471	1544	1511	1381	1408
Mineral oil refineries	151	150	154	155	146	144
Coke ovens	19	21	22	21	16	20
Metal ore roasting and silt	13	14	25	18	11	13
Pig iron or steel	129	133	132	133	95	114
Cement clinker	178	182	201	190	153	153
Glass and glass fibre	20	20	21	23	19	20
Ceramic products	15	15	15	13	9	9
Pulp, paper and board	30	30	29	32	28	30
Other activities	0	0	21	23	20	21
Total	2014	2036	2164	2119	1878	1932

*Data from Cyprus and a few additional installations missing.

Source: Point Carbon (Thomson Reuters)

In turn, allowance demand is dependent on the expected level of emissions from each of the sectors. For the electricity sector, emissions will depend on economic growth, electricity demand, fuel prices, as well as weather. In the industrial sectors, demand is heavily dependent on macro-economic factors. As economies grow, industrial output increases, as does emissions. To a lesser effect, energy efficiency improvements or other abatement strategies can help industrial entities decrease the need for compliance instruments. As we saw in 2011, future electricity sector emissions can also be tied to government policy. In the wake of the Fukushima disaster, Chancellor Angela Merkel decided to phase out nuclear power in Germany. The decision meant that electricity demand would most likely need to be met by fossil fuel generating sources. Examples of EUA price drivers can be found in Table 7.3.

Table 7.3

EUA price drivers

Driver	Impact on EUA price	Reason
Unexpected heat wave	↑	Electricity demand for cooling increases, resulting in more combustion
Prolonged periods of high wind	↓	Increased electricity generation from wind sources, lowers demand for fossil-fuel generated power
Higher GDP forecast	↑	Growing or expanding economy leads to higher demand for electricity and industrial output
Lower natural gas costs relative to coal costs	↓	Low natural gas costs could encourage fuel switching from dirty coal facilities to more efficient combined cycle natural gas plants
Nuclear outages	↑	Increased fossil fuel power production to compensate for loss of non-CO_2 emitting nuclear
Lower oil prices	↓	Lower oil prices result in lower gas prices, making gas fired power production more profitable against coal and reducing the total output of CO_2

Source: Author's analysis

HEDGING AND TRADING

The climate spread

With electricity generating sources contributing the majority of emissions covered under the EU ETS, it is useful to understand the price drivers of the sector and the relationship between the price of carbon and the price of fuel inputs (i.e. coal and natural gas). On average, coal is 2.5 times more CO_2 intensive, or 'dirtier', than natural gas. That is, for the same amount of electricity generation, a coal-fired generator would need 2.5 times more compliance instruments than the gas-fired generator for the same output.

Power generators, especially those operating in areas where coal-fired generation is common, are closely watching their clean dark spreads and clean spark spreads. The clean dark spread refers to the revenue a unit makes from selling electricity after netting out the cost of coal and carbon compliance. Similarly, the clean spark spread is the net revenue from electricity sales, factoring in gas and carbon costs (see Table 7.4).

Table 7.4 **Calculation for clean dark and spark spreads**

Clean dark spread = E – C – (N_{Coal}*P_{CO_2})
Where: E = Electricity price C = Coal price N_{Coal} = Number of compliance instruments to cover coal emissions P_{CO_2} = Price of a carbon allowance/offset
Clean spark spread = E – G – (N_{Gas}*P_{CO_2})
Where: E = Electricity price G = Natural gas price N_{Gas} = Number of compliance instruments to cover gas emissions P_{CO_2} = Price of a carbon allowance/offset

The difference between the clean dark spread and clean spark spread, referred to as the climate spread, is often considered the fundamental driver of the price of carbon in a cap and trade system:

Climate spread = Clean dark spread – Clean spark spread

A negative climate spread indicates that electricity generation from natural gas-fired units is more profitable than electricity generated from coal-fired plants. It may be caused by a rise in coal prices, a drop in gas costs, or an increase in allowance prices; but what's relevant is that a negative climate spread indicates a coal-fired generator would be more profitable if it switched its fuel source to natural gas.

Hedging instruments

At the onset of the EU ETS, nearly all trading occurred OTC. The spot market existed for immediate transfer of allowances and offsets, while the forward market developed for future delivery. Over time, an increased amount of volume migrated to the exchanges. The European Climate Exchange (ECX), which was later purchased by the Intercontinental Exchange (ICE), saw tremendous volume growth and remains the predominant secondary marketplace. Several other exchanges, such as the CME-backed Green Exchange, have emerged to challenge ICE's dominance and provide traders with an alternative venue. From 2009 to 2010, the spot market was plagued by incidences of VAT fraud and allegedly stolen compliance instruments. As market participants lost confidence in spot transactions, traders took comfort in the clearing model, which filtered allowances and offsets as they came through the clearing houses.

Now almost all trading in EUAs and CERs are cleared transactions, both over-the-counter cleared forwards and exchange traded futures. The standardised contract is for physical delivery of 1000 allowances or offsets. While futures contracts are listed for nearly all durations, the most liquid contract month is for the nearest December delivery. Physical settlement of compliance instruments is relatively simple via the electronic transfer of serial numbers in the registry system. Because of this straightforward, effortless process, it is not uncommon for a large percentage of open contracts to go to delivery upon expiration.

Hedging strategies

Hedging strategies will vary from firm to firm, but it's relatively safe to say that the majority of utilities and large industrial entities in the EU ETS deploy some level of hedging strategies to manage their environmental risk. In the power sector, it's not uncommon for a utility to be fully hedged for a full year's worth of generation. Let's take a look at an example where a European utility with coal-fired generation sells forward its power while hedging its exposure to fluctuating fuel and emissions allowance prices. In doing so, the utility is able to lock in a clean dark spread of €5 (Table 7.5).

Table 7.5 **Forward hedging of clean dark spread locks in profit**

In Q1 2012 a utility sold forward Q3 2013 power generation from coal-fired units	
Power sold forward at	€55/MWh
Coal costs locked in at	€38/MWh
Carbon costs locked in at	€12/MWh
Locked-in clean dark spread	**€5/MWh**

Fast-forward to when the power is due and we see that the markets have moved. The utility is now faced with a decision to deliver its own power or purchase it in the spot market to fulfil the forward contract (Table 7.6).

Table 7.6 **Spot clean dark spread is unprofitable**

Now in Q3 2013, the prices of electricity, fuel, and emissions allowances have changed	
Power price	€40/MWh
Coal costs	€30/MWh
Carbon costs	€15/MWh
Spot clean dark spread	**(€5/MWh)**

Since the spot clean dark spread is negative, the utility would be operating out of the money. It therefore decides to buy the power and sell the coal and carbon in the spot market, realising a €10 gain on the transaction. (Table 7.7).

Table 7.7 **Utility will be a buyer of power**

Utility will be a buyer of power	
Power sold forward at €55 is bought in the spot market at €40	€15/MWh
Coal purchased at €38 is sold in the spot market at €30	(€8/MWh)
Carbon purchase at €12 is sold in the spot market at €15	€3/MWh
Spot clean dark spread	**€10/MWh profit**

The allowance–offset swap

In the EU ETS, EUAs and offsets have the same compliance value – one tonne of CO2e – however, they trade at different prices for a variety of reasons. For one thing, the cost of abatement is more expensive in the EU than in the developing world. In addition, EU member states impose limits on the percentage of CERs and ERUs that can be used for compliance, thereby creating a higher demand for EUAs.

Firms that are under their offset quota can take advantage of this price differential by swapping allowances for offsets. In a cash-neutral swap, the trade is volume-adjusted based on the spot EUA–CER (or EUA–ERU) spread. For example, if EUAs were trading at €10 and CERs at €8, a firm could swap EUAs for an additional 20 per cent CER. In a one-for-one swap, EUAs can be traded for an equivalent number of CERs plus cash. Using the previous example, €2 would be included with the transfer of each CER. Figure 7.7 shows the spread between the December 2012 deliveries of the corresponding EUA and CER futures contracts from 2005 to 2012.

EUA–CER spread 2005–2012

Figure 7.7

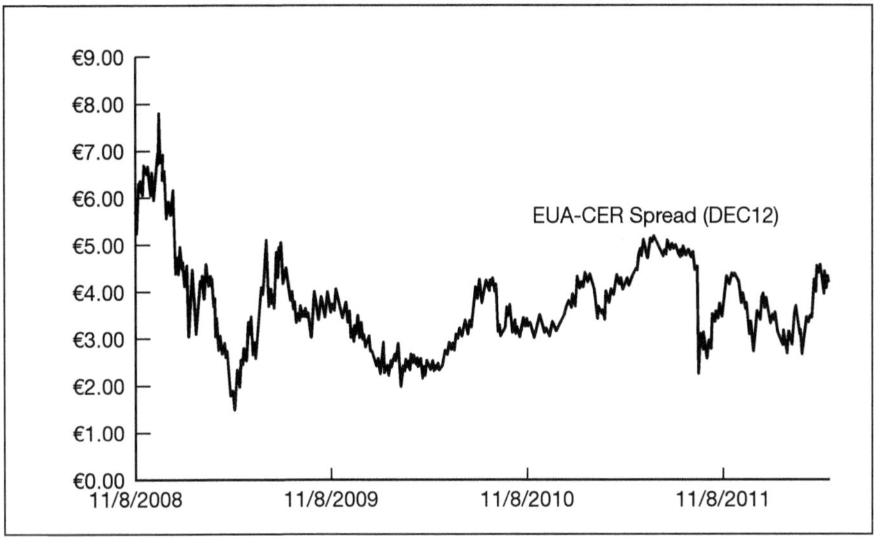

Source: GreenX, a CME Group Company

THE FUTURE OF EMISSIONS TRADING

EU ETS has no sunset clause and will most likely continue beyond Phase III. The outlook for a federal US cap and trade programme essentially died with Kerry–Lieberman in 2010, as the likelihood of another Democrat majority in the House and Senate is not expected anytime soon. So, the US and Canada will rely on their regional markets, with more states and provinces joining in as WCI and RGGI prove successful.

In Asia, there is promise that the world's largest polluter, China, will establish a national cap and trade scheme. The success of six regional pilot programmes (scheduled to launch in 2013) could determine the country's willingness to move forward with a national carbon market in 2015 or beyond. Meanwhile, South Korea continues to make strides towards a compliance market starting in 2015. Assuming the programme gets off the ground, it is likely that companies will be allowed to use CERs to meet their compliance obligations.

Below the equator, Australia is expected to launch its carbon market in 2015 following a 2.5 year trial with a fixed carbon tax. In New Zealand, the second compliance period kicks off in 2013 and will require installations to surrender allowances and offsets to cover 100 per cent of the emissions, up from 50 per cent in the first phase of the programme.

It wasn't so long ago that analysts were forecasting a $2–3 trillion global carbon market. Allowances would be traded freely across international borders, offsets would be the primary mechanism by which wealth would be transferred from the developed to the developing world, and the planet would come together to combat climate change. But with the Kyoto Protocol expiring in 2012, the prospect of such a programme seems unlikely in the near future. The 2011 UNFCCC (United Nations Framework Convention on Climate Change) annual Conference of the Parties (COP) in Durban, however, yielded a somewhat favourable outcome in the fight against climate change as delegates agreed to a roadmap to a legally enforceable agreement to be in place by 2020. It's still unclear what mechanism will prevail in the next rounds of negotiations. So, until then, carbon will continue to be traded in smaller, regional markets.

8

Precious Metals

Jeffrey Rhodes
Global Head of Precious Metals and CEO, INTL Commodities DMCC, Dubai

INTRODUCTION – A PERSONAL VIEW

My career in the financial markets started in 1971 when as a junior in the cash department of the Bowater Corporation, Knightsbridge, I was charged with preparing paperwork for bills of exchange and for the purchasing of foreign currency to pay for imports into the UK of wood pulp. This was when the developed world was coming off the fixed foreign exchange parity system that had been in existence since the Bretton Woods agreement after World War II, and partially floating currencies were allowed. I recall that sterling versus US dollars, or 'cable' as it is still commonly called, was allowed to float between 2.20 and 2.60 and my job was to buy the dollars to match the payment schedules for our large-scale purchase contracts. The amounts were sizeable, as much as $50m a ticket, and it occurred to me that rather than waiting until the contract was due we could or should use the nascent forward foreign exchange markets to ensure that we knew our actual costs well ahead of time, which would of course help in the efficient management of our cash flows. I remember making this suggestion to the Chief Cashier, Mr Richardson, who thought it a good idea, and I had his permission to take it to the company's Financial Director, who will remain nameless, for reasons you are about to hear. My proposal to hedge our large foreign exchange risk in the new world of floating exchange rates was dismissed out of hand as being an unnecessary change to our existing procedures, and who was I anyway to make such suggestions. Rather amusingly, much later in my career, that very same FD of Bowater, who by now was involved in the precious metals industry, came in for a meeting with myself and other senior colleagues to request much larger forward lines to facilitate his company's hedging programme. He never recognised me, but I did him and I took great delight in reminding him of our earlier encounter. The spat with Mr FD of Bowater convinced me that I needed to move to one of the many banks with which we did our forex business if I wanted to develop a career in the financial markets.

This took me to Samuel Montagu, a blue-blooded merchant bank that was one of the five members of the London Gold Fix, held every morning and afternoon at the offices of Rothschild. Samuel Montagu was also a member of the mystical silver fix, which was often compared to 'electing the Pope', comprised three member firms and was held 'in camera' at Montagu's offices daily around noon; it also participated in the daily platinum and palladium quotations.

I joined Montagu as a management trainee under a programme that would see me spend time in various departments before moving into forex dealing. My first stop was in the currency accounts department, where my existing knowledge proved to be of some value, and within a very short period of time I was awarded a number of promotions to the extent that I never completed the management training programme but ended up as a manager of 50 staff at the tender age of 25. However, I had not given up the dream of becoming a dealer, and after writing a paper for the board on the management of the bank's short-term liquidity using gold, I was invited in 1979 to become a bullion dealer. While this was perhaps the most glamorous department in the bank, I was strangely reticent at first; after all, I was giving up a solid position in charge of a large number of staff to become the number three gold trader. Still I took the plunge and, as they say, 'the rest is history'.

Despite my forex background, I really had no idea about gold trading or how to do deals. It was around midday when the chief gold trader and his second in command suddenly announced that they were going to lunch and handed me the gold blotter with instructions 'to make money'. As I said, I was pretty clueless but the other colleagues on the desk were really kind and told me they would look after me. The telephone rang and I answered 'Montagu'. The German voice on the line asked who I was; I answered 'Jeff Rhodes'. 'New, are you?' said the chief dealer of a famous German bank very active in gold back in the late 1970s and early 1980s. 'Yes,' I answered, 'this is my first day, and in fact hopefully this will be my first gold deal.' 'OK, young man, please buy 20 bars of gold [one bar equalled 400 fine troy ounces] for me and call me back.' The protocol then was for bullion banks to deal with each other in amounts expressed in bars, with 10 bars, or 4000 fine troy ounces, being the typical dealing size. I told my colleagues what the client wanted and they helped me to conclude the deal, telling me how important and influential this particular bank was in the gold market. Even on that first day I had enough market 'nous' about me to realise that this kind of buying could move the market higher and so I bought 30 bars, of which 10 were for our own account. On reporting back the order fill to the client, I was told, 'very well done, young man, now buy 20 bars more'. This happened four times in total and when the two senior gold traders returned an hour later after lunch they found me with a 16,000 ounce position with a marked-to-market profit of $100,000 plus. I guess you could say that I had arrived in the international gold market and that I have not looked back since.

In late 1980, I was working late when the Director of Trading asked me if I fancied a three-month stint at Montagu's New York office, an offer I could not refuse. This became closer to two years – the toughest and most rewarding period of my career. As the saying goes, 'if you can make it in New York, you can make it anywhere', and what I learned back in 1981 and 1982 stood me in good stead ever since. When I returned to the UK I was much further up the ladder and eventually became Chief Dealer at one of the world's leading bullion banks.

In 1988 I joined Credit Suisse in London as its Chief Bullion Dealer, but while I had physically left Samuel Montagu, emotionally Montagu never left me and to this day it remains the happiest part of my career. After seven good years at Credit Suisse, at the start of 1995 I was lured away to join Standard Bank in London, enthused by the challenge of helping one of South Africa's leading banking groups to become the first bank from the world's largest gold-producing nation to become a major force in the global gold market. This proved to be a great success, with Standard Bank today one of the world's leading bullion banks. After emerging from the difficult apartheid years, Standard Bank's senior management wanted to build out an international infrastructure, which included establishing a presence in the Middle East; because of my extensive knowledge of the region I was asked in March 1996 to write a business plan and submit an application to the Central Bank of the United Arab Emirates to establish a Representative Office in Dubai. Approval was granted and in February 1997 I flew to Dubai with a briefcase, some good ideas, lots of enthusiasm but little else to set up the office. My initial idea was to stay in Dubai long enough to get things off the ground, perhaps six months at the most, and I had no intention of becoming 'a long-term expat'; however, here I am 15 years later with no burning desire to return to the UK.

I am proud that today Standard Bank has become the market leader in the region's physical gold and silver markets, and after I had taken the bank into Dubai's newly developed Financial Centre Free Zone as a full branch, the time had come to try to 'do it again'. In February 2007, after almost 30 years working for bullion banks, I defected to the other side of the market along with my colleague of 20 years, Barry Canham, to set up a physically based trading business under the umbrella of International Assets Holding Corporation, a US-based financial services company. INTL has grown exponentially in the five years that I have been with the firm, and after merging with FC Stone in 2010 to become INTL/FC Stone Inc. the company ranks number 51 in the US Fortune 500 List, based on gross revenues. I hope readers have found my story of some interest, and perhaps it might act as encouragement for aspiring young dealers from whichever walk of life or background you might come from. My message is work hard, do your best and who knows what you might be able to achieve.

BACKGROUND AND CONTEXT: THE LONDON BULLION MARKET

London is the focus of the international over the counter (OTC) market for gold and silver, with a client base that includes the majority of the central banks that hold gold, producers, refiners, fabricators and other traders throughout the world. Members of the London bullion market typically trade with each other and with their clients on a principal-to-principal basis, which means that all risks, including those of credit, are between the two counterparts to a transaction.

The London bullion market is a wholesale market, where minimum traded amounts for clients are generally 1000 ounces of gold and 50,000 ounces of silver. The OTC market allows flexibility, unlike a futures exchange, where trading is based around standard contract units, settlement dates and delivery specifications. It also provides confidentiality, as transactions are conducted between the two principals involved.

Bullion market history

Records trace bullion transactions in London back to 1684 with the formation of the oldest market member, Mocatta & Goldsmid. It was, however, the introduction of the London Silver Fixing in 1897 and the London Gold Fixing in 1919 that marked the beginning of the current market's structure. The five members of the London Gold Fixing dominated the UK marketplace until 1980 when, fuelled by oil price inflation and spiralling international tension, gold reached $850 per ounce and silver $50. The level of activity and profitability in the market drew increasing global attention, resulting in an influx of international players to London, allowing the city to become the international arena that it is today. The growth in the number and type of market participants, combined with the introduction of the Financial Services Act in 1986, brought about the formation of the LBMA (London Bullion Market Association) in 1987.

Loco London – what is it?

Loco London is an important concept as it represents the basis for international trading and settlement in gold and silver. Most global OTC gold and silver trading is cleared through the London bullion market clearing system, with deals between global parties settled and cleared in London. In the second half of the nineteenth century, London developed as the centre through which gold from the mines of California, South Africa and Australia was refined and then sold. With this business as a base, and supported by the increasing acceptance of the London Good Delivery List, London bullion dealing houses established global client relationships. These clients opened bullion accounts with individual London trading houses. It soon became evident that these 'loco London' accounts, while used to settle transactions between bullion dealer and client, could also be used to settle transactions with other parties by transfers of bullion in London. Today, all such third party transfers on behalf of clients of the London market are processed through the London bullion clearing system. A credit balance on a loco London account represents a holding of gold or silver in the same way that a credit balance in the relevant currency represents a holding of dollars on account with a New York bank or yen with a Tokyo bank.

Key features

Trading unit

For gold, this is one fine troy ounce, and for silver one troy ounce. With gold, the unit represents pure gold irrespective of the purity of a particular bar, whereas for silver it represents one ounce of material where a minimum of 999 parts in every 1000 will be silver.

Loco London spot price

This is the basis for virtually all transactions in gold and silver in London. It is a quotation made by dealers based on US dollars per fine ounce for gold and US dollars per ounce for silver. Settlement and delivery for both metals is two business days in London after the dealing date. From this basis price, dealers can offer material of varying fineness, bar size or form.

Unit for delivery of loco London gold

This is the London Good Delivery gold bar, with a minimum fineness of 995.0 and gold content of between 350 and 430 fine ounces with the bar weight expressed in multiples of 0.025 of an ounce – the smallest weight used in the market. Bars are generally close to 400 ounces or 12.5 kilograms.

Unit for delivery of loco London silver

This is the London Good Delivery silver bar, with a minimum fineness of 999 and a recommended weight between 750 and 1100 ounces, although bars between 500 and 1250 ounces will be accepted. Bars generally weigh around 1000 ounces. Both gold and silver bars must conform to the specifications for Good Delivery set by the LBMA.

Other bullion bars

A variety of smaller exact weight bars is available to wholesale clients in addition to Good Delivery bars. The fine gold content of exact weight bars is determined by their fineness. A client pays only for the fine gold content.

Clearing

The London bullion market relies on a daily clearing system; members offering clearing services utilise the unallocated gold and silver accounts they maintain between each other for the settlement of mutual trades as well as third-party transfers. These transfers are conducted on behalf of clients and other members of the London bullion market in settlement of their own loco London bullion activities. This system avoids the security risks and costs that would be involved in the physical movement of bullion. A bullion clearing member nets out gold transactions, much as banks do in trading foreign exchange. Only the net difference between total purchases and total sales is actually transferred. A bullion clearing bank may take physical delivery of bullion, whereas a foreign exchange clearing bank only takes delivery of foreign exchange in the form of accounting entries. There are currently seven members of the London Bullion Clearing System. Historically the volume of precious metals cleared by the members of the LBMA was kept confidential, but in January 1997 the LBMA released turnover figures for the first time and the latest figures show that in January 2012 the average daily gold clearing was 22.2 million ounces worth US$36.7 billion while the average daily clearing volume for silver was 149.2 million ounces with a value of US$4.59 billion. The highest ever daily average clearing volume for gold was recorded in August 2011, when 25.9 million ounces of gold worth US$45.5 billion was traded. The record in silver was posted in May 2011 when 259.3 million ounces with a value of US$9.53 billion cleared through the London market.

Key features continued

BULLION ACCOUNTS

Unallocated accounts

A bullion account is an account where specific bars are not set aside and the customer has a general entitlement to the metal. It is the most convenient, cheapest and most commonly used method of holding metal. The units of these accounts are one fine ounce of gold and one ounce of silver based upon a 995 LGD (London Good Delivery) gold bar and a 999 fine LGD silver bar respectively. Transactions may be settled by credits or debits to the account, while the balance represents the indebtedness between the two parties. Credit balances on the account do not entitle the creditor to specific bars of gold or silver, but are backed by the general stock of the bullion dealer with whom the account is held. The client is an unsecured creditor. Should the client wish to receive actual metal, this is done by 'allocating' specific bars or equivalent bullion product, the fine gold content of which is then debited from the allocated account.

Allocated accounts

These accounts are opened when a customer requires metal to be physically segregated and needs a detailed list of weights and assays. The client has full title to the metal in the account, with the dealer holding it as a custodian. Clients' holdings are identified in a weight list of bars showing the unique bar number, gross weight, the assay or fineness of each bar and its fine weight. Credits or debits to the holding will be processed by physical movements of bars to or from the client's physical holding.

SUPPLY AND DEMAND

Total supply versus fabrication demand

Gold

Table 8.1 shows that total supply (i.e. primary gold production combined with secondary supply – recycled scrap metal) was 4424 tonnes in 2011, a modest 1.7 per cent higher than 4350 tonnes in 2010. Total fabrication demand was marginally lower in 2011 at 2771 tonnes versus 2784 tonnes in 2010. However, the average gold price rose by 29 per cent from 2010 to 2011, resulting in a massive US$83 billion surplus of supply over demand.

Table 8.1 **Gold supply v. fabrication demand**

Gold (tonnes)	2010	2011
Total physical supply	4350	4424
Total fabrication demand	2784	2771
Supply versus demand surplus/deficit	1566	1653
Average gold price US$	1224.08	1571.64
US$ value of surplus/deficit (million)	61341	83133

Source: Thomson Reuters; table courtesy INTL

Silver

Table 8.2 shows that silver's total supply in 2011 grew by 5 per cent to 1019 million ounces while total fabrication demand rose by 4 per cent to 914 million ounces. Although modest changes, the average silver price in 2011 versus 2010 rose by a staggering 51 per cent, which meant that the supply surplus in US dollar terms grew by 78 per cent to US$3.2 billion in 2011. This figure represents investment buying of what is known as the 'industrial precious metal'.

Table 8.2

Silver supply v. fabrication demand

Silver (million ounces)	2010	2011
Total physical supply	968	1019
Total fabrication demand	879	914
Supply versus demand surplus/deficit	89	105
Average silver price US$	20.1219	30.4200
US$ value of surplus/deficit (million)	1791	3194

Source: Thomson Reuters; table courtesy INTL

Platinum and palladium

Tables 8.3 and 8.4 show that the total supply of platinum in 2011 was barely higher at 7,948,000 ounces in 2011 compared to 2010 while fabrication demand was virtually unchanged at 7,238,000. This resulted in a modest supply surplus valued at US$1.22 billion in 2011, 13 per cent higher than US$1.08 billion in 2010. The average platinum price rose by 7 per cent in 2011 over 2010. Total supply of palladium rose by just under 2 per cent to 9,298,000 ounces in 2011 while total fabrication demand posted a 3.5 per cent gain to reach 8,842,000 ounces. This meant that although the average palladium price surged by 40 per cent, the supply surplus grew by less than 7 per cent, the lowest surplus increase in US dollar terms across the precious metals sector in 2011.

Table 8.3

Platinum supply v. fabrication demand

Platinum ('000 ounces)	2010	2011
Total physical supply	7900	7948
Total fabrication demand	7230	7238
Supply versus demand surplus/deficit	670	710
Average platinum price US$	1608.98	1721.86
US$ value of surplus/deficit (million)	1078	1223

Table 8.4

Palladium supply v. fabrication demand

Palladium ('000 ounces)	2010	2011
Total physical supply	9135	9298
Total fabrication demand	8540	8842
Supply versus demand surplus/deficit	595	456
Average palladium price US$	525.51	733.30
US$ value of surplus/deficit (million)	313	334

Source: Thomson Reuters GFMS Gold Survey and Johnson Matthey Annual Review; table courtesy INTL

Precious metals deficit/surplus

Table 8.5 and Figure 8.1 show that the total value of primary and secondary supply of precious metals in 2011 was US$87,884 billion, which was absorbed by investment demand from both the private and public sectors, with investment fund managers continuing to plough cash into all four precious metals along with the official sector moving to the buy side in gold after almost 30 years of being an important source of selling. Although the fans of the white metals might disagree, this data illustrates perfectly just how much gold dominates the precious metals space. The scary fact is that for gold's record-breaking bull run, which began in the summer of 2001 when the price broke above US$260 per ounce to continue, fresh investment inflows of at least US$100 billion are required, While I am still bullish for 2012, when the music stops there will be nowhere to sit and a US$500 reversal is entirely possible.

Table 8.5 **Precious metals deficit/surplus**

US$ value of deficit/surplus (million)	2010	2011
Gold	61341	83133
Silver	1791	3194
Platinum	1078	1223
Palladium	313	334

Source: Thomson Reuters GFMS Gold Survey and Johnson Matthey Annual Review; table courtesy INTL

Figure 8.1 **Precious metals deficit/surplus**

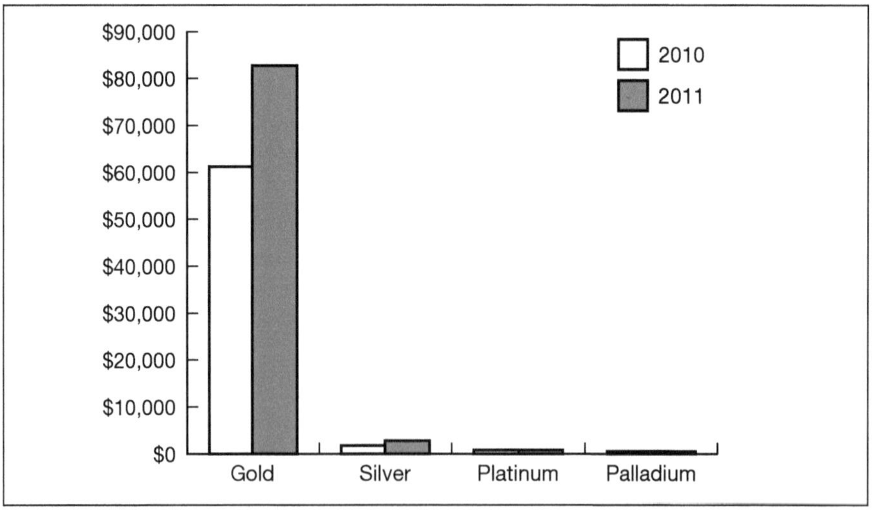

Source: Thomson Reuters GFMS Gold Survey and Johnson Matthey Annual Review, chart courtesy INTL

The message is that holders of gold, either underground (producer), in vaults (public and private investors) or jewellery shops (wholesale merchants) should always have downside price insurance in the form of put options and simply add the premium to their cost base.

PRODUCERS AND CONSUMERS

Gold

Table 8.6 shows that China is the both the world's number one gold producer and second ranking consumer behind India, although recent reports suggest that the world's most populous country may well be about to overtake India to become the top buyer of gold. Australia is the second largest producer of gold, followed by the United States and Russia, while South Africa, for many years the world's biggest source of gold, has slipped to fifth place. India and China on the buy side between them account for 60 per cent of total gold consumption; they are followed by the US, Japan and Italy, with the latter still the world's leading manufacturer of jewellery.

Gold producers and consumers **Table 8.6**

Top five gold producers (tonnes)	2010
China	351
Australia	261
United States	229
Russia	203
South Africa	203
Top five gold consumers (tonnes)	**2010**
India	783
China	509
United States	181
Japan	158
Italy	126

Source: Thomson Reuters GFMS Gold Survey; table courtesy INTL

Silver

Table 8.7 shows that silver's supply geography is somewhat different to gold, with the South American continent dominating the picture. Mexico and Peru are the top two sources of supply, with Chile and Bolivia in joint fifth place, separated by China and Australia in third and fourth place respectively.

Table 8.7 **Silver producers and consumers**

Top five silver producers (million ounces)	2010
Mexico	129
Peru	116
China	99
Australia	60
Chile and Bolivia – equal 5th	41
Top five silver consumers (million ounces)	**2010**
United States	190
China	127
Japan	102
India	94
Germany	40

Source: Thomson Reuters GFMS Gold Survey; table courtesy INTL

Platinum and palladium

Turning to the platinum group metals (PGMs), Tables 8.8 and 8.9 show that producer supply is dominated by South Africa and Russia. In platinum, South Africa is responsible for 76 per cent of total production, with Russia supplying 14 per cent, meaning that 90 per cent of the world's platinum comes from just two countries. While palladium production is shared more or less equally by Russia and South Africa, it is a similar story, with

Table 8.8 **Platinum producers and consumers**

Top five platinum producers ('000 ounces)	2010
South Africa	4635
Russia	825
Zimbabwe	280
United States	210
Rest of the world	110
Total	6060
Top five platinum consumers ('000 ounces)	**2010**
Europe	2110
China	1985
North America	1505
Japan	1155
Rest of the world	1125
Total	7880

Source: Thomson Reuters GFMS Gold Survey and Johnson Matthey Annual Review; table courtesy INTL

Table 8.9

Palladium producers and consumers

Top five palladium producers ('000 ounces)	2010
Russia	2720
South Africa	2575
North America	590
Zimbabwe	220
Rest of the world	185
Total	6290
Top five palladium consumers ('000 ounces)	**2010**
North America	3055
China	1815
Europe	1730
Japan	1475
Rest of the world	1550
Total	9625

Source: Thomson Reuters GFMS Gold Survey and Johnson Matthey Annual Review; table courtesy INTL

the two combining to supply 84 per cent of the total global supply. It is no wonder these two industrial precious metals are more subject to supply shocks than gold or silver, and perhaps explains why the price patterns in the PGMs tend to be different to gold and silver.

PRICING AND PRICE DISCOVERY

Precious metals prices 2001–2011

Figure 8.2 shows that gold is now in the tenth year of an unparalleled bull run that started in the summer of 2001. Silver has posted gains in the annual price for nine out of the last ten years – the exception being in 2009 when a collapse in global economic confidence followed the banking meltdown and financial crisis of 2008. Since 2001 the average price of silver has risen by 596 per cent from US$4.37 to US$30.42 in 2011, when we saw the price reach US$49.50, the highest level since January 1980. The average increase in price between 2001 and 2011 was 23 per cent. The average price of platinum also rose in nine of the last ten years, with 2009 also posting an isolated reversal of fortune. The average price of the noble metal was US$529 in 2001 and in 2011 this had risen by 226 per cent to US$1722, with a yearly average increase of 14 per cent over that period. Palladium has had more of a rocky ride over the last 10 years, with annual average prices falling in five of those years. However, the average price of US$733 in 2011 was still 21 per cent above 2001 and the average increase in price between 2001 and 2011 was 10 per cent.

Figure 8.2

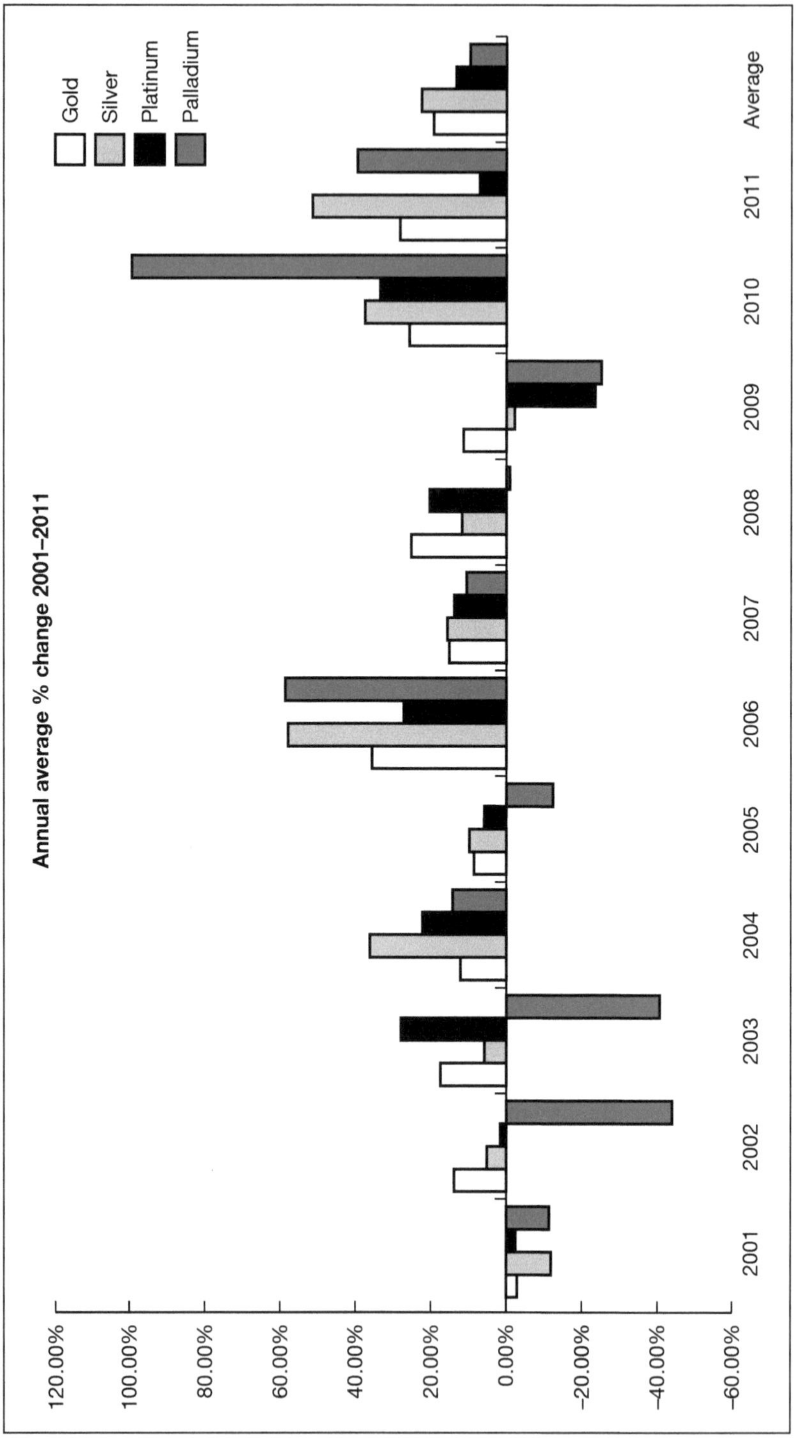

Source: Thompson Reuters GFMS

Global gold prices 2001–2011

Although the key driver of gold prices is traditionally the value of the US dollar, i.e. dollar down, gold up and vice versa, gold has posted impressive gains across all currencies (see Table 8.10). In euro terms, the average price of gold rose by 273 per cent from 2001 to 2011, in yen the increase was 280 per cent, in yuang it was 353 per cent and in Indian rupees the gain was a staggering 436 per cent. Gold has clearly become a mainstream asset class and a credible alternative hard currency in a world where governments have turned to their printing presses to devalue their paper currencies in an effort to stimulate their flagging economies.

Table 8.10

Global gold prices 2001–2011

	2001	2005	2010	2011	2011 v 2001 (%)	2011 v 2010 ($)
Average gold price US$/oz:	$271.04	$444.45	$124.52	$1571.64	480	28
Average gold price euro/kg	€9737	€11521	€29739	€36358	273	22
Average gold price yen/g	¥1058	¥1577	¥3444	¥4018	280	17
Average gold price yuan/g	¥72.13	¥117.09	¥266.15	¥326.61	353	23
Average gold price Rs/10g	Rs4462	Rs6454	Rs18304	Rs23899	436	31

Source: Thomson Reuters GFMS Gold Survey; table courtesy INTL

Figure 8.3

Average gold price US$ 2001–2011

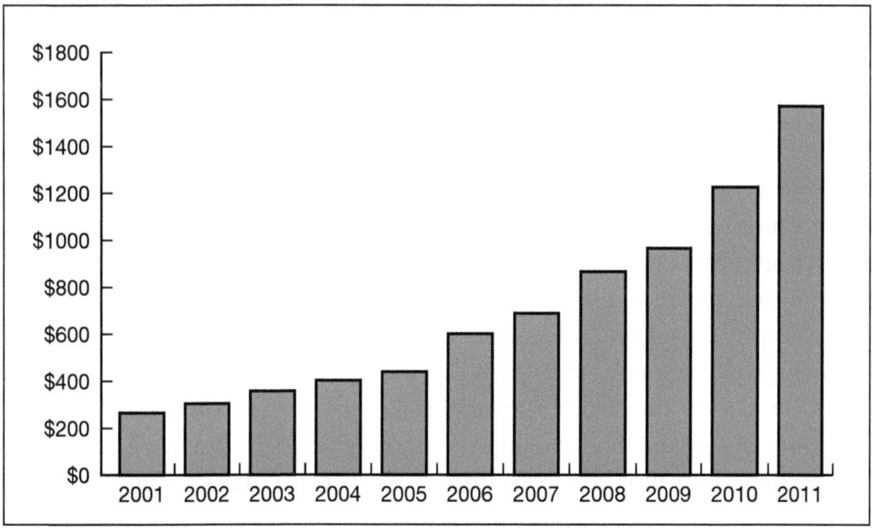

Source: Thomson Reuters GFMS Gold Survey; table courtesy INTL

Gold is on its longest winning streak in history, with the average price in dollar terms rising in each of the last 10 years (see Figure 8.3). In 2001 gold averaged US$271, remarkably similar to the average price of US$275 per ounce achieved by Gordon Brown (the UK Chancellor of the Exchequer) when he flogged off 400 tonnes or two-thirds of the UK's gold reserves in 17 auctions between July 1999 and March 2002.

In 2011 gold posted a series of record highs that peaked at US$1920 in September. The average of US$1571 was 480 per cent higher than 2001, and most pundits are looking for further growth in 2012. The average price increase over the last 10 years has been 22 per cent per annum.

HEDGING AND TRADING INSTRUMENTS

OTC swaps

A gold swap is a spot sale or purchase of metal with a simultaneous purchase or sale of metal at a specified date in the future. The interest cost associated with this method of financing is reflected in the forward price. The swap rate is derived from US$ LIBOR minus the gold lease rate:

The gold lease rate = $ LIBOR minus the gold swap rate

Assume three-month $ LIBOR = 2.5 per cent p.a. and the three-month gold versus $ swap rate is 1 per cent p.a., then the three-month gold lease rate is 1.5 per cent p.a. Therefore the prime gold lending rate for three months is 1.5 per cent p.a. and clients borrowing gold from a bullion bank would pay this 'gold LIBOR' plus a credit spread.

Swaps are the most common gold forward product and are quoted for periods from overnight to five years.

Fixed or outright forwards

All gold forwards are calculated using gold swap rates. These are a function of supply/demand for the underlying metal and the matching money market interest rates. If there is excess demand for gold, then the gold interest rate (see above) will increase and swap rates will be lower. This means that the spread between gold swap rate and money markets rate will widen.

Both producers and consumers can use fixed or outright forward contracts. Producers can hedge future physical production from the mines by matching the production schedule to a strip of fixed forward sales.

Hedging offers producers two important operational advantages:

1. By selling future gold production at a locked in (guaranteed) price, often several years ahead, producers realise a significant premium over the spot price. Because the gold interest rate is typically much lower than $ LIBOR, the gold swap rate is almost always in a steep contango, i.e. the forward price is higher than the spot price. This allows better cash flow and investment planning, stabilises income flow and can improve budgeted revenue.
2. Gold fabricators, principally the gold jewellery industry, try to match their purchases of physical gold with their fabrication schedule. Their requirements tend to be seasonal, peaking at certain times of the year, such as prior to Diwali and the Indian wedding season, Christmas and the Chinese New Year. Instead of waiting until the metal is needed and risking having to pay higher gold prices, the jeweller can buy for fixed forward dates that match fabrication plans if the spot price falls to what is considered to be an attractively cheap level.

Spot deferred contracts

A spot deferred contract is a forward contract without a pre-defined delivery date. While the pricing of a fixed forward deal is based on the known gold swap rate to maturity, the deferred contract will be calculated on a rolling basis using shorter dated rates as requested by the client. These rates can be for varying tenors from overnight to one year or longer. As each short dated forward matures it is rolled for a further period. No settlement takes place until the customer's chosen maturity date. Usually the difference in price between the forward maturity and the prevailing spot price is cash settled. Using deferred forwards introduces an extra element of market risk. Since the final maturity date is unknown, it is not possible to fix the interest components until maturity, which gives rise to an exposure to floating dollar and gold interest rates.

This type of instrument is used by producers who believe that dollar rates are expected to rise in the future and gold lease rates are expected to fall. The producer will roll spot sales on a deferred basis whilst dollar rates have risen and gold rates fallen to target levels. The producer will then use the improved contango, or swap rate to lock in sales until maturity.

Exchange for physicals

While forward gold is traded in the form of swaps, which combine a spot trade (buy or sell) with the reverse forward trade (sell or buy), gold futures can be traded in the form of EFPs (exchange for physicals), which combine a futures trade with the reverse spot trade. EFPs are traded for the same months as gold futures dates. The EFP price represents the difference between the futures price and the spot price for the combined trade and is simply a different way of looking at the basis or the swap rate. The EFP market provides a vital source of liquidity to futures markets and gives a depth to the exchange, encouraging the growth of their contracts. As much as 50 per cent of daily futures volumes can come from EFPs. A futures exchange without an active EFP market cannot be successful.

Options

Hedging is the process of substituting certain, or known, outcomes for uncertain ones. A gold producer, for example, does not know what the spot price of gold will be a year from now, but can hedge future gold sales by selling gold forward at the known one-year forward price. This will enable the cash flow to be determined in advance – at least that part of it that depends on the fluctuating price of spot gold. It will simplify financial planning. The actual spot price of gold a year from now may be higher than the pre-agreed forward rate, or it may be lower. Thus, by hedging and substituting a known price for an unknown one, the gold producer could just as easily suffer an opportunity loss as an opportunity gain. Many in the gold market are looking not for a fixed forward price, but rather for a boundary guarantee. A future seller of gold might want a guarantee that the sales price will not fall beyond a minimum level below which would not be tolerable, but otherwise prefer to remain un-hedged in hopes the market price will rise. Similarly, a future gold buyer might look for a guarantee that the purchase price will not rise above a tolerable maximum level, but otherwise prefer to remain un-hedged in hopes the market price will fall. The gold market creates and sells such guarantee or insurance contracts. In the financial literature (and in the market), these same contracts are also called options. Naturally the market does not provide such insurance contracts for free. Like anything else, they are available for a price – known as a premium. Options are traded OTC and on regulated exchanges. OTC options are typically traded with a bullion bank or market maker with maturity dates to suit the clients' requirements. You can trade long dated OTC options as far forward as 10 years. Exchange traded options are in practical terms options on futures contracts for fixed dates and if exercised become an underlying futures contract; they are American style, meaning they can be exercised into the underlying futures contract at any time prior to expiration. OTC options are typically European style, meaning that they can only be exercised on the maturity date. European options are generally cheaper than American style. Options are regarded in some circles are speculative instruments that help to cause unnecessary and unwanted price volatility. However, the truth is that an option is actually a form of price insurance which is an important tool in managing price risk and exposure.

Although basic option terminology is covered in Chapter 2 (Key Commodities Derivatives), here is a brief recap.

The main elements of an option are the underlying price; the strike price; the expiration date; the contango or swap rate; interest rates and finally and most importantly the implied volatility. This is the secret ingredient and often options traders will take the first five elements as read and simply quote each other the VOL.

Key features

Options

Underlying price

The current underlying price will determine how much the option is in or out of the money. The more out of the money an option is, the lower the option premium. In precious metals, contango rates are important elements in this calculation.

The strike price

The strike price is the price chosen by the client where the buyer has the right to buy (in the case of a call) or sell (in the case of a put) the underlying asset. The lower the put strike (or higher the call strike) the lower the option premium. A higher put strike (or lower call strike) results in a higher option premium.

Expiration/maturity date

The option expiration date is the date at which the option buyers' rights are cancelled. The later the expiration, the more expensive the option premium.

Interest rates

The current interest rate on money is used to determine the cost of financing the option premium for the duration of the option's life.

Implied volatility

This is the measure of anticipated market activity through the life of the option. Higher volatility results in a higher option premium. Out of the money options carry a higher implied 'VOL'.

Commodity futures markets

There are a large number of exchanges around the world that offer futures contracts in gold and silver including:

- COMEX, a division of the New York Mercantile Exchange (NYMEX), now part of Chicago Mercantile Exchange (CME), which is the world's leading futures exchange for gold and silver trading.
- Tokyo Commodity Exchange (TOCOM).
- Dubai Gold and Commodities Exchange (DGCX).
- Multi Commodity Exchange of India (MCX).
- Istanbul Gold Exchange (IGE).
- Shanghai Gold Exchange (SGE).

And many more.

When using futures markets always remember:

- All futures trades require an initial margin paid into the margin account and subsequent variation margins when the price of the commodity changes. Changes are margined on a 'one-to-one' basis.
- Trading futures and managing the position is an intensive process.
- Tight internal controls have to be in place.
- Trading futures in a volatile market carries a high risk.
- Although all futures markets around the world vary in some way depending on local laws and market requirements, the contract specifications and principles of futures exchanges are typically quite similar.

Note: For further background on all derivatives refer to Chapter 2.

Futures markets – pros and cons

- **Pros**: Price transparency; well regulated; low credit risk; low original margin; small size tickets; price volatility.
- **Cons**: Liquidity can be poor; transaction costs; inflexible maturities; price volatility.

Price volatility features as both a pro and a con; it is good for the speculators that thrive on erratic price movements but is bad for the commercial companies that need to hedge their exposure to the vagaries of the international bullion market.

TECHNICAL ANALYSIS

Technical analysis is a method of evaluating markets by analysing statistics generated by trading activity, such as past prices and volume. Technical analysts do not attempt to measure a security's intrinsic value, but instead use charts and other tools to identify patterns that can suggest future activity.

A fundamental analyst studies all aspects of markets including demand and supply, perceived fair value of the asset class and outside influences such as interest rates, foreign exchange rates and macroeconomic data, particularly from the US. The FA then decides whether to issue a buy, sell or neutral recommendation. By contrast, a technical analyst disregards the intrinsic value of the asset and any buy or sell decisions are based simply on price and chart patterns.

In the early part of my career back in the late 1970s and early 1980s I completely ignored the charts, preferring to rely largely on feel and touch while being aware of the demand and supply fundamentals. However, in today's markets, with the advent of programme trading and the 'black box algorithmic' approach, it has become essential to focus on the charts and be well aware of key technical breakout points. This leads me to share with you a trading tip, based on the charts, that has served me well over the latter part of my career in precious metals. Let us review two silver charts, one long term and the other over a much shorter time period. Figure 8.4 shows the long-term chart.

If you are interested in investing/trading in silver, you need to consider timing. Clearly the perfect time to have entered the silver market was in 2009 when silver was just below US$10 in the wake of the credit crisis of 2008, as Figure 8.4 clearly shows.

Since then the silver price has increased dramatically to reach US$49.75/oz in May of 2011, an increase of 400 per cent, putting silver in the premier league of investment assets, and the old adage of 'the trend is your friend' definitely supports the view that silver remains very much in place as an investment for the future.

When should you enter the market? Perhaps the safest approach is to buy on a regular basis, perhaps celebrating special occasions, weddings, birthdays and religious holidays, or using a savings accumulation plan. This would mean that you are investing on an average price basis with the peaks and troughs in the price being smoothed naturally. For the more technically motivated and feistier silver investors, chart analysis can give accurate signals about when you should enter and exit the market. This development is largely due to the increasing involvement of investment or hedge funds,

Figure 8.4

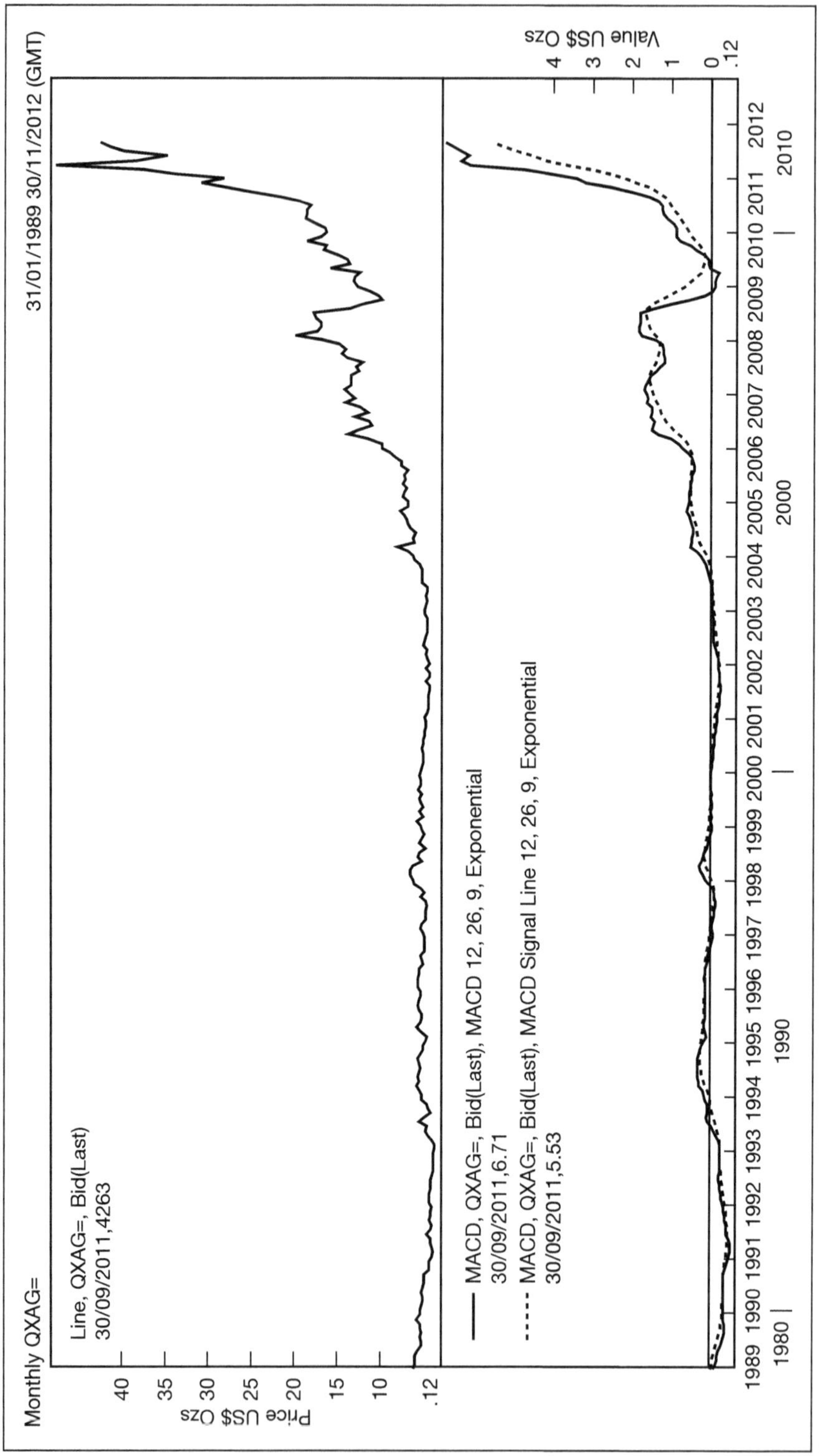

When to invest in silver, long-term view?

Source: Thomson Reuters

tending to use a programme trading approach; these can make the charts self-fulfilling prophecies. I personally like to watch the short-term moving indicators, particularly the 9- and 18-day moving averages and the MACD, with crossovers, either up or down, giving accurate buy and sell signals that pick up all of the major moves in the market. There may be dangers in choppy rather than trending markets, of being whipped in and out, and it is important to identify early what kind of market you are in. Once you get the feel for the market, a focus on short-term momentum can be very profitable, although not without risk.

MACD (source: StockCharts.Com – ChartSchool)

Developed by Gerald Appel in the late 1970s, the moving average convergence–divergence (MACD) indicator is one of the simplest and most effective momentum indicators available. The MACD turns two trend-following indicators, moving averages, into a momentum oscillator by subtracting the longer moving average from the shorter moving average.

The MACD therefore offers the best of both worlds: trend following and momentum. The MACD fluctuates above/below the zero line as the moving averages converge, cross and diverge. Traders can look for signal line crossovers, centreline crossovers and divergences to generate signals.

The MACD line is the 12-day exponential moving average (EMA) less the 26-day EMA. Closing prices are used for these moving averages. A nine-day EMA of the MACD line is plotted with the indicator to act as a signal line and identify turns. The MACD histogram represents the difference between MACD and its nine-day EMA, the signal line. The histogram is positive when the MACD line is above its signal line and negative when the MACD line is below its signal line. The values of 12, 26 and 9 are the typical setting used with the MACD.

As its name implies, the MACD is all about the convergence and divergence of the two moving averages. Convergence occurs when the moving averages move towards each other. Divergence occurs when the moving averages move away from each other. The shorter moving average (12-day) is faster and responsible for most MACD movements. The longer moving average (26-day) is slower and less reactive to price changes in the underlying asset.

The MACD line oscillates above and below the zero line, which is also known as the centreline. These crossovers signal that the 12-day EMA has crossed the 26-day EMA. The direction, of course, depends on the direction of the moving average cross. Positive MACD indicates that the

12-day EMA is above the 26-day EMA. Positive values increase as the shorter EMA diverges further from the longer EMA. This means upside momentum is increasing. Negative MACD values indicate that the 12-day EMA is below the 26-day EMA. Negative values increase as the shorter EMA diverges further below the longer EMA. This means downside momentum is increasing.

Signal line crossovers are the most common MACD signals. The signal line is a nine-day EMA of the MACD line. It trails the MACD and makes it easier to spot MACD turns:

- A bullish crossover occurs when the MACD turns up and crosses above the signal line.
- A bearish crossover occurs when the MACD turns down and crosses below the signal line.
- Crossovers can last a few days or a few weeks, it all depends on the strength of the move.

Now let us focus on a much shorter term silver chart that illustrates perfectly how the MACD performs in trending markets (see Figure 8.5).

As you can see from Figure 8.5, between January and October 2011 there were three buy signals and two sell signals, with the third sell signal occurring later in November, which is not on this chart. The first buy signal in January at US$22 yielded a profit of US$22 or 85 per cent before a sell signal was flagged at US$48 in early May. The market fell sharply until a buy signal was triggered at US$35 later that same month. This US$13 per ounce or 27 per cent profit from the short position was followed by another US$6 gain (17 per cent) before the MACD posted a fresh sell signal at US$41 in September. The market then dropped sharply once again to reach US$32 in October, producing another US$9 or 22 per cent gain. The long MACD base established by this latest buy signal was eventually sold in November at US$35, with a modest US$3 or 9 per cent gain. The fact that this was the smallest profit margin achieved over this period indicated that the trending type of market seen for much of 2011 was waning and since last November silver has entered a sideways trading range which is not ideal for MACD watchers. Nevertheless, MACD devotees would have made in aggregate a return of 160 per cent during 2011, a performance any money manager in the world would have been proud of.

Figure 8.5

When to invest in silver, short-term view?

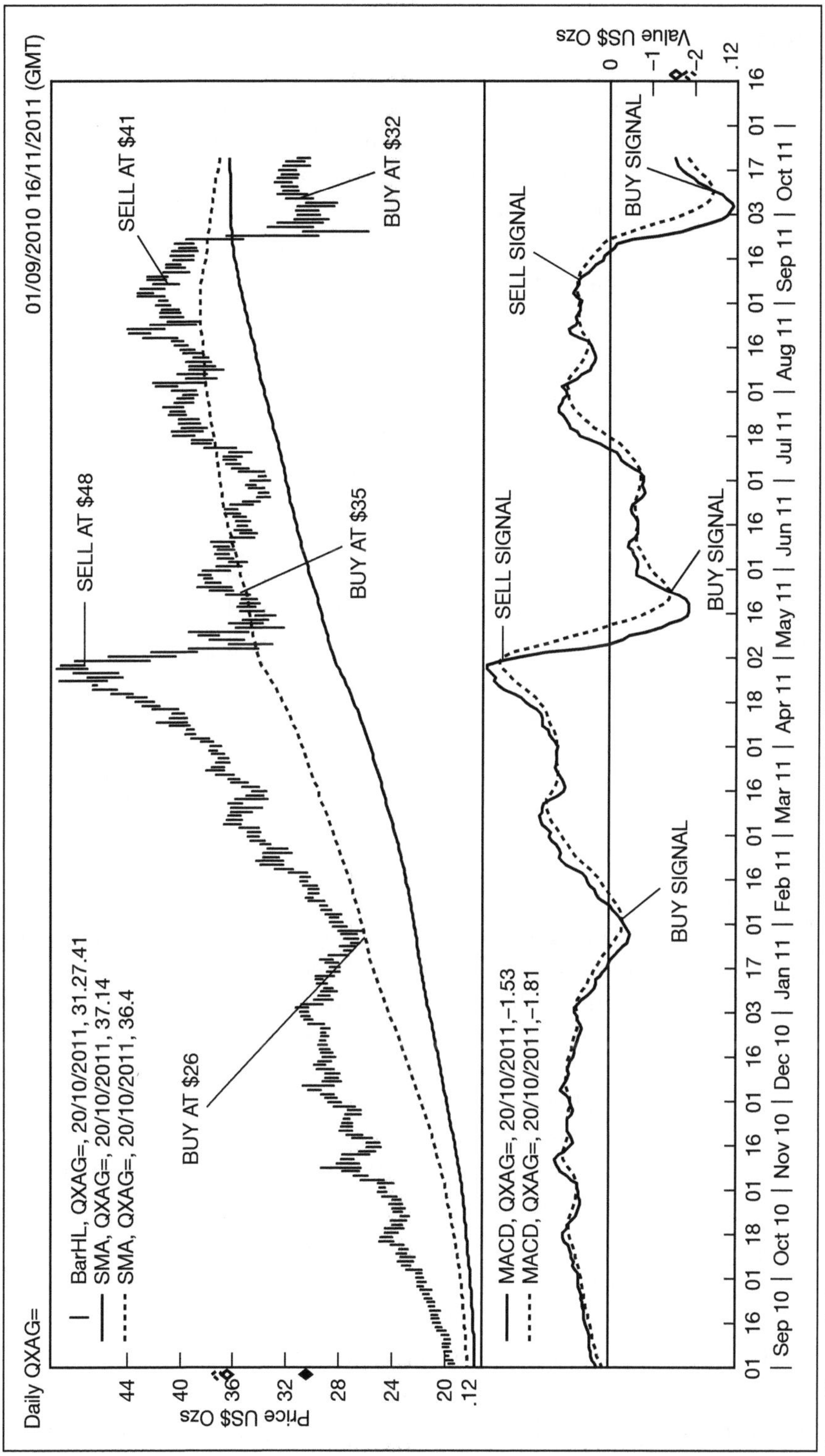

Source: Thomson Reuters

Terminology

Assay The determination of the precious metal content of an alloy, either using a direct method (where the actual precious metal content is measured) or an indirect, instrumental method (usually based on spectrographic analysis) in which the levels of impurities are measured and the precious metal content is calculated by difference.

Bullion The generic word for gold and silver in bar or ingot form. Originally meant 'mint' or 'melting place' from the old French word bouillon, meaning boiling.

Carat Derived from the word for 'carob' in various languages; originally equivalent to the weight of the seed of the carob tree. It has two meanings in modern usage:

- A measure of the weight of precious stones: 1 carat = 0.2053 g.
- A measure of the proportion of gold in a gold alloy, on the basis that 24 carat is pure gold, often expressed as K or k, e.g. 18k is 75 per cent gold.

Doré An unrefined alloy of gold with variable quantities of silver and smaller quantities of base metals, produced at a mine before passing on to a refinery for upgrading to London Good Delivery standard.

Fine weight The weight of gold contained in a bar, coin or bullion as determined by multiplying the gross weight by the fineness.

Fire assay A method of determining the content of a metal (most commonly gold) in an alloy involving the removal of other metals by what is in effect a combination of fire refining (for the removal of base metals) and chemical refining (for the removal of silver) and then determining the gold content by comparing the initial and final weights of the sample. Fire assay can determine the gold content of Good Delivery type alloys to an accuracy of better than 1 part in 10,000. Also known as cupellation or gravimetric analysis.

GOFO Gold Forward Offered Rate. It is the gold equivalent to LIBOR and is the rate at which dealers will lend gold on swaps against US dollars.

Gold Latin name aurum; chemical symbol is Au; specific gravity is 19.32 and the melting point is 1063°C.

Gold/silver ratio This is the number of ounces of silver that can be bought with one ounce of gold.

Terminology continued

Gold standard A monetary system with a fixed price for gold, with gold coin forming the whole circulation of currency within a country or with notes representing and redeemable in gold.

Guinea British gold coin with a nominal value of £1 first issued in 1663, named after gold from Guinea in West Africa. It was unofficially revalued at 21 shillings at the Great Re-coinage of 1696, a value confirmed in 1717. It has a fineness of 916.6 and a fine gold content of approximately 0.25 troy ounces.

Hallmark A registered mark or number of marks made on gold, silver or platinum jewellery and other fabricated products that confirms the fineness, or percentage of precious metal contained in the item.

Kilo bar A popular small gold bar. A 1 kg bar 995.0 fine = 31.990 troy ounces, and a 1 kg bar 999.9 fine = 32.148 troy ounces.

Lakh Indian term for 100,000; used to describe silver orders.

Loco The place, location at which a commodity, e.g. loco London gold, is physically held.

Palladium Chemical symbol Pd; specific gravity is 12.00 and the melting point 1555°C.

Pennyweight Originally the weight of a silver penny in Britain in the Middle Ages; still widely used in North America as the unit of weight in the jewellery trade. 20 pennyweights = 1 troy ounce.

Platinum Chemical symbol Pt; specific gravity is 21.45 and the melting point is 1773°C.

Silver Latin name argentum; chemical symbol is Ag; specific gravity is 10.49 and the melting point is 960°C.

Sovereign British gold coin with face value of one pound sterling, a fineness of 916.6 and a fine gold content of 0.2354 troy ounces.

Tael Traditional Chinese unit of weight for gold. 1 tael = 1.20337 troy ounces = 37.4290 grams. The nominal fineness of a Hong Kong tael bar is 990, but in Taiwan 5 and 10 tael bars can be 999.9 fine.

Tola Traditional Indian unit of weight for gold. 1 tola = 0.375 troy ounces = 11.6638 grams. The most popular sized bar is 10 tola = 3.746 troy ounces. Weights are for 999.0 gold purity.

Terminology continued

Troy ounce The traditional unit of weight used for precious metals, which was attributed to a weight used in Troyes, France, in medieval times. One troy ounce is equal to 1.0971428 ounces avoirdupois.

White gold This is a gold alloy containing whitening agents such as silver, palladium or nickel as well as other base metals. Often used as a setting for diamond jewellery.

9

Base Metals

Fabrice Tayot
Commodity and Energy Specialist for Thomson Reuters, Dubai

Background and context

The mining lifecycle

Rehabilitation and environmental concerns

Characteristics, supply and demand of key base metals: aluminium, copper, zinc, nickel, lead

Pricing and price discovery

Risk management and derivatives

Outlook

BACKGROUND AND CONTEXT

Our history and lifestyle are deeply associated with the history of metal. The truth is, from cave-dwelling ages, to twenty-first century modern society, no progress in industry, transportation or crafts would have been possible without the discovery of copper 6200 years ago.[1]

Metal is commonly defined as a class of substances characterised by high electrical and thermal conductivity as well as by its malleability, ductility and high reflectivity of light. This is a broad definition, but fits perfectly as approximately three-quarters of all known chemical elements are metals, and among them a large majority of base or industrial metals.

So how do we differentiate base metals? Originally, the term base metal was used to refer to metals that easily react with diluted hydrochloric acid to form hydrogen. Now, it refers to the five industrial non-ferrous metals (copper, lead, nickel, zinc and aluminium[2]), which together compose one of the key markets of this new century.

But why is this such an important market?

Firstly, because the supply/demand dynamics of the metals trade has never been stronger than it is today – between the producer of base metals (mostly emerging countries[3]) and the consumer (OECD countries and China[4]). This market reflects perfectly the new shape of world trade, and the growing dependency of the western world on emerging countries' natural resources. Table 9.1 shows metals production in 2011.

Table 9.1 **Metals production in 2011**

Metal	2011 production ('000 tonnes)	Capacity production ('000 tonnes)
Copper	16550	21869
Lead	10328	11126
Nickel	1203	1648
Primary Aluminium	44100	55900
Zinc	13441	14585

Source: USGS and Thomson Reuters

[1] In 4200 BC. Gold was discovered in 6000 BC but did not allow the development of metallurgy. Five other metals were discovered before 0 AD (silver in 4000 BC, lead in 3500 BC, tin in 1750 BC, iron (smelted) in 1500 BC, mercury in 750 BC).

[2] US Customs and Border Protection is even more inclusive in its definition as it includes, in addition to the ones above, many other metals such as iron and steel, tin, tungsten, molybdenum, cobalt, bismuth and cadmium.

[3] 62 per cent of basc metals mines are located in emerging countries (source: Thomson Reuters).

[4] As an example, more than 76 per cent of aluminium consumed in the world is consumed either in the OECD countries or in China.

Secondly, more than ever the mining industry is generating growth. It contributed 1.7 per cent of global GDP in 2009,[5] and in some mining countries, 25–30 per cent of fiscal revenues rely directly on the mining sector (and for eight countries[6] more than 50 per cent of their exports result from mining).

Mining companies have outperformed other industries for the last 25 years. With an aggregated turnover of US$435 billion for the top 40 mining companies (34 per cent increase over 2009) and a net profit up by 156 per cent (US$110 billion),[7] they have multiplied their value 12 times (see Figure 9.1 showing that base metal mining companies have outperformed other sectors).

Lastly, millions of people depend on the metal industry which, including its related activities such as metal production, non-electrical machinery and transport of equipment, was in 2005 employing some 67 million people worldwide.[8]

If base metals have played an essential part in our history, nothing has changed today. With forecast turnover of US$872 billion by 2015,[9] they are, as much as crude oil, the very basis on which our economy is built. Without metals, there would be no houses to live in, no cars to drive and no ships to transport merchandise. The base metal market is a fundamental component of the world economy, making it essential to understand the various features and intricacies of the market.

THE MINING LIFECYCLE

Before being refined and traded, metal needs to be mined. Even with the help of modern technology, mining is still a long and difficult process.

A common definition for mining is simply the process of extracting, through various methods of extraction, useful and/or precious minerals from the surface and the depths of the Earth, including deep sea and seabed. Regardless of the type of excavation, the process usually consists of several distinct steps.

The first stage is the actual **discovery of the ore body**, which is established by many different techniques, including geological surveys and/or satellite surveys, prospecting or exploration of an area to find and then define the size, location and quality (grade) of the ore body.

---

[5] Source: OECD.
[6] Guinea, Dem. Rep. of Congo, Zambia, Niger, Botswana, Namibia, Jamaica, Sierra Leone.
[7] Source: "Mining 2011 – the game has changed" by PWC.
[8] Source: UNIDO estimates for the International Metal Worker Federation.
[9] According to global industry analysts.

Figure 9.1 **Metals and mining equities**

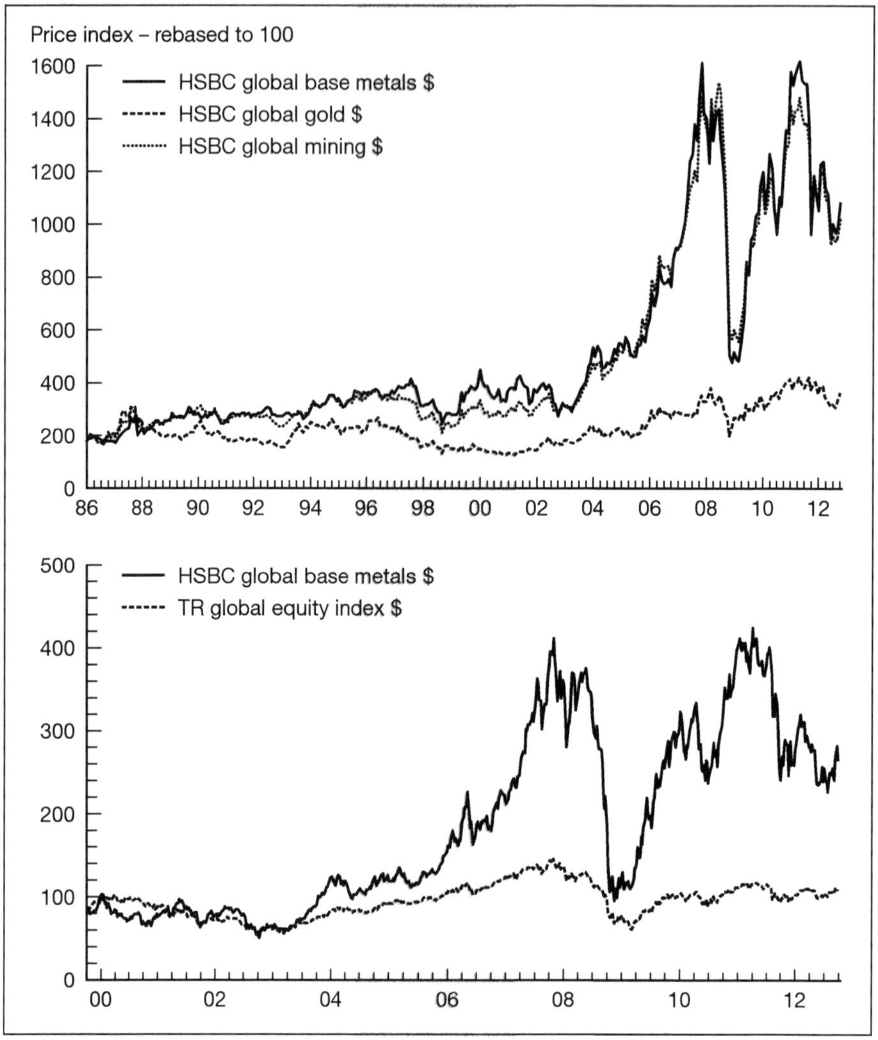

Source: HSBC and Thomson Reuters

The second stage is the calculation of the estimated **value of the deposit**. This estimation is used to determine the hypothetical financial viability of the ore deposit and to identify in advance the main risks (technical and financial) and the different requirements needed to develop the project.

The third stage is usually to source the **funding** for the project. Most financial analysis will be done at this stage and, in a nutshell, this is the moment when investors decide whether or not to invest in a mine. This decision will take into account a large number of factors, including marketability of the ore concentrates, engineering and technical concerns, infrastructure costs, financing rates, the enrichment factor[10] of the ore in the area and legal/environmental issues; but ultimately, as with any industrial investment, the decision depends on the projected profitability of the investment.

The fourth stage of the project, and assuming the finance is in place to **develop** the mine, is where the relevant equipment needs to be sourced and the transport and local infrastructure upgraded, if necessary, in order to progress with the extraction.

The fifth stage is mining and there is a range of different techniques.

- **Surface mining** is carried out by removing (stripping) surface vegetation, earth and, if necessary, layers of bedrock in order to reach buried ore deposits. Techniques of surface mining include open-pit mining[11] and strip mining.[12]
- **Sub-surface mining** consists of digging tunnels or shafts into the earth to reach buried ore deposits and can be generally classified by the type of access shafts used or the technique used to reach the mineral deposit: hard rock mining, bore hole mining, drift and fill mining.[13]

The sixth stage occurs when the ore has been recovered but before the metal can be marketed as an end product. The ore will usually be sold to a refiner for the **concentration phase**. Firstly, the host rock will be removed by either grinding it down to powder and/or a combination of several mechanical and chemical techniques. Secondly, as metals usually bind with other elements during this process to create compounds[14] (also called ores) due to their reactivity, the compounds need to be separated. Reactivity the relative capacity of an atom to combine chemically with another atom – e.g. gold is very un-reactive and does not readily combine with other elements, but copper will easily react with other minerals.

The reactivity of the metal, together with its concentration and the technique used to separate out the compound, will directly affect its commercial viability. Usually, the more reactive a metal is, the harder it is to remove from its ore, and the more expensive it is to process.

Refining is the seventh and final stage of the process, where impurities are removed and the metal is converted into a state allowing fabrication of the end product. Refining consists of purifying the impure metal. It is distinguished from other processes such as smelting and calcining that change the

---

[10] The proportion of a deposit that is economically recoverable.

[11] Which consists of recovery of materials from an open pit in the ground.

[12] Removal of soil and rock (overburden) above a layer or seam, followed by the removal of the exposed mineral.

[13] Drift mining utilises horizontal access tunnels; shaft mining consists of vertical access shafts.

[14] As an example, aluminium itself can be found combined in over 270 different minerals. The most commonly known are bauxite for production of aluminium, chalcocite for production of copper, uraninite for tin, sphalerite for zinc.

chemical nature of the material. There are many processes which may be used, mostly dependent upon the metal itself and the technology available – e.g. fire or electrolytic refining for copper, Parkes or Pattinson process for lead.

At this point the metal is ready to be sold to the market as an end product and will be shipped to a warehouse and/or its final customer; but there is another 'hidden' cost involved in the metal production phase, a cost which influences the profitability of the mine and therefore the cost of metal: the cost of rehabilitation.

REHABILITATION AND ENVIRONMENTAL CONCERNS

As with the extraction of any natural resources, working mines will generally create waste materials and run-off minerals at some point. After a mine has been closed down then comes the time to rehabilitate the land. Due to the heavy engineering and the chemical processes involved in mining, most of the land will suffer environmental damage of some sort. This may include, at various levels, loss of topsoil and erosion, loss of biodiversity, acid rain, movement of significant volumes of rock that could lead to collapsed mines and shafts, and ultimately loss of integrity to anything built over them such as roads or houses. This may occur both during the active mining operations and for years after the mine is closed. Modern mine rehabilitation aims to mitigate those environmental effects even if it is rarely possible to restore the land to its original condition.

The complexity of this rehabilitation has pushed many of the world's most developed countries to adopt really tight regulation to moderate the negative effects of mining operations. These regulations are one of the reasons contributing to the global imbalance between producers (emerging countries with flexible or no regulation) and consumers (developed countries with severe regulations).

Lastly, safety is a constant concern for most countries and operating companies. For decades, mining countries have recorded huge mortality rates:[15] this has led to the adoption of improved safety practices such as timbering and bracing. But regardless of the development of the regulations, new technology and improved safety practices, mining remains a very dangerous and sometimes lethal activity. These improved regulations are mostly followed in Western countries that have to bear a significantly increased cost of production. This can be compared with the often minimal safety regulations in some emerging market countries, leading to yet another imbalance observed on the metal market.

---

[15] The Courrières mine disaster, Europe's worst mining accident, caused the death of 1099 miners in northern France on 10 March 1906, only to be surpassed by the Benxihu Colliery accident in China on 26 April 1942, which killed 1549 miners, according to Marcel Barrois in his article published in *Le Monde*, on 10 March 2006.

CHARACTERISTICS, SUPPLY AND DEMAND OF KEY BASE METALS

Aluminium

More aluminium is produced today than any other base metal,[16] with more than 44 millions tonnes produced by smelting in 2011[17] and a forecast of 51 million for 2012. Figure 9.2 shows the forward price of high-grade aluminium in contango out to 2018. The global market for aluminium is expected to remain strong for the foreseeable future as retail customers are generally eager to buy lighter and more recyclable consumer goods.

Figure 9.2

Aluminium forward curve

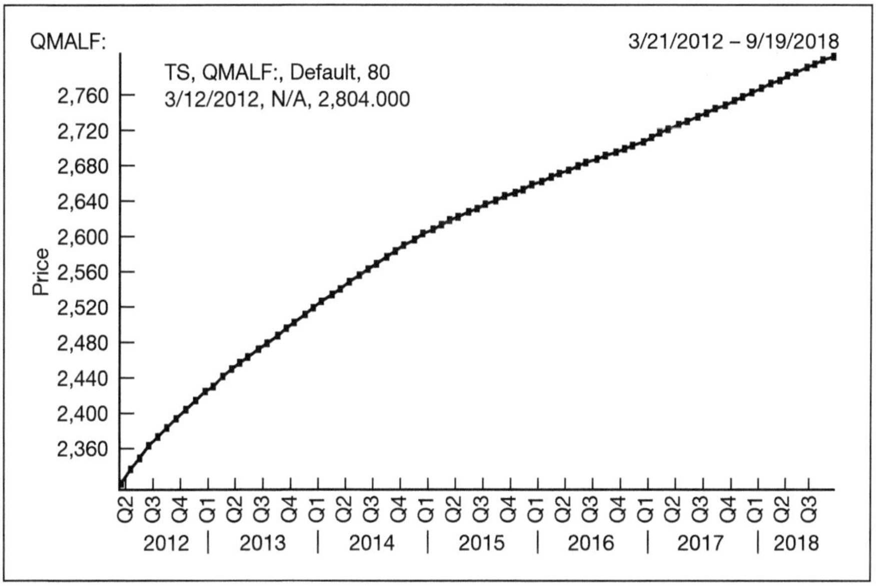

Source: Thomson Reuters Eikon

The impact of the economic crisis in 2008 was hard on the world aluminium sector and the industry is still far from running at full capacity,[18] but the price picked up strongly to US$2328 a tonne due mostly to the growing demand for the metal in developing Asian economies. Figure 9.3 shows the price chart for high-grade aluminium from 1990 to 2012.

Aluminium is used in the construction industry (more than 20 per cent of demand), packaging (18 per cent), and of course the transportation sectors (largest end user of aluminium with 29 per cent), and with a high level of activity in infrastructure development in emerging countries this increasing price trend looks likely to continue.

[16] It even exceeded any other metal except iron (837.5 million tonnes).

[17] Primary aluminium.

[18] 81.78 per cent (source: Thomson Reuters).

Figure 9.3 **Aluminium price from 1990 to 2012**

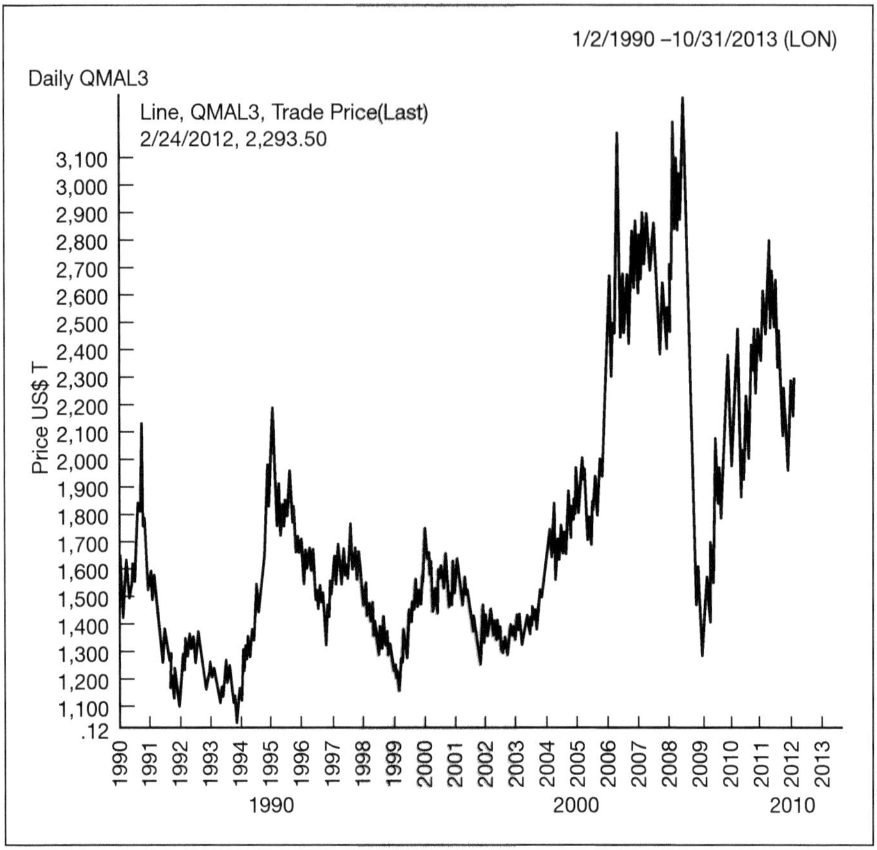

Source: Thomson Reuters Eikon

The primary source of aluminium is from the aluminium ore known as bauxite; this is found worldwide in varying concentrations. Figure 9.4 shows the 2011 world production as a percentage from key producers. The bauxite ore needs to be crushed, dissolved in caustic soda and finally heated at high temperatures and pressures to produce alumina[19] (refining) which can then be converted to metallic aluminium (smelting). Figure 9.5 illustrates this diagrammatically. Approximately 4 tonnes of bauxite will produce 2 tonnes of alumina that in turn will produce only 1 tonne of aluminium. This process is highly energy intensive (between 13,000 and 17,000 kWh for each tonne of aluminium) and smelters are often built in close proximity to power stations. As a result, the price of electricity has a strong impact on production costs.

[19] There are other resources (e.g. alunite, anorthosite) which are technically feasible sources of alumina but not on a commercial scale.

Figure 9.4

2011 bauxite main producers (as % of world production)

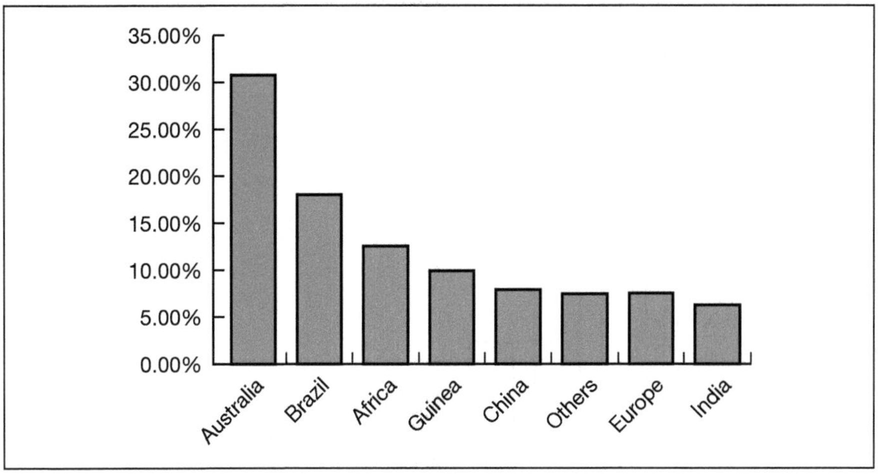

Source: US Geological Survey

Figure 9.5

Aluminium lifecycle

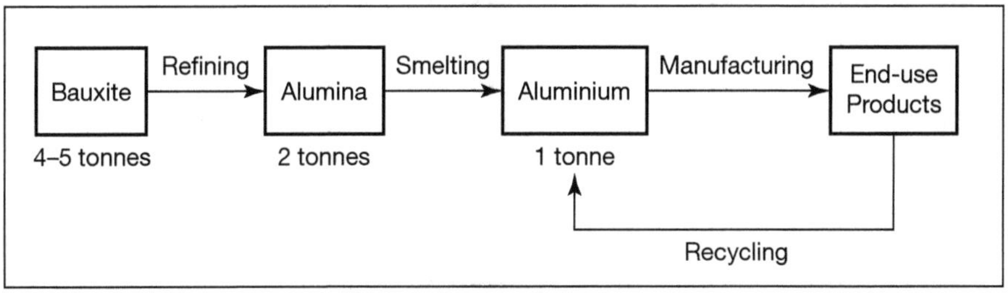

Source: US Geological Survey

Figure 9.6 shows the actual production of aluminium, by country, from the smelting process, with China a clear leader.

The secondary source of aluminium is scrap, or recycled aluminium. Most of this supply will be used in the production of various alloys for the transportation business. Surprisingly, aluminium recycling is a very old business, which started around 1900. Secondary aluminium accounted for 50 per cent of the supply in 1980 and is now over 70 per cent of the supply since the beginning of the 2000s. Part of this success is due to the fact that recycling of aluminium is less energy intensive (approximately 1/20 of the energy) and therefore cheaper to produce than primary aluminium.

Figure 9.6 **2011 primary aluminium producers (as % of World output)**

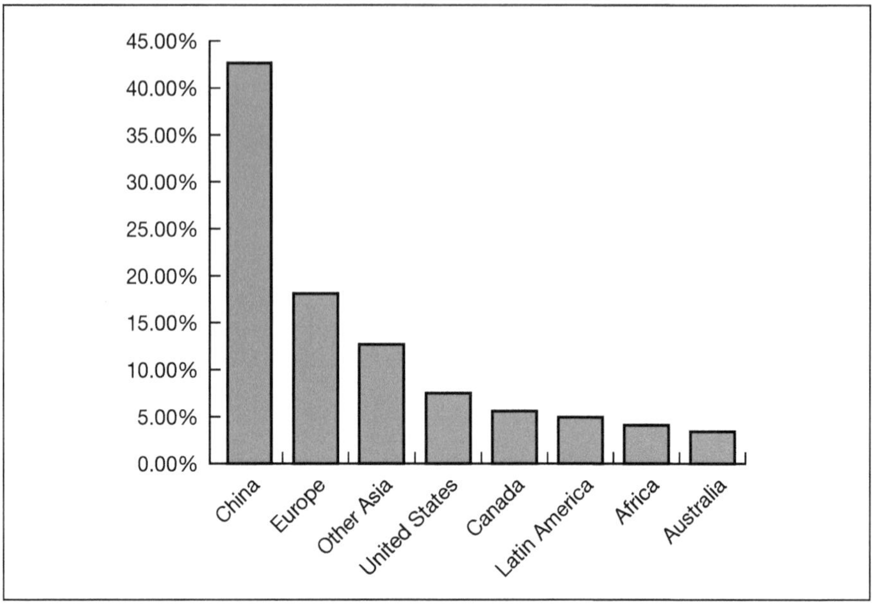

Source: US Geological Survey

Copper

Copper was the first base metal ever discovered and is still widely used. More than 95 per cent of all the copper ever mined and smelted has been extracted since 1900 and the actual production for 2011 is around 16.5 million tonnes.[20] This is mostly used for electronic product manufacturing (65 per cent), construction (25 per cent) and transportation, mostly for car batteries and wiring[21] (7 per cent).

In the last two decades, South America has emerged as the world's most productive copper region. In 2011, about 45 per cent of the world's copper was produced from there, especially from the Andes Mountains, with Chile being the largest producer, accounting for 30 per cent of world production since 2000. Figure 9.7 shows the main copper producers in 2011 as a percentage of world production.

Global copper reserves are vast but only a tiny fraction of these reserves is economically viable using current technology. Various estimates of the remaining copper reserves available for mining vary from 25 years to 60

[20] Source: Thomson Reuters.

[21] The average car contains 1.5 kilometres (0.9 mile) of copper wire, and the total amount of copper ranges from 20 kilograms (44 pounds) in small cars to 45 kilograms (99 pounds) in luxury and hybrid vehicles.

Figure 9.7

2011 main copper producers (as % of world production)

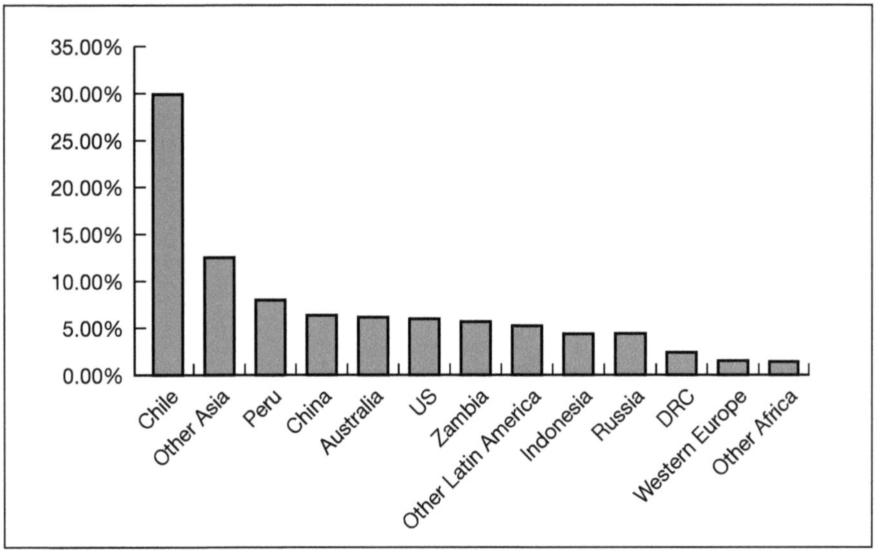

Source: US Geological Survey

years (depending on assumptions such as growth rate and metal intensity of industrial production): this leads to speculation regarding hypothetical peak copper.[22]

In the last few years, mostly because of China's hunger and several operational and project development problems, copper supply has struggled to keep pace with demand.[23] There are a number of new development projects that are expected to deliver additional capacity to meet the moderate demand growth over the medium term.[24] However, the price of copper on the London Metal Exchange (LME) reached several peaks following the decline caused by the credit crunch. Figure 9.8 shows the price of copper from 30 October 2002 to mid-2011. During that period copper reached a low of US$2832 on 17 December 2008 and a high of US$10,160 on 14 February 2011 – a gain of 259 per cent.

High copper prices have also increased copper recycling; this metal is 100 per cent recyclable without any loss of quality. Approximately one-third of all copper consumed worldwide is recycled, and these trends are expected to push the copper balance into surplus in the long term, as displayed by the backwardation of the forward curve (Figure 9.9).

[22] Peak copper is the point in time at which the maximum global copper production rate is reached; when this will occur is a matter of dispute.

[23] World mine output has increased only 1.1 per cent per annum from 2007 to 2011.

[24] 6 per cent increase in global mine supply.

Figure 9.8

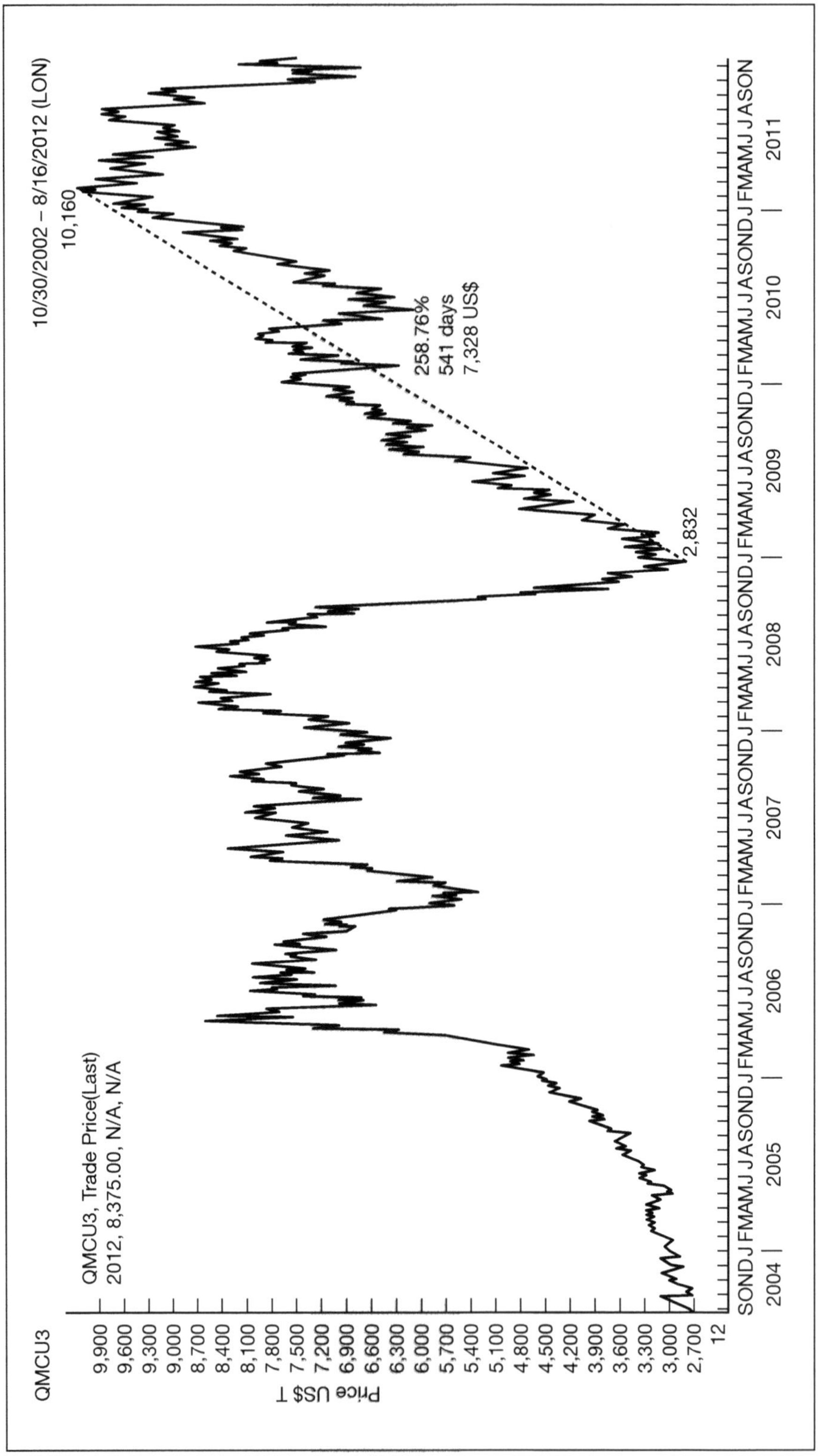

Source: Thomson Reuters Eikon

Figure 9.9

Copper forward curve in backwardation

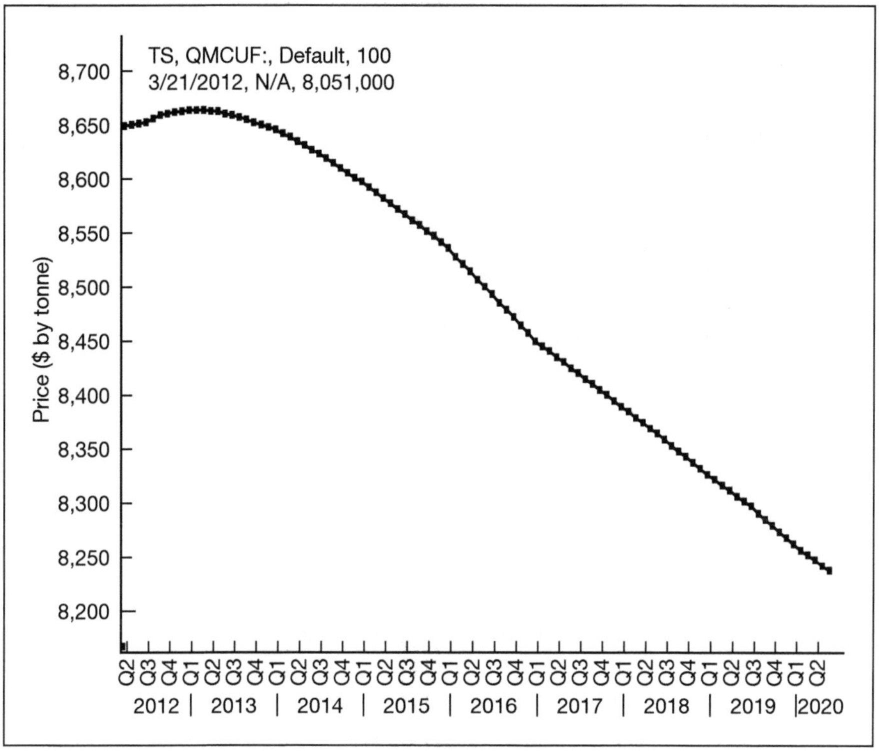

Source: LME data on Thomson Reuters

Zinc

The zinc market is one of the major markets in terms of production – fourth behind iron, aluminium and copper with an annual primary production of about 13 million tonnes (+4 per cent in 2001) and reserve of 250 million tonnes. The primary production represents 70 per cent of the total world production, the other 30 per cent coming from recycled zinc. The level of recycling is increasing each year, and today over 80 per cent of available zinc is recycled. Figure 9.10 shows 2011 zinc production by country as a percentage.

About 50 per cent of our zinc is used for galvanising other metals, coating them to protect iron and steel from corrosion. But it is also used to produce alloys such as bronze and brass, semi-manufactured products such as rolled zinc, and even dietary supplements. Figure 9.11 shows how zinc is used.

Figure 9.10 **2011 zinc producing countries as percentage of world production**

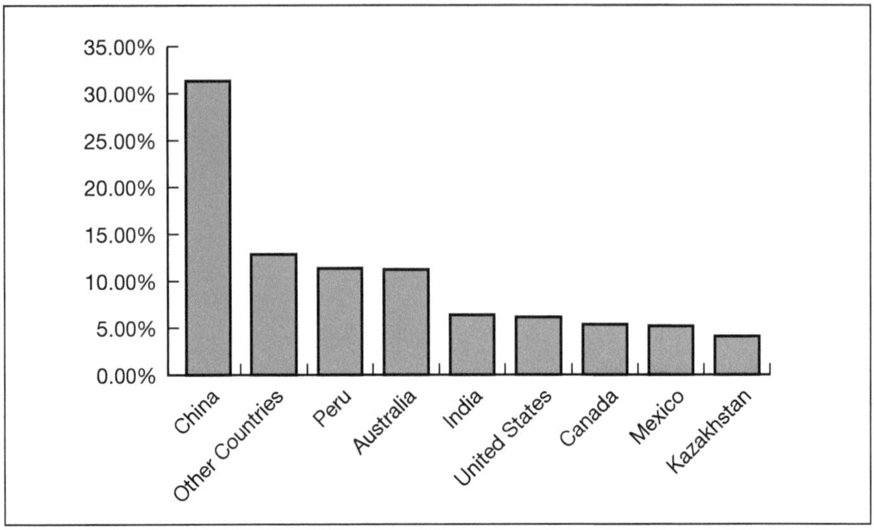

Source: US Geological Survey

Figure 9.11 **Zinc consumption by sector, 2011**

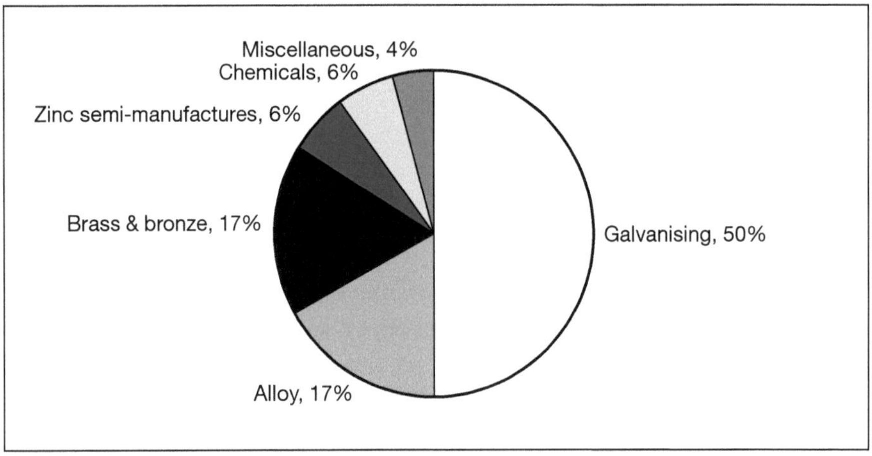

Source: International Lead and Zinc Study Group (ILZSG) (www.ilzsg.org)

For the last three years, declining zinc prices (–39.75 per cent since the peak of 2009) and stock surpluses in LME warehouses have been common. By October 2011 the refined zinc stock surpluses had increased to an impressive 308,000 tonnes compared to 270,000 tonnes over the same period in 2010.[25] Figure 9.12 shows the increasing levels of refined zinc stocks and the poor price performance.

[25] Source: the International Lead and Zinc Study Group (ILZSG).

Figure 9.12

Zinc prices and stock levels since 2005

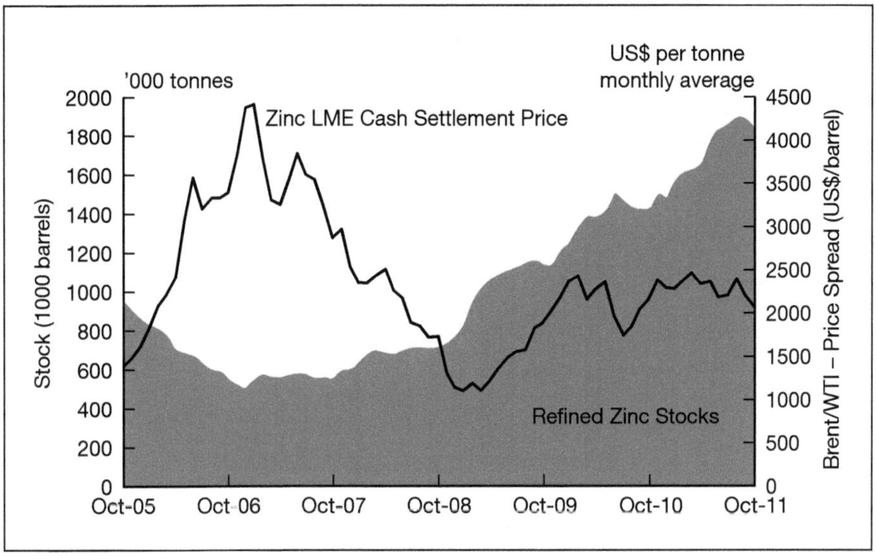

Source: LME and International Lead and Zinc Study Group

Despite the economic uncertainty in Europe and the declining growth in Asia, the surpluses were not driven by falling demand but by increased refined zinc metal output due to rising smelting production in China, India, South Korea and Peru (+2.1 per cent) and the increase in mining.

Nickel

Nickel exhibits a mixture of ferrous and non-ferrous metal properties that can be used in various different industries. The primary production comes mainly from two types of ore deposits, lateritic and magmatic sulfides. Most of the nickel resources on Earth are believed to be concentrated in the planet's core. Figure 9.13 shows the main countries where zinc is mined.

Sixty-five per cent of the nickel consumed in the Western world is used to make stainless steel. Another 12 per cent goes into superalloys – mostly for the aerospace industry – or non-ferrous alloys, both of which are widely used because of their corrosion resistance. The remaining 23 per cent of consumption is divided between steel alloys, rechargeable batteries, catalysts and other chemicals.

The price of nickel surged throughout 2006 and 2007. In April 2007, the metal reached its peak at US$51,600/tonne. This price was so high that the 5 cent US nickel coin became an attractive target for melting, as its metal value was close to 10 cents. The United States Mint, in order to stop the practice, had to implement new rules criminalising the melting

Figure 9.13 **2011 nickel mining production (as % of world mining production)**

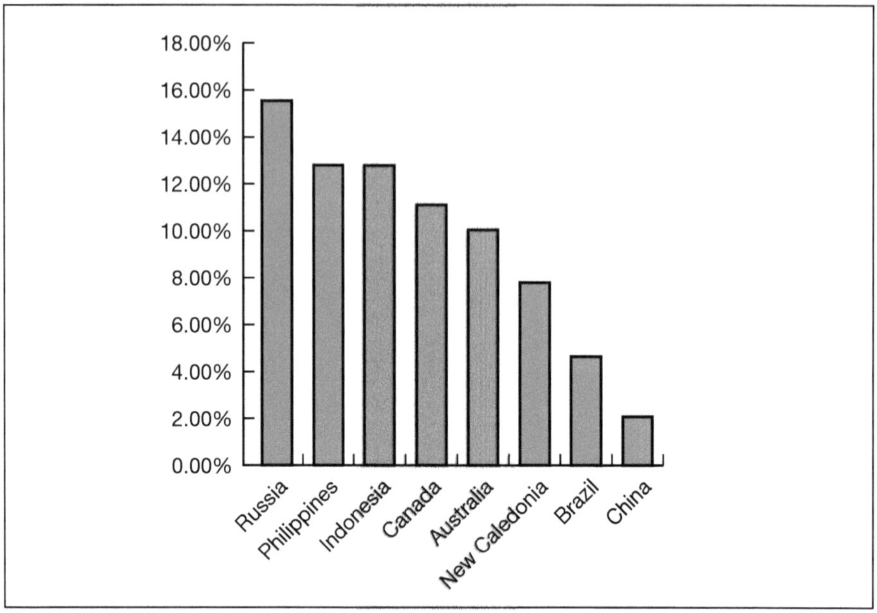

Source: US Geological Survey

Figure 9.14 **Nickel prices 1992 to 2012**

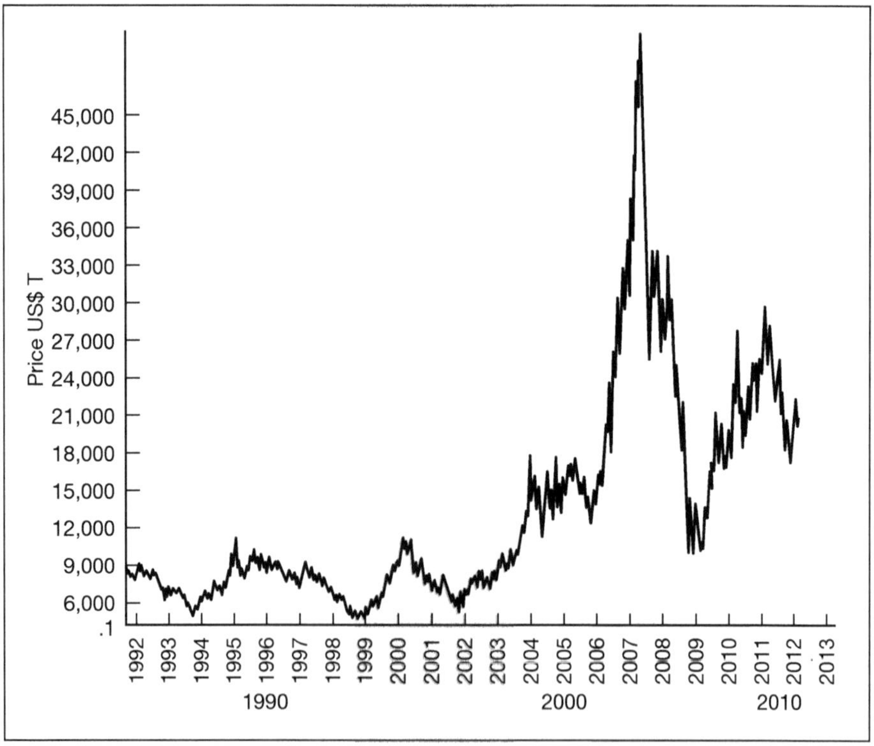

Source: Thomson Reuters Eikon

of nickel coins. Figure 9.14 shows the price variation of nickel. Following the economic slowdown in 2008 and 2009, the price fell, and by 9 January 2009 the metal was trading at US$10,880/tonne.

The two main factors behind the huge drop in price are the level of surpluses and the substitution effect from nickel pig-iron (NPI)[26] stainless steel producers from Chinese – this occurs when nickel prices are too high. However, even at the current price, US$20,175/tonne (25 February 2012), approximately 10 per cent of nickel producers are not making profits, which could force them to stop or at least slow down production, and this may have an impact for 2012.

Lead

Lead, because of its toxic nature, is less used than copper and aluminium. Most lead is used in batteries (over 80 per cent), with the balance used in ammunition and for various other purposes. Its production and consumption has increased to 10.3 million tonnes worldwide, of which 4.5 million tonnes is primary lead. Figure 9.15 shows lead mining production by country.

2011 main lead mining countries (as % of world mining production) **Figure 9.15**

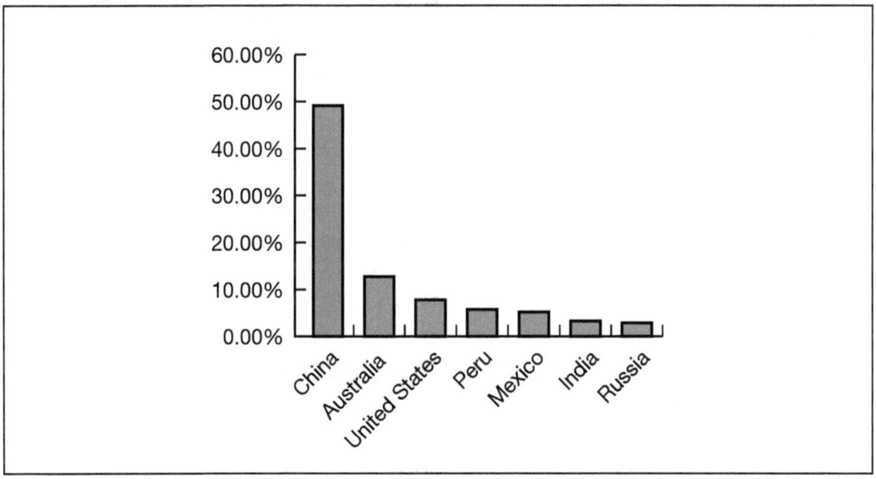

Source: US Geological Survey

As in the copper market, a 'lead peak' is assumed by some analysts. However, in my opinion that assumption should be played down as technology[27] and substitution have reduced the use of lead in many industrial processes, including electronic systems, cable covering, packaging and lead pipes for water and gas.

[26] Low grade ferronickel invented in China as a cheaper alternative to pure nickel for the production of stainless steel.

[27] Fuel cell technology, for example.

Despite its toxic reputation, lead is still widely traded, although on 7 February 2012 the price fell back to US$2190 tonne following two strong years, and the shape of the forward curve seems to indicate that the market is discounting all the fundamentals positively for the coming years. Figure 9.16 shows lead price performance from 1990 to 2012.

Figure 9.16 **Lead prices from 1990 to 2012**

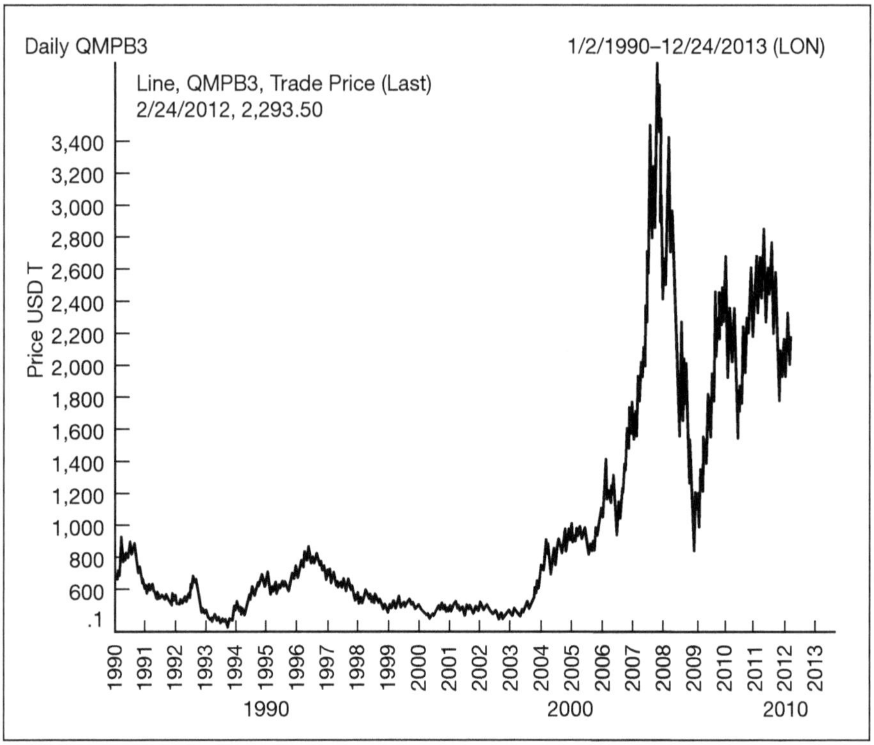

Source: Thomson Reuters Eikon

PRICING AND PRICE DISCOVERY

Pricing

A range of different factors influences the pricing of base metals.

Global GDP growth, demand and supply balance, and the impact of the financial crisis

There are strong parallels between global GDP growth rates and metal prices. Increased demand for industrial investment, new construction, more cars, improvements to transport and communication systems all create a requirement for mining commodities. But any slowdown in the global economy can have the opposite effect. Figure 9.17 shows that historically rich countries with higher GDP per capita tend to consume more metals, therefore the growth of GDP is one of the major price drivers.

Aggregate metal consumption and GDP per capita 1960–2009

Figure 9.17

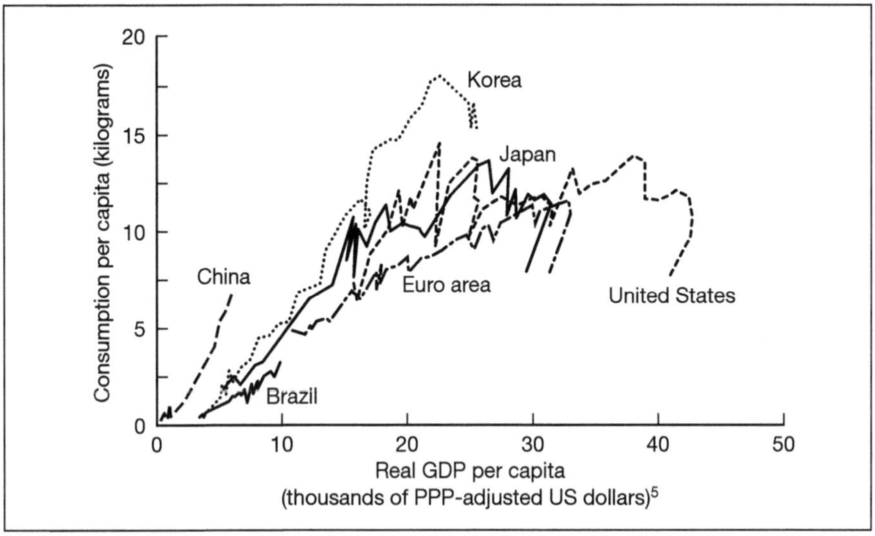

Source: IMF

Following the financial crisis in late 2008 and early 2009, the world GDP growth rate fell from 5.443 per cent in 2007, to 2.785 per cent in 2008 and –0.663 per cent in 2009:[28] this reduced global demand for base metals and their prices, and increased their volatility. Copper prices ranged from US$1679 tonne in April 2000 to US$8685 tonne in April 2008, and then by December 2008 copper fell to US$3072 tonne.

This sharp decline both in GDP growth rate and in the copper price seems to illustrate the usual trend for industrial metals during and after a global downturn. The strong correlation between global macro-indicators and base metal prices is only mitigated to some extent by local indicators, such as GDP growth for emerging countries and favourable economic performance in Asia, as commodity demand in these economies is more elastic than in advanced economies.

Market regulation

One of the features of this market is the impact the various regulations have on the availability of metal. Environmental and safety regulations and minimum wages are among the factors that will impact where and under which

[28] International Monetary Fund, World Economic Outlook Database, September 2011.

conditions the metal can be mined and refined. The current imbalance observed in the market – with production falling in rich countries[29] and most of the new refiners located in China – is a perfect indication of the huge influence of regulation on the production of base metals. Western regulation has economically transferred production to China and the emerging markets. Any new developments there could have huge consequences, for example imposition of minimum wages in China.

Production disruption

Production disruption can manifest itself in several ways – for example cessation of production due to strikes or labour disputes, industrial accidents, natural phenomena – and will usually result in higher prices as the supply chain will be disrupted.

Chinese and Indian demands

In the last two decades, China and, to a lesser extent, India have emerged as two industrial powerhouses. Their rapid industrialisation has made them two of the largest consumers of most industrial commodities and substantial importers of base metals to fulfil their growth.[30] As an example, Chinese demand for metals accounted for two-thirds of world demand growth between 1999 and 2005.[31]

China ranks first and consumes 24 per cent of total world production (nearly 40 per cent of copper and aluminium) of base metals.[32] Its consumption is currently higher than other countries at a similar stage of development, reflecting the exponential growth in its manufacturing sector over the past two decades, and both China and India represent the only foreseeable source of growth in the near future. They are expected to account for more than half of the growth in global copper and aluminium consumption over the next two decades.[33]

It is easy to see how those countries have been a major driver in the recent surge of metals prices and that any change in the growth rate of their GDP, credit liquidity, labour costs or environmental regulation may have significant consequences for prices and should be followed extremely closely (see Figure 9.18).

---

[29] According to the Sustainable Europe Research Institute in 2008, OECD countries were only extracting 32.8 per cent of industrial minerals, China 38 per cent.

[30] In 2007, China was only mining 14 per cent of the copper used in its refineries (source: Mei Zhang 2008 cited in IMF working paper: www.imf.org/external/pubs/ft/wp/2011/wp1186.pdf, p.10).

[31] During that period, China's demand for major metals grew at an average rate of 14.7 per cent a year (source: IMF report 2011).

[32] Sources: IMF and Thomson Reuters.

[33] Source: World Bank Report.

Figure 9.18

China's share of global base metal consumption (%)

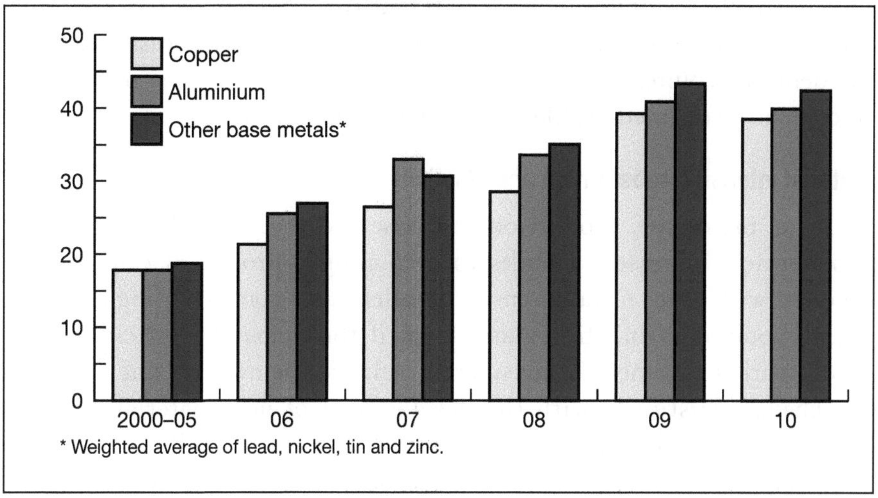

Source: IMF

Exchange rates

As in most of the commodity markets, base metals prices are denominated in US dollars. Therefore any movements in the exchange rate of the end user local currency have a strong influence on the price of metals. If the dollar strengthens against a specific currency, the price will rise (in this specific country) and the demand should logically decrease. On the other hand, if the dollar weakens, the demand will increase. Similarly, an acceleration of US inflation may push producers to raise their prices to protect their purchasing power.

Due to China's influence on the metal market, the Renminbi spot rate is a core focus. Most Western governments are asking for an appreciation of this currency, through a free float mechanism, to protect their commercial balance. However, any appreciation would logically result in a rapid growth in imports of major ore and consequently a rise in the price.

Exploration, capital investment and the issue of 'supply lag'

In our integrated financial market, investors are always looking for the best-performing asset. During an economic downturn, it is difficult to finance new supply capacity as private investors are unwilling to invest in an exploration project, or to upgrade production capacity, without a reasonable degree of certainty regarding the possible rate of return.

Therefore, when prices rise due to new demand it becomes difficult to accommodate the demand with new supply. This delay between new demand and upgrade of production capacity is one of the reasons for rising prices. It can take up to 10 years or longer from the discovery of an economically viable deposit to bringing it to production,[34] when, on the other side, traders react to real-time news every day. As supply cannot easily adapt to the demand requirement, by the time new supply reaches the market, the price trend of the metal is likely to have reached new highs.

Material intensity, substitution and elasticity

As metal prices rise, production costs rise and the possibility of product substitution increases. Thanks to technology, producers can develop products with lesser metal intensity (smaller metal content) using materials such as polymers and fibreglass. Even if the demand elasticity in the metal market is generally considered inelastic (below 1),[35] the situation can change drastically with the development of new materials. Recent developments in this field must be followed regularly. Oddly enough, this issue is affecting the scrap business, but churches and local authorities are affected too as metal theft[36] is booming with high prices.[37]

Operating cost

For a metal such as aluminium the operating cost could rise (or drop) drastically due to variations in bauxite or the electricity price. Both price variables represent more than 50 per cent of the production cost changes but the situation is the same (to a lesser extent) with other base metals.

Hot money

For a few years now, commodities, and among them base metals, are increasingly being seen as part of the diversification of asset allocation for many investors. If the features of the asset – no income yield, high volatility, etc. – still deter traditional investors, many hedge funds see huge profit opportunities in this booming market (Figure 9.19 shows the comparative performance of different assets), with base metals as an asset class continuing to gain acceptance.[38]

Over the last 10 years we have seen speculators entering metal markets in a big way, e.g. copper futures contracts traded on the LME have grown from an average of 15,000 non-commercial long positions to an average of

[34] I will not be discussing the issue of obtaining the permits needed for mining, but it can be an extremely complex and time-consuming process which will add to the delay in bringing new supplies onto the market.

[35] Metal demand elasticity arises only when substitution can arise in the short term.

[36] Copper pipes, wires but also street signs, manhole covers and even works of art.

[37] Source: BBC Radio 4, article by Natasha Grüneberg.

[38] Moreover, various investment funds also use base metals OTC contracts as a bet on the industrial strength of China, and to a lesser extent on the recovery in global industrial activity.

Figure 9.19

Asset performance since 2000

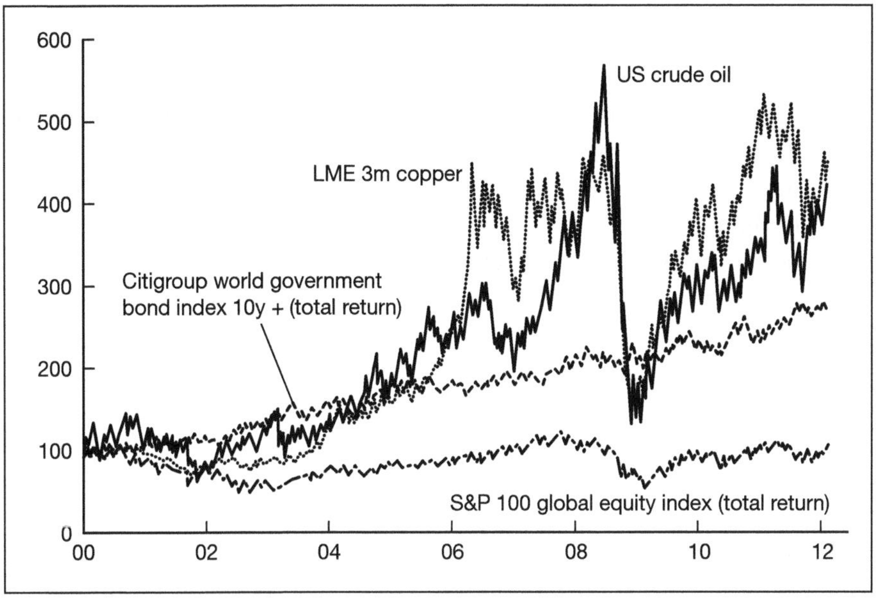

Source: Thomson Reuters Datastream

35,000 currently.[39] Consequently, we experience record high volatility, and rising prices, even when the fundamentals of supply and demand indicated that the price should be low. Fundamentals seem not to be driving the price as they should be.

Nevertheless, it is unclear if speculative funds have such an influence. Many experts have downsized the supposed effects,[40] arguing that there is no evidence of inventory accumulation, but instead external factors influencing the supply/demand balance and inventory level.

In fairness, the truth is maybe between those two stances and careful investors need to follow the amount of speculative money entering the market. Futures markets play a key role in price discovery, and price indexation, even if they do not create shortage/excess of supply. If industrial consumers anticipate a shortage due to the shape of the forward curve, the influence will not be the same as a real shortage of a commodity, but it may influence strong buying pressure. In the same way, a high price for base metals on the LME may push producers to produce more, bringing excess supply to the physical market.

[39] Source: CFTC reports on Thomson Reuters.

[40] Notably Paul Krugman, in the *New York Times*, 7 February 2011.

Price discovery

One of the regular aspects intrinsic to most commodity markets is the need to agree on a fair price for the traded asset.

This process, called the price discovery process, is fundamental as it allows traders to determine if they are paying or receiving a fair price for the desired commodity, if their position is generating profits or loss, and to settle their derivative on a single common price (mark to market). Of course, all of this would not be possible if all trades were made OTC. This is why commodity exchanges play a primary role in the price discovery.

In the base metal market, this key role is played by the London Metal Exchange (LME). Established in 1877, though the market traces its origin back to the opening of the Royal Exchange in 1571,[41] the LME is the world's premier non-ferrous metals market and provides a large range of futures and exchange traded options[42] used for price discovery, hedging and speculation.

Traded on three different platforms ring trading, the inter-office telephone market and electronic trading through LME Select, LME's future and options contracts offer the best liquidity found on the base metal market.[43]

Futures contracts

As with other assets, commodity futures contracts are a commitment to buy or sell a particular metal at an agreed price at a specified date in the future, the quantity and physical specificity (form, quality and shape) of the metal being standardised by the exchange – as opposed to OTC forward contracts which offer more flexibility.

Currently available contracts are:

- Copper A grade;
- Primary aluminium, aluminium alloy and North American special aluminium alloy contract (NASAAC);
- Standard lead;
- Tin;
- Special high grade zinc;

---

[41] Before the exchange was created, business was conducted by traders in London coffee houses using a makeshift ring drawn in chalk on the floor.

[42] At first only copper was traded. Lead and zinc gained official trading status in 1920 and the range of metals traded was extended to include aluminium (1978), nickel (1979), tin (1989), aluminium alloy (1992), steel (2008), and minor metals cobalt and molybdenum (2010). The exchange ceased trading plastics in 2011.

[43] The LME in 2011 has achieved record volumes with 146.6 million lots, equivalent to $15.4 trillion annually and $61 billion on an average business day.

- Steel;
- Cobalt and molybdenum;
- Index contract (LMEX).

The majority of trades conducted on the LME are financially settled[44] and the trades will be offset by taking out an equal and opposite position on the same delivery date – selling 10 contracts will offset an original long position of 10 contracts on the same delivery date, and you pay or receive the difference between the two transactions. However, if held to maturity, all contracts assume physical delivery, so a holder of a long contract receives an LME warrant, while the holder of a short position is required to deliver an LME warrant. An LME warrant is a certificate for a specific tonnage of an approved brand of metal in an LME approved warehouse.

As opposed to other commodity exchanges where futures contracts settlement follows a schedule specific to the commodity, LME's futures contract can be traded for settlement for any date (the prompt date) for up to three months, then weekly for delivery between three and six months, and monthly for delivery of 15, 27 or 63 months forward.

Options

The LME also offers options on the underlying future contract. Common to all commodity markets, an option is the right to buy or to sell an LME futures contract at a pre-determined price at a specified date in the future. It also offers Traded Average Price Options (TAPOs); these are options where the settlement of the underlying contract is against the average (called the Monthly Average Settlement Price) of all the daily settlement prices for a particular month.

These different derivatives can be traded 24 hours a day. However, the most liquid time is during the London afternoon (11:45a.m. to 5p.m.) when the three platforms are open. Outside this period, inter-office telephone market and electronic trading systems are still active.

Ring trading is so called because the LME uses a 6m diameter 'ring' with the traders sitting inside. There are two sessions per trading day, each of them being composed of two rings, where each of the nine metal future and options contracts are traded with a five-minute session for each contract and a kerb session;[45] the morning session gives the official prices at the end of the second ring and the afternoon one provides the unofficial and closing

---

[44] Even if it is possible to use the future contract as a source of supply, more members of the LME will financially settle the contract to either mitigate their risk on a physical delivery or take a speculative position.

[45] During the kerb session, all the metals are trading simultaneously with more than one trader allowed per company inside the ring.

prices. Much of the LME liquidity is passed through the ring and kerb sessions, with the balance through the inter-office telephone market[46] and LME Select.

Beyond the price discovery process, one of the other features of the LME is the presence of a central clearing house that becomes the legal counterparty of each side of the trade, mitigating the default risk for each of them.[47] This feature has been central to the development of the commodity market since its inception and has been used in conjunction with the margining system to increase the volume traded on exchanges.

If not financially settled, the seller has to deliver an LME warrant that can be issued by one of the 400 warehouses approved by the LME. Available in 32 different countries, those warehouses allow the LME to have a global reach.[48] Consequently, the holder of a short position can choose the warehouse where the metal will be delivered and will receive a warrant. The warrant will then be transferred to the holder of the long position, who cannot choose where to receive the delivery. This is why there is a grey market to swap warrants between long position holders. A buyer may try to swap a warrant that is not suitable against a warrant in a more accessible warehouse.

RISK MANAGEMENT AND DERIVATIVES

Base metal derivatives allow price risk to be managed and more precisely controlled, and also profits to be made on speculative positions. As they can be used for different purposes, hedgers and traders will not adopt the same strategy.

Assume you are an aluminium smelter and you wish to hedge (protect) your production against falling prices (also called commodity price risk): you could sell (short) a futures contract on the LME and benefit if prices fell. This would offset the fall in prices received when the goods were actually sold. You could also buy a put option on the same futures contract.

Alternatively, if you were a consumer you could protect yourself from rising ore prices by agreeing a price today for future delivery by using an OTC forward contract, or buying an OTC swap for recurring delivery (paying fixed price, receiving floating).

Theoretically, in a hedging transaction the profit made on the transaction will offset the loss that occurs when the goods are sold. However, if the futures price moves slightly differently from the physical price (because of

---

[46] Transactions done through the inter-office trading system are to summarise 'real' LME contracts, traded OTC but matched, cleared and settled with the usual process.

[47] The risk of the original counterparty defaulting is transferred to the clearing house, which is heavily capitalised, consequently reducing the risk to nearly zero.

[48] More than 95 per cent of LME business comes from overseas.

different physical specificity, location, no future contract on that specific metal), the hedge will be imperfect. This is known as basis risk and is discussed in Chapter 1.

The best way to protect against basis risk is to arrange an OTC forward contract that can be customised to follow the exact characteristics of the asset that requires hedging. This OTC transaction will involve a credit risk for both counterparties; this is the risk that either could default on their obligations – this risk is non-existent in a futures contract due to the presence of the clearing house, and indeed similarly if the OTC transaction is of the 'cleared variety' (see end of Chapter 2). Liquidity risk may be an issue should the holder of the OTC transaction wish to exit before maturity and the counterparty is unable or unwilling to make a fair price. The more 'tailored' the OTC derivative the less likely it is to find a willing counterparty to a secondary trade – this is why exchange traded products are so popular.

Forward curve

A forward curve is a graphical representation of future values over time. A forward price is, in a way, an indicator of supply and demand in the future; to interpret the forward curve is then a way to evaluate market assumptions on supply and demand for the coming years.

When analysing the curve it is important to consider the shape of the curve and the degree of curvature. If prices for future delivery are higher than the actual spot price, then the shape of the curve is described as 'in contango'. The opposite, which occurs when the spot price is higher than the forward price, is known as 'backwardation' (for more information on these technical terms please refer to Chapter 1).

In a contango market, traders are expecting the supply/demand balance to be tighter in the future, and therefore physical prices to be higher. A hedger would therefore buy futures contracts to mitigate the risk on physical delivery and speculators will buy futures to try and generate a profit. This buying pressure will generate an upward trend for future delivery and explain the shape of the curve. The more market participants that expect the balance to be tight, the steeper will be the curve. If the futures prices are felt to be too high, traders will short those positions and break the contango curve of the market.

In a backwardated market, the markets are experiencing high demand and spot prices are equally high. The spot price will therefore move higher than the futures/forward prices and generate the characteristic downward shape of the curve. If the current spot prices are felt to be too high, traders will tend to buy in the future when prices are seen to be cheaper and maybe even to sell and/or deplete their current stocks. If this occurs, the backwardation of the curve is reduced and spot prices will fall.

Studying the forward curve allows market participants to adapt their strategy and mitigate their risk according to the current market expectations of supply and demand. But can it be used as a forecast to future spot rates? No. A forward curve simply shows prices today for delivery on forward dates and because there are many different factors[49] that will undoubtedly change between now and the forward date, forward rates and curves should not be considered as forecasts.

OUTLOOK

So, what should we expect for the coming years? What is the market telling us? The outlook for metals demand is highly leveraged to the macroeconomy, and global GDP growth should give us a good overview of what to anticipate for base metal prices.

Dragged down by the euro crisis and current uncertainties, global growth is projected to be 3.3 per cent in 2012 and 3.9 per cent in 2013.[50] In mid-2012 the advanced economies were growing at 1.2 per cent, whilst emerging countries were growing at 5.4 per cent. This was a full percentage point below the average growth rate from 1995 to 2008.

Can we expect China and India to play the 'white knight'? Apparently not. Even if those two countries are assumed to grow at an impressive pace of 8.2 per cent and 7 per cent respectively (2012) and 8.8 per cent and 7.3 per cent (2013), their growth is slowing down compared to 9.2 per cent and 7.4 per cent (2011). Moreover, due to decisions by the Chinese government, their economic models will be less and less metal intensive, as illustrated in Figure 9.20. All of this combined should ease tension on the base metal market.

However, they are still likely to contribute to world growth respectively 35.1 per cent (from 8 per cent in the 1980s) and 12 per cent. It is estimated that in 2012 emerging markets as a whole will have contributed 82.9 per cent, while America's contribution is expected to decline to 11.5 per cent. Economic power is definitively moving to the East and any difficulties related to economic or government policy in those countries should be followed closely. Figure 9.21 shows 2011, 2012 and 2013 GDP growth by country and the percentage contribution to world GDP growth in 2012. China and India are the biggest contributors to global GDP.

Any forecasts need to be scrutinised in the light of structural changes to the supply and demand equilibrium. The real question should be whether this decelerating GDP growth (as a proxy to base metal demand) will still be higher than base metal supply. Can we expect surpluses to grow or to shrink?

---

[49] For example, geopolitics, weather, social unrest, market psychology.
[50] Source: IMF, World Economic Outlook January 2012.

Figure 9.20

China's real GDP components

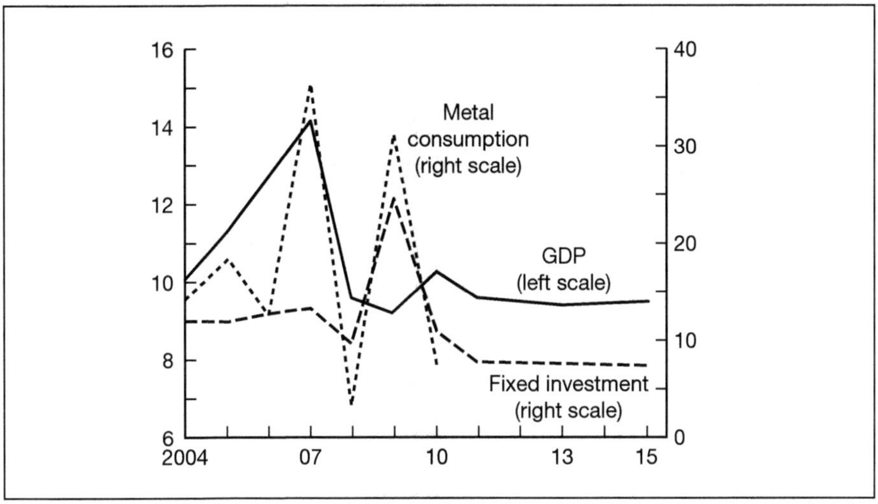

Source: IMF

Over the past decade, prices have increased as global metals markets have struggled to meet the strong demand particularly from China. But due to higher prices since 2009,[51] can we expect supply growth to be more in line with the market? What is the situation for each metal?

Regarding aluminium, the addition of new capacity and the reactivation of idle capacity should boost the supply and generate surpluses in 2012 and 2013 (600,000 tonnes narrowing to 415,000 in 2013[52]). In addition, new plants exploiting low-cost power sources should minimise the upward pressure on aluminium prices from higher oil prices. However, Chinese authorities' efforts to restrain power consumption in the sector may slow the pace of supply growth. Aluminium could also benefit from new production standards in the automotive industry (according to Alcoa, aluminium could soon replace 20 per cent of the copper currently used in cars). Last but not least, even if the inventories held at the LME remain high (on 20 February 2012 they hit a record high at 5.1 million tonnes), they may not be available for immediate consumption. This is due to stockpiling in Detroit and Vlissingen.

Copper is likely to be scarce in the short term. In 2011 demand exceeded refined copper production by about 200,000 tonnes, similar to 2010, and the market still seems to be in a supply deficit for 2012 and 2013 (101,000 and 12,000 tonnes forecast[53]), even with a 6 per cent increase in the global

[51] Higher prices have boosted the industry's cash flow, and generated record capital expenditures in 2011.

[52] Source: Thomson Reuters poll.

[53] Source: Thomson Reuters poll.

Figure 9.21 **China and India, the two strongest contributors to world GDP growth**

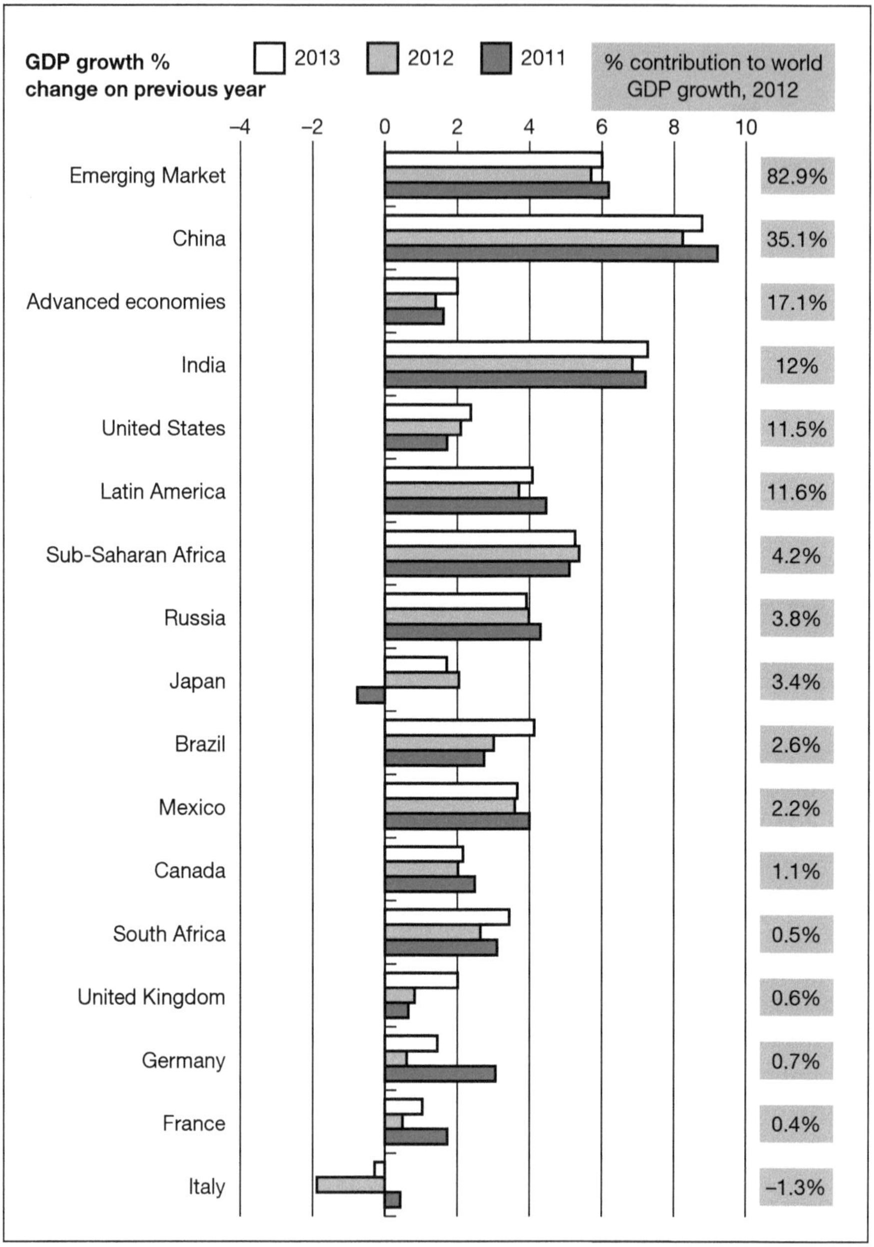

mined copper supply. However, many wonder if global demand will be as strong as in the past due to the economic slowdown, even if China's construction demand is expected to strengthen (new social housing) and Japan's demand may continue to remain high as reconstruction following the earthquake continues.

The zinc three-month contract on LME rebounded in January 2012 to US$2205/tonne but it has since lost 5.67 per cent, trading around US$2080/tonne on 24 February showing that fundamentals are unlikely to improve in the near future. 2011 production was low but is improving, European demand could go down, and surpluses should stay really high (forecast to be 262,000 tonnes and 87,000 tonnes respectively in 2012 and 2013), leaving little space for upside.

The lead outlook is mixed. If global usage increases by 4 per cent to 10.56 million tonnes (despite slowdown in automotive sales and widespread closure of battery production facilities for environmental reasons), rises in global lead mine production of 6.2 per cent to 4.79 million tonnes,[54] and an increase in world refined lead metal production of 7.3 per cent[55] should result in a higher surplus in 2012 at 97,000 tonnes. Nevertheless, this surplus could become a severe deficit in 2013 (18,500 tonnes) if markets in emerging countries keep driving global lead consumption.

The nickel market has moved into surplus since last year as a wave of new capacity reached the market with several large-scale projects in Brazil, Madagascar, New Caledonia and Papua New Guinea. These new developments are, as often happens, the lagged result of the 2007 price spike and could result in a surplus of 60,000 tonnes. However, as approximately 10 per cent of nickel producers are not making a profit at current prices, some of them may halt or slow down production, which could limit the impact of the surpluses and make them shrink to 42,000 tonnes at the end of 2012 and 32,000 at the end of 2013. And finally the current low prices could push buyers to switch from nickel pig-iron (NPI) to nickel, which could provide an upward pressure on the price.

Overall, 2012, and to some extent 2013, should be strong years for supply, but any forecast for demand is still too unreliable. The big uncertainty for the base metal market is of course the Eurozone sovereign debt crisis. If you are expecting only a slow resolution to the European situation through tighter fiscal policy for the coming years, then it could generate negative growth. Another issue is to try and figure out if the US's macro figures will keep on improving. In any case, another round of quantitative easing could push the prices up due to a flow of hot money and possible inflation.

At this stage, the demand growth is still positive and should push the prices slightly up, but any unexpected slowdown could put base metal prices at risk in this uncertain future.

---

[54] Consequence of higher output in China, India and Mexico and the opening of new mines in Tajikistan and Uzbekistan.

[55] Source: ILZSG, September 2011.

10

Rare Earth Elements

BACKGROUND AND CONTEXT

It is almost impossible to open a newspaper without finding a mention of rare earth elements (REEs). The key reason they have impinged upon our consciousness relates to their supply and demand dynamics. Rare earth elements have unique magnetic, chemical and phosphorescent properties that make them indispensable to modern technology. They are found in finished goods such as plasma TV screens, MRIs, iPads, BlackBerrys, DVDs/CDs, hybrid cars, neo magnets, wind turbines and low voltage lighting. As demand for clean energy products and modern technology increases, significant strains are placed on existing REE supplies. We have experienced a form of mild hysteria regarding rare earth prices for the last few years and in 2011 they were hugely volatile. In mid-March 2012 they were still about 25 per cent off their highs and were beginning to creep upwards again as so many of them are almost irreplaceable.

At the time of writing China has over 97 per cent of all known world production – but only a little over a third of global resources. It is beginning to decrease the small amounts available for export via export quotas. This naturally raises concerns that non-Chinese industries and governments that have come to rely on REEs will suffer a scarcity of resources. Export quotas over the last few years have meant that many industries have to pay vastly higher prices for their REE requirements than originally budgeted. On 13 March 2012, President Obama announced that the US, the EU and Japan were launching a World Trade Organization (WTO) case in the hope of curtailing China's control over the global supply of 'rare earth' minerals. Export restrictions from commodity producers – in any country – are amongst the most controversial in world trade.

However, it is difficult to disagree with a country that wishes to keep its own mineral and metal reserves for internal consumption, especially when it is lacking many other natural resources and it has even damaged its own land and water supplies in the process of extracting REE minerals. It is as simple as wanting to build the car that contains the REE rather than export the REE and have someone else build the car in a different country. China now has to try and negotiate a deal. If unsuccessful, the next step would be for the US, EU and Japan to ask the WTO to form a dispute-settlement panel to decide the case, which with appeals could take as long as two years. The Chinese authorities in Beijing have reacted and said that export curbs are necessary to control environmental problems caused by rare earth mining and to preserve supplies of an exhaustible natural resource. According to the official Xinhua news agency, China's Minister of Industry and Information Technology, Miao Wei, said: 'We regret their decision to complain to the WTO. In the meantime, we are actively preparing to defend ourselves.' He added that China's export quotas were not trade protectionism and did not target any specific country.

As can be seen from Figure 10.1, the growth in Chinese consumption and domestic demand will drive demand in the rest of world. If Chinese demand slows markedly there may be more available for export, however the Chinese government currently has structured export quotas to try and protect its home-grown industries.

Figure 10.1

Supply and demand of rare earths

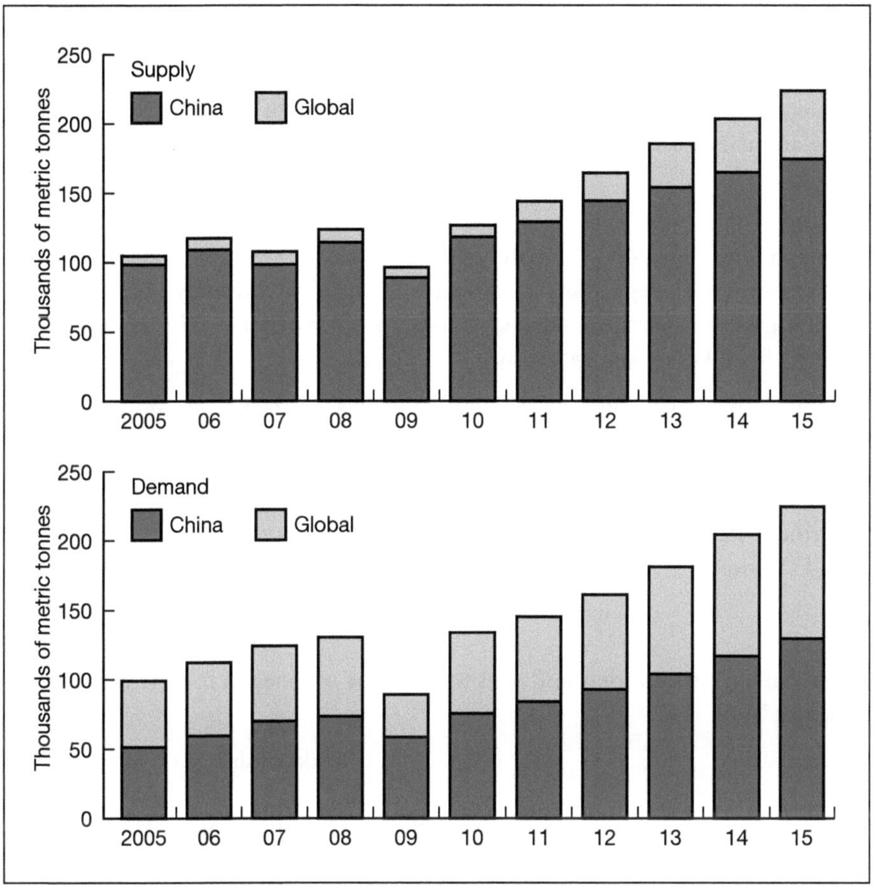

Source: Dudley Kingsnorth/Industrial Minerals Co. of Australia

On 30 March 2012, there was a press announcement from China stating that an official Rare Earth Industry Association would be launched in Beijing on 8 April 2012. One of the main concerns was their defence against the recent WTO action against China but ultimately this will benefit everyone as the authorities seek to exercise more control over this loosely regulated market.

The Ministry of Industry and Information Technology will supervise this association, according to a report in the *National Business Daily*, citing anonymous sources. It is believed that the major functions of this organisation will include providing production guidelines, market research and channels of communication between companies and the government, adding that the association will play a role in influencing rare earth import and export quotas.

Rare earth elements in the media

Here is a selection of some of the more notable quotes from the media.

> 'If China would simply let the market work on its own we would have no objections, but their policies currently are preventing that from happening and they go against the very rules that China agreed to follow.'
>
> (US President Obama, 13 March 2012)

> 'His words, however, imply that he does not really care about the environmental degradation caused by China's disorderly and excessive mining of rare earth materials, as long as US workers and businesses can profit from China's cheap supply.'
>
> (Chen Weihua, commenting on President Obama's quote in *China Daily* US edition, 15 March 2012)

> 'We think the policy is in line with WTO rules. Exports have been stable. China will continue to export, and will manage rare earths based on WTO rules.'
>
> (Chinese foreign ministry spokesman Liu Weimin, 14 March 2012)

> 'Global supply and demand will remain out of balance for the foreseeable future.'
>
> (Mark Smith, CEO of Molycorp Inc.)

> 'The UK government has warned that a global shortage of rare earth metals could hit UK's tech business.'
>
> (Report by the Parliamentary Office of Science and Technology (POST), January 2011; POST no. 368)

> 'The US Dept of Defense is facing a near term shortage of key rare earth materials necessary to support our defense weapons systems, and rare earth magnets are especially critical.'
>
> (Republican Mike Coffman as he introduced a REE amendment to the National Defense Act for fiscal year 2011)

'SHANGHAI – China is building strategic reserves in rare-earth metals, an effort that could give Beijing increased power to influence global prices and supplies in a sector it already dominates.'

(*Wall Street Journal*, 7 February 2011)

'Countries and companies that have or plan to develop industries that need Rare Earth minerals to make products are concerned about China's growing consumption, which they fear will eliminate China's exports of rare earths.'

(W. David Menzie, chief of the international minerals section at the US Geological Survey (USGS))

History

Rare earth elements (REEs) were discovered in the late eighteenth century as oxidised minerals – hence 'earths'. They're actually metals, and they aren't really rare; they are typically widely dispersed but rarely discovered in concentrated amounts which allow for economic mining and production. Rare earths are iron grey to silvery lustrous metals that are typically soft, malleable and ductile and usually reactive, especially at elevated temperatures.

Found in some of the remotest areas on the planet, they are chemical elements that have become indispensable to our current way of life and indeed are used in everything from MRIs to industrial magnets, from communications and wind turbines to your computer or TV screens and even the new breed of eco-friendly cars. The defence applications are even more interesting (see page 249), and research is continuing to establish whether some REEs may be used to treat cancer. To give some idea of context, the battery in a Toyota Prius car contains more than 20 pounds of the rare earth element lanthanum, whereas the magnet in a large wind turbine may contain 500 pounds or more of neodymium.

DEFINITION AND KEY FEATURES

Rare earth elements are defined as the 15 lanthanoid elements plus scandium and yttrium, and their position in the periodic table is shown in Figure 10.2. However, of these 17 elements, promethium is radioactive and is rarely found in nature and scandium is rarely found together with the rest of the REEs. Rare earth elements possess differing ionic radii, producing varying properties, and have been broadly classified into two groups: heavy rare earth elements (HREEs) and light rare earth elements (LREEs).

Figure 10.2 **Rare earth elements in the periodic table**

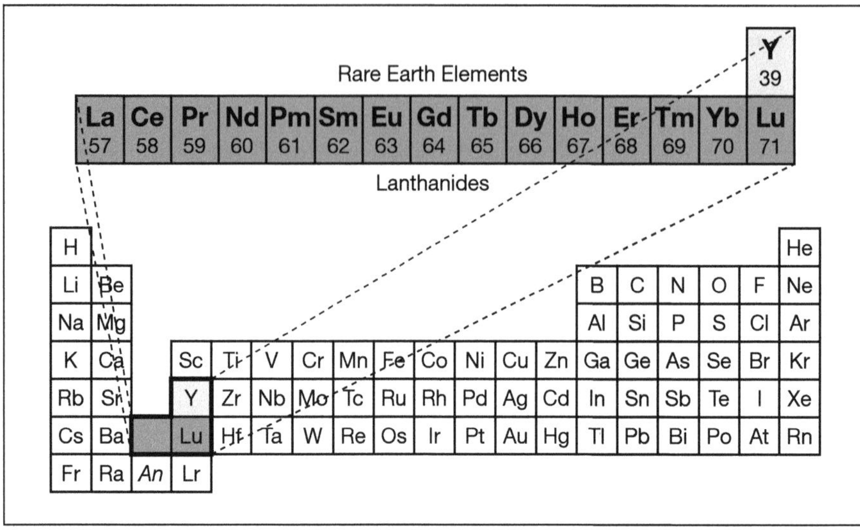

Source: US Geological Survey Fact Sheet 087–02

Key features

Rare earth elements

Light REEs, or the Ceric sub-group, are made up of the first seven elements of the lanthanide series. They are as follows: lanthanum (La, atomic number 57), cerium (Ce, atomic number 58), praseodymium (Pr, atomic number 59), neodymium (Nd, atomic number 60), promethium (Pm, atomic number 61) and samarium (Sm, atomic number 62).

Heavy REEs are the following higher atomic numbered elements from the lanthanide series: europium (Eu, atomic number 63), gadolinium (Gd, atomic number 64), terbium (Tb, atomic number 65), dysprosium (Dy, atomic number 66), holmium (Ho, atomic number 67), erbium (Er, atomic number 68), thulium (Tm, atomic number 69), ytterbium (Yb, atomic number 70) and lutetium (Lu, atomic number 71).

HREEs are scarcer than LREEs, and are more challenging to process, frequently requiring extreme chemical/acid and heat extraction – known as 'cracking'. They will therefore command a higher premium when processed. This makes them more expensive and more attractive to the market.

When eventually extracted from the raw ore, REEs are often sold firstly in oxide form, known as rare earth oxides (REOs), resulting in heavy rare earth oxides (HREOs) and light rare earth oxides (LREOs) or the total deposit may be said to contain a total amount of rare earth oxides (TREOs). The base REO is not the most valuable part of the supply chain but becomes increasingly more valuable as the heavy and light rare earths are separated out and concentrated into metal form. Heavy and light rare earths are commonly found together in deposits and the proportion of light rare earths may well be in excess of 80 per cent of the total.

When separated out, each rare earth element will sell for a different price, so when looking at the economic viability of a deposit it is safer to look at the individual elements and their concentrations rather than get too carried away with whether they are light or heavy rare earth elements.

SUPPLY AND DEMAND

In the 1960s and 1970s China started working to develop the technology for chemically separating rare earths. It was also able to benefit from cheap labour, government support and slack environmental codes of conduct. Consequently, when China started production in the 1980s it was able to undercut everyone else with its cheaper prices. An uncomfortable fact is that now China has a massive global dominance in the production of rare earth elements – over 95 per cent of world production is Chinese. For the last 15 years, industries which use REEs in the fabrication of other goods such as plasma TV screens and magnets have become reliant on imports from China and other lower cost producers. This has led to the situation where there is currently no custom refining capacity outside of China, and REE customers globally are continuing to look for a 'rest of the world' separation solution.

Over the last 10–15 years many existing mines outside of China were 'mothballed'. However, as REE prices rose dramatically in 2011, it became economically viable to give some of these mines a new lease of life, notably in the USA, where the Mountain Pass mine in California was reopened in 2007 by its owners Molycorp Inc.

When the Mountain Pass mine was originally closed in 2002, Baotou, a city in Inner Mongolia (an autonomous region of China), became the world's new rare earth capital. It is here that about 80–85 per cent of all China's rare earths are found, as noted by Mr Chen Zhanheng, Director of the Academic Department of the Chinese Society of Rare Earths in Beijing.

The scramble for REE deposits in China has led to rare earth mines being excavated in an 'amateur fashion', leaving the environment scarred. All rare earth deposits contain the radioactive elements uranium and thorium in varying quantities. It has been reported that some villagers living near Baotou were relocated as their water has been contaminated with mining wastes; this in turn contaminated their crops. It is believed that the mines at Baotou produce about 10 million tons of wastewater annually, with much of it either highly acidic or radioactive, and nearly all of it largely untreated. Mr Chen maintains that the Chinese government is making an effort to clean up the industry, and indeed the 2012 REE export quotas are linked to an environmental cleanup and compliance.

In 2015 the world's industries are forecast to consume an estimated 185,000 tons of rare earths, 50 per cent more than the total for 2010. Figure 10.3 shows just how dominant China currently is; the majority of figures from China must though be considered as estimates. This is due to the fact that a significant proportion of local REE production comes from very small mines – equivalent to your back garden/yard – and their figures may not always be counted in overall government totals.

Figure 10.3 **Supply and demand 2004–2014**

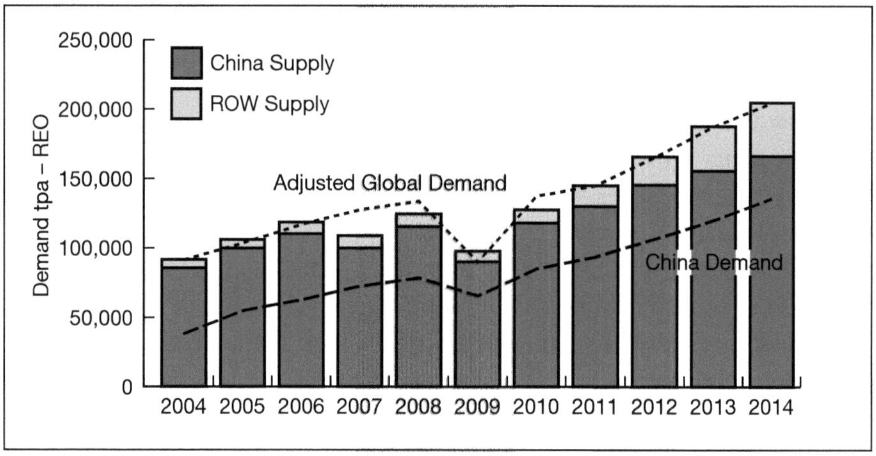

Source: IMCOA, Industrial Minerals of Australia, Pty

Some REEs are scarcer than others and over a prolonged period – up to 15 years – there is a real supply shortfall in elements such as dysprosium, neodymium, terbium and yttrium. Shown in Figure 10.4 is a criticality matrix for the periods 0–5 years and 5–15 years.

WORLD PRODUCTION AND RESERVES

There are other sources of REEs in the rest of the world (Table 10.1). Many of the mining projects are years away from any sort of production. This is due in part to the dominance of China and the sense that the rest of the world could not compete at what, until 2011, were historically low REE prices.

Figure 10.4

Criticality matrix for rare earth elements

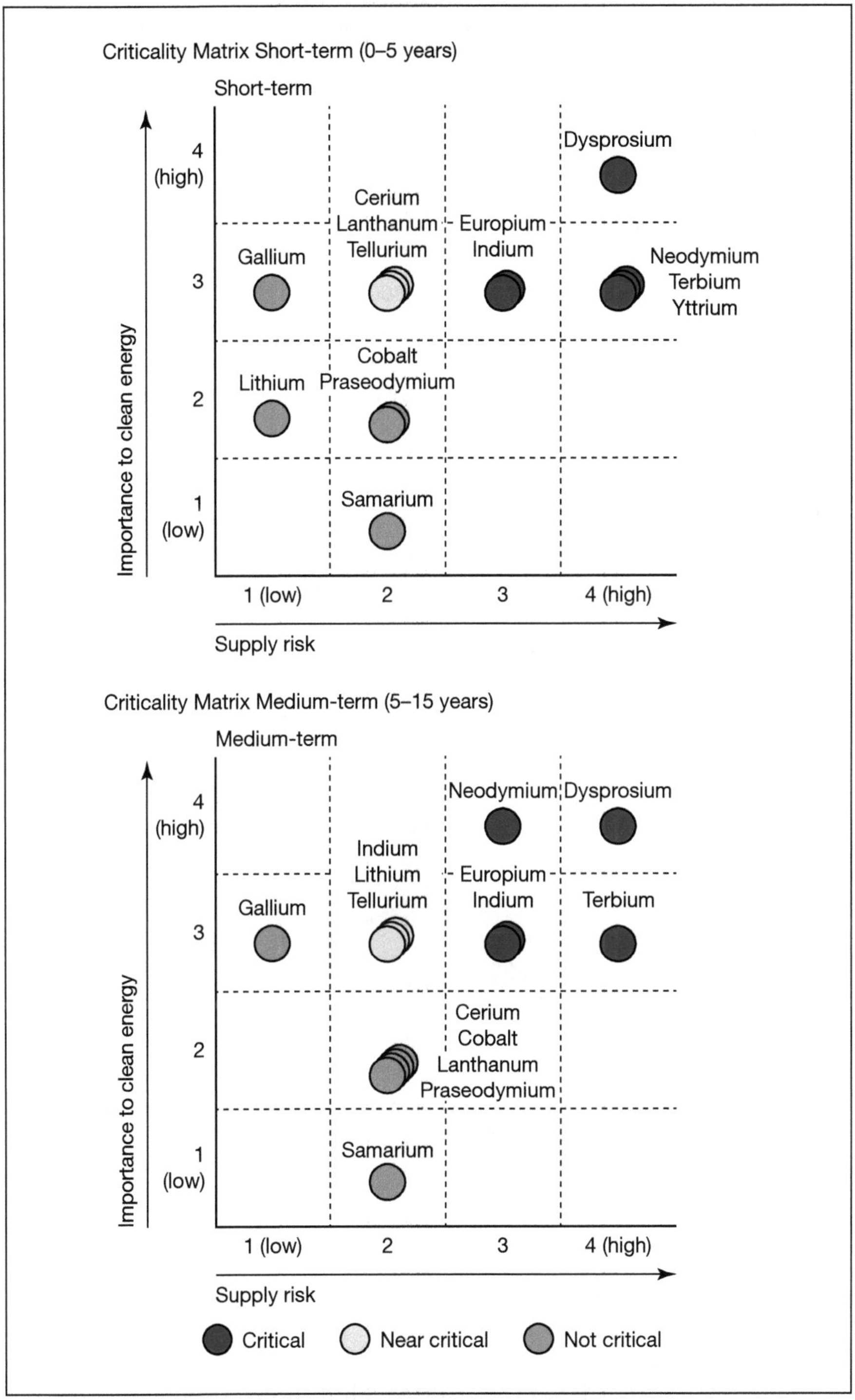

Source: Green Technology Subtrates (US Department of Energy 2010)

Table 10.1 World mining production and reserves

	Mine production 2010	2011	Reserves
United States	–	–	13,000,000
Australia	–	–	1,600,000
Brazil	550	550	48,000
China	130,000	130,000	55,000,000
Commonwealth of Independent States	NA	NA	19,000,000
India	2,800	3,000	3,100,000
Malaysia	30	30	30,000
Other countries	NA	NA	22,000,000
World total (rounded)	133,000	130,000	110,000,0000

In metric tonnes of rare earth oxides

Source: US Geological Survey

Interestingly if you look at Figure 10.5 from the Australian firm Alternative-Energy.com.au, you can see that Australia holds more REE deposits than China, as it also owns the mining operation in Kvanefjeld, Greeland.

Figure 10.5 Key rare earth deposits by country

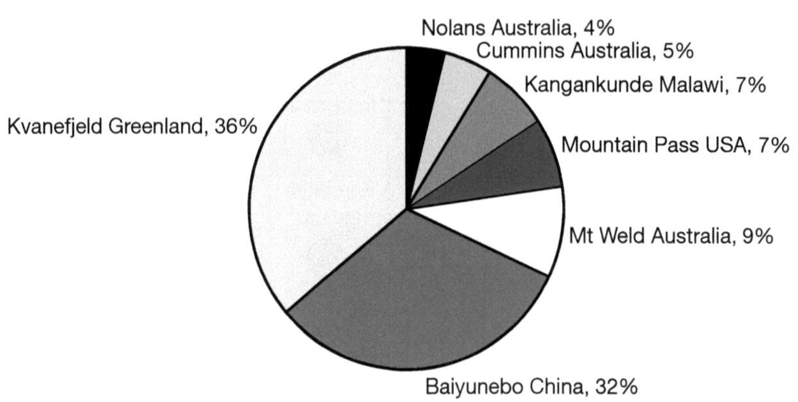

Notes: Baiyunebo is China's major REE province. Australia's Mt Weld deposit is Lynas Corps' (ASX: LYC) very rich deposit and Kvanefjeld is held by Australia's Greenland Energy and Minerals (ASX: GGG)

Source: Alternative-Energy.com.au

Onshore vs offshore REE deposits

There is a continuing discussion relating to whether the deep-sea trenches should be explored for REEs. In 2011 Yasuhiro Kato, a geologist from the University of Tokyo, published his results from a study of Pacific Ocean sea-bed mud (*Nature Geoscience*, 3 July 2011). Good concentrations of REEs were found linked to the hydrothermal vents associated with sea floor spreading. He hypothesised that one square patch of metal-rich mud 2.3 kilometres wide might contain enough rare earths to meet most of the global demand for a year. 'I believe that rare earth resources undersea are much more promising than on-land resources', said Kato, with concentrations of rare earths comparable to those found in clays mined in China. The obvious impediments are the need to drill in deep water, waste disposal, management of the associated radioactive minerals (uranium and thorium) and a host of other practical and environmental issues. The major oil companies have been deep-sea drilling for years, but the other considerations may make this a non-starter.

IMPORTANCE OF CHINA

China is such a dominant player that it is sensible to examine the country's contribution to global rare earth elements. It should be borne in mind that although China has nearly 97 per cent of REE production it has only about 33 per cent of global reserves. The key dilemma facing the rest of the world is that it is going to take many years for existing and new REE discoveries to come to production – in some cases up to 15 years from the original discovery of the ore body. This also assumes that financing is available for the development of these resources. Chinese production is based in nine different provinces, with mostly LREEs being found in Inner Mongolia. The key provinces are:

- Fujian
- Guangdong
- Guangxi
- Hunan
- Inner Mongolia
- Jiangxi
- Shandong
- Sichuan
- Yunnan

Mining REEs is difficult and involves harsh chemical and heat driven reactions that may blight the landscape. In August 2011 the Chinese government introduced a radical new set of environmental guidelines and a mine inspection campaign. This was to combat, amongst other things, the smaller Chinese mines operating as 'leach' mines where high-potency fertiliser is used to dissolve the REE, leaving the land barren and scarred for years. At the time of writing, China's biggest producer, Baotou Rare Earth, has been allocated an export quota but this will only be released to the company if it is found to have complied with environmental regulations and currently it has not succeeded.

The results of the full mine inspection campaign are not yet known but it is admirable for its good intentions. This initiative will most likely decrease the very small amount of Chinese REEs available for export, leading to further shortages in the rest of the world, and increasing the search for viable alternatives and even the recycling of REEs. The giant Baiyun Obo mine in Baotou province in Inner Mongolia is easily recognisable on Google Earth and is currently the centre of the REE industry. China originally used to produce rare earths for export, but as its own domestic economy booms, so does its hunger to keep its own mineral supply.

The Chinese government sets production quotas for the whole REE industry, although, due to the nature of the market and the isolation of some of the mines, actual production is often much higher. On 27 December 2011 the Chinese Ministry of Commerce announced the initial export quotas for individual companies operating in China. Table 10.2 shows the change in the annual export quota for the last few years.

Table 10.2 **Chinese rare earth export quotas**

Year	REE export quota (tonnes)	% change	Demand outside China (tonnes)	Surplus (shortfall) (tonnes)
2005	65,609	0.0	48,000	17,609
2006	61,821	–5.8	53,000	8,821
2007	59,643	–3.5	55,000	4,643
2008	56,939	–4.5	54,000	2,939
2009	50,145	–11.9	25,000	25,145
2010	30,258	–39.7	52,500	(22,242)
2011	30,246	0.0	40,000	(9,754)
2012	31,130	2.9	41,000	(9,870)

Source: IMCOA, Chinese Chamber of Commerce

The announcement for 2012 differed from previous similar announcements in three key areas:

1. The ministry issued separate quota allocations for light (LREE) and medium/heavy (M/HREE) rare earth products, not just for rare earths as a whole.

2. The ministry clearly stated the intended entire export quota for the whole year, prior to making the usual follow-up allocation announcement next summer.
3. The ministry separated individual companies into two groups:
   - The first group received confirmed quota allocations.
   - The second group received only provisional allocations.

Companies were also placed into their groups based on progress towards implementing new Chinese pollution control regulations, with the latter group only getting its allocated quotas if it meets the various requirements by July 2012. Any companies that fail to meet the new requirements will have their quotas reallocated to other companies.

IMPORTANCE OF RARE EARTH ELEMENTS IN TODAY'S MARKETS

Notwithstanding the huge volatile price swings seen over the last year, commodities remain an important part of every investor's portfolio. Rare earth elements are one of the more esoteric commodities yet their use is far more widespread than most realise (Figure 10.6).

Figure 10.6

Uses of rare earth elements

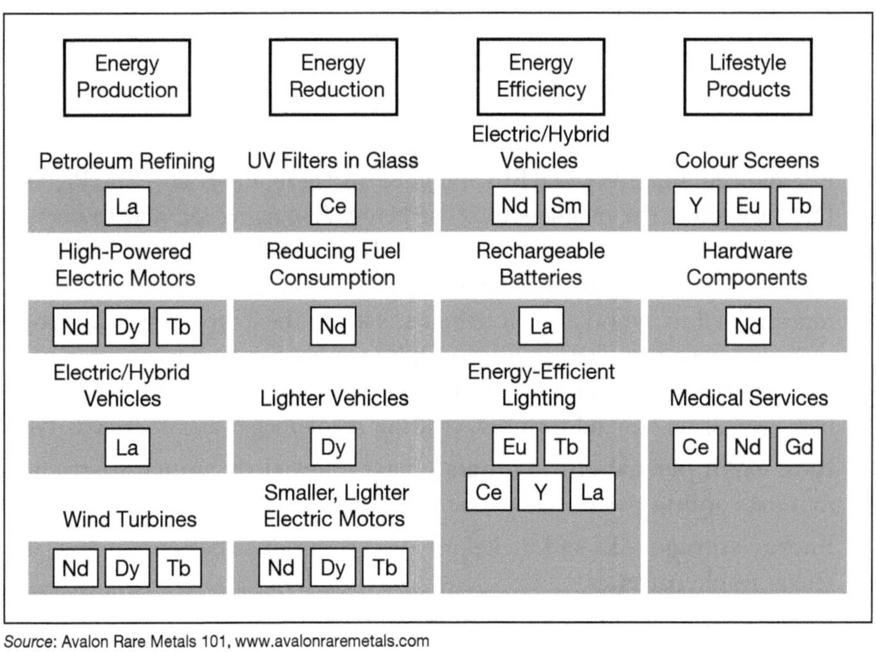

Source: Avalon Rare Metals 101, www.avalonraremetals.com

One of the key resources for rare earth research is a Canadian company called Technology Metals Research (www.techmetalsresearch.com) and I am indebted to them for the following section on both REE usages as process enablers and technology building blocks.

Process enablers

1. **Fluid cracking catalysts** – La and Ce are added to the catalytic compounds used to convert heavy crude oil into the various petroleum products. This is due to their valuable ability to link with hydrogen atoms in the long chain hydrocarbons.
2. **Automotive catalytic converters** – used to reduce pollutants and emissions from vehicle engines. CeO_2 is used in this process together with some of the platinum group metals.
3. **Polishing** – considerable amounts of CeO_2 and oxides of lanthanum and neodymium are used to create the quality finish on polished glass, TV screens, computer displays, iPads, iTouches, together with mobile phone screens and wafers used to produce silicon chips.

Technology building blocks

REEs are incorporated into other alloys and compounds used to engineer components, which may then be used to manufacture other complex products. Relatively small amounts of REEs are used but their presence is critical, examples include:

1. **Permanent magnets** – REEs included in these alloys are Nd, Pr, Sm, Dy; they allow the magnets to resist being de-magnetised and to operate at higher temperatures. They are used in electrical generators, and high-performance electric motors. Some of these permanent magnets and generators are used in hybrid electric vehicles, such as the Toyota Prius, although there has been some research into finding substitutes given the potential high prices of REEs. Permanent magnet motors are now being used in the new generation of wind turbines, creating many megawatts of electricity.
2. **Rare earth permanent magnets** – have allowed the miniaturisation of motors, cordless power tools, loud speakers and hard drives.
3. **Energy storage** – La and nickel are used to produce batteries, especially rechargeable batteries.
4. **Phosphors** – compounds of Eu, Y and Tb are used to produce phosphors whose materials emit light after being exposed to UV radiation and electrons. Uses include liquid crystal displays (LCDs), light emitting diodes (LEDs) and fluorescent lamps. These are more energy efficient and much brighter.

Table 10.3 lists the individual rare earths and their uses.

Table 10.3

Rare earth elements and their usage

Atomic No Initial	Rare Earth Element LIGHT (LREE)	Selected usage
57 La	Lanthanum	High refractive index glass, hydrogen storage, battery-electrodes, camera lenses, catalytic cracking catalyst for oil refineries
58 Ce	Cerium	Chemical oxidizing agent, polishing powder, yellow colours in glass & ceramics, catalyst for oil refineries
59 Pr	Praseodymium	Rare earth magnets, lasers, carbon arc lighting, glass & enamel colourant, glass for welding goggles & firesteel products
60 Nd	Neodymium	Rare earth magnets, lasers, violets colours in glass & ceramics, ceramic capacitors
62 Sm	Samarium	Rare earth magnets, lasers, neutron capture
	Heavy (HREE)	
63 Eu	Europium	Red & blue phosphors, lasers, mecury vapour lamps, NRM relaxation agent
64 Gd	Gadolinium	Rare earth magnets, high refractive idex glass, lasers, x-ray tubes, computer memories, neutron capture, MRI contrast agent
65 Tb	Terbium	Greenphosphors, lasers, flourescent lamps
66 Dy	Dysprosium	Rare earth magnets, lasers
67 Ho	Holimium	Lasers
68 Er	Erbium	Lasers, vanadium steel
69 Tm	Thulium	Portable x-ray machines
70 Yb	Ytterbium	Infrared lasers, chemical reducing agent
71 Lu	Lutetium	PET Scan detector, high refractive index glass
39 Y	Yttrium	Yttrium-aluminium garnet (YAG) laser, high temperature superconductors, microwave filters

Source: The Matrix Partnership

DEFENCE USES OF RARE EARTH ELEMENTS

As the world becomes a more volatile and dangerous place, the use of rare earth elements for defence purposes is growing. They are key ingredients for the very hard alloys used in armoured vehicles and projectiles that shatter upon impact into thousands of sharp fragments. REE substitutes can be used in some defence applications; however, it has been established that these substitutes are not quite so effective and there are fears that this will compromise military capabilities. Some of the key uses of REEs in defence technology are:

- Lanthanum – night vision goggles.
- Neodymium – laser range finders, guidance systems, communications.
- Europium – fluorescents and phosphors in lamps and monitors.

- Erbium – amplifier in fibre optic data transmission.
- Samarium – permanent magnets stable at high temperatures; precision guided weapons; 'white noise' production in stealth technology.

REE PRICING AND PRICE DISCOVERY

The last few years and months have seen increasing volatility, with the REE sector exhibiting extreme behaviour. One of the core issues in this market is how long it will take from the discovery of economically viable concentrations of TREOs to the end of the supply chain where it can be delivered in the final form to purchasers.

As previously mentioned, over 95 per cent of world production lies with the Chinese, indicating that the rest of the world is lagging far behind. However, it wasn't always this way. Mountain Pass in California, USA, was a well-known REE producer for many years, but it was put into stasis when the Chinese inundated the market and made the mining of the REE economically unviable. Mountain Pass only came back into production in 2007. The supply chain for rare earth production is shown in Table 10.4.

Table 10.4 **Supply chain for rare earth production**

Mining	Milling	Hydro-metallurgy	Separation	Refining	Products
From the ground to crushed ore	Grinding and benefication of REE minerals	Cracking the REE minerals to produce mixed REE oxides concentrate	Separating and purifying the individual REE oxides	To meet specific downstream technology applications	Permanent magnets, LEDs, consumer electronics

Source: The Matrix Partnership

However, given the financial incentives, potentially high prices and increasing demand for REEs, many countries have now started prospecting for the ores or taking existing plants out of mothballs. Some have found REE reserves, but it may take 10–15 years from initial discovery to the final marketplace. Obviously some organisations are ahead of the curve, but at the time of writing only a very small handful are excavating ores and producing the REOs.

KEY STEPS TO PROJECT COMPLETION

Industrial Minerals of Australia (IMCOA) has taken the time to tabulate the steps involved in a REE project (see Table 10.5, which illustrates the process, and Figure 10.7, which gives an idea of time scale).

Table 10.5

Key steps to REE project completion

1. Establish resource – appoint geological consultants, to establish grade of deposit – legal and commercial due diligence 2. Understand/evaluate mineralogy – identification of minerals, availability of REE within them 3. Scoping study – required to justify undertaking the Definitive Feasibility Study (DFS) 4. Pilot plan: benefication – demonstrate viability, generates data for DFS 5. Pilot plant: extraction – produce samples for evaluation 6. Pilot plant: separation – generate data for Environmental Impact Statement 7. Environmental approval – preparation, public review and environmental approval 8. Letters of intent (LOIs) – customers will require mutual trust and letters of intent 9. Definitive feasibility study and funding – funds raised on basis of DFS 10. Engineering, procurement, construction and start-up – variety of procedures to get plant to full operating capacity

Source: Industrial Minerals, 2011

There are a number of mining and exploration companies active in this sector and I am indebted to Gareth Hatch and the specialist firm Technology Metals Research for their TMR Advanced Rare Earth Project list, shown in Table 10.6 (an abbreviated version as at February 2012).

Table 10.6

TMR Advanced Rare Earth Project Index

Project	Location		Owner(s)
Araxá	BRA	Minas Gerais	MBAC Fertilizer Corp.
Bear Lodge (Bull Hill Zone)	USA	Wyoming	Rare Element Resources Ltd
Bokan (Dotson/ I & L Zones)	USA	Alaska	Ucore Rare Metals Inc.
Buckton	CAN	Alberta	DNI Metals Inc.
Çanakli I	TUR	Burdur	AMR Mineral Metal Inc.
Clay-Howells	CAN	Ontario	Rare Earth Metals Inc.
Cummins Range	AUS	Western Australia	Navigator Resources Ltd & Kimberley Rare Earths Ltd
Dubbo Zirconia Project	AUS	New South Wales	Alkane Resources Ltd.
Eco Ridge	CAN	Ontario	Pele Mountain Resources Inc.

▶

Table 10.6 continued

Eldor (Ashram Zone)	CAN	Quebec	Commerce Resources Corp.
Foxtrot	CAN	Labrador	Search Minerals Inc.
Hastings	AUS	Western Australia	Hastings Rare Metals Ltd
Hoidas Lake	CAN	Saskatchewan	Great Western Minerals Group Ltd
Kangankunde	MWI	Balaka	Lynas Corporation Ltd
Kipawa	CAN	Quebec	Matamec Explorations Inc.
Kutessay II	KGZ	Chui	Stans Energy Corp.
Kvanefjeld	GRL	Kujalleq	Greenland Minerals and Energy Ltd
La Paz	USA	Arizona	Australian American Mining Corporation Ltd
Montviel (Core Zone)	CAN	Quebec	Geomega Resources Inc.
Mount Weld CLD	AUS	Western Australia	Lynas Corporation Ltd
Mount Weld Duncan Deposit	AUS	Western Australia	Lynas Corporation Ltd
Mountain Pass	USA	California	Molycorp Inc.
Nechalacho	CAN	Northwest Territories	Avalon Rare Metals Inc.
Niobec	CAN	Quebec	IAMGOLD Corp.
Nolans Bore	AUS	Northern Territory	Arafura Resources Ltd
NorraKärr	SWE	Småland	Tasman Metals Ltd
Sarfartoq (ST1 Zone)	GRL	Qaasuitsup	Hudson Resources Inc.
Steenkampskraal	ZAF	Western Cape	Great Western Minerals Group Ltd
Strange Lake (B-Zone)	CAN	Quebec	Quest Rare Minerals Ltd
Tantalus	MDG	Diana	Tantalus Rare Earths AG
Two Tom	CAN	Labrador	Rare Earth Metals Inc.
Wigu Hill	TZA	Morogoro	Montero Mining and Exploration Ltd
Xiluvo	MOZ	Sofala	Southern Crown Resources Ltd
Zandkopsdrift	ZAF	Northern Cape	Frontier Rare Earths Ltd & Korea Resources Corp.

NB: This list is based on the relative in situ quantity of REOs as a fraction of the overall mineral resource and the relative physical distribution of the specific rare earth oxide as a fraction of the total rare earth oxide.

Source: Technology Metals Research, Advanced Rare Earth Project List, www.techmetalresearch.com

If you then consider that each of the listed organisations in Table 10.6 is at a different stage of development, there must be a range of time horizons before each of these projects 'comes to market'. Figure 10.7 incorporates the data and indicates potential timelines for some of the projects listed.

Figure 10.7

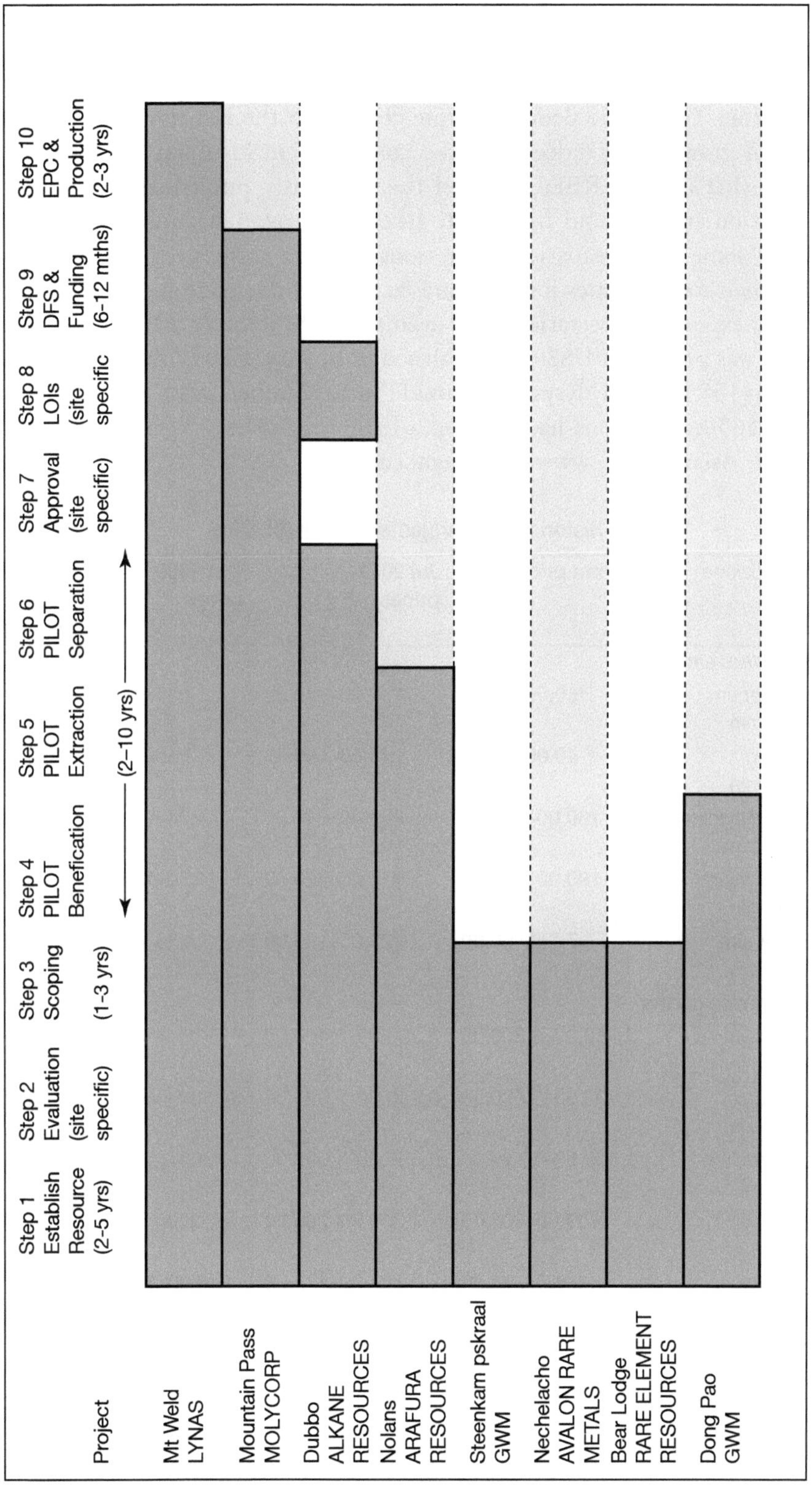

Source: Avalon Rare Metals 101, www.avalonraremetals.com

Pricing

Fundamentally, pricing will be determined by the market, based on a range of factors. Given the poor economic climate in the last few years and the lack of growth and indeed reduced consumption for many manufactured items that include REEs, some of the previously published forecast consumption and demand figures are likely to prove inaccurate. Table 10.7 shows some more realistic assumptions. However, my personal opinion is that their forecast rates for 2015 are far too low. Demand for specific REEs has far exceeded expectations. For example, in September 2011 neodymium oxide was pricing at US$400/kg, although by March 2012 this had reduced to US$155/kg, and dysprosium oxide in September 2011 was trading at US$1565/kg, and this had reduced a little to US$1450/kg in March 2012 (*Source*: Asian Metal, www.asianmetal.com).

Table 10.7 **Historical and projected prices (US$/kg)**

Metal oxide	Current prices	Jul 2011 prices	Oct 2009 prices	AVL 2015 forecast
Light rare earths				
Lanthanum 99% min	**50.00–52.00**	147.00–149.00	4.40–4.90	17.49
Cerium 99% min	**40.00–45.00**	148.00–150.00	3.50–4.00	12.45
Praseodymium 99% min	**160.00–170.00**	237.00–240.00	14.20–14.70	75.20
Neodymium 99% min	**190.00–200.00**	315.00–320.00	14.70–15.20	76.78
Samarium 99% min	**77.00–80.00**	127.00–130.00	4.25–4.75	13.50
Heavy rare earths				
Europium 99% min	**3,780.00–3,800.00**	3,380.00–3,400.00	470.00–490.00	1,392.57
Terbium 99% min	**2,800.00–2,820.00**	2,900.00–2,920.00	340.00–360.00	1,055.70
Dysprosium 99% min	**1,400.00–1,420.00**	1,500.00–1,520.00	105.00–110.00	688.08
Gadolinium 99% min	**100.00–105.00**	200.00–205.00	5.00–5.50	54.99
Yttrium 99.999% min	**88.00–93.00**	167.00–172.00	10.00–10.50	67.25
Prices are indicative and basis FOB China.				

Source: Metal-Pages.com, 12 January 2012, www.avalonraremetals.com

Following the recent announcement of the establishment of a Chinese trade association for the rare earth industry, Jack Lifton, of Technology Metals Research, wrote on 1 April 2012:

> **'Since Chinese domestic demand for consumer goods utilizing rare-earth-containing components in general, and HREEs in particular, is growing and may well be the fastest growing market in any one nation or even region for such goods, this means that Chinese HREE prices in the short term will immediately come under pressure and then trend upwards. However I think that when China is finished consolidating and remediating the environmental damage caused by the HREE extraction techniques used and by illegal mining it is possible that China may make the decision that it should seek to source HREEs from outside of China, because it may not be possible to increase, or even maintain, current HREE production rates and levels safely from the ionic clays.'**

HEDGING AND TRADING

How does an investor get exposure to the REE markets or indeed hedge an exposure? Investors have the possibilities of buying/selling the physical rare earths themselves, but there are difficulties as there are no formal REE commodities exchanges. There are also very few intermediaries as the end product often goes straight to the end user. Trade magazines are a good source of data as there is no open trade in these minerals (see www.metals-pages.com). REEs are also not exactly the type of commodity that you can store easily. Another issue will be lack of liquidity and the absence of a large number of market makers.

The only real alternative for would-be investors is to purchase the shares (stocks) of the mining and production companies in the rare earth sector. Pure plays in an individual metal are rare but most firms publish the nature of their REE deposits and you would be able to get a good idea of the range of their REEs and ratio of heavy:light rare earths. However, any investment in any share will open you up to stock market risk – and this in itself may be unwelcome. Shown below – and purely for information – is a short list of rare earth companies that have been identified by Technology Metals Research as some of those most likely to succeed – not of course that this is a recommendation in any form, or a solicitation to buy/sell.

For illustration, I have included historic charts of the share price performance of:

- Tasman Rare Metals Ltd (Figure 10.8)
- Avalon Rare Metals Inc (Figure 10.9)
- Lynas Corporation Ltd (Figure 10.10)
- Great Western Minerals Group (Figure 10.11)

Figure 10.8

Tasman Rare Metals Ltd share prices

Source: Tasman Rare Metals Ltd, CVE:TSM, courtesy Google Finance, 15 March 2012

Figure 10.9

Avalon Rare Metals Inc share prices

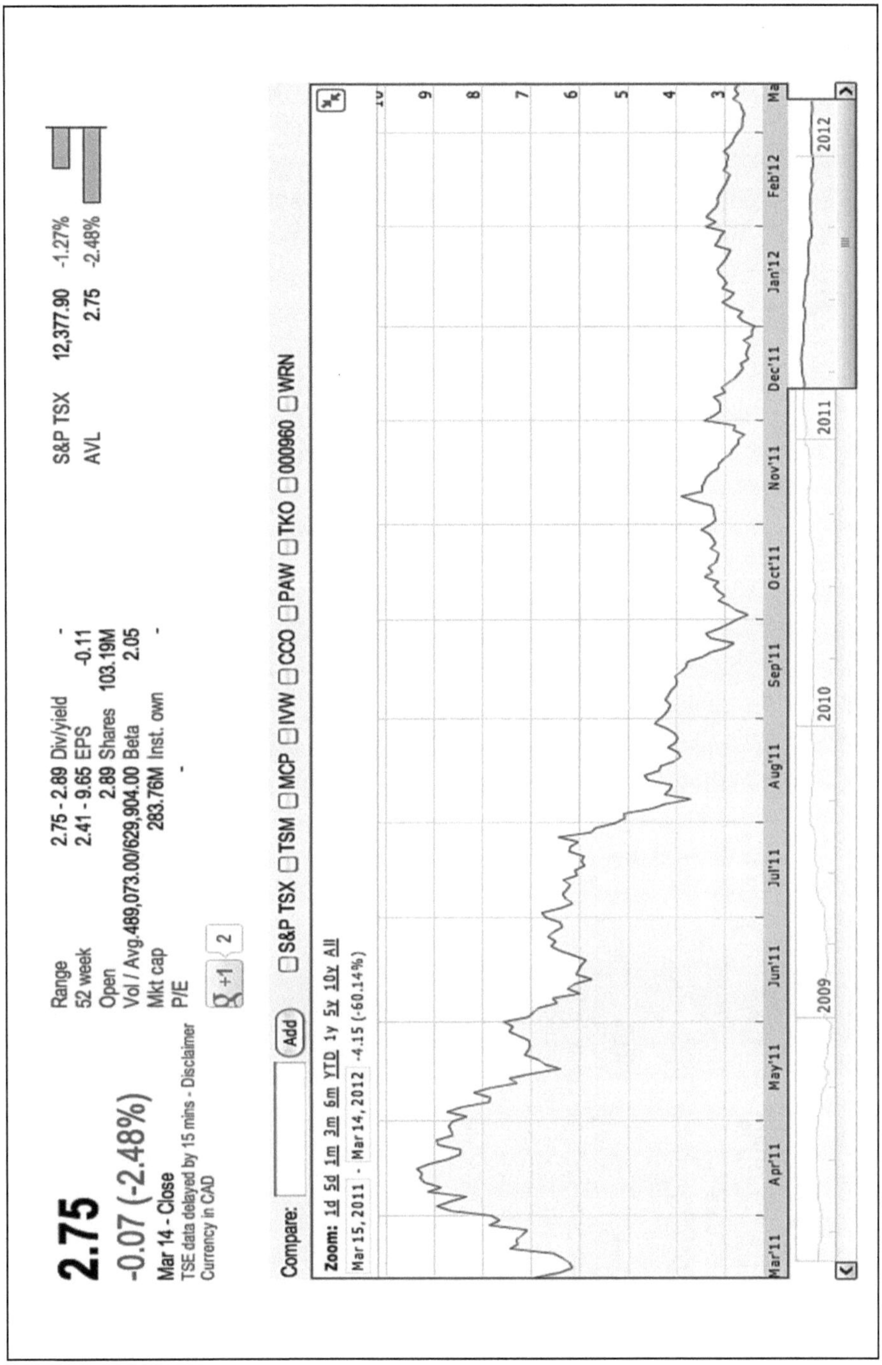

Source: Avalon Rare Metals Inc, TSE:AVL, courtesy Google Finance, 15 March 2012

Figure 10.10

Lynas Corporation Ltd share price

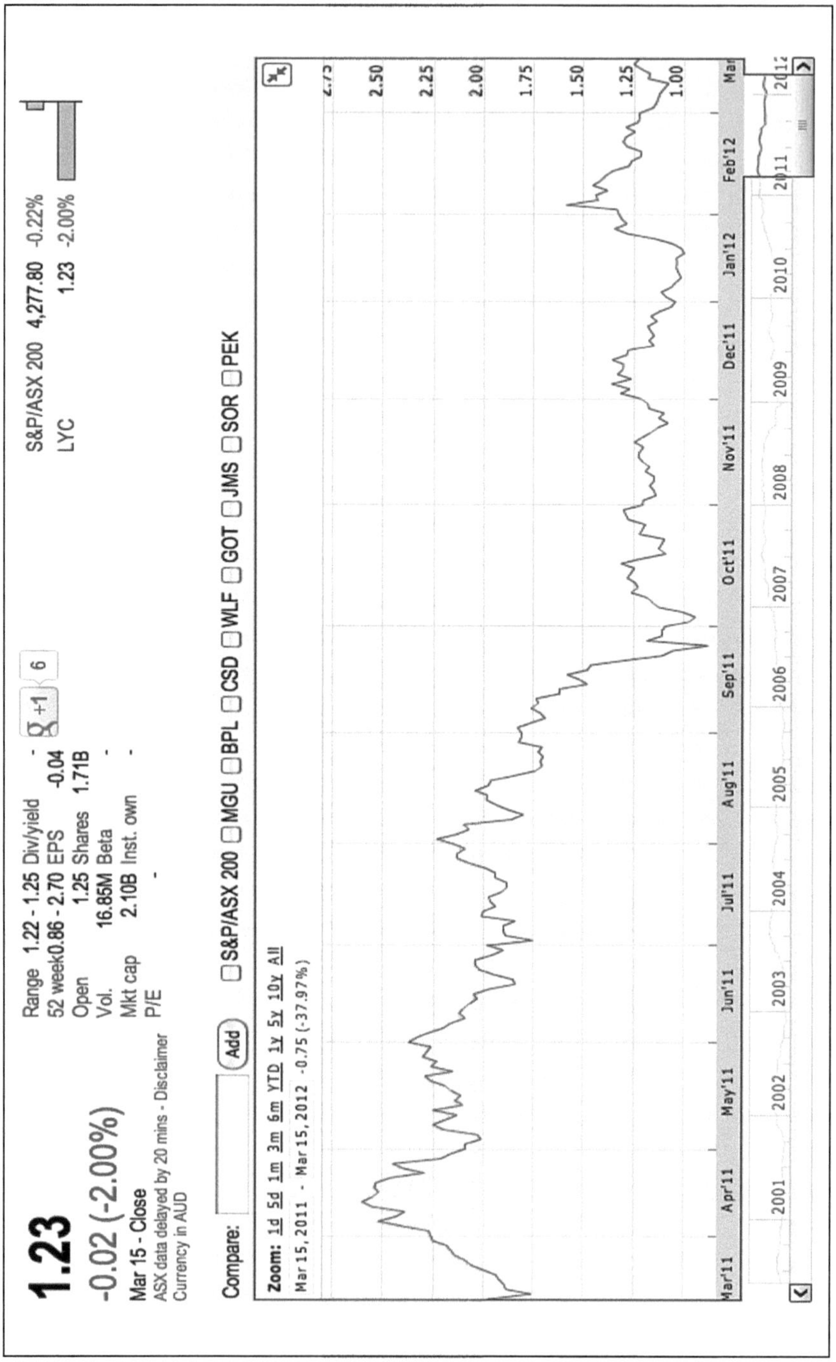

Source: Lynas Corporation Limited, ASX:LYC, courtesy Google Finance, 15 March 2012

Figure 10.11

Great Western Minerals Group share price

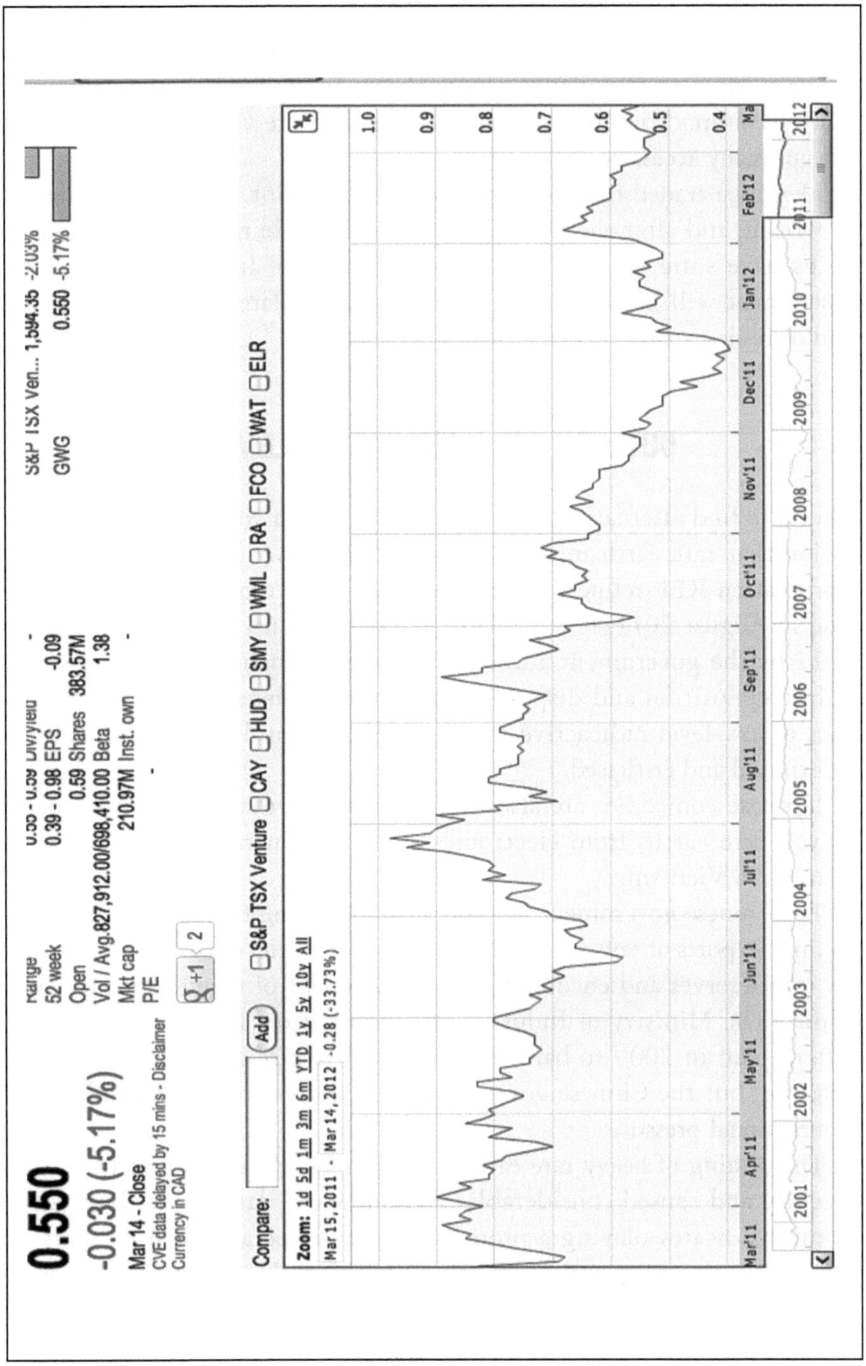

Source: Great Western Minerals Group, CVE:GWG, courtesy Google Finance, 15 March 2012

An investment in private equity or in a hedge fund might also achieve the desired effect, although there are the necessary management and performance fees to factor into any analysis. In contrast to the other more mature commodities markets, the REE markets are very 'frontier' and there are not many access points.

Exchange traded funds do provide an entry point. However, at the time of writing and after the UBS and Société Générale rogue trader incidents, ETFs have suffered increasingly bad press. The likelihood is that this instrument will become either very heavily regulated or be re-engineered and/or re-designed.

OUTLOOK FOR RARE EARTH ELEMENTS

Efforts to find alternative REE supplies have been complicated by the pollution that rare earth mining and processing may cause. The new Lynas Corporation REE refinery in Malaysia was to have been ready for production in August 2011; it was finally granted a licence at the end of January 2012 by the government authorities but since then there has been much public opposition and dispute as the disposal plans for the thousands of tons of low-level radioactive waste the plant would produce annually are scrutinised and criticised.

Japanese companies are also finding it harder than originally hoped to recycle rare earths from electronics and to begin rare earth mining and refining in Vietnam.

The Chinese government has said with increasing frequency that it wants to limit exports of raw rare earths so as to protect the environment, conserve its own reserves and encourage the development of manufacturing within China. The Ministry of Industry and Information Technology circulated a draft plan in 2009 to ban the export of five rare earths, including dysprosium, but the Chinese government later retreated from this idea under international pressure.

The mining of heavy rare earths has been largely unregulated until very recently and caused considerable environmental damage, with organised crime syndicates playing a prominent role in operations that dump acid into local waterways and cause other pollution. The Chinese government has taken a series of steps between 2010 and 2011 to try to limit production, close illegal mines and consolidate the industry under the control of state-owned enterprises.

11

Food and Agriculture

Douglas Hansen-Luke
Managing Partner, HLD Partners
With featured section on 'Agriculture in Africa – Focus on Zambia'
by Bruce Danckwerts, Managing Director, New Venture Farm Ltd, Zambia,
and Marc-Henri Veyrassat, AF Founder and Managing Director,
African Resources Capital

BACKGROUND AND CONTEXT – WHAT IS AGRICULTURE?

In Egypt the word for bread, 'aish', is the same as that for 'life'.[1] It is this metaphysical linkage which explains why investment in food is so emotive a subject and one that brings most strongly to the fore the complicated environmental, ethical and political issues related to so many commodities. This chapter addresses the demand and supply outlook for agriculture, the structure of the industry, ways to invest and the ethical issues that have to be carefully navigated in this sector.

What is included within the definition of agricultural commodities and what is not? Dairy, grains, livestock and oils are discussed as well as the food supply chain: land, farming, farming companies and distributors. Water is dealt with in Chapter 12.

Demand for food is increasing at twice the rate of supply. Is this sustainable and what investment is required to match the two? This question is dealt with extensively within the chapter and the entire agricultural value chain studied with the aim of providing theory and practical examples of whether or not it is possible for supply to meet demand. Marc-Henri Veyrassat and Bruce Danckwerts have worked on the ground in African food production for over 20 years and contributed a significant part of this chapter. Africa is one the world's greatest bread-baskets and yet is currently unable to feed itself; Marc-Henri's and Bruce's case study on Zambia looks at the challenges and opportunities that this presents.

The key messages from this chapter will give the general reader an overview of the fundamentals of the global food industry, an awareness of the issues that it faces and a description of the different ways to invest in these most vital of commodities.

Perhaps the biggest point to remember, however, is that there is currently enough food to feed all 7 billion people on this planet. There should also be enough to feed the 2 billion new mouths set to join us by 2050. Despite starvation, malnutrition and concern over food security, the world currently produces 2800 calories of food per person per day compared to our average need of 2250.[2] The fundamental problem of food is not scarcity but that some people eat too much and that far too much of what is produced is in the wrong place or wasted.

Nutritionists (and governments) have been giving guidance for years on what a balanced meal should contain and Figure 11.1 shows the new US symbol for healthy eating.

---

[1] Quoted from Chris Patten, 'What Next?', 2008.

[2] Source: http://www.nhs.uk/chq/pages/1126.aspx? Average calorie needs: 2500 calories per day for men and 2000 calories per day for women. Current production: Green Economy, UNEP, 2011.

Figure 11.1

FDA recommended daily diet: 1992 and 2011 food images

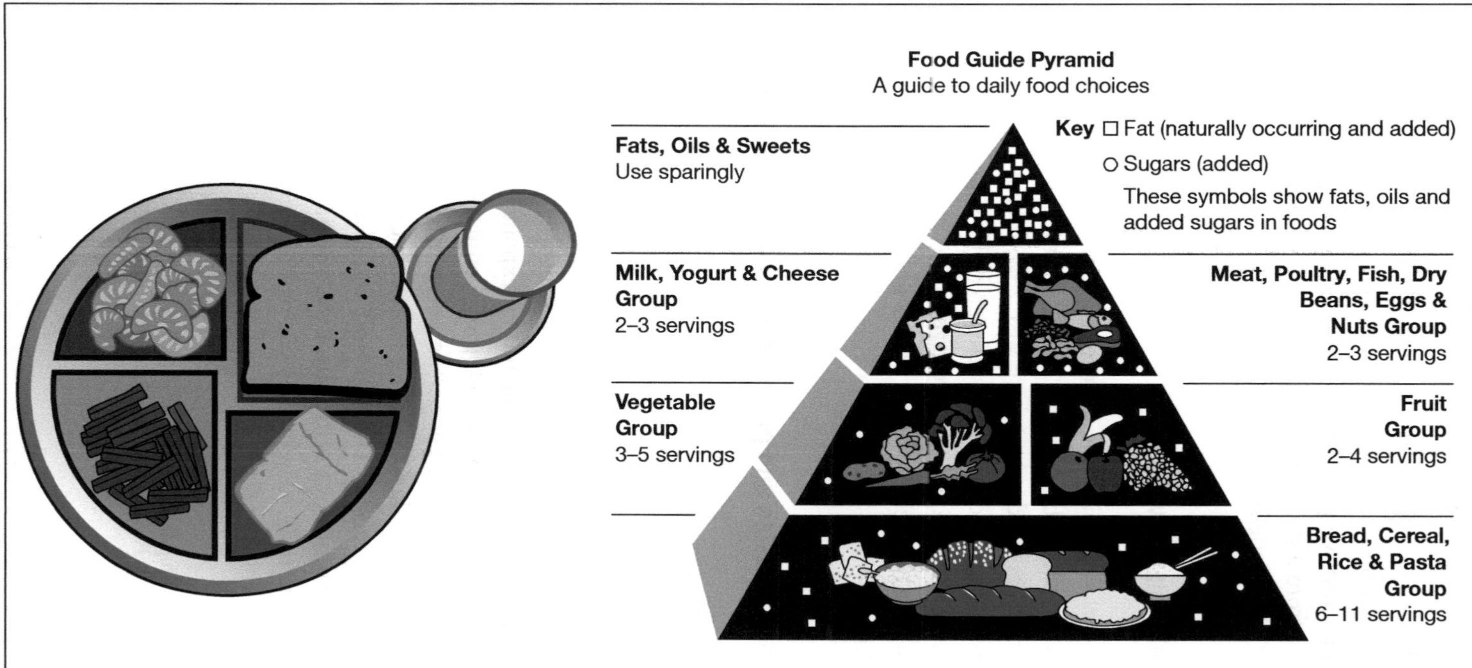

Source: US Department of Agriculture

DEMAND

Food is a need before it becomes a want. Everyone needs to eat to survive and nutritionists argue that the average man should consume 2500 calories per day and women 2000. Beyond this level of calorific intake, then, food moves from a necessity to an economic want. Base-case forecasts for demand to 2050 include both of these factors.

Population growth

The world's population is forecast to grow from 7 billion today to 9 billion individuals by the year 2050.[3] From this simple forecast it can be seen that farmers need to produce just 29 per cent more food over the next 25 to 30 years to accommodate this growth. When the 'want' element of food demand is included, however, then the increase in demand is far greater. Rising income creates new wants and urbanisation creates new tastes as fashions change.

Changing tastes and preferences: the wealth effect

As people become richer it is clear that food is not just about need but also about taste. If food was only about necessity or about the optimum allocation of resources then food manufacturers could simply produce pills designed to meet all of our dietary needs, but this has never happened.

In almost all countries a rise in income leads to an immediate increase in demand for meat protein and an exponential demand for feed. The FAO forecasts that by 2050 developing countries will increase their meat consumption from 30kg per person per year to 44kg[4] (see Figure 11.2).

Table 11.1 makes clear that the production of meat is incredibly resource intensive in terms of inputs and water and requires up to 10 times the inputs per unit of calorific output as vegetable sources. Indeed, if the world became entirely vegetarian, we would switch from food shortage to an instant surplus and the price of commodities would plummet.

---

[3] Source: UN Population Division, 3 May 2011.

[4] Source: *How to Feed the World in 2050*, UN; FAO, 2009.

Figure 11.2

Response of meat consumption to changes in income

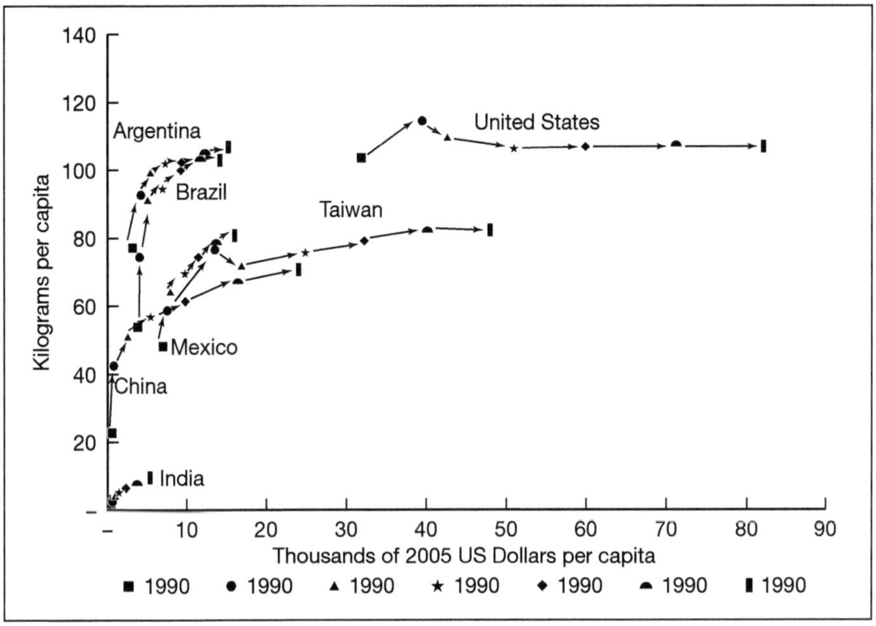

Source: FAO

Table 11.1

Feed to food conversion

Species	Kilo feed per kilo product	Virtual water requirements litres/kg
Fish Farming	1.5–2.0	N/A
Poultry	1.8–2.4	3900
Rice	N/A	3400
Pork	3.2–4.0	5469
Beef	10	15000

Sources:
Feed – Council for Agricultural Science and Technology, 1999;
Water – Hoekstra 2010; International Expert Panel on Virtual Water Trade, 2003

India is an interesting example of a country that has partially bucked the correlation between growing wealth and increased meat consumption. India's 1 billion people are predominantly Hindu and in that religion the purest form of diet is vegetarian or even vegan. Vegetarians will be encouraged by India's lead in showing that increasing wealth does not always mean an increase in meat consumption.

The wealth effect: malnutrition to fit to obesity to fit

Another interesting element of food demand is to chart the impact of income on malnutrition and obesity. The poorest 1 billion people on the planet who live on less than US$2 a day are chronically malnourished. There are also at least another 1 billion of the world's population who are chronically obese and consume a far greater share of the world's food than their 2250 daily calorific needs. The impact of malnutrition is not only an immediate one of death and disease but even those who survive are permanently affected. It is estimated that 25 per cent of the world's children are physically stunted because of malnutrition and the physically stunted on average have an IQ 15 per cent lower than the population norm.[5]

As income rises and people break out from the poverty trap the first impact of more food is to eliminate these physical and mental limits, as illustrated in Figure 11.3.

Thereafter, however, the increased consumption of meats and processed foods relatively quickly leads to an uptake in rich man's diseases like cancer and diabetes. In richer countries where the definition of poor is an income 30 per cent below the median, it is immediately apparent that the relatively less poor are far more likely to be prone to obesity. This impression is borne out by the facts, as shown by the example of the US (Table 11.2).

Figure 11.3 **The global shift from childhood stunting to adult obesity as national income rises**

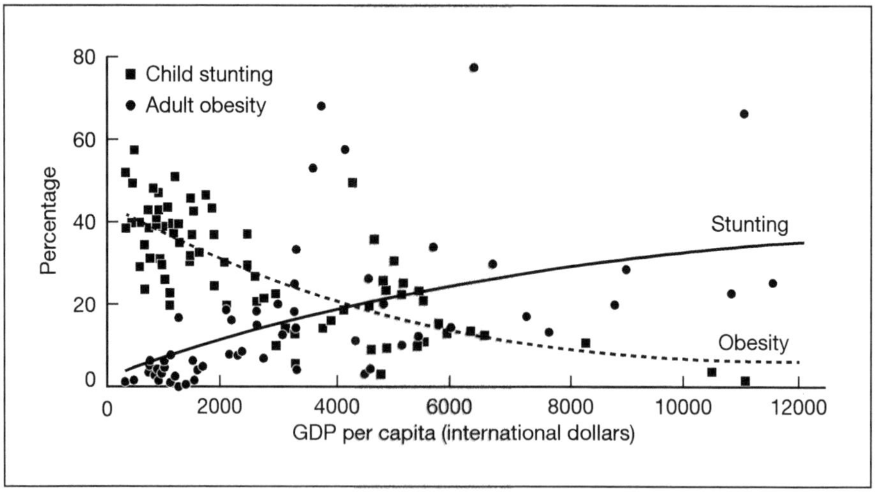

Source: WHO World Health Statistics

[5] *A Life Free From Hunger*, Save the Children, January 2012.

Table 11.2

US obesity rates by annual income among national adults aged 18 and older

	2008	2009	2010 (1 Jan–30 Sep)	Change 2008 vs. 2009	Change 2009 vs. 2010
	%	%			
National adults	25.5	26.5	26.7	1.0	0.2
Annual income					
Less than $36,000	30.0	30.9	31.3	0.9	0.4
$36,000–$89,999	25.8	26.9	27.0	1.1	0.1
$90,000 or more	21.1	21.4	21.7	0.3	0.3

Source: Gallup-Healthways Well-Being Index

Finally, once an individual's income rises to the absolute top of the world's income pyramid, then food consumption declines back towards the levels needed for efficient digestion, intake of meat is reduced and food is more likely to be organic or 'whole' and unprocessed.

What are the implications of the wealth effect on global food demand? It is clear that there are caveats to the simplistic view that more wealth means greater meat consumption, but with the world's current demographic profile the overall generalisation holds true.

Urbanisation

By 2050 it is projected that 70 per cent of the world's population will live in urban areas. This also affects the demand for food.[6] Food has to be transported further from 'farm to fork' and is more likely to be processed and branded than when sold in rural areas. This may not necessarily increase the actual demand for agricultural inputs but it does mean that the overall demand for food expressed in value will rise. It is also possible that demand for agri-produce will rise because the transportation, processing and storage involved in moving food to the cities results in greater waste and hence a need to order more. This would count as an inadvertent increase in demand or as an increase in supply-side inefficiencies and will be discussed further in the next section.

Combine this with the increase in global population and changing tastes and preferences and the UN's FAO estimate is that demand for food will rise by 70 per cent by 2050.[7] In concrete terms this involves an increase in demand of 1 billion tonnes of cereals and 200 million tonnes of meat.

[6] Ibid.
[7] Ibid.

Demand for biofuels

The FAO figures could be a significant underestimate. The rise of biofuels has had a huge impact on the demand for agricultural produce. Around 40 per cent of all US corn production is now used as inputs for the refining of biofuel.[8] Predicting future demand for biofuels is a difficult proposition as so much is determined by perceptions of climate change, resulting government policy and the feedback loops created by taxes and subsidies on consumer and producer behaviour.

The most that can be said is that if current trends continue then demand for agriculture commodities for fuel could take up as much as 70–80 per cent of the annual US corn crop by 2020. Such an increase in agri-demand, including that already forecast given population growth, rising wealth and urbanisation, will have serious ramifications for the world's ability to supply sufficient food to reduce hunger. Later in this chapter ethical issues will be discussed, but for now it is worth noting that the environmental benefits of the US biofuel programme are hotly contested and most scientists would count them as only marginally positive. On the positive side, the experience of Brazil with biofuels has shown a clear net reduction in emissions combined with a national ability to also meet the rising food demand for agriculture.

In total the latest estimates for the overall growth in demand for agricommodities including population growth, wealth effects, urbanisation and fuel usage are that demand will increase by 86–100 per cent.[9]

SUPPLY

So, the demand for food is going to rise by at least 1.9 per cent per annum to 2050 and the demand for agricultural commodities for biofuels by even more. Compared to this, the mainstream supply forecasts are a cause for major concern. Between 2010 and 2030 it is estimated that the supply of food will grow by 1.3 per cent per annum and then fall to an even lower 0.8 per cent to 2050.[10]

The great agricultural productivity gains of the 1950s and 1960s appear to be over – easily accessible land is now intensively farmed. Now, for more land and production, the industry needs to address the challenges of the emerging and frontier markets where agriculture is often at an inefficient subsistence level and producing areas inaccessible or not yet connected with global trade routes.

---

8 *The Guardian*, 10 January 2012.

9 Global Harvest Initiative, 2010, Tilman and Hill, University of Minnesota, 2012, *Proceedings of the National Academy of Sciences* (PNAS).

10 J. Bruinsma, 'The Resource Outlook to 2050. By how much do land, water use and crop yields need to increase by 2050?', FAO, 2009.

Another hit to supply is the remarkable level of waste associated with food production. It is said that in both mature and developing markets up to 40 per cent of food is wasted.[11] In mature markets this is often either in the supermarket, where 'sell-by' dates mean that produce is taken off the shelves, or it is food wasted in people's homes or restaurants. In developing countries the waste in foodstuffs is of a similar level but more usually associated with pre-market difficulties. In Africa it is not unusual to see food rotting at the sides of the roads because there are no storage facilities available nearby or transport to take the food to market.

This section on supply locates the largest food-producing areas of the world, describes their level of productivity and their level of connection with global trade flows. The section concludes with a discussion of the weather and its impact on agricultural commodities, the potential to increase supply faster than forecast and the options for reducing wastage.

Areas of food production and their levels of productivity

By and large the production of cereals centres on North America, South America, Russia, the Ukraine and Australia. For soybeans it is the US and Brazil and for palm oil it is South East Asia and West Africa. Cocoa, coffee and tea are spread over South Asia, East Africa, West Africa and Central and South America. Livestock is raised wild or placed in feedlots in Australia, North America and Southern America. Chickens are produced locally almost everywhere and fish-farming for salmon and prawns is big business in Norway, Scotland, Chile and Indo-China.

Table 11.3 illustrates some of the starkest productivity comparisons between nations for cereal production.

Table 11.3

Cereal output (kg per hectare)

Country	Region	2009	Productivity gap
Zimbabwe	Africa	313	28.9
Kazakhstan	Russia & FSU	1254	7.2
Nigeria	Africa	1598	5.7
Australia	Asia Pacific	1764	5.1
Russian Federation	Russia & FSU	2279	4.0
India	South Asia	2471	3.7

[11] Kevin Hall and colleagues at the National Institute of Diabetes and Digestive and Kidney Diseases, 2009.

Table 11.3 continued

Pakistan	South Asia	2803	3.2
Argentina	Latin America	3167	2.9
Israel	Arabian Peninsula	3250	2.8
Brazil	Latin America	3526	2.6
South Africa	Africa	4395	2.1
Saudi Arabia	Arabian Peninsula & Levant	5212	1.7
China	Asia Pacific	5460	1.7
Japan	Asia Pacific	5920	1.5
New Zealand	Asia Pacific	6922	1.3
Korea, Rep.	Asia Pacific	7073	1.3
United States	North America	7238	1.2
France	Europe	7460	1.2
Egypt, Arab Rep.	Africa	7635	1.2
Netherlands	Europe	9032	1.0

Source: HLD Partners; World Bank

Accessibility

The ability of land or sea to produce agricultural commodities is but the first step. The second and third are to process that commodity and transport it to market.

Kazakhstan and Mongolia both have significant potential to grow cereals and support livestock. Kazakhstan has the world's 8th largest landmass and the 70th largest population. In Mongolia there are more yaks than people and the population density is amongst the lowest in the world. Such places can have low levels of productivity and a relatively old stock of capital or infrastructure. Investing to address both will have a major impact on production but investment in storage and logistics are even more important. Kazakhstan, Mongolia and large parts of Africa are poorly served by road and rail and are often many miles from the sea, by which the largest part of global trade is conducted.

There is another kind of inaccessibility, which also reduces supply. The European Union's Common Agricultural Policy and the North American Free Trade Area promote trade within their own borders but reduce access to supplies from other markets. After the collapse of the Doha trade talks in 2008, the visible market for many of the world's farmers was that much smaller. If demand can only be seen locally, then supply will not rise to exceed that level.

Another problem is being able to overcome local obstacles to production even if the global market is there. Emerging and frontier markets are not only inaccessible but their level of civil or soft infrastructure may severely inhibit supply. A particularly prominent example of this was the 2010/2011 civil war in the Ivory Coast which drove coca prices close to all-time highs as nations around the world imposed sanctions on the regime of Laurent Gbagbo.

Definition

The problem with physical and market inaccessibility can be summed up very simply: the right food is in the wrong place.

Weather and agri-commodity supply

Another major determinant on supply is the weather. The droughts of 2008 and 2010 caused prices to shoot to unprecedented levels and were contributors to significant civil unrest. In the case of North Africa in 2011, food price increases were a significant factor in the 'Arab Awakening' and the fall of a number of governments.

Weather impacts on supply in a random manner but there is an inverse relationship to climate change. Desertification and the warming of certain areas of Africa is reducing the available area of food production faster than can be compensated for by increased production in the Northern Hemisphere.

Furthermore, most weather models predict that climate change will increase the volatility of weather patterns. Farmers are able to manage their crops and actions in relation to long, slow changes but less so when extremes in weather hit them. One model presented at the World Summit on Sustainable Development in 2002 provided the alarming prediction that climate change could increase global malnutrition by 26 per cent by 2080.[12]

Productivity enhancers and waste reducers

The fastest way to increase supply would be by knowledge-sharing and the promotion of best practice techniques between farmers and countries. The Netherlands with its long experience of irrigation and horticulture has output levels 7 times greater than Kazakhstan and 29 times higher than Zimbabwe. It is often assumed that such differences are accounted for simply by the use of superior fertilisers, or steroids in the case of livestock, or genetic modifications. This is partly but not wholly true.

---

[12] 'Climate Change and Agricultural Vulnerability', International Institute for Applied Systems Analysis, 2002.

The UN's Environmental Programme issued a study in 2011 which stated that food production could rise to 3200 calories per person per day by 2050, if farmers moved away from 'business as usual' to a less intensive green model and also moved to attack waste. They acknowledged that this may mean a reduction in industrialised farming outputs but noted that 70 per cent of production still comes from traditional farming where sustainable methods would increase yields.

Not all improvements need necessarily be green. A brilliant example of low-tech knowledge-sharing is the use of mobile markets in Africa. By text and phone calls, farmers are told when and where the next market will be and the price that buyers will pay. This simple form of communication has led to a far higher rate of supply of foodstuffs in all areas where it has been used.

Waste is perhaps the simplest and most certain way to invest in food and agriculture. The industry's high rate of wastage has already been referred to in this chapter. In developing countries, areas where waste can be reduced are primarily in storage and transport. Cold storage is important, as are silos that offer dry, secure and pilfer-free conditions. In mature countries some of the simplest approaches are for governments or supermarkets to extend sell-by dates, for shops and restaurants to distribute left-overs to food halls and for households to be better educated on nutrition and waste.

INDUSTRY STRUCTURE

Before investing in agriculture it is important to understand the structure of the industry. There is nothing comparable to it anywhere else in the world and, other than water, there is nothing more material to our well-being.

The industry has 1 billion suppliers and 7 billion end users but it has fewer than 1000 processors and distributors in between. Surprisingly, at the narrowest point in the supply chain, fewer than 10 firms dominate the commodities market (Figure 11.4). This leads to a huge concentration of power in the hands of very few.

The value chain for arable commodities is shown in Figure 11.5, and can be divided into roughly six categories.

To match the limited number of traders in the agri-commodity world there are also a small number of traded commodities. The trading part of the industry is primarily conducted in commodities markets, of which the Chicago Mercantile Exchange is by far the largest, as shown in Table 11.4.

Commodities to trade

Figure 11.4

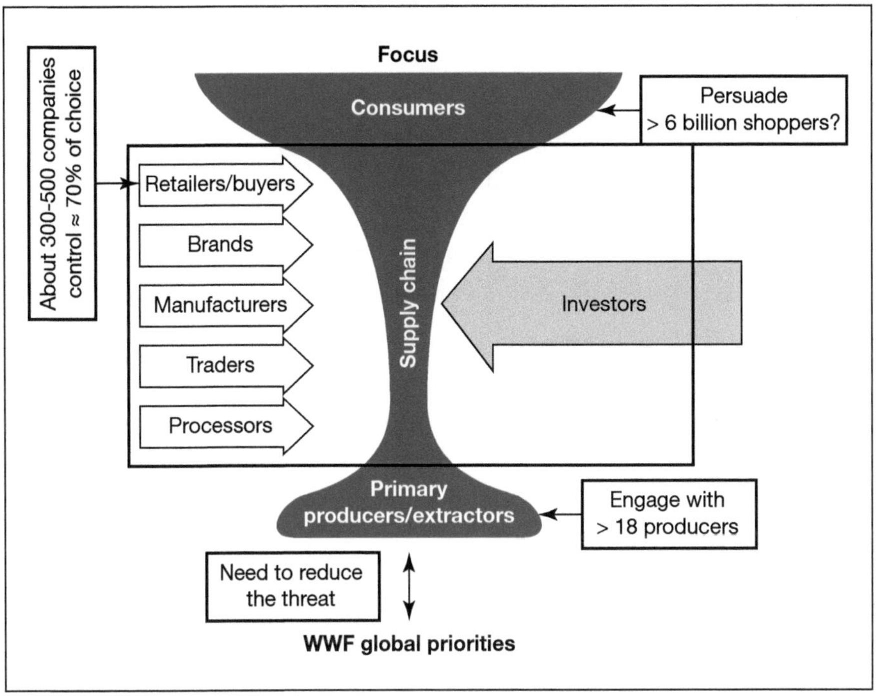

Source: World Wildlife Fund

Value chain for arable commodities

Figure 11.5

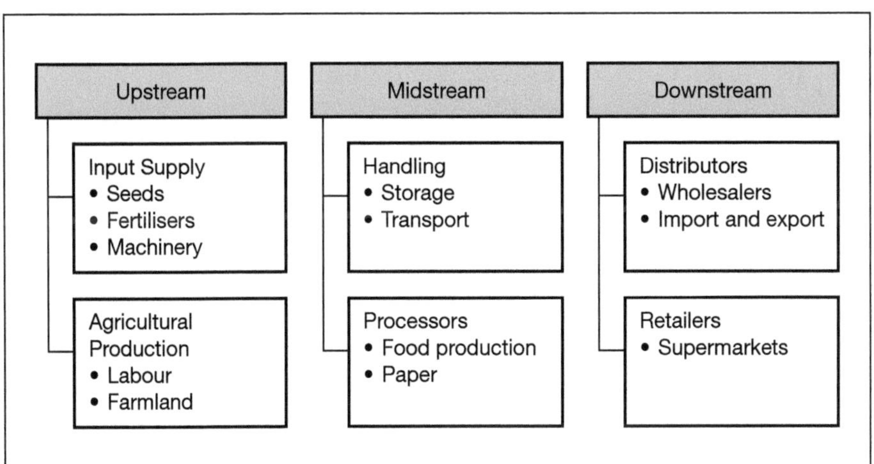

Source: A Guide To Understanding The Value Chain, Brent Gloy, Department of Applied Economics and Management, Cornell University

Table 11.4

CME agricultural commodity slate

Product name	Code	Contract		Charts		Last	Change	Open	High	Low	Globex Volume
Corn	ZCK2	May 12	OPT	~	v	**649'2**	+4'6	645'4	652'0	645'4	32838
Soybeans	ZSK2	May 12	OPT	~	v	**1365'4**	+16'0	1350'2	1369'4	1349'4	40883
Soybean Oil	ZLK2	May 12	OPT	~	v	**54.81**	+0.85	53.96	54.90	53.93	34560
Soybean Meal	ZMK2	May 12	OPT	~	v	**373.1**	+3.0	370.2	374.5	370.1	16732
Wheat	ZWK2	May 12	OPT	~	v	**649'4**	+3'2	647'6	653'0	646'2	15852
Live Cattle	LEM2	Jun 12	OPT	~	v	**121.175**	-1.000	122.225	122.400	120.900	8440
Lean Hogs	HEM2	Jun 12	OPT	~		**92.300**	–0.525	92.825	92.900	92.000	4273
Feeder Cattle	GFK2	May 12	OPT	~	v	**153.500**	–1.200	155.075	155.225	153.375	918
Class III Milk	DCJ2	Apr 12	OPT	~	v	**16.01**	–0.30	16.32	16.32	16.01	278

Source: www.cmegroup.com

200 million contracts are traded annually in grains and oilseeds, with an average notional value per day of US$124 billion.[13] Around 60 per cent of agricultural trade at the CME relates to underlying goods, whereas the remainder is financial speculation. The large trading houses partake in both real and speculative trades, whereas investment banks like Barclays Capital or Goldman Sachs confine themselves to speculation and would argue that they provide useful market liquidity.

Other important commodities markets include cocoa and palm oil, and if not traded by the CME then they are likely to be found on the NYSE Euronext platform.

Since the food crisis of 2008 there has been a growing awareness amongst politicians and the public of the food and agri-industry's structure and the level of concentration. These issues are discussed in the chapter's final section on the ethical issues involved with dealing or investing in agriculture.

INVESTING IN AGRICULTURE

The FAO believes an additional US$30 billion a year needs to be invested in agriculture to bring about the enhancements in output to meet growing demand.[14] To an individual US$30 billion is a not inconsiderable sum. To the capital markets this is almost a rounding error! Global equity markets are valued at levels between US$40 and US$70 trillion and several trillion dollars were pushed into buying out the banks, their bad loans and in quantitative easing during the period from 2008 to 2012. For agriculture itself it is likely that far larger amounts than US$30 billion per annum could already have been mobilised. Aside from planned private sector investment, every major government and multilateral institution has mobilised funds for food security. The Chinese have been investing in natural resources for over five years and food is very much viewed as a part of this. The World Bank in 2008 and the Islamic Development Bank in 2010 both announced that food was a major priority. The subject has been aired at more than one G20 meeting and the Sovereign Funds of the Gulf have each laid plans for securing food security or even sovereignty.

With such a large amount of interest and a need of only US$30 billion a year, there is a significant risk of a wall of money flooding this sector. With this as a distinct possibility it is important to realise that the returns from investing in agriculture will be huge for those first able to do so well. For those that follow the first-movers there will be volatile returns and the potential for the significant misallocation of resources.

[13] CME Media Room, 4 January 2012.
[14] D. Hallam, Buying Land in Developing Nations, VoxEU, 2009.

Investment instruments and vehicles

Between 2005 and 2010, despite the substantial rise in commodity prices, holders of agri-commodity futures would have made a return.[15] This is because of the cost of carry of futures and the need to roll them over on a quarterly basis. From 2000 to 2010 investors in agricultural land in the US and UK would have doubled their money. Agricultural equities, however, increased their value by more than fourfold. Figure 11.6 shows that the Dow Jones Agricultural Index (DXAGP) has outperformed both the S&P 500 (SPX) and the Morgan Stanley World Equity Index (MWXO).

This was partly due to the bidding war surrounding Potash Inc. (a major component of agricultural equity benchmarks), but can be principally accounted for by the ability of operating companies to continuously improve their efficiencies and sales margins. An analogous example would perhaps be the rise of the share price of Apple over the last decade, compared to the continuously falling unit price of technology commodities such as DRAM (dynamic random access memory) or TFT-LCD (thin-film transistor liquid crystal display) screens.

So what are the different ways of investing in agriculture? A comprehensive although not exhaustive list would include agri-futures, real estate, listed agricultural equities, private equity and agricultural debt.

Commodity futures

The futures traded in Chicago are quarterly. Each future relates to the agreed price and delivery of a specified amount and quality of a standard commodity. There are also options on each of the futures.

Theoretically, the agri-commodity should be delivered at the end of that quarter. In actuality, only a small percentage of contracts is ever physically delivered. Even genuine end users of agricultural commodities use the contracts as a means to hedge price changes in crops that they will buy and have delivered directly from the producer.

Futures should trade at a premium to current spot prices as they are purchased on 'margin' rather than the entire value of a contract. The interest earned on cash that would have been locked up in the contract as well as the cost of physical storage if actual delivery had been taken need to be added to the contract price to determine the 'fair value' of a commodities contract. In more common parlance, the difference between the futures market price and the spot price is taken as an indication of sentiment or weight of market opinion. If the futures are above fair value then traders are betting the market index will go higher; the opposite is true if futures are below fair value.

[15] Michael C. Litt, 'The Great Grain Robbery', Arrowhawk, 2010, www.arrowhawkpartners.com/document.php

Figure 11.6

Returns to listed agricultural companies versus the market

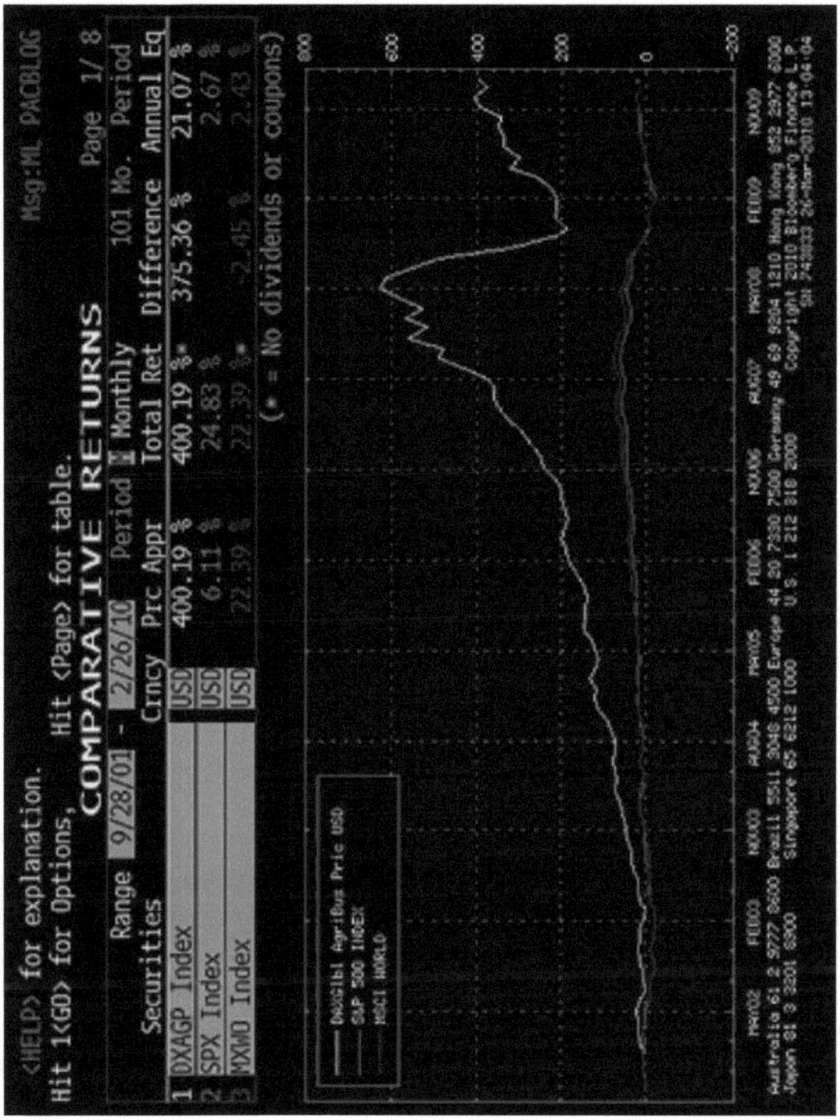

Source: Bloomberg

The CME states the following in relation to fair value:

> 'The actual futures price will not necessarily trade at the theoretical price, as short-term supply and demand will cause price to fluctuate around fair value. Price discrepancies above or below fair value should cause arbitrageurs to return the market closer to its fair value.'

In actual fact, most agri-commodity futures since 2004 have been priced above their fair value. Arbitrage that 'should have been caused' has not. Instead the 'right to own' agricultural exposure has cost investors around 15 per cent per annum whilst the 'insurance' for producers has been coming free. Some have surmised that this is an early example of the excess of money deployed to the relatively tight financial markets that represent agriculture.[16]

Over the last decade the cost of carry and rolling agri-commodity futures has meant that investors were unable to benefit from the continuously rising prices of the underlying assets.

To trade these commodity futures you need to be a member of the exchange but through them institutions, funds and individuals can participate in one of the most liquid markets in the world.

Real estate

Investing directly in real estate has shown strong returns but involves a far higher degree of cost, labour and research. Unlike futures, every single transaction is unique and will have its own risk–reward characteristics. Office or residential property is valued on the rental stream associated with it, which in turn hinges on the revenue potential or desirability of a particular location. It is relatively easy to assess the revenue potential of farmland. It can be measured by the expected yield or production of the land multiplied by the going or future price for that production. Of course the calculation may be easy but the vagaries of weather and agriculture mean that the price of agricultural land must be based on long-term averages with an acceptance of near-term volatility.

Other factors that influence the price of land are its access to water and to markets. These two elements are essential no matter how attractive the land is in its own right.

And finally the value of agricultural land cannot be divorced from politics and international and national trade rules. The latter is another form of access to market. The former, politics, is more about the level of subsidy or otherwise provided to farmers and the stability and predictability of the legal framework in which they operate.

---

[16] Ibid.

Listed equities

As previously mentioned, the returns to listed equities were considerably higher than those of commodities and land. The difference can perhaps be accounted for by the application of human capital to the market price of commodities or the productive capacity of land. Companies are able to capture innovation and competition continually drives the need for efficiency.

Through agricultural equities, investors can benefit from liquidity, proven and standardised valuation methodologies and diversified exposure across a number of products and geographies. However, there is also the possibility of a substantial revaluation of the sector in the same way that emerging market valuations and futures premiums have increased over the past decade. Doug Hawkins of Hardman & Co. has calculated that although agriculture represents around 6 per cent of global GDP, it occupies only around 3 per cent of market capitalisation.[17] As investors become increasingly focused on agriculture the limited supply of agricultural equities could result in rapid increases in prices.

To invest in agricultural equities, however, is not entirely simple. There are few agri-companies that do not have interests in other areas. Nestlé and Unilever are two examples of agricultural giants that also have numerous non-food and agriculture interests.

Private equity funds and direct investments

Due to the absence of many 'pure-play' agricultural companies, there is a growing interest in private equity fund or direct investment in agriculture. Several billion dollars have been committed towards this purpose by Gulf investors and their agents are currently scouring the world to find suitable opportunities.

Private equity allows investors to harness the uplift from profit-maximising companies and to harvest the premium required for an illiquid holding. Each deal can be individually negotiated, structured and priced. This can provide very high and attractive returns but it does require a heavy time commitment and the involvement of experts. As companies and projects can take many years to actually deploy the investments, investors must be patient and not have any calls on their funds in the meantime.

If public equities have produced a long-run return of 8–12 per cent then the rate of return for private equity is closer to 12–20 per cent. One expert US private equity investor recently stated that to invest in agricultural private equity in Africa they would stipulate a minimum expected return of 30 per cent.[18]

[17] Doug Hawkins, *The World Agriculture Industry: A Study In Falling Supply and Rising Demand*, Hardman, 2010.

[18] SII Conference, Cape Town, March 2012.

Improving production, reducing waste and accessing more international markets could indeed generate such returns that the additional risks around agriculture were worth accepting. In reality, however, many investors are still hovering on the sidelines. In late 2008, Daewoo Logistics of Korea announced the long-term lease of 1.3 million hectares in Madagascar. Such a deal was unprecedented in terms of its scale and ambition. Within four months the government of Madagascar had been toppled. The coup that caused the change of government was at least partly driven by the accusation that the country's birthright had been sold to foreigners.[19]

To avoid such risks, a number of institutions are looking to work with development and multilateral agencies that can offer some kind of sovereign or institutional protection and with operating companies that have actual on-the-ground experience of work in agriculture. This structure significantly reduces risks but its additional complexity in terms of co-ordination and communication means that speed of decision-making can be adversely affected.

Debt

A way to gain exposure to agriculture, food and related infrastructure is via debt. Financial institutions like Rabobank and Calyon provide a significant proportion of the liquidity required by trading houses, and Islamic finance houses are particularly keen to earn a return on these non-financial assets.

Longer-term debt opportunities can be established through the purchase of mortgages or securities related to them, to corporate debt rather than equity or through infrastructure financing. The returns available for lending agriculture-related irrigation, storage or transport are not high but they can be locked in for the long term and often come with the implicit or explicit guarantee of government.

Other interesting methods of investing in agriculture can come from supplier financing or through revenue-sharing. Both microfinance organisations and input manufacturers offer loans to farmers to purchase seeds and fertilisers. Indian organisations wishing to avoid the accusation of being land-grabbers have turned to agreeing production shares with producers, or of investing in companies and not real estate. In this way they do not challenge domestic sovereignty or ownership but still maintain an economic interest in agriculture.

Investing throughout the value chain

The foregoing has described the different ways in which investment exposure can be achieved in agriculture. It is also worth briefly describing the part of the 'farm-to-fork' value chain that is currently viewed as most attractive, and the instruments most suited to invest in it. This is shown in Table 11.5.

---

[19] http://news.bbc.co.uk/1/hi/world/africa/7952628.stm.

Table 11.5

Arable value chain

Value chain	Investment needs	Method	Examples
Inputs	Water, seeds and fertiliser	Private or listed equity. Debt/ microfinance	Listed: Potash, Monsanto
Production	Land, labour and machinery	Private equity and mortgages	Listed machinery suppliers: John Deere Listed banks with large agri-mortgage exposure
Handling	Storage and transportation	Private equity, infrastructure or trade finance	PE Funds, infrastructure or agri-specialists and CP for trading houses or Islamic banks
Processing	Milling, slaughtering or pressing	Private equity and infrastructure	Co-investment with trading houses, food specialists or through listed branded food companies
Distribution	Wholesaling and transportation	Private equity	Refrigerated storage companies and shipping lines
Retail	Shops	Private and listed equity	Dominant local or global retail powerhouses. E.g. Migros or Tesco

Source: HLD Partners

AGRICULTURE IN AFRICA – FOCUS ON ZAMBIA

(I am indebted to my colleagues, Marc-Henri Veyrassat and Bruce Danckwerts, who have been working in Africa for many years, for this featured section on agriculture in Africa.)

Zambia seldom makes the headlines, especially when it comes to major investments in agricultural land. A few investments have been made, with variable degrees of success, yet the country has some of the best potential in the region, with reliable rainfall, plenty of water for irrigation and hydro-electric power, and possibly the most politically acceptable form of land ownership in Africa, so it would be fair to conclude that some investors are missing the boat.

Investors who typically think solely in terms of mono-culture prairies, such as exist in Brazil and the black earth regions of Eastern Europe, will certainly be disappointed with all that Zambia has to offer. However, by adopting a different approach, some investors have shown that Zambia's agricultural sector is a compelling business case.

Lager beer consumption in Africa has been growing faster than the Chinese economy and a major South African brewery needed to source more malting barley. To everyone's surprise, yields and quality of barley grown in Zambia (under winter irrigation) proved outstanding. So much so that the firm is now working with existing commercial farmers to expand the industry and a malting plant is earmarked for 2013. Not only are these farmers capable of growing barley of excellent quality, they can do so at a price that makes them competitive within the region, also providing exports to neighbouring countries. This investment will encourage the development of a new enterprise on existing farms, so no human populations will be displaced. It also has important environmental advantages over many of the land-grabbing investments in other parts of the world. By exporting value-added processed food, Zambia will be able to produce an export of sufficient value to withstand the cost of transport. All by-products will remain within the country, to be recycled into other products, and of course the investment creates more local employment.

This symbiosis between a large investor and groups of existing commercial farmers should prove attractive to other commodities (particularly livestock) in Zambia. Use Google Earth to fly over Mkushi (S13 49 E29 21), Chisamba (S15 00 E28 18), around Lusaka (S15 29 E28 14), Mazabuka (S15 50 E27 56) and Choma (S16 42 E26 57). A quick glance at the centre pivot circles shows that there has been considerable investment in irrigation on these farms – there has also been widespread adoption of drip irrigation, but this does not show up so clearly. Closer inspection reveals that there is still a significant amount of these farms that is under-utilised. This land could be brought into production of specialist crops with suitable food-processing partners. Again, when one looks closely at these farms one notices that a feature of this region is that most farms are broken up by poorly drained valleys (*Dambos* in the local language, very similar to the *vleis* of South Africa). These valleys would provide a useful resource for high-value crops such as livestock development. Worldwide, animal protein consumption is growing rapidly as more people make the step up out of poverty. This protein can be supplied the 'Brazilian' way, by shipping vast tonnages of soybeans to China for the Chinese to use to feed their own pigs and chickens. Another suggestion is producing the protein in a high-value way in Zambia, by growing the meat on marginal land and by shipping the end product overseas. An ancient trade has been operating whereby the Horn of Africa provides meat (particularly in the form of goats) to the Middle East (particularly during religious festivals). A modern approach would be to export pre-packaged or possibly pre-cooked meat products directly to retailers around the world. This would require not only exportable meat surplus, but also investors in the meat processing part of the value chain. The brewers' 'chicken and egg' model shows that there is a way of producing an exportable surplus where no industry existed before.

Furthermore, there is no reason why food-processing companies cannot invite small-scale farmers (on communal land) to contribute to the required production. However, we would caution that such practices come with an important caveat: companies buying produce from small-scale farmers must shoulder the responsibility of monitoring the land-use techniques of these farmers and ensure that the best possible practices are adopted. Many Zambian soils, being ancient, are fragile. A few years of reckless, badly implemented agriculture can do serious harm.

Zambia's cotton industry is entirely based on small-scale agriculture. They have learned to herd cats, a technique that investors adopting the brewers' approach would find useful. Farmers are notoriously independent – which is part of their strength, but also part of their uncooperative weakness. In order to lend money to their small-scale producers, the cotton industry learned to group them in clusters, whereby all the members in that group would guarantee the loans of the whole cluster. They soon discovered that these clusters have another, more important, function and that was as a means of disseminating knowledge. It is much more challenging to produce 600 hectares of mixed crops than it is to produce 10,000 hectares of monoculture – which is why prairie farming has so often been the model of choice for agricultural investors. By adopting the brewery/cotton industry approach an investor can tap into the innovation of these individual farmers and use clusters of them to disseminate that knowledge and to supply mutual support. Farmers working together to produce a commodity for export no longer feel that they are in competition with their neighbour; instead they feel united with their neighbour and their processor to produce an internationally competitive product of which they can all be proud.

In addition, no investment should be considered without giving due consideration to the economic and political environment of the country in question. African agriculture is no exception. There are various reasons why Africa has not developed as rapidly as it could. Some will argue that inadequate government policy takes the lion's share of the blame, while free market policy, imposed by the international community, comes a close second. The free market remains a myth in agriculture, with subsidies distorting the sector on a worldwide basis. As Eric Reinert points out in his book *How Rich Countries got Rich and Why Poor Countries stay Poor*, no industrialised nation developed an industry without first closing its doors to foreign competition. Any interference in the free market is dangerous and Zambia can give both good and bad examples of how to go about it. Former President (1964–1991) Dr Kenneth Kaunda's use of permanently subsidised parastatal companies, staffed with political appointees, clearly was (and remains) the wrong way. On the other hand, it makes sense for Zambia to be self-sufficient in wheat. By keeping out foreign imports of subsidised wheat – sometimes traceable to food aid received by neighbouring countries

– the government gave the agricultural sector sufficient confidence to invest, primarily in the irrigation and harvesting equipment necessary for wheat production, with the result that Zambia is now self-sufficient in wheat and able to export small quantities within the region.

In the Zambian sub-tropical climate wheat suffers too much disease if it is grown under summer rainfall; therefore it needs to be grown under winter irrigation and, as such, it cannot be competitive with South American or subsidised Australian wheat on the world market. Yet it remains a valuable industry to Zambia. In the same vein, locally produced wheat is competitive with imported, non-subsidised wheat. In other words, careful use of trade restrictions may be necessary to help some of the sectors mentioned in this section to grow to a size and sophistication that will allow them to compete on regional and possibly world markets.

Two current projects clearly illustrate that there are different ways to invest in Zambian agriculture. The first involves the planting of palm oil on a floodplain (see Google Earth S11 45 E30 49). Although this project, being undertaken by a Zambian company, is behind its initial, ambitious target, it could prove unique in that it will be the first palm oil plantation in the world not replacing indigenous forest. It is also in an area of very low population and could have a definite positive impact on the surrounding community. This should be contrasted with an attempt to grow 160,000 hectares of Jatropha (bio-diesel) in the Mpika district of Northern Zambia (see Google Earth S11 52 E31 26). This project seems to be delayed and there are concerns about the footprint that will be required for the venture, and the possible impact on natural woodland of that area.

In conclusion, although Zambia has yet to attract large-scale, global agricultural investors, there are real opportunities that exist to develop value-added products in collaboration with existing farmers, both large (commercial) and small scale. Such synergies are more environmentally sound than many of the 'land-grabbing' projects in other parts of the world, as they will promote multi-cropping operations on widely distributed farms; they will enhance local employment, leave the by-products in the country of origin to be recycled, and will only use transport infrastructure (and transport energy) to ship high-value products. Crops as diverse as wheat, barley, soybeans, tobacco, cotton, rice, sugar, maize, citrus, nuts, fruits and vegetable, and animal protein from cattle, pigs, chickens, goats, fish, wildlife and dairy, could all be developed in a similar manner. Industrial investors and financial institutions that choose to follow the brewers' model will be in a perfect position to gain strong support from all stakeholders – politicians, local communities, land owners, environmentalists and shareholders. It just takes long-term vision.

THE ETHICS AND SOCIAL EQUITY OF FOOD INVESTMENT

Even the recent James Bond novel, *Carte Blanche*, bases its plot around food and taps the moral ambivalence that many feel about the making of money or holding of power based on access to food.

Food lies at the cutting edge of moral philosophy and economics. There is already more than enough food in the world to feed us all. If we all became vegetarians then both hunger and increases in global warming would be eliminated. Given these facts should government step in and control who eats what and where?

Control of food and agriculture

There are a few who see this as a practical possibility and point to the experience of the United Kingdom during its period of war-induced rationing in the 1940 and 1950s. Then the overall standard of health and (non-conflict) life expectancy increased for the population as a whole. Although most do not want to see their food controlled or transferred to other nations, there is a disquiet that non-elected trading companies hold such an extraordinary degree of market power and that just one or two firms control access to the best seeds and inputs.

Biofuels v. energy security

By contrast, biofuels is an industry very much influenced by electoral considerations and where the ethics and social equity of agriculture are particularly open to challenge.

> **'I'll be the president who harnesses the ingenuity of farmers ... to free this nation from the tyranny of oil once and for all.'**
>
> (Barack Obama, 4 January 2008)

Every four years, in chilly January, Iowa holds the first caucuses of the American presidential campaigns. It is also the state which most benefits from farming subsidies for biofuels. It is considered electoral suicide to argue that payments made to farmers do little to reduce global warming and a lot to increase the price of corn. Instead if climate change cannot be used to justify subsidies then oil security is. It is perhaps worth pointing out here the connection between oil and food prices. Oil is the biggest input to fertilisers and the cost of agricultural transport. If oil goes up so do food prices and if biofuel is used as an alternative to oil then food prices will go up even faster.

Outside of American presidential politics many did eventually highlight the choice between feeding people and feeding cars. The *Journal of American Physicians and Surgeons* published a report in spring 2011[20] which claimed that nearly 200,000 people may have starved as an indirect result of American biofuel subsidies. This argument combined with the crisis around the US Federal deficit meant that in September 2011 the Senate passed a bill to remove biofuel subsidies at the pump. Simultaneously, however, the President pledged US$500 million of subsidies for next-generation biofuel growth.

Government policy and subsidy

Of course the Americans aren't the only nation to protect or subsidise their farmers. The European Union's Common Agricultural Policy has long held food prices artificially high in Europe whilst simultaneously blocking entry for far less well-off Third World farmers. Indeed, almost every country in the world has some form of food policy which favours domestic farmers against international competition and national consumers. And among farmers it is a truism that the richest farmers receive the largest subsidies.

Government policy seldom has the impact that the framers of legislation expect and the unintended consequences can be dramatic. It has been claimed by some but denied by others that the Fed's policy of easy money following the 2008 financial crisis pushed up global food prices to unprecedented levels. The transmission mechanism is thought to be the commodities markets, oil or general inflation. Low interest rates in the US, Europe and Japan have made it far cheaper to borrow and thus speculate in agricultural futures. This, it is argued, drove up their prices. Another alleged transmission mechanism is that the low US rates and the US Treasury have allowed the US dollar to depreciate and thus pushed up the dollar price of oil and increased the cost of farming inputs. And, finally, in a period of general inflation the price of real assets, land and food, are likely to increase most in nominal terms. Are the mature economies deliberately inflating their way out of debt despite its accompanying effect of pushing millions into hunger?

Food security and food sovereignty

The linkages between monetary policy and food prices are yet to be conclusively proved but food and food security was without doubt an integral part of the 'Arab Awakening'.

---

[20] Indur M. Goklany, 'Could Biofuel Policies Increase Death and Disease in Developing Countries?'.

The 2010 Russian and Ukrainian wheat harvests failed and this, combined with bans on exports, pushed up global food prices. This exacerbated Arab leaders' fears about food security and resulting political instability. They raced each other to put in orders to boost their food stocks only to see this competition push up prices further. The claims of protesters that their governments did nothing for their people appeared to be vindicated and the governments fell.

This example of misdirected policy serves as a warning to governments set on food security for their people or even food sovereignty. The ability for a government to secure food for its people is an essential test of its legitimacy but it can also quickly become a zero-sum game if all governments hoard simultaneously. Food sovereignty – the wish to own and control food resources – has had a curious history. Saudi Arabia decided in the 1970s that it must be self-sufficient in wheat. It set up irrigation plants and was so successful that it became the world's seventh largest wheat exporter. Even though it was willing to pay the huge cost for this food sovereignty programme, the kingdom was unable to fight nature and gave up production 2007 after it became apparent that it depleted water resources at an alarming rate.

In the last five years, military organisations around the world have been briefed and played war games around hypothetical food and water wars. Looking at the history of Africa, where conflict and resource scarcity have been so often linked, this is sound strategy. An even sounder strategy for food security is the multilateral approach espoused by the G20, the World Bank and the Organisation of Islamic Conferences.

Sourcing, GM food, organic and Halal foods

Not all ethical issues around food are government-based, however. Bottom-up concerns and ethically founded changes to tastes and preferences are also driving agriculture and investment.

Amongst the richest populations there is an increasing demand for the healthiest and most environmentally sound food products. This demand brings with it a requirement that consumers see where their food has been sourced. Questions may be asked about the cost and carbon footprint of imported food or worries expressed over the extent to which genetically modified food is safe.

Not all of these concerns can be simultaneously addressed. There are trade-offs. The fastest way to reduce global hunger is probably by the more widespread use of genetic modifications and increased trading and thus transportation of food. The UN Environmental Programme may believe that green farming can feed the world's population by 2050 but organisations like the World Wildlife Fund see the need to expand sustainable mass fish and livestock farming rather than boosting land-intensive organic farming.

Another change in demand that will affect the food industry and the focus on sourcing is the growth of the world's Islamic population. There are currently over 1.5 billion Muslims and their population and income are growing faster than any other group. If Halal food is available then that is the food that Muslims must eat. With increased wealth, global trade and transparent sourcing, more and more Muslims are able to demand and be supplied with Halal food. So at least there is one ethical factor that can be directly and positively translated into an investment opportunity.

CONCLUSION

Food security requires food investment. They are not contradictory goals. Due to its essential nature, food cannot be divorced from public policy and politics but investment requires profit. This chapter has aimed to describe the global supply and demand dynamics for agriculture, to provide an insight into its structure and to illustrate the different ways to invest in the sector.

Investment is required, but not a huge amount, and there are many ways in which that investment can be profitable. The opportunities in Africa, particularly, have been well explained.

There are also, as our section on ethics highlighted, many pitfalls and difficult issues that must be surmounted before investment in agriculture and an equitable feeding of the world's population can be assured. Just US$30 billion of extra investment is all that is required to satisfy basic nutritional needs. If the right framework can be constructed then it is likely that far more than this will be invested and that current concerns about food can be addressed profitably and at least partially resolved before 2050.

12

Water

BACKGROUND AND CONTEXT

Whilst researching this chapter, I searched on the Internet for 'water as a scarce resource', finding information from the World Health Organization (WHO) website (www.who.int).

Ten facts about water scarcity

1. Water scarcity occurs even in areas where there is plenty of rainfall or freshwater. How water is conserved, used and distributed in communities, and the quality of the water available, can determine if there is enough to meet the demands of households, farms, industry and the environment.
2. Water scarcity affects one in three people on every continent of the globe. The situation is getting worse as needs for water rise along with population growth, urbanisation and increases in household and industrial uses.
3. Almost one-fifth of the world's population (about 1.3 billion people) lives in areas where the water is physically scarce. One-quarter of the global population also live in developing countries that face water shortages due to a lack of infrastructure to fetch water from rivers and aquifers.
4. Water scarcity forces people to rely on unsafe sources of drinking water. It also means they cannot bathe or clean their clothes or homes properly.
5. Poor water quality can increase the risk of such diarrhoeal diseases as cholera, typhoid fever and dysentery, and other water-borne infections. Water scarcity can lead to diseases such as trachoma (an eye infection that can lead to blindness), plague and typhus.
6. Water scarcity encourages people to store water in their homes. This can increase the risk of household water contamination and provide breeding grounds for mosquitoes – which are carriers of dengue fever, malaria and other diseases.
7. Water scarcity underscores the need for better water management. Good water management also reduces breeding sites for such insects as mosquitoes that can transmit diseases and prevents the spread of water-borne infections such as schistosomiasis, a severe illness.
8. A lack of water has driven up the use of wastewater for agricultural production in poor urban and rural communities. More than 10 per

cent of people worldwide consume foods irrigated by wastewater that can contain chemicals or disease-causing organisms.

9. Millennium Development Goal number 7, target 10 aims to halve, by 2015, the proportion of people without sustainable access to safe drinking water and basic sanitation. Water scarcity could threaten progress to reach this target.
10. Water is an essential resource to sustain life. As governments and community organisations make it a priority to deliver adequate supplies of quality water to people, individuals can help by learning how to conserve and protect the resource in their daily lives.

At the time of writing this chapter (7 March 2012) the global population has just passed 7,026,522,800 and counting (see the World Population Clock www.worldometers.info, with daily births approximately 300,000). If population growth increases continuously at the existing rate we can expect a near doubling of the population to 13 billion by 2060. Many of these individuals will live in areas where water is in short supply and there are compelling reasons to manage this very scarce resource.

Figure 12.1 shows the scarcity of water resources as at 1975: you can see that the areas of water stress, whilst important, are comparatively few.

Contrast this with a later forecast for 2025 (see Figure 12.2) and the stressed areas now include all of North Africa, China and India.

Water is one of the riskiest assets, and one of the least understood resources. Most commodities are available for optional consumption, or indeed there may be a series of alternatives – e.g. beef instead of poultry, or wheat instead of corn – but there is no alternative to water. As human beings our physical bodies are made up of approximately 70 per cent water. Even comparatively recently, no one was worried that there might not be enough water to drink, especially in Europe and North America.

According to the FAO, the Americas have the largest share of the world's total freshwater resources. In a typical year 1000 cubic metres of water are required per inhabitant as a minimum to sustain life and ensure agricultural production in climates that require irrigation for agriculture. The FAO also recognises that 33 countries depend on other countries for over 50 per cent of their renewable water resources, including Vietnam, Ukraine, Argentina and Uzbekistan; all are important in food production yet will be susceptible to drought and water shortages. The four richest water resource countries are Russia, Canada, Brazil and Indonesia.

Figure 12.1

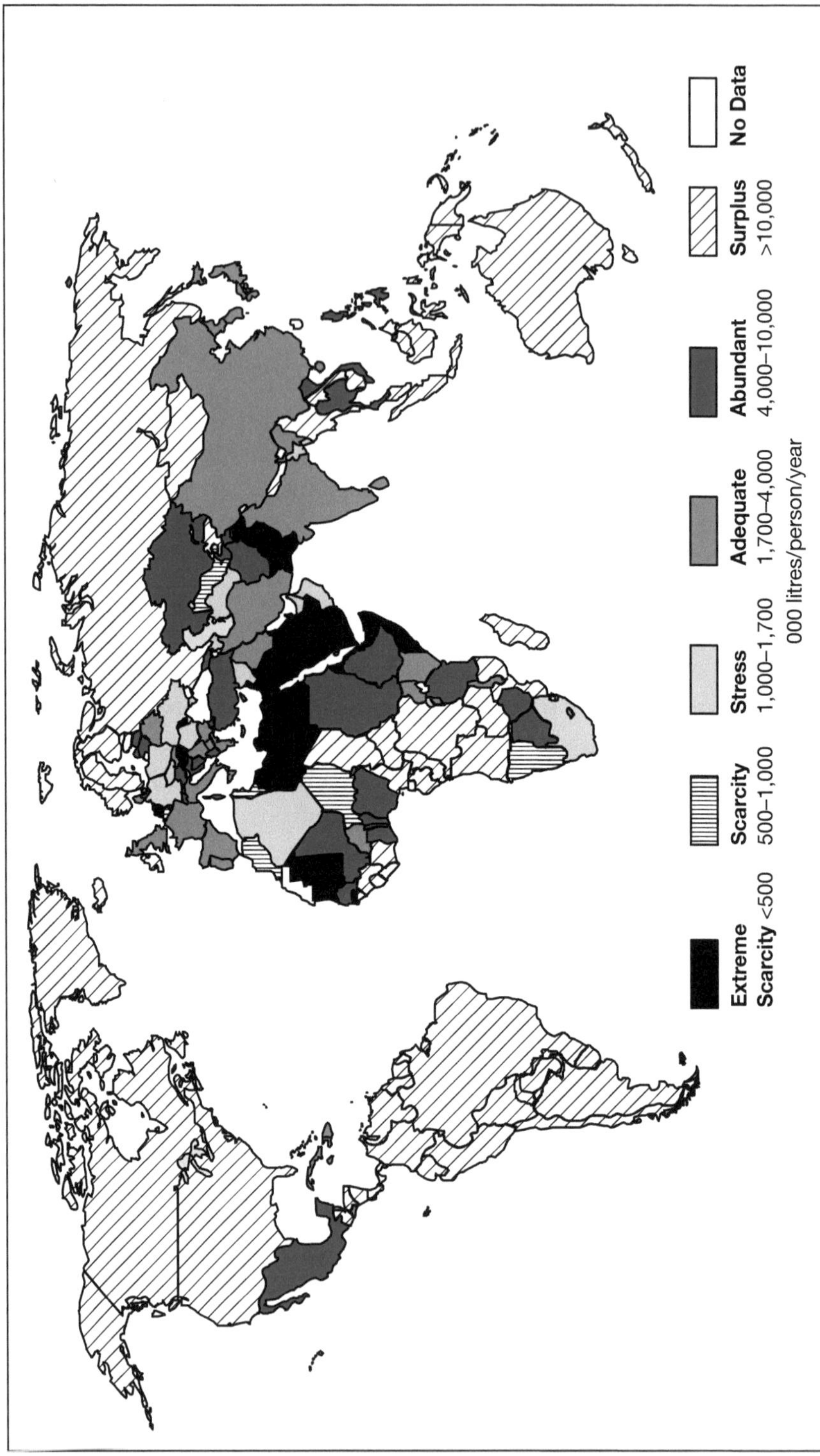

Global per capita water availability 1975

Source: Grail Research

Figure 12.2

Global per capita water availability 2025

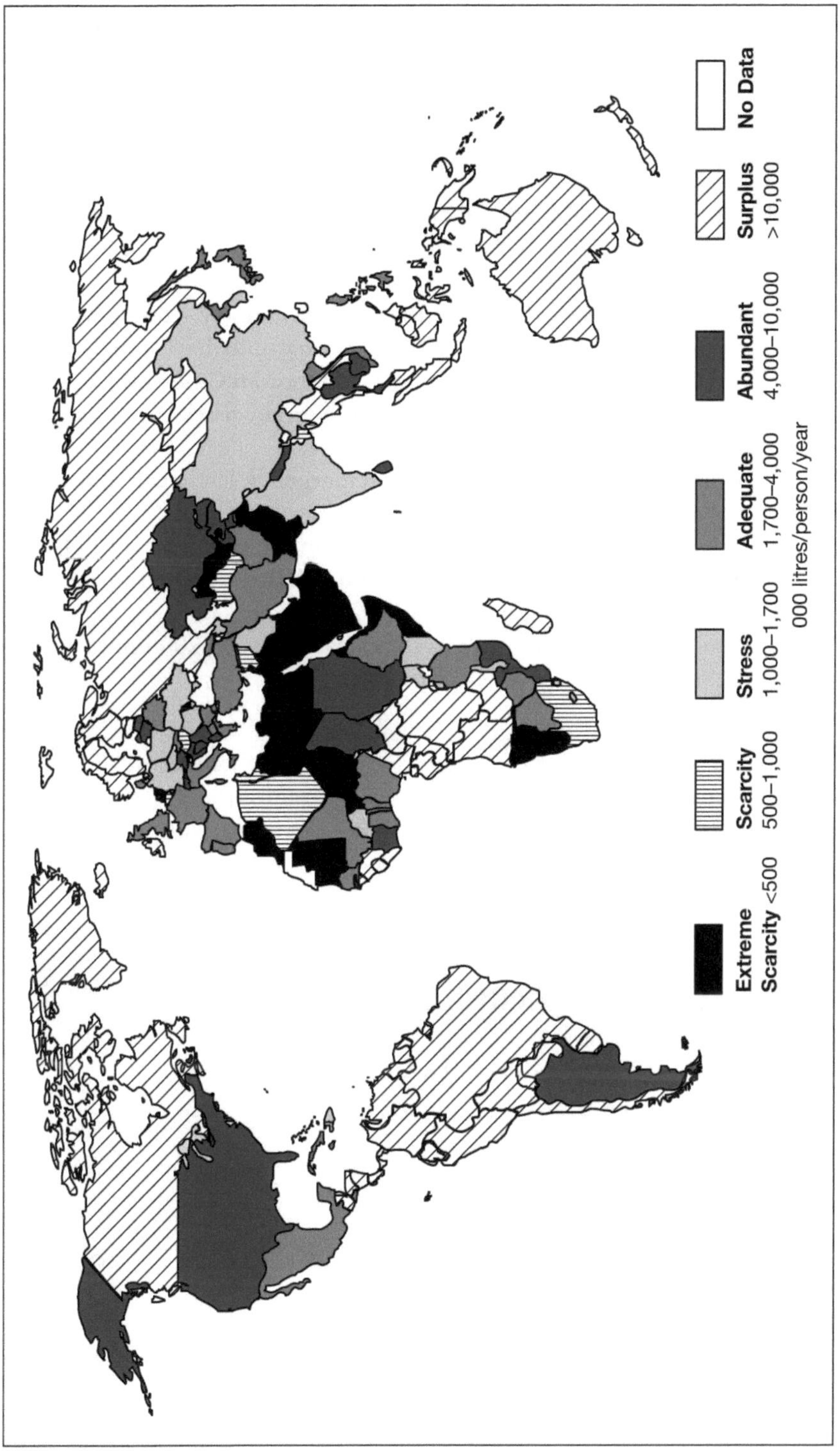

Source: Grail Research

The 2030 Water Resources Group published a document in 2009 entitled, 'Economic Frameworks to Inform Decision Making'. This noted that by 2030, in some developing regions, water demand would exceed supply by 50 per cent. This article appeared in *The Daily Mail* in the UK on 4 October 2011:

> 'The tiny Pacific Island nation of Tuvalu, located midway between Australia and Hawaii, has declared a state of emergency due to a severe shortage of fresh water.
>
> 'Officials said today that some parts of the country – the fourth smallest in the world with a population of 11,000 – may only have a two-day supply.
>
> 'New Zealand's Foreign Minister Murray McCully said his country was working with the Red Cross to deliver aid workers and supplies as quickly as possible.
>
> 'He said Tuvalu first declared the emergency last week and the situation had deteriorated since then.
>
> 'Meteorologists have warned that it is unlikely to rain until December, and workers for the Red Cross said that it has not rained properly in the country for at least six months.
>
> 'Usually the 10 square mile country has between 200mm to 400mm of rainfall per month.'

Definition and key features

Many of us will remember the statistic that the surface of the earth is mostly covered with water – in fact 75 per cent of the surface is water, of which approximately 97 per cent is in the seas and oceans, 2.4 per cent is in the polar ice caps and glaciers, and 0.6 per cent is freshwater.

THE WATER CYCLE AND CLIMATE CHANGE

Water exists on Earth in different states:

- Freshwater;
- Saltwater;
- Ice/snow;
- Rain;
- Vapour.

Figure 12.3 from the US Geological Survey illustrates the continuous cycle of water in the environment.

Figure 12.3

The water cycle

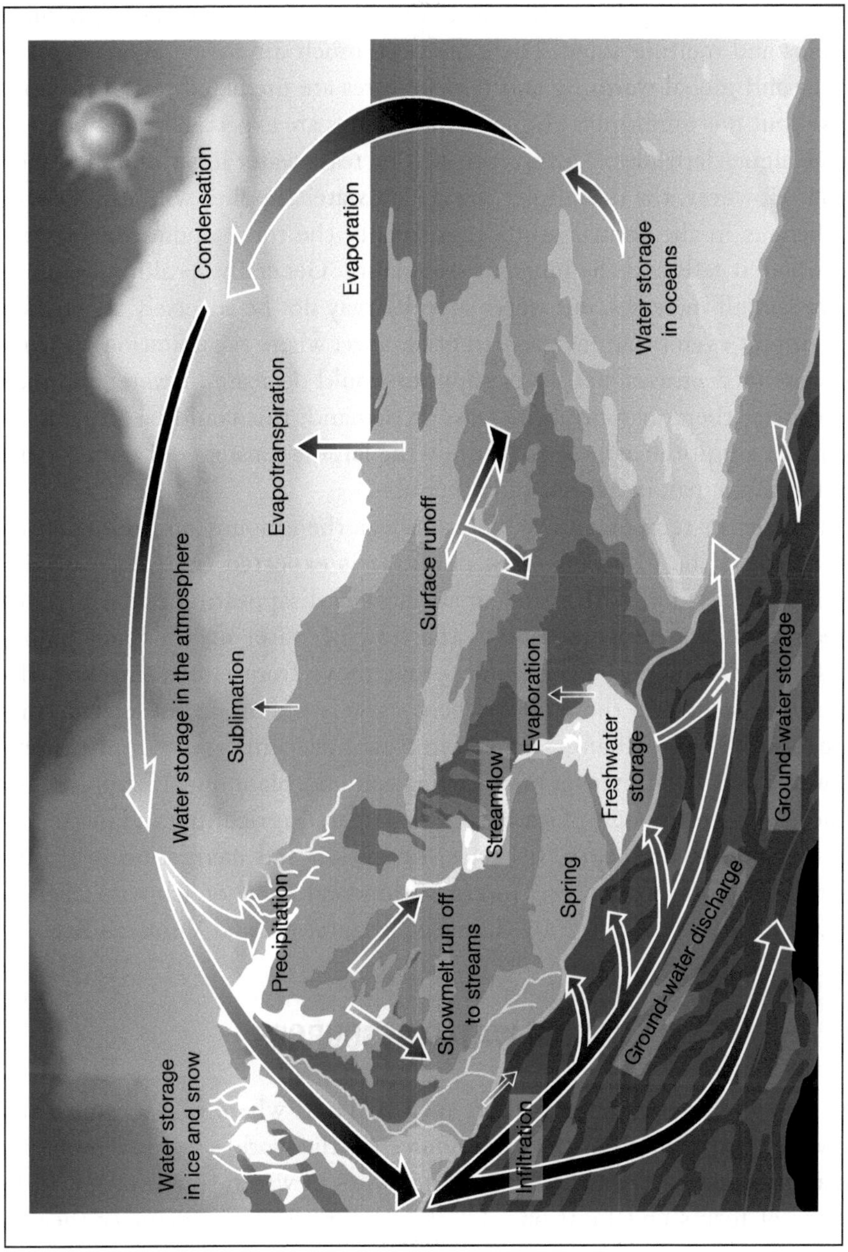

Source: US Geological Survey

Water availability is greatly affected by changes in temperature, rainfall patterns and melting snow. There has been much discussion about climate change and global warming and temperatures are predicted to rise in most areas – but not uniformly. Higher temperatures are expected in inland areas and at higher latitudes. This in turn will increase water loss through evaporation. However, the overall net impact on water supplies will also depend on changes in the annual rainfall, especially the total amount of rainfall and where it falls and the inherent seasonality. Generally speaking, in areas where rainfall increases, our water supplies may not be adversely affected or there might even be an increase. In other areas where precipitation remains the same or decreases, net water supplies would decrease. If water supplies deteriorate, there may be an increase in demand; this could be an issue of particular significance for agriculture – the largest consumer of water – and also for municipal, industrial and other uses.

Increases in temperature will also affect the amount and duration of snowfall and the resultant snow cover. It is expected that glaciers will continue retreating, with many small glaciers disappearing entirely. Peak 'streamflow' – a measurement of the flow of water over a fixed point, measured in cubic feet per second – may move from late spring to early spring/late winter in those areas where snow is important in determining water availability. Changes in streamflow have important implications for water and flood management, irrigation and planning. If supplies are reduced, off-stream users of water such as irrigated agriculture and in-stream users such as hydropower, fisheries, recreation and navigation could be most directly affected (source: Intergovernmental Panel on Climate Change (IPCC), 'Climate Change 2007: Impacts, Adaptation, and Vulnerability').

MAJOR WATER RESOURCES

But just how much water is there on Earth and where is it? Table 12.1 shows the distribution of the main sources of the world's water. The Earth has approximately 1.4 billion cubic kilometres of water, spread over a wide variety of forms and locations. Of this water, the vast majority (nearly 97 per cent) is saltwater in the oceans. The world's total freshwater reserves are estimated at around 35 million cubic kilometres. Most of this, however, is locked up in glaciers and permanent snow cover, or in deep groundwater, inaccessible to humans (see Table 12.1).

Table 12.1

Distribution of the world's water

	Distribution Area (10^3 km^2)	Volume (10^3 km^3)	Per cent of Total Water (%)	Per cent of Fresh Water (%)
Total water	510,000	1,386,000	100	
Total freshwater	149,000	35,000	2.53	100
World oceans	361,300	1,340,000	96.5	
Saline groundwater		13,000	1	
Fresh groundwater		10,500	0.76	30
Antarctic glaciers	13,980	21,600	1.56	61.7
Greenland glaciers	1,800	2,340	0.17	6.7
Arctic islands	226	84	0.006	0.24
Mountain glaciers	224	40.6	0.003	0.12
Ground ice/permafrost	21,000	300	0.022	0.86
Saline lakes	822	85.4	0.006	
Freshwater lakes	1,240	91	0.007	0.26
Wetlands	2,680	11.5	0.0008	0.03
Rivers (as flows on average)		2.12	0.0002	0.006
In biological matter		1.12	0.0001	0.0003
In the atmosphere (on average)		12.9	0.0001	0.04

Source: Shiklomanov 1993 (I.A.Shiklomanov, 'World Fresh Water Resources' in *Water in Crisis: A Guide to the World's Fresh Water Resources*, pp. 13–24 (Gleick, P.H. (Ed.) 1993))

POPULATION PRESSURES

Are we correct to treat water as a commodity? It is a scarce but also a renewable resource – just not immediately. Is it similar to oil and copper, or poultry and wheat? Water in the context of this book is water that can be used for human consumption whether it is for drinking, or agriculture, or to a lesser extent industry or even power generation.

With a population of over 7 billion people on the planet, water is in demand; the agriculture industry and its consumption of water for the production of meat and vegetables is rising, and there is increasing competition for water from biofuel crops. As the population becomes richer less cereals will be eaten and more meat will be required. The production of meat is very water intensive. It takes around 3000 litres of water to produce enough food to satisfy one person's daily dietary need. This is a considerable amount, when compared to that required for drinking, which is between two and five litres.

One way to evaluate what water we have and what we have left is to examine the impact of human activities on rainfall, surface and groundwater stocks, soil moisture, and so on.

An early effort to evaluate these uses estimated that humans already use over 50 per cent of all renewable and 'accessible' freshwater flows (S.L. Postel, G.C. Daily and P.R. Ehrlich, 'Human Appropriation of Renewable Fresh Water', *Science* 271 (1996): 785–788). Surely we can continue indefinitely without any effect on future availability because of the renewability of water? However, according to Meena Palaniappan and Peter H. Gleick, in their chapter entitled 'Peak Water' in *The World's Water, 2008–2009*, while water itself is renewable, many uses of water will degrade its quality to such an extent that this theoretically 'available' water is practically useless. Improving the quality of this water for reuse will require the input of energy, technology, biological treatment, or dilution with more water.

RENEWABLE VERSUS NON-RENEWABLE RESOURCES

The key difference between renewable and non-renewable resources is that renewable resources are flow (or rate) limited; non-renewable resources are stock limited (P. Ehrlich, A. Ehrlich and J.P. Holdren, *Ecoscience: Population, Resources, Environment*, San Francisco: W.H. Freeman and Company, 1977).

- **Stock-limited resources**: These are notably fossil fuels that can be depleted without being replenished – certainly on a time scale of practical interest. What we mean here is that it took millions of years for stocks of oil to accumulate and will need many millions of years to accumulate new stocks. How long oil now lasts depends on our ability to find it, the rate we use it, and the cost of removing and using it.
- **Flow-limited resources**: Flow-limited resources may be virtually never-ending over time, because their use does not diminish the production of more resources. For example, solar energy is limited in the flow rate. Our use of solar energy has no effect on the next amount produced by the sun, but our ability to capture solar energy is a function of the rate at which it is delivered.

Water is a unique resource that demonstrates characteristics of both flow-limited and stock-limited resources, mainly due to the wide range of forms and locations for freshwater. This duality of water has implications. Overall, water is a renewable resource with rapid flows from one form to another, and the production of water typically has no effect on natural recharge rates. However, many of the stocks of water are fixed or isolated stocks of local water resources that can be consumed at rates far faster than natural rates of renewal – or for which the rate of recharge is extremely slow. Most of these are groundwater aquifers – often called 'fossil' aquifers because of their slow recharge rates – but some surface water storage in the form of lakes or glaciers can also be used at rates exceeding natural renewal, a problem that may be worsened by climate change.

With the immense amount of seawater covering the planet, it is unfortunate that only about 0.5 per cent of water available on the earth is drinking water – potable.

The Rime of the Ancient Mariner by Samuel Taylor Coleridge, published in 1798, laments this in the text of his verse:
'Water, water everywhere, nor any drop to drink'.

Water 'backstop'

A relevant concept to both water and oil is the 'backstop' price of substitutes – i.e. the price of the substitute capable of replacing or expanding the original source of supply. For example, as oil production peaks and then declines, oil prices will increase in the classic 'supply/demand' economic response. Prices will then continue to increase until the point when a substitute for oil becomes more economically competitive, when prices will stabilise at the new 'backstop' price.

Likewise for water, as cheaper sources of water are depleted, more expensive sources must be found. Ultimately, the 'backstop' price for water will be reached. Unlike oil, however, which must be backstopped by a different, renewable energy source, the ultimate water backstop is still water, from an essentially unlimited source – for example, desalination of ocean water. The amount of water in the oceans is limited only by how much we are willing to pay for it and the environmental constraints of using it. In some regions, desalination is already an economically competitive alternative, particularly where water is truly scarce, such as certain islands in the Caribbean and parts of the Gulf Co-operation Council.

AFRICA

Africa is going to be the key to unlock the various water (and agricultural) challenges that we will all face as our population and urbanisation increase.

Shown in Figure 12.4 is the rainfall data for Africa, and for most of the countries suffering water stress Africa is the nearest neighbour with surpluses. The equatorial prominence in the mid-to-south of the continent, coupled with numerous sources of large rivers and lakes, make the African continent a unique water deposit for Asia and the Arabian Gulf.

Figure 12.4 **Rainfall in Africa**

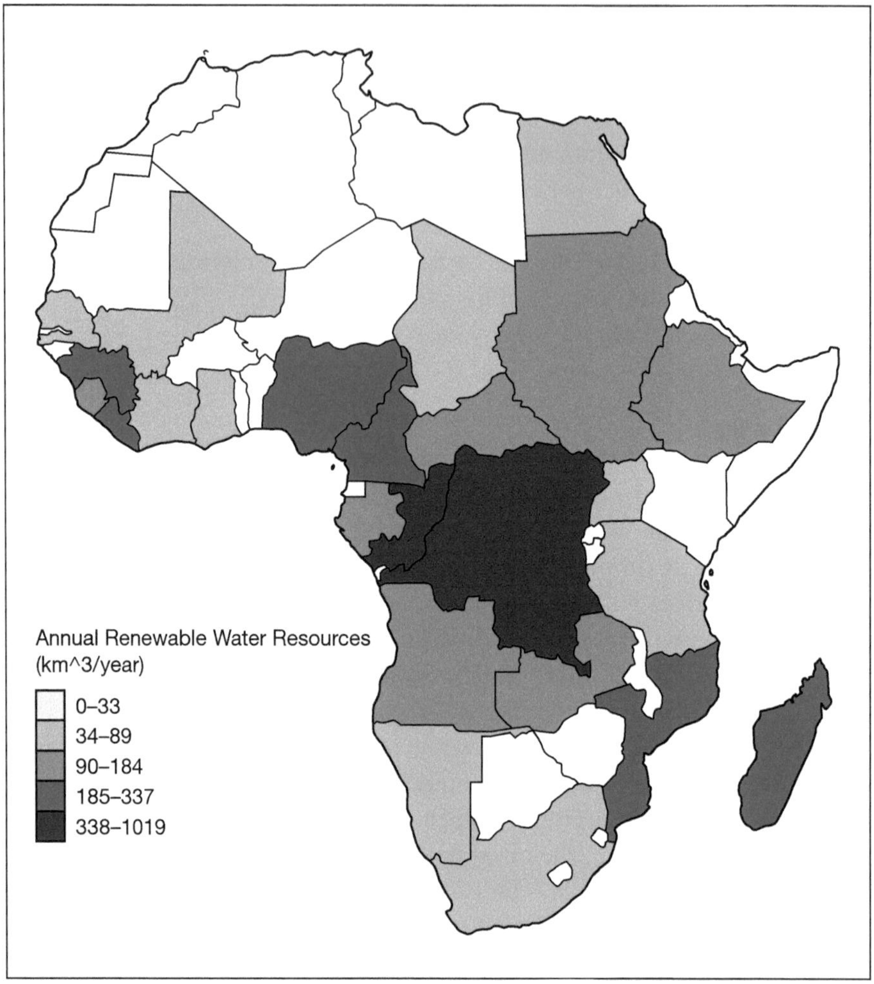

Source: Based on data from Gleick, The World's Water 1998–99, Table 1

Example

How is water consumed?

Using India as an example, let's look at the activities that consume the most water. In Figure 12.5 it is clear that bathing, going to the toilet and washing clothes accounts for over half of daily usage.

Figure 12.5

Domestic water consumption in India

% Water Usage for Domestic Activities[1]

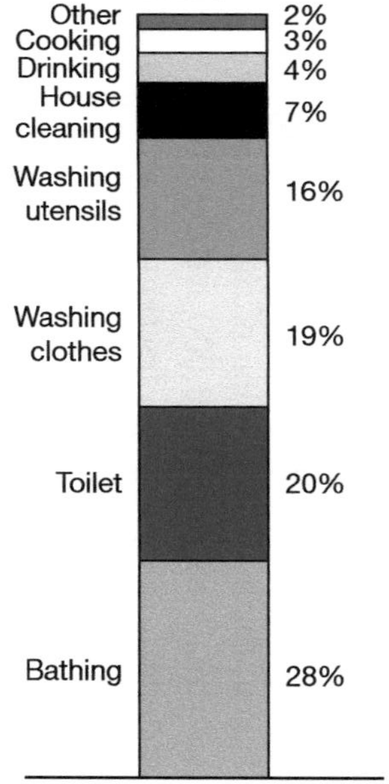

Per Capita Income[2], 2000-2050E ($)

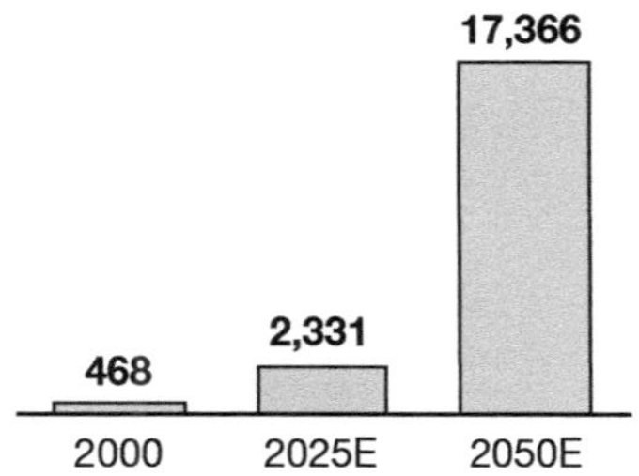

Urban Population as a % of Total Population, 2007-2050E

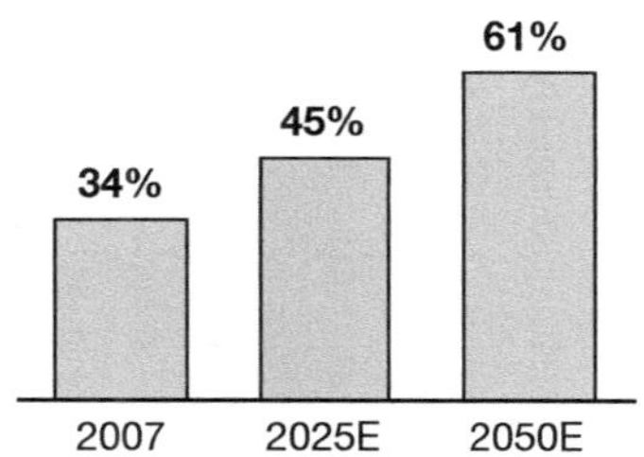

Impact on Water Stress

- Domestic contribution to the total water consumption is projected to increase from 5% in 2000 to 11% by 205
  - Domestic consumption of water is expected to triple from 2000 to 2050
  - Per capita water consumption is expected to double from 89 litres/day in 2000 to 167 litres/day by 2050
- Cities are facing severe water shortage
  - In 2005, 65% of households across 7 major cities faced water deficiency
  - Cities are reaching out to distant water sources, e.g., Delhi and Chennai receive water from rivers that are 250 km and 450 km away, respectively
- Untreated sewage from cities is leading to severe water pollution
  - Only 31% of the ~9,275 million litres per day of wastewater generated by 23 metropolitan cities is treated
  - Severely polluted stretches in 18 major rivers identified by the CPCB[3], were located in and around large urban areas

Note: [1]Data for Ahmedabad, Delhi, Hyderabad, Kanpur, Kolkata, Madurai, and Mumbai; [2]Per capita Income has been taken to be GDP per capita; [3]Central Pollution Control Board, Source: 'India's Water Future to 2025–2050: Business as Usual Scenario and Deviations', International Water Management Institute; India Census 2001; 'Water Poverty in Urban India: A Study of Major Cities', Jamia Millia Islamia; 'Troubled Waters', Development Alternatives; 'Dreaming With BRIC's: The Path to 2050', Goldman Sachs, 2003; 'Urban and Rural Areas 2007', United Nations; 'Water Supply – The Indian Scenario', IEA India; 'Status Of Water Treatment Plants In India', Central Pollution Control Board; Population Division of the Department of Economic and Social Affairs of the United Nations Secretariat

Source: Grail Research, 'India – The Water Story', 2009, www.grailresearch.com

WATER CONVERSION AND DESALINATION

Naturally there are great incentives to convert seawater into freshwater for agriculture or into potable clean drinking water. The reader may be aware of these schemes:

- Transporting an iceberg from one of the poles to areas of water shortage, e.g. Texas;
- Desalination of seawater.

Iceberg transportation

In the 1970s an engineering graduate named Georges Mougin had an idea. He suggested that icebergs floating around in the North Atlantic could be tethered and dragged south to places that were experiencing a severe drought, such as the Sahel of West Africa. Mr Mougin received financial backing from a Saudi prince, H.E. Mohammad al-Faisal, but most 'experts' at the time scoffed at his idea and the whole scheme was eventually shelved.

However, in 2009 French software firm Dassault Systèmes contacted Mr Mougin and suggested to him that he model the whole idea on a computer. Using 15 engineers to attack the problem, the team concluded that towing an iceberg from the waters around Newfoundland to say the Canary Islands off the north-west coast of Africa could be done, and would take under five months, though it would cost nearly US$10 million.

In the simulation, as in a real-world attempt, the selected iceberg would first be fitted with an insulating skirt to stave off melting; it would then be connected to a tugboat (and a kite sail) that would travel at about 1 knot (assuming assistance from ocean currents). In the simulated test, the iceberg arrived intact having lost only 38 per cent of its 7 ton mass.

A real-world project would of course require hauling a much bigger berg; experts estimate a 30 million ton iceberg could provide fresh water for half a million people for up to a year. There would also be the problem of transporting the water from the berg in the ocean to the drought-stricken people. The high costs for a similar operation would most likely come from the price for the skirt, five months of diesel fuel for the tugboat, the man hours involved and then, finally, distribution of the fresh water at the destination. Scientists estimate that some 40,000 icebergs break away from the polar ice caps each year, though only a fraction of them would be large enough to be worth the time and expense of dragging them to an area experiencing drought.

Whilst in my opinion this is an interesting idea, it does bring into focus a key question: just who owns the icebergs? Can anyone just take away an iceberg? Are we then opening up the ice shelves and polar regions to indiscriminate blasting to loosen icebergs?

Desalination

In ancient times, many civilisations used this process on their ships to convert seawater into drinking water. Today, desalination plants are widespread. Even in the Seychelles where average rainfall is in the region of 2100mm per annum, the construction of desalination plants is being considered, as storage of rainwater is still a challenge.

Definition

Desalination

Removal of salt (sodium chloride) and other minerals from the seawater to make it suitable for human consumption and/or industrial use. The most common desalination methods employ reverse osmosis in which salt water is forced through a membrane that allows water molecules to pass but blocks the molecules of salt and other minerals.

(*Source*: www.businessdictionary.com)

Recent forecasts suggest that in the Middle East alone US$135 billion will be required by 2019 if rising demand is to be met and old water infrastructure is to be replaced. The heart of the challenge is that desalination demand is set to increase on several levels, and with it the energy required to maintain water supplies.

Desalination relies primarily on natural gas, which is an efficient resource but an increasingly hard one to obtain. As water demand continues to grow, it could magnify all these strains on natural gas to unprecedented levels.

Key features

Desalination

Reverse osmosis

Involves seawater being forced through a semi-permeable membrane that traps salt and other impurities on one side and allows water filtration through a microscopic strainer. This is the 'greenest' approach but it does not work well in the Arabian Gulf areas due to the very high salinity of the water.

Thermal distillation

Involves processes that boil the saline water and collect the purified vapour. Multi-stage flash (MSF) distillation is an extension of this.

Electrodialysis

Involves the removal of salts by separating and collecting their chemical components through electrolysis and is more suited to salty groundwater than seawater.

Currently, more than 13,000 desalination plants are in operation around the world. At the time of writing the largest plant is the new Jubail II Industrial Zone in Saudi Arabia's Eastern Province. Opened in 2009, the plant produces 800,000 cubic metres of water per annum. In Dubai, United Arab Emirates, the Jebel Ali Desalination Plant produces 300 million cubic metres of water annually through the utilisation of multi-stage flash distillation. Shrinking groundwater supplies and more advanced desalination techniques have brought a massive desalination boom to the UAE, leading firms to spend more than US$13 billion on new plants and expansions between 2007 and 2010. Other multibillion-dollar projects are scheduled to undergo construction in the next few years.

Globally, the most common desalination process is reverse osmosis, which is the process commonly used on cruise ships and navy vessels to supply very pure water. The recent technological advances have improved the cost effectiveness of the process such that the reverse osmosis process is now only about half as expensive as the distillation process. The filtration process removes 95 to 99 per cent of dissolved salts and inorganic material.

PROCESS OVERVIEW

Reverse osmosis

Typically, the seawater is pre-treated before the reverse osmosis process begins, to extend the life of the semi-permeable membrane. This filtered water is then pumped through a range of micro-filters and then pushed through these membranes under pressure, removing the salt from the seawater. Approximately 50 per cent of the feed water taken from the source becomes product water. The remaining 50 per cent is returned to the source, with concentrated salts.

A post-treatment stage of the product water involves adding alkalinity to the soft processed water. A similar treatment stage is used for soft dam waters as this prevents corrosion in the distribution system. In keeping with other treatment methods, chlorine is also added for cleansing and maintenance of the distribution system (see Figure 12.6).

Multi-stage flash distillation

The raw seawater is pumped through heat exchangers in the stages and warms up. When it reaches the brine heater it is already near boiling point and additional heat is added. Water then flows back through the valves into stages that have ever-decreasing pressure and temperature. This processed

Figure 12.6

Seawater reverse osmosis desalination process

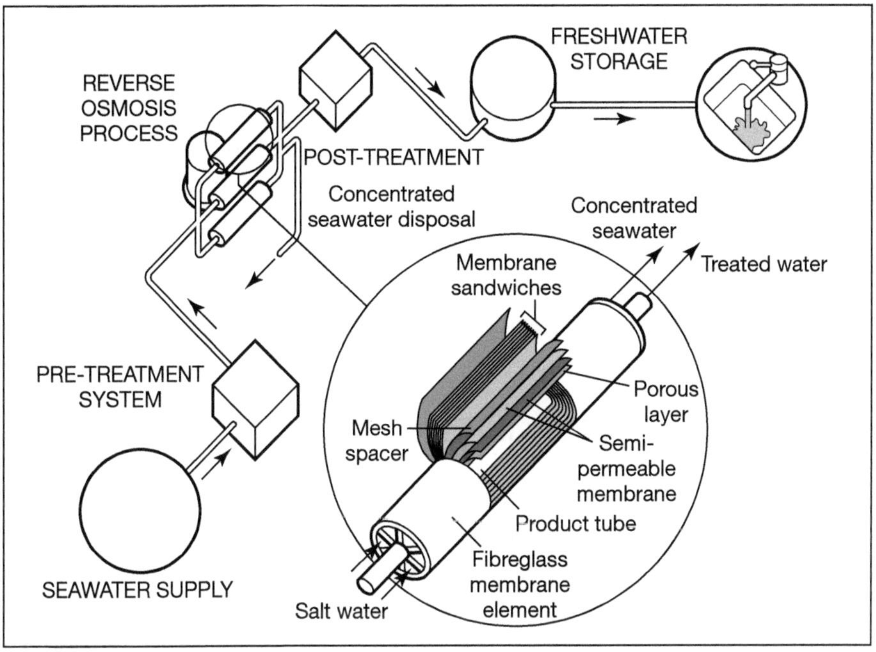

Source: watersecure.com.au

seawater is now called brine, to distinguish it from the inlet water. At each stage, as the brine enters, its temperature is above the boiling point and a small fraction of the brine water boils ('flashes') to steam, thereby reducing the temperature until an equilibrium is reached. The resulting steam is a little hotter than the feed water in the heat exchanger. The steam then cools and condenses against the heat exchanger tubes (see Figure 12.7).

Figure 12.7

Multi-stage flash distribution desalination

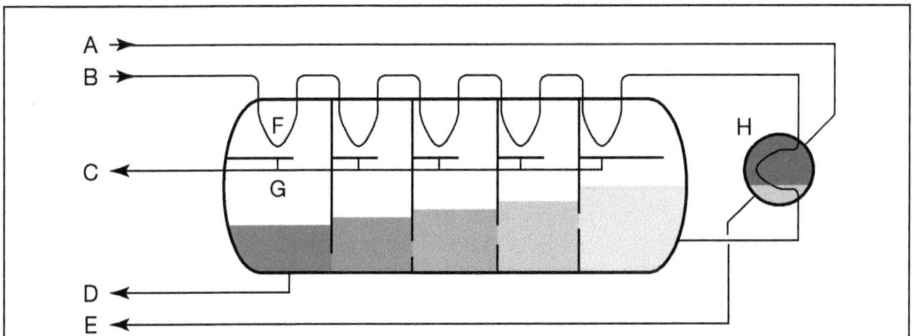

Source: Wikipedia

Each desalination method has its supporters and critics: but generally MSF distillation plants, especially large ones which are often combined with power plants in a co-generation configuration, are seen as more cost-effective – in some parts of the world. Waste heat from the power plant is used to heat the seawater, providing cooling for the power plant at the same time. This reduces the energy needed by one-half to two-thirds, which drastically alters the economics of the plant, since energy is by far the largest operating cost of MSF plants. Reverse-osmosis plants, which are MSF distillation's main competitor, require more pre-treatment of the seawater and more maintenance, as well as energy in the form of work (electricity, mechanical power) as opposed to cheaper low-grade waste heat.

PRICING AND PRICE DISCOVERY

Although we understand instinctively that water is a valuable commodity there is no universal pricing for this, yet! Consequently it is problematical to invest in the raw material, which only leaves us with the possibility of investing via equity, bonds or ETFs with the organisations that are involved in the supply chain for clean potable water. There are no futures or options markets yet, and many of the world's major water providers are governmental, though there are occasional commercial operators.

Four major water exchange traded funds (ETFs) have been launched since 2005, with combined assets of over US$1.3 billion, according to Morningstar Inc., an independent data provider (www.morningstar.com). The key water ETFs all hold stock in publicly traded companies that mostly deliver water 'services' (e.g. crop irrigation systems) and have water as only part of their mainstream activities.

A recent article in *The Wall Street Journal* by Liam Pleven (5 December 2011) notes that up until end November 2011, these four major water-focused ETFs had mixed returns, shown in Table 12.2.

Table 12.2 **Performance of four water-focused ETFs**

		Total return			
Name	Ticker	Year to date	Three years (annualised)	Five years (annualised)	Assets (mils.)
PowerShares Water Resources	PHO	–9.0%	8.9%	–0.6%	US$852
PowerShares Global Water	PIO	–17.3	14.0	–	257
Guggenheim S&P Global Water Index	CGW	–5.9	15.3	–	196
First Trust ISE Water Index	FIW	–4.5	14.2	–	59
S&P 500		1.1%	14.1%	–0.2%	

Source: Morningstar Inc.

It is clear that one of the key challenges facing investors is how to invest in water as a pure holding, rather than it being just part of the overall portfolio within the ETF, and trying to find liquid independent stocks.

CONCEPT OF 'PEAK WATER'

Experts predict that we are approaching, or possibly have passed, the point of global maximum production of oil, or 'peak oil'. The implications of reaching this point for energy policy are profound, for a range of economic, political and environmental reasons.

However, are we now approaching a comparable point of 'peak water', at which we run up against natural limits to availability or human use of freshwater?

Thus far, the concept of 'peak water' has focused on local water scarcity and challenges. In areas where water is scarce, the seeming nature of water constraints and their implications are already apparent. As the costs of transporting bulk water from one place to another are so high, if a region's water use exceeds its renewable supply it will begin to tap into non-renewable resources such as slow-recharge aquifers. Once extraction of water exceeds natural rates of replenishment, the only long-term options are to reduce demand to sustainable levels, move the demand to an area where water is available or shift to increasingly expensive sources, such as desalination.

A few exceptions to the economic limits on transporting water exist. Bottled water, for example, is sometimes consumed vast distances from where it was produced because it commands a premium far above normal costs. Growth in bottled water consumption may expand in some markets, but overall, long-distance transfers of bulk water are not likely to become a significant export in commercial markets.

FUTURE DEVELOPMENTS

Highlighting the link with agriculture, Saudi Arabia made headlines in late 2011 when it announced that the government would stop buying wheat from local farmers by 2016, as part of a drive to reduce farming and conserve limited water resources.

This move is the most recent acknowledgement of a familiar problem: Saudi Arabia is using its groundwater 10 times more quickly than it can be replenished. The Gulf Co-operation Council (GCC) nations consume an average of 850 cubic metres of water per capita each year, compared to a global average of about 500 cubic metres and a UK average of 165 (source: *Financial Times*, 5 October 2011). They have also considered nuclear desalination plants with a view to them being on-line by 2020.

In the words of Nick Butler, who chairs the Kings Policy Institute at Kings College London, and Ian Pearson, a strategy consultant and former UK government minister:

> 'Across the world water needs to be found, conserved, managed, cleaned and delivered. Where no alternatives are available, desalination must be developed and deployed. Water needs to be protected from the dangers of disease and the threat of global terrorism. The skills to manage water are therefore of huge value, providing they can be improved and expanded.'
>
> (*Financial Times*, 17 August 2011)

INTRODUCTION TO THE MATRIX PARTNERSHIP

The Matrix Partnership is based in Dubai, UAE, and has a broad business platform. Matrix provides strategic advisory services to leading financial institutions and asset managers, focused across the spectrum of the commodity complex, including energy, mining and metals and agricultural commodities. The company also provides best-in-class financial and commodities training to a range of industry groups: exchanges, multinationals, governmental organisations, financial institutions – including banks and asset managers, information and infrastructure providers.

Matrix is focused on the Middle East and Africa (MEA) region and emerging markets. Matrix draws upon significant experience of our two principals, Gary King and Francesca Taylor, and their deep fundamental knowledge of the energy chain and derivatives and financial markets. The principals have extensive international senior management and board level experience in financial, asset management and commodity/natural resource companies.

The Matrix Partnership offers advisory services in the following areas:

- Direct investments and structuring and marketing of private equity and commodity hedge funds.
- Entry strategies and joint ventures/strategic alliances in emerging markets.
- High-level evaluation and screening of oil and gas projects for energy companies and private equity funds.
- Bespoke in-house commodities, derivatives and financial training.

For further information, please contact:
info@matrixpartnership.biz
tel: +971 504587785
www.matrixpartnership.biz

Weights and Measures for Commodities

Name	Abbreviation	Weight	Used for
Fine troy ounce	oz	31.103 grams	Gold
Bar	bar	400 troy ounces ~ 12.5kg	Gold – Good Delivery Bar
Troy ounce	oz	31.103 grams	Silver
Bar	bar	750 to 1100 ounces	Silver – Good Delivery Bar
Barrel	bbl	42 US gallons, 35 imperial gallons	oil
Long ton	t	2240 lbs (1016.047 kg)	Coal
Tonne/Metric tonne	tn	2204 lbs (1000.00 kg)	Coal, Rare Earths,
Kilograms	kg	2.2lbs	Rare Earths, Metals
Avoirdupois ounce	oz	28.4 grams (1/16 of lb)	agriculture
Bushel	1 bushel	Wheat/Soybeans – 60 lbs	agricultural items
	1 bushel	Corn/Rye – 56 lbs	agricultural items
	1 bushel	Barley – 48 lbs	agricultural items
	1 bushel	Oats – 38 lbs	agricultural items
Carat	Ct	200 mg	Diamonds
Point	Pt	100 points in each carat	Diamonds
kilowatt	kW	1000 watts	electricity
megawatt	MW	1000 kilowatts	electricity
gigawatt	GW	1000 megawatts	electricity
terawatt	TW	1000 gigawatts	electricity
thousand cubic feet	1 Mcf	1000 cubic feet	Natural Gas
billion cubic feet	1 Bcf	1,000,000,000 cubic feet	Natural Gas
trillion cubic feet	1 Tcf	1,000,000,000,000 cubic feet	Natural Gas
Cubic meters	m^3	1 litre = 1 kg	Water

Index